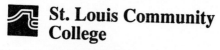

St. Louis Community College

Forest Park
Florissant Valley
Meramec

Instructional Resources
St. Louis, Missouri

THE NILE

◆

THE NILE

Histories, Cultures, Myths

edited by
Haggai Erlich and Israel Gershoni

LYNNE
RIENNER
PUBLISHERS

BOULDER
LONDON

Published in the United States of America in 2000 by
Lynne Rienner Publishers, Inc.
1800 30th Street, Boulder, Colorado 80301
www.rienner.com

and in the United Kingdom by
Lynne Rienner Publishers, Inc.
3 Henrietta Street, Covent Garden, London WC2E 8LU

Library of Congress Cataloging-in-Publication Data
The Nile: histories, cultures, myths / edited by Haggai Erlich and
    Israel Gershoni.
        p.   cm.
    Includes bibliographical references (p.   ) and index.
    ISBN 1-55587-672-2 (hc. : alk. paper)
    1. Nile River Valley—Civilization.
DT115.N45   1999
962—dc21   99-21066
                                                                CIP

British Cataloguing in Publication Data
A Cataloguing in Publication record for this book
is available from the British Library.

Printed and bound in the United States of America

      The paper used in this publication meets the requirements
 ∞ of the American National Standard for Permanence of
      Paper for Printed Library Materials Z39.48-1984.

    5 4 3 2 1

In memory of David Ayalon,
1914–1998

Contents

Acknowledgments

The Nile: Histories, Cultures, Myths was first conceived as a conference held at Tel Aviv University and the Hebrew University of Jerusalem in May 1997. Our general idea—to gather historians of Egypt, Sudan, and Ethiopia to initiate an all-Nile scholarly dialogue—was approved by friends and colleagues who joined the steering committee: Nehemia Levtzion, Yoram Meital, Ehud R. Toledano, Gabriel Warburg, and Joachim Warmbold. We thank them all, and in particular Tami Sarfatti, the conference coordinator, who personally made it a memorable event. We also want to thank all those who sponsored the conference and this book: Yoram Dinstein, then president of Tel Aviv University; Dan Amir, the rector; Marcello Daskal, the dean of humanities; and Shulamit Volkov, head of the School of History. Professor Levtzion of the Hebrew University, then head of the Van Leer Jerusalem Institute, came forward with generous help, as did Dror Ze'evi, head of the Herzog Center for the Study of the Middle East and Diplomacy, Ben Gurion University.

The conference was attended by forty scholars from Egypt, Eritrea, Ethiopia, Europe, Israel, Sudan, and the United States. All of them presented papers, each adding a new special dimension to our main all-regional, multicultural theme. Most papers were of the same quality and value as those eighteen we selected for this volume. It is with the deepest appreciation that we thank all the historians and friends who contributed to our project. We also want to thank Rachel Yurman and Lydia Gosher for their professional preparation of the manuscript, and Lynne Rienner and her staff for seeing this volume to press with both pleasantness and efficiency.

—*Haggai Erlich*
Israel Gershoni

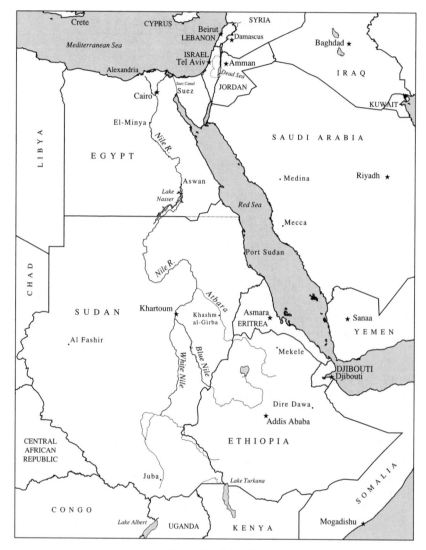

The Nile Basin

1

Introduction

Haggai Erlich & Israel Gershoni

The Nile River is one water system, but it is not a homogenous geo-graphical, climatic, or ecological unit. It originates in the broken high-lands of Ethiopia, land of the Blue Nile, and in the vast areas of great lakes and huge swamps of central Africa and southern Sudan, the lands of the White Nile. The two rivers unite, then flow into the narrow valley of Egypt, bringing life to humankind and society from their very incipience. The Nile's geographical versatility has always been the theater of human diversity. Over centuries, the peoples living along the river shaped vari-ous cultures, practiced different religions, spoke many languages, and made the Nile basin a vast symbolic space of countless experiences and identities. The Nile was not only a reality of geography and waters but an arena of multiple human concepts, myths, and discourses. It was the en-vironment of intercultural dialogues, of the continuous interplay between mutual recognition and denial, assimilation and rejection. The river was one of the first human cognitive maps that interpreted the symbiosis of ecology and life by molding it into concepts and images. It was one of the earliest cradles in which humans coped with nature, a space in which ex-periences were organized and translated into ideas, practices, beliefs, and orientations.

The Nile, as both the site of early beginnings as well as the space of mysterious diversity, has captured the human imagination since the earli-est civilizations have resided along its banks. The enigma of its sources, the life it gave to barren areas, and the capricious nature of its vital flow have produced endless speculation and legends. The realities and myths of the river personified have been retold and reproduced from early ancient times to the present.

The geographical diversity of the Nile can be conveniently categorized and identified. In this volume we shall confine ourselves to the territories of Egypt, Ethiopia, and Sudan. For Egypt, "the gift of the Nile," the river was the source of life as well as the backbone connecting its upper regions with the lower country. For Ethiopia, the Blue Nile, known as the Abbay, was a huge gorge, disconnecting provinces and stealing away precious waters. For Sudan, the midland, the river was both a bridge and a barrier. Indeed, in its dual role as both bridge and barrier the Nile also provided a shared context for the evolution of historical relations between these three regions.

By its natural cyclical rhythms and its ever imposing presence, the Nile embodied continuity and harmony. Its physical forces shaped and influenced the nature of the riparian civilizations. Cultural forces, however, worked in noncyclical rhythms to create multifaceted human transformations that, in their turn, produced the countless images of the Nile. Conceptualizing the river was often a matter of defining one's identity, of both one's self and the other. Cultural representations of the Nile acquired different forms and contents and were multiplied continuously in space and time. From ancient times to the medieval period, and then to the modern and the contemporary eras, among the Egyptian delta, the Sudanese sudd, and Ethiopia's Lake Tana, the Nile always meant different things to different peoples. It often also managed to foil those who strived to unify it, to render it one-dimensional, to mobilize it to serve a single identity or cause. These included builders of ancient civilizations, disseminators of monotheistic religions, imperial conquerors, local modern nationalists, revolutionary visionaries, missionaries, scientists, travelers, distant romantic admirers, Orientalist observers, and contemporary advocates of Afrocentrism. They, and others, tried in vain to create, by practice or by imagination, one Nile, one reality, one legend.

Our volume takes note of the concepts and representations molded by proponents of monolithic unity. However, it is primarily devoted to reflecting the Nile's rich diversity, to recording its many voices. Our Nile is a heterogeneous entity, a polysystem of cultures, interpretations, representations, and dialogues. It is a world of varied symbolism with different, often competing modes of memory, rituals, ceremonies, and artistic expressions, all describing the supposedly same Nile but creating different portraits, reflecting human diversity in continuous change. In this spirit, two interrelated themes seem to stand out. The first is that cultural, geographical, and historical barriers separated the Nile's major cultures, underlining their distinctive identities but also hampering shared experience, mutual understanding, and cooperation. The second is that myth, mystery, and misconceptions were magnified where direct communication lagged behind.

The world of Nile symbolism is indeed imbued with hope and gratitude to nature, but also with anxiety, fear, and suspicion. Perhaps the last
episode of mystery, embodying the old anxieties, occurred in 1987. After
several years of drought in Ethiopia, the waters of Lake Nasser sank to an
unprecedented level. Production of electricity in the Aswan High Dam's
station had to be halted, and predictions in Egypt and abroad were so
alarming that experts believed that the river was about to virtually dry up
due to climatic changes. Mother Nature, to be sure, soon sent the relief of
rain, but could people cope with such eventualities by emancipating themselves from their own inheritances of myths and misunderstandings?
Could the Egyptians, Sudanese, Ethiopians, and other children of the great
river join together in a common effort, build a better future for their rich
human diversity?

The literature on the Nile is vast and varied. Practically everything
published on the Nile's countries, historical or artistic, scientific or ficti-
tious, reflects the centrality of the river in their stories. However, academic
discussion of the Nile, its human ecology and history, has tended to be
fragmented, essentialist, and reductionist. It appears that too little has been
done to combine history, anthropology, political science, and strategic
studies to provide the multidimensional insights into the human story of
the greater Nile. Scholars and observers of Egypt tended, not unjustifiably,
to relate the river to the Middle East, to the land of Islam, to the Mediterranean. They neglected its southern section, the Nile's backyard, almost
entirely. Historians of the Sudan linked it to Egypt, Islam, and Africa but
rarely discussed its Ethiopian relations. Ethiopianists, on their part, tended
to make their observations in the context of Ethiopia's uniqueness, and
have begun only lately to relate them to the broader African context. They
seldom resorted to Ethiopia's Oriental, Egyptian, Middle Eastern contexts.
Indeed, in the generation previous to today's these branches of knowledge
seemed to have drifted further apart. Perhaps this was partly due to contemporary politics. During the 1950s, both Emperor Haile Selassie and
President Gamal Abdel Nasser diverted their national orientations elsewhere. Emperor Selassie first opted to turn his back on an increasingly
revolutionary Middle East, finally breaking the sixteen-centuries-old institutionalized affiliation of Ethiopian Christianity with the Egyptian Coptic
Church in June 1959 and making African diplomacy his major sphere of
political interest. President Nasser broke away from the modern concept of
Nile Valley unity, which had motivated Egyptian nationalism from the late
nineteenth century, and reoriented his politics on Arab nationalism and the
regional politics of the Fertile Crescent and the Arab-Israeli conflict. Si-
multaneous structural changes in the academic world seemed to combine
and widen the gap. The emerging African studies departments of the 1960s

embraced Ethiopian history, absorbing it in their very core. This African-ization of Ethiopian history was justified from every scholarly angle except for the resulting overmarginalization of the very vivid Eastern dimension of the country's culture and foreign relations. Ethiopianists of the previous generation were usually trained to link their findings to the general studies of sub-Saharan Africa, and far less to those of Egypt, Sudan, the Red Sea Basin, and the Arab East. To a certain extent this was also the rule for Egyptian and Sudanese historiographies. Here the academic paradigm to ignore the Ethiopian connection fostered during the 1950s was not only convenient in terms of scholarly training and immediate political relevance, but it also seemed to echo the old Islamic tradition: "Leave the Ethiopians alone as long as they leave you alone." Silhouetted against this background, our volume is an attempt to capture the gist of interrelations in both their cultural and practical dimensions. The very convergence here between scholars of Egypt, Sudan, Islam, and the Arabs on the one hand, and of Ethiopianists, Africanists, and historians of Christianity and of Ethiopian Judaism on the other, is an innovation in itself.

The idea behind the present volume could therefore be defined as re-establishing eye contact. As will be mentioned in some of the chapters, local tradition on all sides worked to blur such contact. The emergence of modern national identities and revolutionary ideas did little to demystify old mutual concepts. However, a renewed endeavor to analyze both historical relevance and cultural attitudes will, hopefully, better clarify the legacies of the past.

Our first chapter, "The Spread of Islam and the Nubian Dam" by David Ayalon, focuses on a very significant military event of the seventh century. As conquering Arab armies thrust forward from the Arabian Peninsula, creating the basis for the Muslim world empire, they were, for a very long time, checked only on the banks of the Nile at a point not far from today's Aswan High Dam. The Nubians, a Christian people of military valor and skill, defeated the Muslims and were able to maintain their power up to the thirteenth century. Egypt, as an Islamic state, was unable to spread institutionalized Islam beyond the metaphoric "Nubian Dam" prior to Muhammad 'Ali's conquest of the Sudan during the 1820s. Ayalon surveys the relevant Islamic literature and its readiness to admit failure. He also analyzes the far-reaching consequences for both Islam and Egypt.

We were fortunate that David Ayalon, one of the greatest historians of medieval and late medieval Islamic societies, contributed to our volume. His chapter here is the last fruit of his unique scholarship. Ayalon's observations underline a major theme in our book, that no single culture has ever managed to disseminate itself throughout the entire Nile basin. Islam, in its heyday, like earlier and later civilizations and systems from the early pharaohs to modern Western imperialists and contemporary national revolutionaries, was forced to cope with such barriers along the river.

Ayalon notes that the victory of the Christian Nubians was recognized legally by Islam. Perhaps more important, and more clearly recognized by Islamic tradition, was the ability of Christian Ethiopia to maintain its independence and check Islamic political influence from the direction of the Red Sea. The fact that the Christian Ethiopian empire controlled the Blue Nile region constituted another cultural barrier along the river. It was bridged by the speculated assumption that Ethiopia was in a position to threaten the very life of Egypt, a myth that agitates politics to this very day. In the next chapter, "Ethiopia's Alleged Control of the Nile," Richard Pankhurst demystifies this idea. He exhausts the relevant literature and Ethiopian chronicles, discussing in detail the issue during Ethiopia's golden Solomonic period of 1270–1527, which corresponded to Egypt's golden age under the Mamluks, 1250–1517. Pankhurst concludes that no concrete effort had been undertaken by the Ethiopian emperors to interfere with the flow of the river, but the myth influenced Ethiopian-Egyptian medieval and early modern multifaceted relations for centuries. Pankhurst also discusses the spread of the myth to Christian Europe and its treatment and gradual demystification by later observers and scholars.

Paul Henze, in his chapter, "Consolidation of Christianity Around the Source of the Blue Nile," summarizes several local traditions and myths related to the introduction of Christianity in this strategically vital area by Mary and Christ themselves. He then analyzes the early spread of the Ethiopian Church in the Blue Nile area during the thirteenth century, and exemplifies its later processes of consolidation as reflected in the history of the local monastery of Mertule Maryam, the home of Mary, established in the fifteenth century. Henze's vivid narrative acquires a new dimension in view of Ayalon's Nubian Dam. The region of the Blue Nile was inhabited by pagans such as the Wayto, the Agaw, and the Gumuz peoples, who fell under Ethiopia's Christian emperors of the Solomonic period some six centuries after Islam was halted near Aswan. What if Islam had defeated the Nubians? What would have prevented the spread of the Islamic empire across the Blue Nile? How different would our entire story be?

But the region of the Blue Nile fell to Ethiopia, and Ethiopian Christianity added a cultural, religious dimension to the ensuing Ethiopian-Egyptian politics. A collection of tales of the miracles of the Virgin Mary was incorporated into Ethiopian literature by transmission through the Egyptian Coptic Church and translated from Arabic into Ethiopic (Ge'ez) during the reign of Emperor Dawit (1388–1413). The latter, as we are told by Pankhurst, fought with Egypt's Mamluks who threatened to block the Nile. According to the stories, the Virgin advised David, in response to his prayers, to block the river prior to his marching to meet the Egyptians in the battlefield. When the Muslims witnessed the resulting low level of the Nile in Egypt, they appealed to the emperor for peace. (A new version of the "Miracles of Mary" was introduced into Ethiopia during the second half of the nineteenth century, a period of renewed Ethio-Egyptian conflict.)

Another aspect of religious history gives Steve Kaplan an opportunity to discuss the Ethiopian-Egyptian cultural connection. In his chapter, "Did Jewish Influence Reach Ethiopia via the Nile?" Kaplan examines the sources and literature of the Falasha's origins, and criticizes the proponents of the Nilotic theory. Kaplan believes that Beta Israel's Judaism stemmed from the very culture and history of Christian Ethiopia and was not the result of outside influences. He thus criticizes the Judaeocentric approach to Falasha history, as well as the ideas of Afrocentrists who perceive ancient Egypt to be the origin of integral African culture. Was the Nile such a tremendous cultural gateway or, with all its "dams," was it the geographical home of a cultural variety interconnected primarily by myth and blurred eye contact?

Nehemia Levtzion sheds new light on this central question. In his "Arab Geographers, the Nile, and the History of *Bilad al-Sudan*," Levtzion examines the perceptions held by medieval Muslim scholars such as al-Idrisi (twelfth century) and al-Bakri (eleventh century) of the river's sources. They combined Ptolomey's ancient theory about the sources in *Iabal al-Qamar* (Mountains of the Moon) (mainly al-Idrisi) with their knowledge of Western sub-Saharan Africa, and described a river that combined the Senegal, the Niger, the Shari, and Bahr al-Ghazal. It was only in the fourteenth century, Levtzion asserts, that such imaginative descriptions of the Nile disappeared from Islamic geographic literature. His findings do indeed correspond with those of our previous contributors. Prior to the Mamluk period in Egypt, only rarely did individual Muslims penetrate beyond the Nubian Dam or cross Ethiopia. The entire region south of Egypt was occasionally referred to by Muslims as the "land of *al-habasha*," Ethiopia. They knew much more about the "land of the Sudan (the blacks)" to the west and stretching to the Atlantic than about the peoples of the White and the Blue Niles (the latter, as mentioned earlier, came under Christian rule in the thirteenth and fourteenth centuries).

"Up the River or Down the River? An Afrocentric Dilemma," by Yaacov Shavit, addresses the issue of cultural barriers, but it also introduces us to a new world, that of images of the Nile as seen by distant outsiders. Shavit provides a rich introductory description of the Nile's ancient image as the creator of Egypt and then addresses the river's place as perceived by today's Afrocentrists. Like Kaplan, he mentions "Nile Valley Afrocentrism," the idea that the Nile River was, in ancient times, the cradle of one homogenous, interdynamic African civilization, which in turn gave birth to a universal human culture. Shavit presents the dilemma inherent in the assumed African Nile dialectic: Was inner Africa the main source of "down the river" influence, or was it "up the river" from the great Egyptians to the inner Africans? Analyzing the importance of this argument for the Afrocentric contemporary message, Shavit also attempts to refute its scholarly premise. His arguments about Nile dams and barriers are indeed much in line with a major theme of this volume.

Benjamin Arbel also discusses the Nile's image as perceived by distant outsiders but takes us back in time from today's Afrocentrists to the great early modern European cultural revolution. In "Renaissance Geographical Literature and the Nile," he first succinctly summarizes the ancient and medieval European concepts of the great river, describing them as religious and mythical. The legend of Prester John, for example, the fabled Christian Ethiopian anti-Islamic crusader, was spread in medieval Europe and blended with the image of the Nile as a mysterious godly creation. The Renaissance, Arbel contends, brought about a fundamental change. Rediscovering the outside world while emancipating their own rational and scientific concepts, Europeans made the Nile a renewed subject of scholarly curiosity. Travelers to Egypt, Sudan, and Ethiopia brought home what became the modern discipline of geography and its branches, such as the Portuguese Francisco Alvarez's sixteenth-century descriptions of Lake Tana and the sources of the Blue Nile, which heralded the demystification of the blocking myth mentioned earlier by Pankhurst. The new literature and cartography produced during the Renaissance in various European languages, says Arbel, constituted a revolution in the direction of modern research.

The change in attitude toward science also created a whole new world of mysteries, albeit scholarly ones. It heralded the nineteenth-century drive to solve the riddle of the Nile's sources, as well as the twentieth-century drive to control its waters. Yet these modern mysteries, as discussed below, could not do away with ancient and medieval legacies. For many, insiders and outsiders alike, they would be recycled and blended to form renewed mixtures of reality and myth. In "The Legend of the Blue Nile in Europe," Emery van Donzel returns to Pankhurst's subject of Ethiopia's alleged ability to block the Nile. He mentions some of its early Ethiopian and Egyptian sources, then analyzes the history of this myth in Europe. Van Donzel traces the early spread of the myth beginning in the second half of the fourteenth century, surveying many late medieval accounts that describe the Europeans' desire for aid in their struggle with Islam from a legendary Ethiopian Prester John, and how it contributed to the notion that Egypt might be deprived of the Nile's waters. In the spirit of Arbel's chapter, van Donzel moves to post–Renaissance European sources. Here again, he provides a detailed tour through the literature, quoting travelers, missionaries, explorers, and geographers, completing the picture up to the late nineteenth century. The idea that Ethiopia could destroy Egypt by diverting the Nile, he shows, remained intact and was recycled as a blend of mythical religious messages and new scholarly findings. Among his various sources, van Donzel mentions the writings of seventeenth-century Hiob Ludolf. This German "father of modern Ethiopian studies," he asserts, believed the myth of blocking the Nile to be an example of wishful thinking.

The idea, however, that Ethiopia might destroy Egypt never died. It remained as one element of an everlasting Islamic dichotomy of Ethiopia, the polarized attitudes of which are discussed later by Haggai Erlich. Joachim Warmbold provides a glimpse of European, Western Christian concepts, also similarly polarized. At one end, the image of savagery was to motivate missionaries, imperialists, and fascist aggressors. At the other end, however, was the Ethiopian image of innocence, justice, and purity. Warmbold's "The 'Gondar Utopia'" is a fascinating reflection of a modern version of Prester John's image of Christian purity in medieval Europe. Warmbold summarizes a novel by a late eighteenth-century German proponent of enlightenment and liberalism in which an Ethiopian prince who learned tyrannical despotism while touring Germany was toppled at home by a constitutional revolution (inspired by the neighborly Nubians). For the author of this Ethiopian utopia, a new enlightened regime in Gondar was to serve as a model for liberal Germans.

Uoldelul Chelati Dirar bases his contribution on the same European amalgam of old myths and new modern scholarship. In his chapter, "The Nile as a Gateway for Missionary Activity in Abyssinia," he explains how the paternalistically exoticized image of Ethiopia's black, Semitic, Christian purity created in the minds of nineteenth-century European missionaries the idea that Abyssinia was the proper gateway for their all-African enterprise. Moreover, the idea of the Abyssinian bridgehead enhanced and recycled the old myth that the river Nile was the gateway to the entire continent beyond Ethiopia. Though the idea of Ethiopia as a missionary springboard to the rest of Africa did not materialize, missionaries played an important role in local modern transformations. The concept of the Nile as a geographical corridor into Abyssinia ran headlong into the barriers mentioned in our earlier chapters, and proved painfully futile. Yet the Nile as a metaphor remained strongly engraved in people's minds, and missionaries turned its discovery into a part of their spiritual legacy in spreading their word in remote lands. Their archives, says Uoldelul, are filled with material attesting to their pioneering role in scholarly exploration, a fact not really consonant with the mythical symbolism they continued to attach to the Nile.

Bairu Tafla examines a rich variety of Ethiopian oral traditions, old and modern texts, in his chapter, "The Father of Rivers: The Nile in Ethiopian

Literature." He asserts that the Blue Nile, or Abbay, "our father" in Amharic (stemming from Abbawi, in the classical language of Ge'ez, meaning "fatherly"), was central in Ethiopia's culture and history. The fact was reflected in endless tales, proverbs, poems and novels, private names and symbols. Together with Islam and the Red Sea, the river was the factor that turned Ethiopia's foreign relations in the direction of the Middle East. In analyzing this connection, however, Tafla, much like Kaplan, Shavit, Uoldelul, and others, sees the Nile more as a conceptual bridge than as a geographical channel of cultural exchanges. Relations with Egypt were by far the most important factor. If the medieval Egyptians regarded the lands to the south as *al-habasha,* medieval Ethiopians considered Egyptians to be their only partners in sharing the great river. Tafla discusses the most important institution linking the two countries: the Ethiopian Church, whose head, the *abun,* was an Egyptian Coptic bishop from the fourth century to 1950. He also analyzes Ethiopia's image of Egypt, mentioning major turning points such as the 1876 war between the armies of Emperor Yohannes and Egypt's Khedive Isma'il.

In his discussion Tafla moves from the traditional to the modern, and from the external to the internal. The image of the Nile, he asserts, is also a factor in Ethiopia's developments. Not as important as in Egypt or Sudan, the river was, nevertheless, Ethiopia's "father of rivers"—personified, worshipped, loved, hated. The river, a huge gorge, was admired for its natural might. But rather than uniting economy, culture, and peoples, it was a major geographical obstacle dividing communities, depicted by modern and contemporary Ethiopian intellectuals and authors as an arrogant thief of soil and cattle, a traitor that steals Ethiopia's waters and divides her sons.

Flowing toward Egypt, the Nile acquires much different symbolic patterns, those of life and unity. In her chapter, "Brothers Along the Nile: Egyptian Concepts of Race and Ethnicity, 1895–1910," Eve Troutt Powell examines an early stage in the evolution of Egyptian modern nationalism: the definition by Egyptian intellectuals of their new modern identity via the concept of "Nile Valley unity," meaning Egypt's embrace of the Sudan. The British, whose Anglo-Egyptian army had conquered the Mahdiyya Islamic state in Sudan (1896–1898), opposed the idea of Egyptian-Sudanese unity and, as Troutt Powell explains, mobilized the science of anthropology and ethnography to refute the Egyptian claim. They allowed a British anthropologist to analyze the anatomy of soldiers of southern Egyptian origin to prove that they were decendants of ancient Egyptians, racially distinguished from fellow Sudanese. In rebuilding a racial scientific Nubian Dam, the British colonialists were also aided by extensive ethnographic research conducted by their Lebanese agent Na'um Shuqayr. The latter published a voluminous description (in Arabic) of Sudanese tribes, underlining their cultural uniqueness. But, according to Troutt Powell, the pioneers of Egyptian nationalism, led by the luminary intellectual Ahmad Lutfi al-Sayyid, who viewed the common Egyptian-Sudanese history as one of deprivation and a yearning for modern national citizenry, insisted on a common Nile Valley human identity. The author ends on a critical note, however, noting some similarity between Lutfi al-Sayyid's ignoring of the Sudanese's own voice and British paternalism.

In his chapter, "Egypt, Ethiopia and 'The Abyssinian Crisis,' 1935–1936," Haggai Erlich attempts to summarize the mutual images and concepts exposed by a traumatic watershed. The Ethiopian side is dealt with quite briefly. Facing their destruction by Benito Mussolini in 1935, the Ethiopians had little effort to spare for reflection on their traditional attitudes of suspicion and fear, which stemmed from a sixteenth-century traumatic Islamic conquest. The Egyptians, however, who experienced quite a critical year in 1935 themselves, had ample time to discuss Ethiopia, primarily as the antithetical image of Mussolini. Erlich analyzes the Egyptian perception of Ethiopia through what he describes as the three main components of the Egyptian soul: Islam, modern Egyptianism, and Arabism. Each of those identities, he asserts, held a different image of Ethiopia, each wavering between polarized concepts. Egypt's debate on Ethiopia revealed a rich variety of nuances in 1935 and was indeed a discussion of Egypt's own identities and options. These attitudes, ranging from a radical delegitimization of Ethiopia on one hand, to cordial friendliness on the other, resurfaced and were recycled in later decades, continuing to shape Egyptian Nile policy to this very day.

Israel Gershoni's contribution, "Geographers and Nationalism in Egypt: Huzayyin and the Unity of the Nile Valley, 1945–1948," analyzes the special role of geographers in the intellectual and scientific enhancement of national ideologies. He describes the role of Egyptian geographer Sulayman Huzayyin, who devoted his career to shattering the Nubian Dam barrier and providing evidence that the entire Nile Valley (differentiating from "the Nile heights" of Ethiopia) was the home of one Egyptian-Sudanese nation. Gershoni describes Huzayyin's important work to develop Egyptian geographical studies, and analyzes his dilemma in being both a proponent of a nationalist ideology and a scholar of professional integrity. As a geographer, says Gershoni, Huzayyin combined his research of the physical aspects of the Nile Valley with an analysis of ethnography, culture, history, and contemporary politics, so as to provide a scholarly dimension to the central ideological premise of modern Egyptian nationalism. This aspect of his work culminated in 1945–1948, the period in which the issue of Egyptian-Sudanese unity became a pivotal factor on the Anglo-Egyptian agenda. Huzayyin's conclusion, that Egypt would never be able to separate itself from Sudan, and that Egyptian-Sudanese unity—

a matter of virtual existence—was inevitable, was indeed consonant with the prevailing atmosphere in Egypt of the 1940s.

Within half a decade, however, a fundamental change took place. The new revolutionary regime in Egypt began its historic reorientation away from Egyptianism and the unity of the Nile Valley, toward Arabism and a strategic focus on the Fertile Crescent and the Arabian Peninsula. In 1953 an Anglo-Egyptian treaty recognized Sudan as a separate entity embarking on national independence. Robert Collins, in his chapter described below, argues that Nasser initiated construction of the Aswan Dam as both a particular Egyptian solution to an all-Nile problem, as well as a political spectacle aimed at eternalizing his revolution. Yoram Meital does not enter the hydropolitical sphere but delves deeply into the worlds of culture, myth, and identity. In his chapter, "The Aswan High Dam and Revolutionary Symbolism in Egypt," he shows how the erection of the dam was closely connected to shaping the regime's major objectives. The monumental enterprise was to become the foundation for a comprehensive economic transformation, as well as a landmark on the revolutionary road to human progress. Its construction was to be depicted as the embodiment of the anti-imperialist struggle, the molding of a new, emancipated society. The story of the dam and the symbolic aura built around it reflected the entire revolution as perceived by Egypt's new leadership. Meital analyzes the metaphoric images of the dam as manifested in literature, art, music, and other cultural fields. The Aswan Dam became a historical signpost, a site commemorating the Nasserite phase in Egyptian history. Simultaneously functional and symbolic, a magnified monument of eternal irreversible duration, it would remain not only a mere hydropolitical "Egyptian" solution but also a legacy of revolutionary myth.

In "The Nile in Egyptian-Sudanese Relations: 1956–1995," Gabriel Warburg offers a succinct analysis that complements the chapters by Troutt Powell, Gershoni, and Meital. The Nile, he says, was a major factor in shaping the four stages of modern Egyptian-Sudanese relations. The first was the pre-1955 period marked by Egyptian ideological consensus regarding unity with the Sudan. Warburg describes how the British used their control of the Sudanese Nile to threaten the Egyptian nationalists in order to thwart the idea of unity. The second stage, Warburg says, began in 1952 when the new revolutionary regime accepted Sudanese independence and turned, in the very same spirit, to the building of the Aswan Dam. He describes the tension between the states prior to their signature of the new water agreement in 1959 and explains Sudanese policy against the background of internal political changes. Sadat's return to Egyptianist, Nilocentrist concepts, and Sudan's newly formed anti-Soviet policy, paved the way for a third stage of near cordiality between the two countries beginning in the early 1970s. It was manifested by various agreements, most importantly their mutual efforts to cope with the Nile, culminating with the start of construction of the Jungelei Canal in 1978. The fourth stage, marked by an acute deterioration in relations, is the present situation. Beginning in the mid-1980s, Sudan re-embraced a radical Islam of the sort that, a century earlier, had motivated its leadership and society during the formative Mahdiyya era. Warburg describes the new anti-Egyptian spirit, the deterioration of the situation in Christian southern Sudan, and the ensuing collapse of the Jungelei project, and warns that the tendency of the Islamic radicals in Khartoum to threaten Egypt with the Nile waters might prove counterproductive.

As part of the 1959 Egyptian-Sudanese agreement, some 50,000 inhabitants of the region to be covered by Lake Nasser were transferred to Khashm al-Girba in eastern Sudan in 1964. There, in an area irrigated by another new dam, they were to undergo profound transformations stemming from revolutionary planning, changes that included the establishment of twenty-two new villages, the generous distribution of good irrigated land, and a new town called New Halfa. In "Removing the Nubians: The Halfawis at Khashm al-Girba," Ismail Abdalla looks at the project from the perspective of thirty years and considers it a complete failure. The revolutionaries of the 1960s wanted to build a new model of future society and boost their newly regained national confidence, yet they ignored the wishes of the people they led. In retrospect, he says, neither nature nor people were ready to change that rapidly. Expectations of the water reservoir proved too high, and the resettled Halfawis adhered to their old values and habits. Describing the multifaceted failure, Abdalla concludes that no changes, instituted from the top downward, can succeed without full consideration of the people in question, their culture, and their long historical experience.

Abdalla's chapter dwells on the dynamism between continuity and change, humans and nature, ideas and realities, history and myth. It also brings us back to our point of departure; the Nubians of Wadi Halfa, in their seventh-century victory over the army of Islam, re-emphasized and eternalized the human diversity of the Nile basin. Their fate is indeed a reflection of the vicissitudes of history and the inevitability of change—the descendants of those ancient, invincible warriors who have become the transferrable objects of modern revolution.

If all our chapters underlined human diversity, "In Search of the Waters of the Nile, 1900–2000" by Robert Collins calls for unity of action; it is a succinct but authoritative summary of the river's twentieth-century history of hydropolitics. The Nile basin, Collins determines, is a single comprehensive hydrological system and should have been coped with as such. But in this respect, the twentieth century has been a two-stage story.

This was primarily a British story during the first half of the century. Though Egypt had controlled Sudan during the nineteenth century for short periods, the British brought the two countries under the same rule in

1898. By abolishing the Nubian Dam, they were in a position to create a comprehensive hydraulic plan. Collins analyzes their failure, partly due to lack of vision, proper technology (such as an attempt to dig a canal in southern Sudan), and their strategic interest in preventing Egyptian-Sudanese unity. Collins says they were also overly reluctant in their approach to the Blue Nile, their relevant schemes foiled by Ethiopian procrastination, suspicion, and finally by the Ethiopian preference for American expertise and interests. The Americans finally provided the best comprehensive scheme for the entire Nile system in the 1950s, but it was not to materialize for political reasons.

The second stage, Collins says, was primarily an Egyptian-Ethiopian failure, beginning with the Nasserite revolution in Egypt and the ensuing strategical decision to build the Aswan High Dam. The idea behind the dam was to create both a political achievement and a water reservoir in Egyptian-controlled territory. It necessitated an agreement with Sudan (1959) but resulted in ignoring Ethiopia and shelving the proper all-Nile hydraulic solution. Collins goes on to describe the Egyptian-Ethiopian diplomatic failure to reach an understanding, as well as the failure of the renewed Egyptian-Sudanese effort to build the White Nile Canal in southern Sudan during the 1980s. To Collins, this has been a sad century of rivalry and ignorance, of the failure of humankind to unite in order to tame nature, and he warns that the leaders of the Nile communities must reach an understanding and work out a comprehensive plan to tap the waters of the Nile, or face inevitable disasters.

The twenty chapters in this collection far from exhaust the subject. Entire areas of major relevance are excluded. The entire scope of medieval Egyptian and early modern Nile history is mentioned only indirectly. For example, the Nile was probably more important to the Mamluks' conceptualization of Egypt and its regional affiliation than to their Ottoman successors. If true, was this also because Ethiopia was strong and prosperous during the days of the earlier period but weak and disunited during the later one? Ethiopian history and concepts are discussed primarily in their medieval and early modern contexts. But what of their twentieth-century transformations? What of the Ethiopian-Egyptian religious dialogue, its Islamic and Christian dimensions, and their Nile legacies? What of Sudan, presented here solely in its modern and contemporary perspective? What of the Nile factor during the Mahdiyya formative period, during earlier Sudanese periods and cultures? What of other riparian histories and cultures, their attachment to the great river, their relations with their close and distant neighbors upstream? What of the voices of peasants, nomads, fishermen, traders? What of women, their vision of Mother Nature, their concepts of the eternal river, their role in the histories and the myths?

Academically, we must admit to having attempted to open a single door. Personally, we believe it is not for us to say how the barriers should be removed. Transferring the Nubians did not move the metaphoric dam, nor did it bring neighbors closer together. Barriers of all sorts, we believe, should be addressed and recognized in order to ensure, rather than combat, diversity. Sober leaders and people of goodwill must establish eye contact and continue the effort to turn diversity into a basis for recognition, cooperation, and mutual enrichment.

Part 1

◆

Peoples and Identities
in Medieval Times

2

◆

The Spread of Islam and the Nubian Dam

David Ayalon

The Nile Valley forms an essential component of the lands of Islam in general and of their North African part in particular. Yet the Arabization and Islamization of the portion that we now call Sudan has been slow and is not yet completed. By far, the main reason for this phenomenon is that the Arab thrust along the Nile in the very early decades of Islam's existence was checked by what I call the Nubian Dam, a term I shall explain further on. For centuries that check was followed by an infiltration of nomads, not all of them Arab or Muslim. Then came military attacks on Nubia from the north, haphazard by the Ayyubids and much more determined by the Mamluks. The culmination of those attacks was that of Muhammad 'Ali, in the early nineteenth century, which opened a new page in the history of Egypt and its southern neighbors.

The study of the Nile Valley in early Islam should be conducted in close connection with two major factors: its place within the Muslim expansion as a whole, and its place in the expansion within the African continent. Not long after its early thrust, Islam faced four major fronts: (1) the Christian Byzantine front, especially in northern Syria, southeastern Anatolia, and northern Iraq (extended by a very important naval element in the Mediterranean Sea); (2) the Central Asiatic front and its extensions; (3) the Indian front; and (4) the African front.[1]

The most important fronts for quite a long time were the Christian Byzantine and the mainly pagan Central Asiatic fronts. In a civilization that relied more and more on slave armies, the Central Asiatic front proved to be the most beneficial. From the Central Asiatic front the fair-skinned Mamluk armies, which formed the backbone of Islam's might, were recruited for a very long period. The Byzantine front and its Christian continuators

17

were the most dangerous, with the largest and most threatening attacks coming from that direction. The pagan Indian front, with its immense human reservoir, was only marginal in the supply of Mamluks, and even this only for quite a short period.

The African front is of the greatest interest within the subject of this volume, and it includes, of course, the Nile Valley, which served as a huge source of slaves and for a considerably longer period than the three other fronts. The African front served both the civilian and the military markets, and the contribution of its black soldiers, who served mainly in the infantry, was of the highest importance. However, because of the discrimination against the blacks in the armed forces, which was much greater there than in civilian life, these soldiers have not received the attention and tribute that they deserve. And, therefore, it is far more difficult to reconstruct the history, the functioning, and the inner working of the black armies than for the white Mamluks. In this context it should be pointed out that the black eunuchs belong to a different category.

This is the extent to which the whole African front, lying to the south of Islam's conquests, figures in the general panorama of that religion's military drive, particularly in the first three or four centuries of its existence. However, Egypt and the Nile Valley, which form an essential part of the African front, figure in yet another formidable way during the earliest part of that drive.

A most astounding feature of the military expansion of Islam shortly after its birth was its swiftness. When it halted, the Arabs were already hundreds of miles away from their points of departure. This was the case with their thrust against Byzantium, Central Asia, the Maghrib, and Spain. Furthermore, in all of those faraway fronts, the struggle continued. The only outstanding exception was the Arab advance along the Nile, where they were brought to a lengthy standstill as soon as they tried to march beyond Egypt.

The absolutely unambiguous evidence and unanimous agreement of the early Muslim sources is that the Arabs' abrupt stop was caused solely and exclusively by the superb military resistance of the Christian Nubians. That is what I call the Nubian Dam. The array of those early sources includes the two most important chronicles of early Islam, al-Tabari (d. 926)[2] and al-Ya'qubi (d. 905);[3] the two best extant books on the Muslim conquests, al-Baladhuri (d. 892)[4] and Ibn al-A'tham al-Kufi (d. 926);[5] the most central encyclopedic work of al-Mas'udi (d. 956);[6] and the two best early sources dedicated specifically to Egypt, Ibn 'Abd al-Hakim (d. 871)[7] and al-Kindi (d. 961).[8]

All of the above-cited sources attribute the Nubian success to their superior archery, of which I shall bring some examples. To this central factor should be added the combination of the Nubians' military prowess and Christian zeal; their superior acquaintance of the terrain; the narrowness of the front line that they had to defend; and, quite possibly, the series of cataracts situated at their back, and other natural obstacles. What follows is a sample from al-Baladhuri's evidence.

> The Nubians fought the Muslims very fiercely. When they encountered them they showered them with arrows, until all of them were wounded and they withdrew with many wounds and gouged eyes. Therefore, they were called "the marksmen of the eye." . . . A Muslim participant in the fighting on that front said: "I took part twice in the war against the Nubians during the reign of 'Umar b. al-Khattab, and I never saw a people fiercer in war than they are. I saw repeatedly one of them saying to the Muslim: 'Where would you like me to put my arrow into you?' and sometimes one of our brave youngsters would say jokingly 'in this place,' and would not miss the target. One day they went out against us and met us in battle array. We wanted to decide the battle by launching a single [concentrated] charge with our swords but we could not anticipate them. They shot at us until [our] eyes were gone. A hundred and fifty gouged eyes were counted. We said, therefore, that nothing is better than making peace with these ones."[9]

Al-Mas'udi, in giving the account of the Muslim-Nubian fighting, goes as far as stating that the Nubians shoot from strange bows. The people of Hijaz and Yemen and the rest of the Arabs learned archery from them. They are called by the Arabs "the marksmen of the pupil of the eye."[10] I do not accept or reject the assertion of al-Mas'udi about who were the earliest teachers of the Arabs in the use of the bow, the main weapon of the cavalryman, who formed the backbone of the armies in medieval Islam. What that assertion certainly proves is the immense impact that the Nubian bow and its users, who brought them to a halt, made on them. What might support al-Mas'udi's claim is that the great ability of the Nubians as archers was already recognized by the pharaonic Egyptians as well as by the Meroites.[11]

What is particularly worth noting is that the account of the military ability of the Nubians was sometimes accompanied in the Arab sources by expressions quite similar to those that they used about the valor of the Turks who top the list of peoples of military excellence among Islam's adversaries.[12] However, the Nubians were not allowed to join the topmost Muslim units, especially after the creation of the Mamluk armies. Fair-skinned Christians were enlisted in those armies even before the upsurge in their numbers at a later time.

The basic difficulty in the study of the first two or two and a half centuries of the history of Islam is the paucity of the contemporary source material pertaining to that formative period. The information that has come down to us through the eyes of later sources is, to no small extent, partisan, especially when we consider that Islam developed and expanded through internal adversities and struggles at least since the death of the prophet Muhammad. However, there is nowadays a growing tendency among some Islamicists to put much more stress on that obvious partisanship than is warranted.

In my view, the correct way to study that difficult period is first to review the data that, by reasonable considerations, seem to be correct and reliable, and only afterward to relate to it the data that are more questionable. To the best of my conviction, the Nubian account is an excellent case in point. What is so significant about the evidence of our sources is that it is given by the Nubians' enemies (evidence that is called so aptly in Arabic *shahadat shahid min ahlihi* [an evidence by a person of the people in question]). This act carries a lot of weight for one cannot see any reason for the Arabs to praise the Nubians so highly, along with their admission of their own failure in the field of battle. At the same time it is a great tribute to the objectivity in this case of the Muslim sources, and it also enhances considerably the chances of the reliability of their accounts, at least about the Muslim expansion in other fronts, and perhaps much more beyond that.[13]

Additional conclusions that emerge from the sources mentioned include the following:

1. The orders to advance in Egypt both southward along the Nile and westward along the Mediterranean coast were given by Caliph 'Umar b. al-Khattab ('Umar I) (634–644), and there is no indication that the caliph, or the commanders on the spot, gave preference to one direction over the other.

2. The concentrated attacks in the Nubian front were made by a no lesser person than 'Amr b. al-'As, the conqueror of Egypt, its first de facto if not formal governor, and one of the greatest commanders of early Islam. They lasted until his dismissal and replacement by another great commander, 'Abdallah b. Sa'd in the reign of Caliph 'Uthman (644–656). For him it was easier to admit the military failure and sign with the Nubians the famous treaty, where both sides were given a more or less equal standing.

3. The awe and respect that the Muslims had for their Nubian adversaries are reflected in the fact that even a rather late Umayyad caliph, 'Umar b. 'Abd al-'Aziz ('Umar II 717–720), is said to have ratified the Nubian-Muslim treaty out of fear for the safety of the Muslims ("he ratified the peace treaty out of consideration for the Muslims and out of [a desire] to spare their lives").[14] This implies that in the capital of Islam the memory of the feats of the Nubians was still alive and that the danger of

an attack by them was not considered to be a matter of the past even more than half a century after the treaty signing.

The obvious question that arises is how the removal of the Nubian Dam—had it been carried out by the attacking Muslims and the march of their armies into Nubia and beyond—would have affected the Muslims' more crucial advance along the Mediterranean coast in the direction of the Maghrib and Spain. The answer is that the chances of weakening the Arab thrust from Egypt westward were very great indeed, with all the negative consequences for Islam resulting from that weakening. Although, as already stated, the fear of the Nubians was still quite considerable in the reign of the Umayyad caliph 'Umar II, it must have diminished with the march of time because of the decline of the Nubian military power and also because there was not much to look for south of Aswan.

The treatment of Nubia by the Ayyubids, a few years after their coming to power in Egypt (1169), is most revealing. Saladin, the founder of the Ayyubid dynasty in Egypt, who threw off his allegiance to his patron, the Zangid Nur al-Din, at least actually, if not formally, feared the retaliation of that patron and looked for a place of refuge for himself and for his family. His first choice fell on northern Nubia. It was conquered temporarily by his elder brother, Turanshah, in 1172. Speaking of the Ayyubid siege and capture of Ibrim, the major town in that area, Ibn al-Athir said: "[Ibrim's] people were powerless in fighting the Muslim army, because they did not possess shields which could protect them from the arrows of the Muslims and from their other weapons. They therefore surrendered the town."[15] The Ayyubids soon discovered the inadequacy of that place as a safe and self-supporting shelter, and Turanshah moved in 1170 to the prosperous Yemen, where he established the south Arabian branch of the Ayyubid dynasty, which was replaced in 1229 by the Rasulids.

The process of the decline of the Nubians' military might from the early seventh to the late twelfth centuries has still to be reconstructed. In the seventh century the Nubian archery stopped the Muslims, whereas in the twelfth century it was the Muslim archery that played a major role in defeating the Nubians. The subjugation of Nubia was carried out by Sultan Baybars I, who turned it into a vassal state.

Another factor that might contribute to the delay in conquering Nubia from Egypt is mentioned by P. M. Holt, in his important chapter "The Nilotic Sudan." In a note to that article he says: "It has been suggested (in a private conversation) that the Arabs might have found it more convenient to leave Nubia outside the Muslim empire, as a source of slaves, and especially eunuchs, since enslavement and mutilation within the frontier were forbidden."[16] What is certainly true about this suggestion is that the Muslims did have a problem when they conquered lands that previously served as a source of supply of slaves and eunuchs. However, we do not know the extent of the flow into Egypt of either slaves or eunuchs originating from Nubia and its immediate neighborhood. There are some indications that they might have come from more western regions.[17] Furthermore, although most of the eunuchs were imported, we know of castration, and on no small scale, within the boundaries of Islam. Further study is needed for establishing more precisely the weight of that factor.

Finally, a brief reference will be made to the very well-known evidence of al-Maqrizi (d. 1442) about the seventh-century treaty (the *baqt*) with the Nubians. It would appear that later authors did not show much readiness, certainly not enthusiasm, for relating the prowess and skill of the Nubians in their fight against the armies of Islam. Already Yaqut (d. 1229), in his classical geographical dictionary, dilutes the unequivocal statements of the early sources almost beyond recognition. In his entry under "Dunqula" all he has to say is that the eye of one of the Muslim leading fighters was hit.[18] In his entry under "Nuba" he says about its inhabitants: "They shoot with arrows from *Arab* bows."[19] But al-Maqrizi goes much further than that. He simply wipes out any trace of the fighting qualities of the Nubians in spite of the fact that he quotes two of the seven early authors I mentioned, al-Baladhuri and al-Mas'udi. What is more, from al-Maqrizi's presentation one cannot understand at all why the Muslims accorded the Nubians such generous and quite unique terms.[20] There is no doubt that the cause of al-Maqrizi's attitude was his strong antagonism to the Christians.

One reason, and certainly not the only one, for Islamicists' ignoring or greatly underestimating the evidence of the early Muslim sources about the Nubians' valorous resistance is their heavy reliance on al-Maqrizi's evidence, which, considering its fullness and detailed character (especially about the terms of the *baqt*), is justifiable in itself.

NOTES

This chapter summarizes my article "The Nubian Dam," *YSAI,* vol. 12 (1989): pp. 372–390 (reprinted in *Islam and the Abode of War,* London: Variorum Reprints, 1994), and of a passage in my "Aspects of the Mamluk Phenomenon," part 1, in *Der Islam,* vol. 53 (Berlin, 1976), especially pp. 201–202 (reprinted in *The Mamluk Military Society,* London: Variorum Reprints, 1977).

　　1. Ayalon, "Aspects," pp. 207–204.

　　2. Al-Tabari, *Ta'rikh,* pp. 5–15, 2593.

　　3. Al-Ya'qubi, *Ta'rikh,* pp. 4, 15–180.

　　4. Al-Baladhuri, *Futuh al-Buldan,* pp. 6, 14–237.

　　5. Quatremère's translation into French of the Persian translation of Ibn al-A'tham's *Kitab al-Futuh* in "Mémoire sur la Nubie" in *Mémoires Géographiques et Historiques sur l'Egypte et sur quelques Contrées Voisines,* pp. 39–41. Unfortunately, in the Hyderabad edition (1968–1975) of Ibn al-A'tham's work, the relevant

part is missing and is replaced with a summary of the Persian translation. However, the very last lines of the original work in Arabic, which are essential for the thesis presented here, were not lost (see Ayalon, "The Nubian Dam," p. 381, n. 23).

6. Al-Mas'udi, *Muraj,* vol. 3, pp. 3, 11–39.

7. Ibn 'Abd al-Hakim, *Futuh Misr wa-Akhbaruha,* pp. 2–3, 18–170, 188, 609.

8. Al-Kindi, *Kitab al-Wulat,* p. 5–11, 12.

9. Al-Baladhuri, *Futuh-al-Buldan.*

10. Al-Mas'udi, *Muruj,* vol. 2, pp. 4, 8–383.

11. Shinnie, "Christian Nubia," pp. 564–565. See also Adams, *Nubia,* p. 451.

12. Ayalon, "The Nubian Dam," p. 383.

13. There is a tendency among some Islamicists to minimize the dimensions and importance of the Muslim army's attempt to break through the Nubian front. This is a mistaken approach. Within the framework of the present subject it would be worthwhile to collect the views of the Islamicists who studied it and have them comment. These views were by no means identical. As far as I know, however, none of them goes as far as I do in stressing the significance of that army's setback on that front, either in its general Islamic setting or in its more limited Nile Valley setting.

14. Ayalon, "The Nubian Dam," pp. 387–388.

15. Ibn ad-Athar, *al-Kamil fi al-Ta'rikh,* p. 387.

16. Holt, "The Nilotic Sultan," p. 328.

17. Al-Istakhri, *Kitab Masalik w'al-Mamalik,* pp. 39–41; al-Ya'qubi, *Kitab al-Buldan,* pp. 345, ll. 11–19.

18. Yaqut, *Mu'jam al-Buldan,* p. 92.

19. Ibid., pp. 323, ll. 6–7. Thus Yaqut turns the whole story upside down. According to him it was the *Arab* bow and not the Nubian that figured so prominently in that encounter!

20. Al-Maqrizi, *al-Khitat,* vol. 1, pp. 199, ll. 35–202, l. 23.

3

◆

Ethiopia's Alleged Control of the Nile

Richard Pankhurst

Si dice che il Soldan, re dell'Egitto,
A quel Re di tributo e sta suggetto;
Perch'e in poter di lui del camino dritto
Levare il Nilo e dargli altro ricetto;
E per questo lasciar subito afflito
Di fame e tutto quel distretto.
—Ludovico Ariosto, *Orlando Furioso*

Ethiopia and Egypt, linked but also divided by the Nile,[1] were in contact since the dawn of history. They were mutually interdependent. Egypt's prosperity depended on Nile water and silt from Ethiopia, which occurred mainly in the summer for agriculture. Christian Ethiopia depended on the Coptic Church of Egypt, from where the Ethiopian *abun* (patriarch) was selected. Egypt was thus dependent on Ethiopia for its material existence, and Ethiopia was dependent on Egypt for its spiritual existence.

This mutual dependency was, however, unstable. The Nile flow varied from year to year, for climatic reasons, whereas the *abun's* arrival depended on the vagaries of Egyptian efficiency and goodwill, which, after the Arab conquest in the early seventh century, was problematic. One other element entered the equation: Ethiopia's supposed ability to control the Nile flow and thereby pressurize Egypt. This assumed that Ethiopian power was long a major international interest, creating pride for Ethiopians, fear for Egyptians, and hope and wonder for European Christendom.

FAILURE OF THE ETHIOPIAN RAINS AND THE NILE FLOOD

The first interruptions in Ethiopian rainfall are reported in the *Masahaf Senkesar,* or "synaxarium."[2] Ethiopian wickedness is supposed to have

25

caused two droughts, when God "restrained the heavens" so that it "could not rain." This happened during the time of the Coptic patriarch Joseph (831–849) and again during the time of Patriarch Gabriel (1131–1149).[3] Whether these droughts actually occurred, and influenced the amount of water reaching Egypt, has still to be ascertained.

The question of the interruption in the Nile's flow supposedly first came to the fore in Egypt around 1089–1090, during the reign of Fatimid sultan al-Mustansir. The subsequent Arab writer al-Makin reports that the flood failed to reach Egypt, and the sultan accordingly sent Patriarch Michael of Alexandria to Ethiopia with a request that the Ethiopians restore the stream, which they did. The Ethiopian monarch's name is not given, but he was probably a member of the Zagwe dynasty. He reputedly ordered a mound to be broken, whereupon the water in Egypt rose three cubits in one night.[4]

This account, though written long afterward, was accepted by the seventeenth-century German scholar Hiob Ludolf. He declares that al-Makin, a "creditable" author and secretary to the rulers of Egypt, could not possibly have "invented such an incident," for "had it been an untruth" he would have been "in fear of being contracted." Ludolf also considered the possible objection that the Nile's failure might have happened naturally, the river being dammed up by tree trunks, mud, and stones, driven by force, and heaped together by the river in the narrow passage of the water. He replied that such "remarkable" blockages "rarely or never" occurred in "large or violent Rivers" and that "if Nature could effect so much, what might not be accomplish'd by Art?"[5]

The above argument is not, however, fully convincing. The Nile's failure could have occurred for natural reasons other than those Ludolf mentioned. It could have been due to drought in the highlands, as reported earlier, or to vegetation growth in the Sudanese lowlands. It may also be questioned whether Ethiopian rulers then possessed the technical ability to construct a "mound" able to block the river.

BRUCE'S STORY ABOUT KING LALIBALA
AND SALT'S COMMENT

The idea of diverting the Nile to pressurize Egypt is alleged to have developed two centuries later, during the reign of the Zagwe emperor Lalibala (1172–1212). This claim rests, however, on entirely uncorroborated statements by the eighteenth-century Scottish "explorer" James Bruce. He asserts that Lalibala's reign coincided with "a great persecution" in Egypt of Christian "masons, builders and hewers of stone." The monarch supposedly collected a "prodigious number" of them, with whom he attempted to realize one of "the favourite pretensions of the Abyssinians" by "turning the Nile out of its course" to stop it being "the cause of the fertility of Egypt." Recalling that Egypt was controlled by Muslims, enemies of Lalibala's religion, the Scotsman remarks that "if it was in the power of man to accomplish this undertaking," it could have fallen into "no better hands" than those whom Lalibala gave it, for they had been "driven from their native country by those Saracens who now were reaping the benefits of the river" in place of those they had forced "to seek habitations far from the benefit and pleasure afforded by its stream."[6]

Wishing to "famish Egypt," Lalibala, according to Bruce, "found, by an exact survey and calculation," that there ran "on the summit, or highest part" of Ethiopia, "several rivers which could be intercepted by mines." Instead of flowing northward to the Nile, they could thus be "directed into the low country southward" and not reach Egypt at all.[7] Elaborating on the river's supposed diversion, Bruce asserts that "people of the country" had informed him that the king had actually "intersect[ed] and carr[ied] into the Indian Ocean, two very large rivers" that had "ever since flowed that way." Lalibala, he claims, had also "carried a level" to Lake Zway, where "many rivers" emptied themselves at the beginning of the rains and would have "effectually diverted the course of them all."[8]

This work was stopped, Bruce claims, by Lalibala's death. Signs of the ruler's activities, he asserts, could nevertheless be seen in his day. He substantiates this statement by reference to the alleged observations of a Shawan prince, Amha Iyasus, "a young man of great understanding" with whom he had "lived several months in the most intimate of friendship." The chief assured him that Lalibala's earthworks were still "visible" and were "of a kind whose use could not be mistaken." The prince "had himself often visited them."[9] No such earthworks have, however, been seen by any traveler, nor is there any visible sign that any river was ever reversed to run into the sea. The diversion of even a stream from the Nile area to the Indian Ocean would in fact have been virtually impossible. Bruce attempts elsewhere to explain why the alleged Lake Zway plan was abandoned. Contradicting his earlier statement that this was due to Lalibala's death, he cites Amha Iyasus as offering an entirely different explanation. The chief had reportedly stated that:

> in a written account which he had seen in Shoa, it was said that this prince [Lalibala] was not interrupted by death in his undertaking, but [had been] persuaded by the monks, that if a greater quantity of water was let down into the dry kingdoms of Hadea, Mara, and Adal, increasing in population every day, and even now, almost equal in power to Abyssinia itself, these barren kingdoms would become the garden of the world; and such a number of Saracens, dislodged from Egypt by the first appearance of the Nile's failing, would fly thither, that they would not

> only withdraw those countries from their obedience, but be strong enough
> to over-run the whole kingdom of Abyssinia.[10]

No Ethiopian written account, such as Amha Iyasus supposedly mentioned, has ever been reported; nor is any attempt to divert the Nile included in Lalibala's *Gadl* (Acts).[11]

Bruce also supports his statements about Lalibala's earthworks by reference to the early sixteenth-century Portuguese traveler Francisco Alvarez.[12] He cites Alvarez as stating that the Portuguese ambassador
Roderigo de Lima, who had come to Ethiopia in 1520, had seen "the remains" of the king's "vast works" and had "travelled in them for several
days."[13] No mention of this is, however, given in the Portuguese narrative.[14]

Bruce's story is thus a much flawed story: it contradicts itself and is
almost implausible. Yet it was accepted by the early nineteenth-century
British traveler Henry Salt, who asserts that Lalibala was "very distinguished" for "a successful attempt to turn the course of the Nile." Salt
thought that this was also recorded in "Arabian histories of Egypt" around
1095. Not knowing when Lalibala lived, he confused the latter's alleged
closure of the Nile with the entirely unconnected failure of the waters in
Egypt two centuries earlier.[15] Though seemingly endorsing Bruce's claims
about Lalibala, Salt also took up an almost contradictory position, for he
observes that the idea of diverting the river perhaps sprang from the "ignorance of the times." His own view was that the "only source of a river"
over which Lalibala had any "command" was, "in all probability," not the
Nile at all, but its tributary, the Takazze, which began near Lasta.[16]

We may conclude that Bruce's uncorroborated assertions are unconvincing and that Salt was correct in asserting that Lalibala had no direct
control over the country through which the Nile flowed. There is in fact no
evidence that the monarch ever contemplated, let alone effected, any diversion of the river.

Ethiopian tradition, though silent on Lalibala's supposed attempt on
the Nile, claims that the last of the Zagwe rulers, Na'akuto La'ab (deposed
1270), wished to deflect the Takazze. In *Gadl,* written many centuries
later, he asserts that the Egyptians refused to pay their accustomed tribute
to Ethiopia, whereupon the monarch prayed that the flow of water to the
Nile be stopped for three years and seven months. God reportedly listened:
Egypt was struck by famine, and its population declined. The Egyptian
ruler then dispatched messages to the king, promising tribute and begging
him to resume the river's flow.[17]

Two comments deserve to be made. First, it was the Takazze, not the
Nile, that was reportedly blocked. Second, there is no suggestion that the
king did anything beyond prayer.[18]

THE EMPERORS OF ETHIOPIA'S GOLDEN ERA (1270–1540)

The idea of diverting the Nile, rather than the Takazze, apparently dates from the reign of Emperor 'Amda Seyon (1312–1342). This was a period, according to the Arab historian al-Maqrizi, when the Mamluk sultan of Egypt, al-Nasir Muhammad ibn Qala'un, was in conflict with his Coptic subjects and demolished several of their churches. The Ethiopian monarch, who according to al-Maqrizi's dating, was probably 'Amda-Seyon, reportedly dispatched an embassy to Egypt and threatened its ruler with diverting the Nile.[19]

The Ethiopian embassy apparently increased Egyptian awareness of the significance of Ethiopia's location at the source of the Nile. The Egyptian courtier Ibn Fadlallah al-'Umari reports that the Abyssinians claimed to be "the guardians of the course of the Nile" and furthered "its regular arrival out of respect" for the Egyptian sultan.[20]

It should be emphasized that al-Maqrizi's claim is only that 'Amda-Seyon threatened to block the Nile, not that he actually attempted to do so. Al-'Umari's assertion is likewise only that the Ethiopians considered themselves guardians of the Nile and acted out of respect for the sultan, not that they could in fact interfere with its flow, or had tried to do so.

Conflict with Egypt erupted during the reign of 'Amda-Seyon's son, Emperor Sayfa Ar'ad (1342–1371), who "assumed the role," as British historian J. S. Trimingham says, "of protector of the Patriarch of Alexandria."[21] He made war, according to the Ethiopian royal chronicles, in Upper Egypt,[22] but, significantly, did not attempt to divert the Nile, presumably considering even a faraway campaign less arduous. The first Ethiopian ruler alleged to have actually interfered with the Nile was Sayfa Ar'ad's son, Emperor Dawit (r. 1380–1412), who was reportedly also in conflict with the Egyptians. This is, however, not mentioned in the principal Ethiopian chronicles, but only in a little-known version. It claims that, because of the imprisonment in Egypt of Patriarch Yohannes of Alexandria, Dawit held back the Nile waters. The Egyptian ruler responded by sending the emperor important gifts. Peace was reportedly re-established and the patriarch freed.[23] Support for the view that Dawit had in fact attempted to stop the Nile is expressed in several hagiographies, cited by Tadesse Tamrat, who notes that they insist that one of Dawit's strategies was to divert the flow of the Nile.[24] It should, however, be reiterated that Dawit's alleged Nile diversion does not figure in most of the chronicles, is not mentioned in any Egyptian source, nor is there any archaeological evidence that it ever took place.

The idea that Ethiopian rulers could divert the Nile was subsequently voiced during the reign of Emperor Yeshaq (1413–1430) by an Italian,

Pietro of Naples, who visited the country as envoy of the Duke of Berry. Pietro was quoted as stating, in 1432, that "if it pleased Prester John," the Ethiopian ruler, the latter could make the river go in "another part" of the country. The monarch had not done so, he added, because of "many Christians living on the banks of the Nile."[25] Pietro makes no reference to Emperor Dawit's earlier supposed "holding back" of the river, which, had it occurred, would doubtless have been mentioned. His report claims only that the Ethiopian ruler had the power of diverting the Nile, and states expressly that he had refrained from so doing.

The Nile question reportedly came to the fore again during the reign of Emperor Zar'a Ya'qob (1434–1468), when the Copts in Egypt were again persecuted and an important church destroyed. The patriarch of Alexandria, Yohannes XI, appealed, according to the Ethiopian royal chronicle and a text of the *Ta'amra Maryam* (Miracles of Mary), for support.[26] The emperor, according to an Egyptian source, sent the Egyptian ruler, Sultan Jaqmaq, a strongly worded message that reached Cairo in November 1443.[27] Complaining of Egyptian repression, it drew the sultan's attention to the fact that the Nile rose within Ethiopia and that Zar'a Ya'qob had the power to divert it, and only refrained for fear of God and in consideration of the sufferings a diversion would produce.[28] Zar'a Ya'qob's threat, which is not made in either of the above-mentioned Ethiopian texts, thus asserts only Ethiopia's ability to divert the Nile. So far from actually diverting it, the monarch is said to have deliberately refrained from doing so.

Support for the view that the Ethiopian ruler could control the Nile flow was expressed in the following century, during the reign of Emperor Lebna Dengel (1508–1540), by an Ethiopian monk, Abba Raphael. He told the Venetian scholar Alessandro Zorzi, in 1522, that the Ethiopian monarch could take the water of the Nile from the Muslims "so that it did not reach Cairo," but he would not do so because he feared that they "would ruin the churches and the Christian monks who are in Jerusalem and those in Egypt of which there are many."[29] Abba Raphael's claim, like Zar'a Ya'qob's threat, was thus qualified, in this case by fear of reprisal, and shows that the Ethiopian ruler was not in fact interfering with the river.

The above evidence shows that claims about Ethiopia's supposed ability to control the Nile were made for seven rulers: Lalibala, Na'akuto La'ab, 'Amda Seyon, Sayfa Ar'ad, Dawit, Zar'a Ya'qob, and Lebna Dengel. The evidence about the first, Lalibala, is too problematical to be considered seriously. Na'akuto La'ab reportedly did no more than pray, while four other rulers, 'Amda-Seyon, Yeshaq, Zar'a Ya'qob, and Lebna Dengel, reportedly refrained from any action, either on account of scruples or expediency. Only one ruler, Dawit, is supposed to have actually blocked the river, but evidence on this is far from conclusive. Threats were occasionally made but apparently never implemented. Claims of Ethiopia's ability to divert the Nile thus proved to be no more than roars of a paper lion.

EUROPEAN PERSPECTIVES

Ethio-Egyptian belief in the possibility of diverting the Nile duly percolated to Western Christendom. Many European Christians, preoccupied with the Crusades, were predisposed to accept any story offering support against the Saracens. The myth of Prester John,[30] a supposedly powerful Eastern Christian ruler, seeking to fight with Islam on behalf of European Christianity, was a popular early expression of the, "Let's get someone else to fight our wars for us," syndrome.

European pilgrims to the East returned with reports of the power and wealth of Prester John. They spoke of his riches, the strength of his army, and his ability to divert the Nile, to reduce their Muslim enemies in Egypt to destitution. Such ideas, though today perhaps considered genocide, captured European imagination. Largely devoid of reality, they nevertheless framed the opinions of the age.

Reports on Ethiopia's supposed influence over the Nile began as early as the reign of Emperor 'Amda-Seyon. Two Italians, Jacopo of Verona and Niccola of Poggibonsi, traveled to Jerusalem in the 1330s and returned with interesting reports. Jacopo claimed that Prester John was able to remove the Nile waters from the Egyptians.[31] Niccola agreed that the sultan feared Ethiopia's control over the river and stood in awe of the Prester, whom he considered "the best lord in the world."[32] This statement seems to show that the ruler had never utilized his assumed power over the river.

The Nile story was taken up shortly afterward by a Frenchman, Philippe of Mezières, who claimed that an Ethiopian ruler—he did not specify who or when—had deviated the river and caused a major Egyptian famine. The Egyptians, he added, were so afraid of the Ethiopians that they allowed them to pass through their territory free of tax.[33] Variations on this theme were published by a number of European travelers throughout the fifteenth century. They appear to have included Archbishop Giovanni, a cleric involved in the East,[34] the French pilgrim Guillebert of Lannoy,[35] and Anselmo Adorno, a man of Genoese descent who resided in Bruges.[36]

Many people in Europe were soon convinced that the Ethiopians could be mobilized to defeat the Saracens. This belief, Taddesse Tamrat observes, was "seriously considered by the strategists of the later Crusades."[37] The possibility of diverting the Nile was voiced at both the popular and governmental levels. Tuscan storyteller Andrea da Barberino

(1370–1432) made reference to it in his *Guerin Meschino*.[38] The Grand Master of Rhodes, John of Lastic, wrote to Charles VII of France about it in 1448.[39] Two years later, Alfonso of Aragon urged Emperor Zar'a Ya'qob to direct his attention to the Nile, "which ran to Cairo."[40] Fra Mauro's *mappamondo* (map of the world), completed in Venice in 1460, featured a drawing of imaginary gates, with which the Prester could supposedly block the river and deflect it into the Sudanese desert.[41]

European visitors to the East meanwhile continued to write of the possibility of diverting the river. Statements to this effect were made by the Flemish author Joos van Ghistle, who declared that Ethiopians in the Holy Land were therefore exempt from taxation and entitled to carry crosses;[42] the Belgian, Georges Lengherand, of Mons, who affirmed that the Nile flood took place by permission of the Prester;[43] the Frenchman, Jehan Thénaud, who agreed that it was because of the latter's control of the Nile that the sultan paid the Ethiopian ruler regular tribute;[44] and the German pilgrim Arnold von Harff, who reported that Christian Abyssinians arrived in Jerusalem "with banners unfurled . . . into the Temple of Christ."[45]

Such ideas, in the early sixteenth century, reached the Portuguese, then expanded into the East. They stirred the imagination in particular of their famous governor of India, Affonso d'Albuquerque. He conceived the ambition, around 1513, of piercing through "a very small range" of Ethiopian hills to divert the Nile "into another bed" and "destroy irrigation" in "the land of Cairo." To this end he requested his sovereign, Manoel I, to send him workmen from Madeira, skilled in cutting rocks and digging irrigation trenches. Albuquerque was, however, soon recalled, and his Nile plans were abandoned.[46]

Belief that the Nile could be diverted nevertheless continued to hold sway throughout the early sixteenth century. It found expression in the Italian poet Ludovico Ariosto's epic *Orlando Furioso* of 1516, which reiterated that Prester John had the power to cut the river and reduce Cairo and its neighborhood to famine.[47]

The arrival in Ethiopia of the Portuguese diplomatic mission in 1520, and the publication in 1540 of Alvarez's report on it, represented an important development. It vastly expanded European knowledge of the country and led to its steady demystification. European interest in the diversion of the Nile accordingly began to wane. Speculation tended thereafter to focus more on Ethiopia's military might, which Alvarez had witnessed, than on the country's reputed control over the river.[48]

European belief in Ethiopia's supposed ability to divert the river nevertheless died slowly. It was voiced by two notable early seventeenth-century travelers to the East. William Lithgow, a Scotsman, claimed, in 1616, that the Turkish sultan paid the ruler of Ethiopia an annual tax of 50,000 gold coins "lest he impede and withdraw the course of Nylus, and so bring Aegypt to desolation."[49] A decade or so later, a Spaniard, Antonio of Castelon, likewise reiterated that the Ethiopian ruler had control over the Nile, for which reason his subjects were exempt from taxation in Turkish territory.[50]

The coming to Ethiopia of the Jesuits, and their "discovery" of the source of the Nile in April 1618, was of major importance.[51] It removed much of the mystery still surrounding both the Nile and the land in which it flowed. This made the difficulty of diverting the river increasingly apparent. The new, postmedieval view was stated succinctly by a leading Jesuit writer, Baltazar Tellez. He emphatically declared that the Nile, with its immense mass of water, could not be redirected over the vast area suggested, particularly as it was the site of steep and rugged mountains.[52]

Later in the century, the German scholar Hiob Ludolf was greatly intrigued with the question "whether it be in the power of the Abyssine Kings to divert the Course of the Nile, that it should not overflow Egypt." He discussed the matter with his Ethiopian friend and informant, Abba Gorgoreyos. Asked if he knew the story of Patriarch Michael of Alexandria reportedly dispatched to Ethiopia over half a millennium earlier, Gorgoreyos replied in the negative. He stated, however, that he had "heard from persons of great Credit" that "not far from the Cataracts of the Nile, all the Land toward the East" was "level," and that, but for a single mountain, the river would "rather flow that way, than into Egypt."

Gorgoreyos believed that if this mountain were "digg'd through, a thing to be done with pains and difficulty," the river's course might be "turn'd and carry'd into the Red-Sea." This, he thought, was well known to both the Turks and the Portuguese, and that it was for that reason that the Ethiopian emperors had obtained "advantageous Conditions from the Saracens." Gorgoreyos added that it was said that an Ethiopian emperor once had "an intention" to divert the Nile "and had commanded his Subjects to undertake the Work" but had been "prevail'd upon to desist at the entreaty of the Egyptian Christians."[53]

Despite his admiration for Gorgoreyos, Ludolf accepted the latter's views on the Nile only reservedly. Probably influenced by the Jesuits, he doubted the country's ability to divert the river. He admitted that the question had perplexed him but was inclined to believe that the task of raising "a Mole or Dam of Stones" required "so much toyl and labour" that it was in no way agreeable to "the nature of the Abessins." He felt moreover that it was "unlikely that so vast a River, so long accustom'd to a declining and headlong Course," could be diverted. He argued that, if the Ethiopian monarch really controlled the Nile, he would "have had all Egypt at his Devotion," for the Turks would "deny him nothing." Moreover, if the project had been practicable, he wondered why the Jesuits had not persuaded the Ethiopians to make use of "that Power which Nature had put into their hands," and why they had not used "Threats rather than Intreaties and Bribes" to obtain the facilities they enjoyed at the Red Sea ports by the favor of their Turkish governor.[54]

Despite these reservations, the German scholar felt that the Nile diversion might be possible, not from the Ethiopian heartland, which lay "many Leagues distant from the Sea," but rather, as Gorgoreyos had suggested, from territory near the cataracts, namely, toward Sudan. Such action, he declared, was, however, no longer politically possible, for the Ethiopian monarch had ceased ruling the areas where the river could be redirected. Ludolf therefore concluded that what might have been done in the past was no longer possible. It was not that "the nature of the place" obstructed the river's diversion but that the Emperor lacked "the Power" to carry it out or had "no inclination" to do so. Were it were not for that, Ludolf could not think it either "absurd" or "improbable" that the Ethiopian rivers might be conveyed through the sandy lowlands to the north and thus produce a "vast diminution of the *Egyptian* Stream." To do so, it would, however, be necessary to employ "skilful Artists" to survey the area and establish the places "most proper to carry off the Water."[55] Ludolf was the last serious student of Ethiopia, prior to the modern era, to take the Nile diversion seriously.

By the early eighteenth century the idea that the Ethiopians could divert the Nile was largely rejected in Europe. This is apparent in the writings of the French cleric Abba Joachim Le Grand. Writing in 1726, he declared that Abyssinia was "most full of mountains," some so high that the Alps were "mere hills in comparison," while the Nile lay over a hundred leagues from the Red Sea.[56] After reviewing all available historical data, he declared: "We do not pretend that a canal cannot be dug from the Nile to the Red-Sea, but the Abyssinians cannot do it."[57]

Belief in the possibility of diverting the Nile nevertheless lingered on in Ethiopia. Early in the eighteenth century Emperor Takla Haymanot (1706–1708), infuriated that a French ambassador, Lenoir du Roule, and Murad, an Armenian trader, had been detained by the Muslim rulers of Sennar, wrote a strong protest to the pasha of Cairo. In it he declared that the detention violated "the law of nations," and continued: "We could very soon repay you in kind if we were inclined to revenge the insult you have offered to the man Murad on our part; the Nile would be sufficient to punish you, since God hath put in our power his foundation, his outlet, and his increase, and that we can dispose of the same to do you harm."[58]

The Egyptian pasha was probably not impressed, for the belief that the Ethiopians could divert the Nile had by then evaporated. Bruce was emphatic about this. Writing a little over half a century later, he declares that "no sensible man in Abyssinia" believed that the diversion of the Nile was possible, "and few [believed] that it had ever been attempted."[59] Such was the traveler's final judgment, and that of his generation.

CONCLUSION

The medieval belief that the rulers of Ethiopia could divert the waters of the Nile, and thereby ruin Egypt, exercised a major and long-enduring influence over Ethiopians, Egyptians, and Europeans for half a millennium. Threats were made, fears expressed, prayers uttered, hopes voiced, and travelers' tales published. The myth that the Nile had, or could, be redirected by the misnamed Prester John became a feature of Ethio-Egyptian statecraft, a question of direct relevance to the Coptic Church, an item on the agenda of Christian European diplomacy, and even, far away, a subject of Italian creative literature.

There is, however, little evidence that the Ethiopians ever made plans for the diversion of the Nile, let alone that they executed them. Variations in the annual flow of water reaching Egypt were due to erratic rainfall in the Ethiopian highlands rather than any action on the part of Ethiopia's rulers. One may even doubt whether changing the course of the Nile, however much desired, or feared, ever lay within the technological possibilities of the time.

NOTES

1. Following medieval practice and the writings of James Bruce, the term *Nile* is used here for the Abbay, or Blue Nile, which supplies the bulk of the water and silt reaching Egypt. The existence of the White Nile is irrelevant to the issues discussed in this chapter.

2. On this text see Budge, *The Book of the Saints,* vol. 1, p. xi.

3. Ibid., vol. 1, pp. 185–186; vol. 3, 800–801.

4. Al-Makin, *Historia sarracenica,* p. 358. See also Ludolf, *New History,* p. 41; Perruchon, *Vie de Lalibala,* p. xxi; Le Grand, *Voyage historique,* pp. 215–216; Lobo, *Voyage,* p. 216; and Cerulli, "Il volo," p. 36.

5. Ludolf, *New History*, pp. 41–42. See also Cerulli, "Il volo," p. 36.

6. Bruce, *Travels,* vol. 1, p. 529.

7. Ibid., p. 530.

8. Ibid.

9. Ibid., p. 531.

10. Ibid., pp. 530–531.

11. Perruchon, *Vie de Lalibala.*

12. Bruce, *Travels,* vol. 2, p. 150.

13. Ibid., vol. 1, p. 531.

14. Beckingham and Huntingford, *Prester John.*

15. On Salt's error, see also Perruchon, *Vie de Lalibala,* p. xxi.

16. Salt, A *Voyage to Abyssinia,* p. 473, n.

17. Rossini, *Gli atti di re Na'akueto La'ab,* Tipografia del Senato, Roma, 1943, pp. 110–112, 228–229.

18. Hecht, "Ethiopia Threatens to Block the Nile," p. 5.

19. Quatremère, *Mémoires géographiques et historiques sur l'Egypte,* p. 275. See also Basset, "Etudes," p. 434; and Trimingham, *Islam,* pp. 70–71.

20. Gaudefroy-Demombynes, *Ibn Fadl Allah Al-'Umari, Masalik al-Absar fi Mamalik al-Ansar,* p. 30. See also Trimingham, *Islam,* p. 71.

21. Trimingham, *Islam,* p. 73.

22. Basset, "Etudes," p. 94. See also Tamrat, *Church and State in Ethiopia 1270–1527,* 1972, p. 253.

23. Guidi, "Due nuovi manoscritti della Cronaca Abbreviata di Abissinia," p. 360.

24. Tamrat, *Church and State in Ethiopia,* p. 256.

25. Kammerer, *La Mer Rouge, l'Abyssinie et l'Arabie depuis l'antiquité,* p. 303. See also La Roncière, *La Découverte,* p. 110; and Cerulli, "Il volo," p. 34.

26. Perruchon, *Les Chroniques de Zar'a Ya'eqob,* pp. 56–57, 88; Cerulli, *Il libro etiopico dei miracoli di Maria,* pp. 124–125.

27. Tamrat, *Church and State in Ethiopia,* p. 262.

28. Al-Sakhawi, *Al-Tibr al Masbuk,* pp. 47–72; Wiet, "Les Relations," pp. 124–125; Cerulli, "Il volo," p. 35; Tamrat, *Church and State in Ethiopia,* p. 263, n.

29. Crawford, *Ethiopian Itineraries,* p. 145.

30. See for example Slessarey, *Prester John;* and Beckingham and Ullendorff, *The Hebrew Letters of Prester John.*

31. Cerulli, *Etiopi in Palestina,* vol. 1, p. 117.

32. Ibid., 127.

33. Ibid., p. 156.

34. Ibid., pp. 205, 211.

35. La Roncière, *La Découverte,* p. 111; Cerulli, *Etiopi in Palestina,* pp. 218–219, 221–222; Cerulli, "Il volo," p. 34.

36. Cerulli, *Etiopi in Palestina,* vol. 1, pp. 261–263.

37. Tamrat, *Church and State in Ethiopia,* p. 256.

38. Cited in Cerulli, "Il volo," pp. 33–34.

39. Le Grand, *Voyage historique,* pp. 245–246; Cerulli, "Il volo," p. 34–35. See also Rossi, *Storia della Marina,* p. 125.

40. Cerulli, "Il volo," p. 35.

41. Wiet, "Les Relations," pp. 123, 132–3; Cerulli, "Il volo," p. 34. See also maps in La Roncière; *La Découverte;* and Crawford, *Ethiopian Itineraries,* between pp. 20 and 21.

42. Cerulli, *Etiopi in Palestina,* vol. 1, pp. 293, 298.

43. Ibid., p. 286.

44. Ibid., pp. 357, 365.

45. Letts, *The Pilgrimage of Arnolf von Harff,* p. 178. See also Cerulli, *Etiopi in Palestina,* vol. 1, pp. 371, 381.

46. De Birch, *The Commentaries of the Great Dalbuquerque,* pp. 36, 207. See also Le Grand, *Voyage historique,* pp. 215–216; Lobo, *Voyage,* pp. 216–217; Beckingham and Huntingford, *Prester John,* p. 2; and Cerulli, "Il volo," p. 36.

47. Cerulli, "Il volo," p. 33.

48. Cerulli, *Etiopi in Palestina,* vol. 1, p. 416.

49. Ibid., vol. 2, pp. 61, 75.

50. Ibid., pp. 61, 80–81.

51. See discussion in Caraman, *The Lost Empire,* pp. 103–109.

52. Le Grand, *Voyage historique,* pp. 216–217; Lobo, *Voyage,* p. 217; Ludolf, *New History,* p. 41. For Jesuit references to the Nile see Beccari, *Rerum Aethiopicarum Scriptores Occidentales,* p. 1250.

53. Ludolf, *New History,* p. 42.

54. Ibid., pp. 42–43.

55. Ibid., pp. 43–44.

56. Le Grand, *Voyage historique,* p. 216; Lobo, *Voyage,* p. 217; Cerulli, "Il volo," p. 36.

57. Le Grand, *Voyage historique,* pp. 216–217; Lobo, *Voyage,* p. 217.

58. Le Grand, *Voyage historique,* p. 174; Lobo, *Voyage,* p. 185; Bruce, *Travels,* vol. 2, pp. 526–527. See also Cerulli, "Il volo," pp. 36–37.

59. Bruce, *Travels,* vol. 3, p. 715.

4

♦

Consolidation of Christianity Around the Source of the Blue Nile

Paul Henze

LEGENDS

The Blue Nile has its source at Gish Abbay in the middle of Gojjam. Here a sacred spring, which is said to flow from a pool under a nearby mountain, trickles out to form a small brook. The brook soon gathers enough strength to become a small stream, the Wetet Abbay (the Milk Abbay), which flows northward across the Gojjam plateau and into Lake Tana at a place along the papyrus-edged shore south of the island of Deq. In the rainy season the brown silt it carries colors the normally bluish water of the lake for a great distance from the shore. According to tradition, the river remains intact as it flows through the lake to its outflow at the northern edge of Bahr Dar. As it leaves the lake it passes a series of small islands. On one is the monastery of Debra Maryam. The river then flows for several miles, relatively broad and smooth, to the Tisisat Falls. After tumbling spectacularly over a broad expanse of vertical ledges, it plunges into a deep cleft so narrow that the Portuguese were able, relatively easily it appears, to construct a stone bridge across it. Visitors still use it to walk up to the hillside to view the falls. Racing out of this cleft into its ever deepening gorge, the Blue Nile flows first east, then south, and finally west, circling the immense Gojjam plateau and gathering tributaries all the way.

After my first travels in the region more than a quarter century ago, I wrote:

> To judge by the legends linked to it, Ethiopian history has revolved around Lake Tana. Emperor Menelik I, son of King Solomon and the Queen of Sheba, is said to have come to the eastern shore of the lake

39

when he arrived in Ethiopia from Jerusalem bringing the country's first *tabot* [sacred tablet]. This *tabot* was allegedly kept for 600 years on the island of Tana Cherqos before being transferred to Axum. . . . Legend also has it that Frumentius, who brought Christianity to Ethiopia, found his way to Lake Tana, established a church where Jewish rites had previously been observed, and was buried on Tana Cherqos. . . .

When did this lake really become Christian? Rather late, in comparison with most of northern Ethiopia, though one of the most diligent of modern Ethiopian scholars has concluded that "there seems to be no doubt that a Christian community existed in the area before the end of the Zagwe dynasty" [i.e., before 1270].[1] The body of Emperor Yekuno-Amlak (r. 1270–85), who restored the Solomonic line, is kept in the *eqabet* [treasury] of the Church of St. Stephen on [the island of] Daga, but there is no tradition that this long stone church itself dates from that time.[2]

When I visited the island monastery of Tana Cherqos on the eastern shore of Lake Tana a few years ago, the monks took our party to admire the monastery's most sacred feature: a large boulder with a broad, gently curving top where they told us the Virgin Mary had rested on her way from the Holy Land to Egypt. Like some of those on other islands of Tana, abbots at several Gojjam monasteries relate that they were founded by the legendary Axumite twin kings, Abraha and Atsbaha. There is no reason to believe that these entertaining myths can be anything but apocryphal. Nevertheless, they reveal a serious concern with legitimacy and demonstrate the universal human preoccupation with roots.

In Axumite times and during the still little-understood period following the collapse of the great northern Ethiopian empire, the entire region around Lake Tana and the upper Blue Nile was in all likelihood inhabited by the pagan ancestors of the Wayto, who live by fishing and hunting from their reed boats on the lake; by the Agaw, the dominant pre-Semitic people of the Ethiopian highlands who survive in a substantial district (Agawmeder) in central Gojjam; and by the Gumuz, who live in the lower country to the east, the Metekel, extending all the way to the Sudan lowlands. The Agaw, whose traditions cite Wag and Lasta as the region from which they originally migrated outward, may have gradually pushed the Gumuz westward during the late prehistoric period. The pagan kings of Gojjam whom Ethiopian emperors fought from the late thirteenth century to the beginning of the fifteenth were Agaw.

There are scraps of evidence that traders from the north were coming into this region in Axumite times. Through the centuries, vague knowledge of Judaism and Christianity must have filtered in. The Agaw seem to have had a proclivity toward Judaism, and some, for example the Qemant,[3] still profess it. The whole issue of Falasha origins remains cloudy and controversial. It seems unlikely that any systematic Christian penetration began before the thirteenth century. Christianization accelerated in the fourteenth century during the reign of the great warrior king 'Amda-Seyon. There is good reason to conclude that many of the island monasteries of Lake Tana were established during this reign. He is said to have favored Debra Mariam, and his son became abbot at Mandaba. Not long afterward the great monasteries on the eastern edge of the Gojjam plateau within the great bend of the Blue Nile were probably established: Dima, Debra Worq, and Mertule Maryam. We know that Christian missionaries came into this region with the armies of Emperor 'Amda-Seyon and his successors. Christian influences also penetrated from the east across the Nile.[4]

INITIAL VISITS TO MERTULE MARYAM

I have visited all of these northeast Gojjam monasteries several times. They continue to be active centers of Ethiopian religious life. Their manuscript libraries have still not been thoroughly studied. Because of its location and the remains of a large European-style stone building reliably attributed to Empress Eleni, Mertule Maryam is physically the most impressive. Eleni was a Hadiya princess who married Emperor Zar'a Ya'qob, outlived him for the better part of a half century, and played an important role in Ethiopian political life during the reigns of Emperors Baeda Maryam and Lebna Dengel.

Mertule Maryam has seldom been visited and never systematically studied. However, what is known of its history, and what can be reasonably presumed, makes it an appropriate focus for discussion of the consolidation of the Ethiopian Orthodox Church in the upper Blue Nile region. The monastery is located in the northeastern part of Gojjam in a region called Nebese or Enebese. It crowns a sizable hill around which a substantial country town of perhaps 1,500 inhabitants clusters, primarily on the north and west side of the hill. To the east, cultivated fields that belonged to the monastery stretch over gently sloping landscape to the edge of the main Nile gorge.[5] An ancient trail leads down into the gorge here and across the Nile into Amhara Saynt over the Daga Ford. Farther north a bridge attributed to the Portuguese used to carry a trail into Begemder. Long broken, it is appropriately called the Sabbara Dildi.[6] The region of Nebese has apparently been thickly settled for centuries and is interlaced with trails that are still in daily use. Except in isolated locations along gorge sides, there is no original forest left. There are no large villages. Small groups of farmsteads dot the entire region.

I first attempted to visit Mertule Maryam in the early 1970s when I lived in Ethiopia. I was successful in reaching Dima and Debra Worq and visited several country churches along the way but was unable to reach

Mertule Maryam because of rain and lack of time.[7] Seventeen years later, in February 1989, I finally reached Mertule Maryam with a party of Ethiopian officials and friends. In the interim a road from Bichena to Mota and on to Bahr Dar had been completed. We covered the distance from Addis Ababa all the way to Debra Worq in a day, stayed in a friendly traditional inn there overnight, visited the monastery atop its hilltop (hence the name, "The Mountain of Gold"), and drove onward the next morning. When we reached the roadside town of Gundawein, we learned that a side road had recently been completed from there to Mertule Maryam by a Norwegian reforestation project. It led us easily over a rolling landscape of yellow stubblefields and through fords across small streams for about 30 kilometers.

We had a sense of entering a medieval painting as we neared the town, for it is surrounded by a considerable growth of trees, and beyond rises the monastery hill. Crossing the broad red-earth marketplace, we were able to follow a track up to the monastery gate. There we were welcomed by the tall young abbot in a deep burgundy velvet robe, Memhir Habte Mikael Tadesse. He was happy to lead us on a tour of his establishment.

The great stone ruin at the east end of the compound caught our eyes as soon as we came within the walls. It was impressive beyond all our expectations. Several sections of stone wall rose to a height of almost 10 meters. Two tall, intact arches were edged with beautiful floral-pattern carvings. There were other arches, doors, and windows that were framed in smooth-cut blocks, some with scroll and scallop ornamentation. There were three bays in the great ruin, which the abbot called a church, but our doubts were aroused by ends of wooden beams protruding from walls that had obviously supported a second story. Windows in the back (east) wall gave a hint of a third story. The structure looked more like a palace than a church. There also appeared to be two or three fireplaces framed with carved stone edging and topped with mantels, one with a striking sun design. But it was hard to be sure, for great piles of fallen stones had accumulated on the floor of the ruins. In places the debris was at least a meter and a half deep. It was impossible to determine what kind of floor the building had originally had and whether paving or tile remained. We saw no crosses, no inscriptions.

The *memhir* then led us to the nearby large round church, the principal one of the monastery. It smelled pleasantly of incense from recent services. Its sactuary (*maqdas*) walls were covered with good-quality paintings. One side had apparently been painted in the eighteenth century, the other in the early nineteenth. Outside, not far southeast of the round church, we were taken to a place where a hole more than a meter deep had been dug. Less than half a meter below the present surface, a corner of old foundations had been exposed—several narrow tiers of finely cut stone totaling over half a meter in height with scroll designs resembling some of those at Day Giyorgis in Jirru in northern Shoa.[8] We first speculated that the huge ruined building had originally extended into the area occupied by the round church and that stones from it had been used in construction of the later church. Or had there been another structure here built of cut stones? The corner faced out toward the southeast, away from the ruins.

We asked Memhir Habte Mikael about the history of the monastery. He said a church had first been built in the reign of the twin kings, Abraha and Atsbaha (fourth century A.D.). It became a *gadam* (monastery) in the fourteenth century. He said it possessed twelve *tabots*. The south end of the great ruined building was crudely roofed with tin and used as an *eqabet*. At the abbot's beckoning, monks unlocked a rough door and brought out a succession of icons, manuscripts, crosses, and vestments for us to admire, of which the most spectacular was an enormous blue velvet robe said to have belonged to Ahmad Gragn, the Muslim ruler of Adal who ravished the Ethiopian highlands in the early sixteenth century. The abbot did not know how the monastery had gained possession of it.

Memhir Habte Mikael led us to a new building on the north side of the compound and explained that it was not yet finished but was intended as a museum. It had been started several years before, but no work had been done for two years because crops in the region had been poor and people could not contribute money for it. He said they planned to move all their treasures into it, have it connected to electricity, and hoped to attract tourists. Habte Mikael told us he was a native of the region, had been educated at Mertule Maryam, and had never traveled any farther than Bahr Dar. He appeared younger than the majority of the monks we saw at the monastery and impressed us as remarkably enterprising. It was encouraging to see the Ethiopian Orthodox Church putting this kind of man in charge of an ancient monastery. We were due in Bahr Dar that evening, so we left in the early afternoon with our curiosity whetted but far from satisfied. It was clear that Mertule Maryam deserved much further study.

MERTULE MARYAM IN 1993 AND 1995

The opportunity to investigate Mertule Maryam more extensively followed after the fall of the Derg and the opening up of travel in the Ethiopian north. In November and December 1993 Stanislaw Chojnacki and I organized a small party of foreigners and Ethiopians for a three-week journey to investigate churches and monasteries in Wag, Tigray, Lasta, and Gaynt. Time was short when we finally crossed the "Chinese Road" and reached Bahr Dar after spending a day exploring the monastery of Tara Gadam and the cave of Washa Andreas in the forested hills above Addis Zemen. We were determined in the next two days to spend as much time as we could at Mertule Maryam. The road from Bahr Dar was in good condition, and it was apparent as we traveled that the crops had grown well this year. Everywhere people were stacking and threshing teff, wheat, and barley. We reached the monastery town at four in the afternoon and took austere rooms at the Abraha Atsbaha Hotel.

Memhir Habte Mikael Tadesse was still in charge of the monastery and came down to the hotel to welcome us. He told us that they had gathered money to complete the new *eqabet*/museum and their treasures had been moved in from their cramped room at the south end of the great ruin. He escorted us up to the monastery and took us for a long walk in splendid evening light along the outer periphery of the walls on the southern and eastern side of the compound. The slopes here encompassed a vast area of ruins that also extended along the crest of the hill to the east. The walls of several roofless, large Lasta-style, two-story round stone houses rose in several places. Whatever the history of the present town on the north side of the monastery hill may be, it is clear that in earlier times there was a very substantial settlement to the south and east, now almost entirely abandoned. Some of the structures had been built with mortar. On the hilltop a number of buildings, some inhabited by nuns and hermits, contained cut stones that looked as if they had been taken from the large ruined building inside the monastery walls. As the sun began to set, we came back into the monastery precincts through the south gate. Memhir Habte Mikael assured us everything would be ready for us to examine in the *eqabet* at 7:30 the following morning.

We were up at dawn on December 8, drank tea in the bar where a photograph of Haile Selassie hung on the wall, and drove up to the monastery past houses where women were fanning hearth fires for breakfast. The morning *qedasse* (mass) was still in progress when we walked through the monastery gate, but the *memhir* was waiting. He had the new building opened and told us we were free to examine everything in it. The monk in charge was eager to be helpful and allowed us to photograph as we wished. We made a preliminary assessment of the icons, crosses, manuscripts, vestments of many kinds, various other kinds of church paraphernalia, and some objects that had belonged to various kings and princes and had been donated by them, including some portraits. Only the vestments and ceremonial umbrellas were hung; icons, crosses, and manuscripts were stacked in piles. It was impossible to make anything like a complete inventory in the limited time we had, but we gained a good enough impression of the monastery's holdings to know that a longer return stay would be rewarding.[9]

During our next visit in January 1995, we had the good luck of arriving at the time of the greatest feast of the year, Tir Maryam. We planned the visit to be able to do a more systematic investigation of the ecclesiastical and historical material preserved in the monastery as well as to examine and measure the great ruin more thoroughly than we had done before, remaining over a period of four days. Memhir Habte Maryam Tadesse was no longer at Mertule Maryam, however. He had been called to serve in the patriarchate in Addis Ababa. His replacement was another young monk, Eserunan (Chief Teacher) Haile Maryam Tagale. There was an aura of holiness about him, but he seemed less sure of his authority than Habte Maryam had been.

We found ourselves in the kind of situation so often encountered at Ethiopian religious establishments. Our letters from the bishop of Gojjam in Debra Marqos carried little weight. Historic monasteries often feel independent of central authority. We were told we could not examine manuscripts or take photographs. Then we were requested to pay 500 birr to see anything. Fortunately Bahru Zewde, then director of the Institute of Ethiopian Studies at Addis Ababa University, had joined our party. He set about negotiating, stressing the value to the Institute of Ethiopian Studies of having an accurate record of the monastery's holdings.[10] Meanwhile we visited the lively Saturday market with sellers and buyers filling the vast marketplace. Thousands of people were streaming into the town, mostly on foot, some on horses, mules, and donkeys, from all directions, not only to the market, but for Sunday's festivities. Many hermits and beggars were also in evidence. At the end of the afternoon Bahru came to tell us that he had reached an agreement with the monastery: for a payment of 200 birr we would be allowed to spend as much time as we wished in the *eqabet* and to take pictures and notes without restriction. Our party rushed to record inscriptions and photograph.[11]

Sunday provided a rewarding climax to the whole visit. The night service was coming to an end when we came into the monastery compound shortly after sunrise. Monks and pilgrims were dozing under the old cedars in the yard, roused periodically by hermits making their own impromptu sermons. We spent the first part of the morning examining and measuring the ruined building and for the first time crawled into the interior of the old *eqabet,* a narrow warren of walls and shelves extending upward three stories. At midmorning the priest in charge of the *eqabet*/museum opened a locked chest and brought out several manuscripts we had not yet seen. There were two *Tamre Maryams* with excellent illustrations, two fifteenth-century manuscripts in bad condition, an *Orit* (Old Testament), and a Book of Henoch noteworthy only for its *harag.*[12] A pile of loose parchment sheets contained three very fine illustrations from a magic book. We photographed and described these treasures and then moved to the round church to photograph its paintings. It was now empty but still heavy with the odor of incense from the night's service. Shortly before noon the monastery burst into life.

A procession formed to take the *tabot* to a *tabal* (sacred spring) at the edge of town. Priests, monks, nuns, and hermits joined in, followed by pilgrims. Drums throbbed, rhythmic chanting rose in intensity and was punctuated by bursts of ululations of the women. *Imbyltas* (horns) sounded as the procession proceeded down the hill, across the marketplace, and off into a maze of side streets, gathering enormous numbers of people along the way. After services at the *tabal,* the *tabot* returned in the afternoon with a crowd of more than 10,000 accompanying it. Joyous cheers rose at each stop or turn of the procession, drums were beaten with continually greater intensity, jesters in baboon pelts and monkey tails cavorted as the multitude made its way back up the hill. We raced ahead and climbed to the balcony of the *eqabet*/museum to watch the return of the *tabot* to the church. Boys climbed high into the trees for a better view. Surges of ululation and drumming reverberated from the walls of the great ruin. Ethiopian flags fluttered in the breeze. It was as magnificent a medieval scene as I have witnessed in Ethiopia—centuries away from the concerns of politicians in Addis Ababa!

Not long after the *tabot* was back in the church, our party was invited to come to the *senbet* (Sabbath meeting house) outside the compound walls on the north for the concluding feast of the day. More than 200 special guests were gathered in the long hall, men seated along low tables on the right side, women in their traditional finery on the left. Our party was brought to a raised platform on the left in front, while the abbot, the senior monks, and high-ranking guests were seated on the platform opposite. Waiters brought in huge trays of *injera* (pancake bread) and *brindo* (raw beef); *qay wat* was ladled out of large casseroles. *Tej* was poured for most of the guests, but there was also bottled beer for those who preferred it. The trays kept being refilled throughout the banquet. Food that remained would be distributed to the enormous horde of beggars and cripples waiting outside the *senbet* when the festivities were finished.

There were speeches. The monastery's historian recounted its founding by Abraha and Atsbaha. At the same time, with the peculiar illogic characteristic of much traditional Ethiopian Church history, he related that Christ himself, when a young man, had served here as a priest. Christ asked that the monastery be made especially sacred to the memory of his mother, so it was called Mertule Maryam—"Home of Mary."[13] The *memhir* and a visiting monk made short speeches and then I was asked to speak on behalf of our party. I praised Ethiopia, peace, the beauty of Gojjam, the importance of the monastery for preserving treasures and traditions, and thanked the monks for their hospitality. Our Addis Ababa University graduate student assistant translated. There was great applause. He then gave a summary of Professor Chojnacki's life in Ethiopia and devotion to study of Ethiopian art. More applause. There were blessings by the *memhir* as the banquet came to an end.

The next morning we drove back to Gundawein and from there to a country school at Eneseqol, where we left our vehicle in the care of a group of four friendly young teachers and set out on a long trek into the Goncha Gorge to visit the monasteries of Wafa Yesus and Getisemani, both of them perhaps older than Mertule Maryam. In spite of the account of its founding, other monasteries in this region claim seniority over Mertule Maryam, and there has apparently always been rivalry among all of them.[14] I will now summarize what little seems to be known of the history of Mertule Maryam.

HISTORY AND TRADITIONS OF MERTULE MARYAM FROM TRAVELERS' ACCOUNTS

Mertule Maryam has been rarely visited, and few travelers have left a record of their visits. The first European to have seen it appears to be the Portuguese Pero de Covilhao to whom Father Francisco Alvarez, who did not go to see it himself, attributes his brief reference to it.[15] A hundred years later the Portuguese Jesuit Manoel d'Almeida visited the site and left an extensive description in his *Historia geral de Ethiopia a Alta ou Abassia*.[16] James Bruce did not travel in this part of Gojjam. The first modern-era traveler to visit Mertule Maryam was the Englishman, C. T. Beke, who came upon the site unexpectedly in 1842 and was so impressed with the ruins that he presented a paper to the Society of Antiquaries on return to London.[17] The Italian *Guida dell'Africa Orientale Africana* has a brief reference:

> From Dibo continue westward . . . and arrive at Martula Mariam, altitude 2750 m, famous for the ruins of a church built by the Roman Jesuit P. Bruno Bruni during the time of Susenios, and for other buildings of that period or a little later. It was built using materials from a rock church that had been possibly built by Egyptians for Empress Elena, the widow of Baeda Mariam. Today's church of Mariam has interesting pictures.[18]

The French Minister in Addis Ababa in the early 1920s, M. de Coppet, published an account of a visit at that time, which is among the meager sources on Mertule Maryam that the Englishman Stephen Bell was able to find twenty-five years ago. The explorer, C. F. Rey, who did not actually see the monastery, attributes the rebuilding of it for Emperor Susenyos in the sixteenth century to Pero Paez (Pais), the Spanish missionary in Portuguese service, and summarizes Beke's account:

> Dr. Beke discovered there an edifice, the walls of which were in a perfect state, built of stone in the form of a Roman cross. The interior was

adorned with carvings of freestone of exquisite workmanship, as fresh and sharp as if recently executed. The current tradition was that the work had been executed in the early 15th century before the arrival of the Portuguese, and even before the Muslim invasion.[19]

The British consul at Dangila, Major Cheesman, likewise did not visit the monastery but passed near it:

We passed Martola Mariam, with its ancient ruined church on a hill, said to be the oldest in Gojjam, contemporary with, but a little later than, the Cathedral at Axum. I did not interrupt our journey to see it, as my face was turned toward the Abbay, but it has been visited by Europeans from time to time and I have seen photographs of some fine sculptures on the stone walls which suggest that they were the work of the Portuguese.[20]

The great modern specialist in Ethiopian medieval history, Tadesse Tamrat, did not include Mertule Maryam in his travels in search of historically interesting manuscripts in the 1960s, though he found significant material at Dima and Debra Worq. No other Ethiopian scholars are known to have done any research in this far northeastern corner of Gojjam. Stephen Bell, then working at the Institute of Ethiopian Studies at Addis Ababa University, trekked to Mertule Maryam in 1967 and was told by an official of the Ethiopian Ministry of Culture of plans to do some elementary protective work to preserve the ruin from further deterioration. It was never undertaken.

The intrepid Englishwoman, Diana Spencer, who explored so many ecclesiastical sites in Wollo and Gojjam in the late 1960s and early 1970s, stopped at Mertule Maryam en route to the Goncha Gorge in January 1973 during the celebrations of Tir Maryam but seems to have been shown only a small portion of its treasures.[21]

Stephen Bell gave a paper summarizing his observations and researches relating to Mertule Maryam at the Eighth International Conference of Ethiopian Studies in Addis Ababa in 1984. Drawing primarily on d'Almeida and Beke, he attempted an outline of the history of the monastery.[22] Until further research has been done, it will be difficult either to confirm, supplement, or alter many of the tentative conclusions he reached, though some seem to me debatable. What follows is an attempt to summarize what may be known of the monastery's history, drawing on Bell's researches and other sources.

The first church at Mertule Maryam is attributed to Empress Eleni, a favorite wife of Emperor Zar'a Ya'qob (r. 1434–1468), whom he married about 1445. A princess from the kingdom of Hadiya in the south, she was one of those extraordinarily talented and politically astute women who appear in Ethiopian history every century or so. The chronicler of Zar'a Ya'qob's reign says of her:

> She was accomplished in everything: in front of God, by practicing righteousness and having strong faith; by praying and receiving Holy Communion; as regards worldly matters she was accomplished in the preparation of food, in her familiarity with books, in her knowledge of the law, and in her understanding of the affairs of state.[23]

She was neither the mother of Zar'a Yak'ob's son and successor, Baeda Maryam, nor did she marry him (as some accounts say). The complex court intrigues of the time resulted in the death of Baeda Maryam's own mother about 1462 and several years of alienation from his father. The two, however, became reconciled, and Zar'a Ya'kob designated Baeda Maryam his successor before his death in 1468. Having no mother himself, Baeda Maryam gave Eleni the title of queen mother and apparently relied on her support and advice. She "occupied this position of great influence throughout the reign of Baeda Maryam [1468–1478], and apparently gathered a huge political patronage in the whole kingdom."[24] During the confused period following Baeda Maryam's death, she was for a time eclipsed but soon reasserted herself and apparently lived beyond the first decade of the sixteenth century, participating in affairs of state during the minority of Emperor Lebna Dengel (1508–1540).

Baeda Maryam felt a special attachment to the monastery of Atronsa Maryam in Amhara Saynt, endowed it, and was buried there.[25] Empress Eleni had a stronger orientation toward Gojjam. Alvarez reports that the kingdom of Gojjam belonged to her and that when she decided to build a church at Mertule Maryam she ordered Pero de Covilhao to come there to advise on the construction of its altar.[26] He says she was buried there. He gives no date, but reports: "There was great rumour and talk at the Court about the death of Queen Elena. They said that since she had died all of them had died great and small, and that while she lived, all lived and were defended and protected; and she was father and mother of all."[27]

When did Empress Eleni decide to build the church at Mertule Maryam? Was there already a monastic establishment there? Did Eleni have only a church built, or perhaps also a palace? Did she reside there? On the basis of available information, these questions can only be speculated upon. Bell dates the completion of Eleni's edifice about 1510. This seems late, but construction may, of course, have been started considerably earlier and taken several years. We do not know when Covilhao went there.[28] In any event the first building had a short life, for according to d'Almeida it was destroyed by Ahmad Gragn at the end of the 1520s or early 1530s, rebuilt at least in part at the initiative of Lebna Dengel or his successor Galawdewos (r. 1540–1559), and again ravaged by Oromos in the 1560s.

It then seems to have remained largely a ruin for half a century but must have retained its sacred standing and probably continued to shelter a monastic community. D'Almeida reports that the hill was "all clothed and peopled by so many cedars and wild olives that they cover it entirely and number over two thousand."

The emperor Susenyos (1607–1632) decided to rebuild it—perhaps out of respect for the memory of Eleni but also because he was first offered the crown at Mertule Maryam in 1604. Susenyos had an adventurous life, having been captured when young by the Oromo and then released. He had to fight his way to the throne. He decided to ally himself with the Portuguese and accepted conversion to Catholicism, which resulted in enormous domestic tension and eventually brought about his downfall. After Mertule Maryam was rebuilt, he encouraged the Jesuits to establish themselves there, which they did in 1627.[29] Perhaps, as the *Guida* states, the rebuilding was undertaken by the Jesuit Bruni. Or did Pero Pais also have a part in it? The Jesuits cannot have enjoyed the place long, for Susenyos abdicated five years after they are said to have been established in Mertule Maryam in favor of his son, Fasilidas, who expelled the Jesuits and re-established traditional Ethiopian Orthodoxy. Mertule Maryam reverted to the control of the Orthodox Church.

The next two centuries are a blank in the monastery's history. Further research in chronicles may be revealing, though so far no historical material on the monastery itself has come to light at Mertule Maryam. Archaeology seems more promising as a means of shedding light on the entire history of Mertule Maryam and on life in the region. Professional examination of the ruins themselves and probes in the entire monastery area might produce valuable information.

A CHALLENGE FOR ARCHAEOLOGISTS

The survival of ancient cedars and olives in church groves and the existence of occasional stands of what appear to be original forest in isolated locations in northeast Gojjam provide evidence that a thousand years ago the area must have been heavily forested.[30] D'Almeida's reference to more than 2,000 cedars and olives on the hill on which Mertule Maryam is located does not match the situation today, though there are still perhaps 150 old trees in and around the monastery compound. Some may be several hundred years old, but many no longer appear healthy. D'Almeida's statement that trees were originally planted around the monastery seems improbable. There is little evidence of deliberate planting of trees around Ethiopian churches and monasteries. For the most part they are survivors of original forests and where enough trees are left, they replant themselves.

We know that medieval Christian missionaries often chose pagan forest glades, especially on hilltops, for churches in order to give the new

Christian faith the benefit of continuity. The pagan beliefs they aimed to supplant centered around nature worship and animistic practices. For example, the people of a district were described as worshipping "the rocks, trees, or rivers. They did not know God except very few [among them]. They lived by eating, drinking, and committing adultery all their lives."[31]

Many accounts in chronicles attest to hilltop locations of secular and religious authority, for example: "Tekla Haymanot came to a hill called Bilat. This was the headquarters of the sorcerers and here they sacrificed the blood of cows and goats. . . . There lived their king and the witch-doctors, the diviners, and all the men of magic worshipped him."[32]

Thus, these energetic Christian missionaries cleverly attracted the inhabitants of an area to new kinds of ceremonies at sacred places with which they were already familiar. Like that of Debra Worq, the hill on which Mertule Maryam was established is prominent and visible from afar. It would seem to be the kind of place where early inhabitants of the region might have gathered. A hilltop site such as this may have been a fortified strongpoint before it became a primitive religious site and then a monastery. Elementary archaeological investigation should be able to determine whether it was occupied earlier than the fourteenth century for secular or religious purposes.

Why did Eleni choose the site for her church and/or residence? Perhaps she wished to have a site with no past, one attributed only to herself. Possible, but it seems more likely that an existing monastic community or country church would have drawn her attention to the location. No traditions of a previous church have come to light, however. All the monks tell us is that the site was chosen by Christ, that he served there, and that the monastery was originally established by Abraha and Atsbaha. These claims are so common throughout the region that they cannot be given any particular weight for Mertule Maryam. On the other hand, the tradition that Mertule Maryam became a *gadam* in the fourteenth century supports a hypothesis that there might have been a religious establishment there before Eleni's time. Yet, this tradition may be merely an invention to support a claim of antiquity as great or greater than Debra Worq and Dima.[33] The extensive manuscript libraries said to exist at both these monasteries have never been thoroughly studied. There may be materials in them that would shed light on Mertule Maryam.

While greatest interest attaches to the enormous ruined building at Mertule Maryam, other parts of the compound might also repay exploratory excavation and reveal foundations of earlier structures, even comparatively primitive ones. But it is at the great ruin that even the most elementary and preliminary archaeological investigation could produce information most easily. How were the foundations constructed? What do they reveal of construction techniques? Was the early seventeeth-century building reconstructed on the foundations of the earlier one? Is there a difference in construction techniques between the original structure and the reconstruction of the time of Emperor Susenyos? Is there evidence in the present ruin of incorporation of parts from the first? Is all the present ornamentation from the second building—or was some reused from the original?

There are many other questions about building techniques—who were the builders: Egyptians, Portuguese, Italians? Do the stone-cutting methods provide evidence? What kinds of tools were used? What is the nature of the mortar? What does the ornamentation reveal? There is beautiful stone carving and a great variety of designs. But there is no conventional Christian symbolism in any of them. No inscriptions have been found. Much of the ornamental carving consists of scrolls and floral patterns. There is also the intriguing row of figures high on the west side of the central hall. They do not seem to have religious character, nor do they readily reflect a direct relationship to known ornamental figures in Mediterranean countries. Is there evidence of a connection to ornamentation and statuary from India, Syria, Palestine, Egypt, Byzantine monuments in Turkey, or from Armenia or Georgia?

Then there is the question whether the great ruin was actually a church. The fact that it is traditionally referred to as a church is weighty. But the building itself has little immediate resemblance to a church. At least half of it is missing, of course. The entire western side is gone, much of it apparently used in construction of the present large round church. Would a systematic examination of the stones used in the round church reveal those that were probably taken from the ruined building? There are also other cut stones in the rectangular church at the west end of the monastery compound built at Haile Selassie's instigation as well as in buildings outside the walls of the monastery compound. Perhaps inscriptions or a stonecutter's or mason's marks could be discovered on some of them.

If the great ruin were indeed a church, it might have been of the classic ancient basilica style—rectangular, with a relatively low two-sided sloping roof in an east-west direction. It is very difficult to envision what sort of roof the original building might have had. What is clear is that the building had at least a second story, perhaps even a third. Existing windows on the east and south side and remains of wooden rafters protruding from the west wall of the largest room, some still a meter or more in length, are evidence of that. But there is no evidence of stairs. Were there stairs in the destroyed section of the building, or would more careful investigation of the existing ruin discover evidence that there were wooden stairways?

Carefully cut wooden beams still exist in considerable numbers. There are well-preserved lintels above many windows and doors. They should be examined for tool marks and cutting techniques. Dendrochronological methods could provide information about the time when the wood was cut.[34] The same is true of pollen analysis. Pollen analysis in many parts of the world is now providing reliable information about forest cover, domestication of crops, changes in agriculture and food use, and climate changes. It is beginning to be relevant to the study of pre-Axumite and Axumite civilization.

Some tentative answers to many of the most elementary questions about Mertule Maryam would in all likelihood be provided by a small team of archaeologists working for at least a period of a few weeks. On the basis of preliminary work, plans and priorities for more systematic investigation could then be made. The first task would probably be to remove sections of the great quantities of fallen stones and other debris, examining everything for remains of pottery, metal, coins,[35] and wooden remains.

A modicum of elementary excavation would make it possible to determine what kind of floor the building had and whether it was all on the same level. Were there underground passages? Was anyone—such as Empress Eleni—buried here? The floor might give evidence of internal partitions that are no longer visible. The ruin already shows evidence of division into separate rooms that seems unlikely for a church but much more likely for a palace or an administrative building. A palace might, of course, have had a chapel. A lady as pious as Eleni is reported to have been would probably have had a private chapel. Covilhao was brought to Mertule Maryam to advise on the construction of an altar. Was it in the present ruin, or at another location?

One of the best indications of sophisticated construction techniques is the presence of well-designed drainage outlets at several points in the walls. These should be compared with similar features of buildings in areas where the builders may have come from. The intriguing incipient excavation not far southeast of the round church should be extended. The foundations exposed there appear to extend far toward both the north and the west. Further digging would not be difficult.

Unfortunately, medieval archaeology has not yet aroused much interest among Ethiopians or foreigners concerned with the country. The attraction of finding primate and human remains that shed light on the origins of humankind in Ethiopia is too great. So is the prospect of uncovering more about the development of agriculture and civilization, the origins of Axum, and the history of this first great Ethiopian empire. Paleontology and Axum will doubtless continue to be the priorities for archaeologists in Ethiopia. It is impossible to argue that they should not be. But we must also hope that a few archaeologists and historians will be tempted to learn more about the medieval period, including all aspects of life at the time: religion, politics, daily life.

Far too little is known about the extension and consolidation of Axumite rule over the center and south of the country and the related process of Christianization. Too little is known of the influence of outsiders on Ethiopian life during this and earlier periods, not only Europeans and people from the eastern Mediterranean but influences from as far away as Persia and India. Who carved the spectacular churches of Lalibela? The rockhewn churches there show a remarkable ornamental, though nonfunctional, adherence to the most important features of Axumite architecture, but there is also evidence of foreign influence. The churches of Lalibela are at least four centuries earlier than the present ruins of the great building at Mertule Maryam, but given the conservatism of Ethiopian civilization, some continuity would not be surprising.

Archaeological investigation at Mertule Maryam would have to be approved by the religious authorities in Addis Ababa and in Gojjam and be undertaken with careful attention to the sensitivities of the resident clergy. Our experience at the monastery in recent years gives reason to believe that with diplomacy and sensitivity, work could begin and proceed with both the permission and cooperation of the abbot and the monks. They are unlikely to have objections to tasks such as extension of the digging that has already taken place near the round church or in clearing of the debris from the ruin and stabilization of walls. They would probably have little concern about excavations outside the walls to the south and east, an area of substantial population sometime in the past. Modest monetary contributions to the maintenance and operation of the monastery would undoubtedly have a positive impact. If the entire undertaking were presented as primarily an effort to preserve the site and honor the memory of those who have devoted their lives to it in the past—Empress Eleni as well as generations of abbots, priests, and monks—it is likely that archaeological investigation could proceed successfully for several years. The results would in all likelihood shed light on the late medieval and early modern history of the entire upper Blue Nile region.

NOTES

1. Tamrat, *Church and State in Ethiopia,* p. 190.
2. Henze, *Ethiopian Journeys,* pp. 256–257.
3. Gamst, *The Qemant.*
4. Tamrat, *Church and State in Ethiopia,* is by far the most substantial source on its subject available in English. See especially pp. 189–205.
5. Although the monastery's lands must have been taken from it as a result of the Derg's 1975 "land reform," in 1995 the monks spoke of the land as belonging to them. Perhaps local authorities have restored it since the fall of the Derg. In any event, proclamations from distant Addis Ababa have not necessarily been implemented in remote rural regions such as this.

6. For descriptions see Cheesman, *Lake Tana and the Blue Nile,* pp. 268–272.

7. See Henze, "The Land of the Blue Nile," in *Ethiopian Journeys,* pp. 236–268.

8. Tiered foundations are a familiar feature of Axumite buildings in northern Ethiopia dating back to the pre-Christian era. At Day Giyorgis, on the top of the *amba* (flat-topped mountain) above the Monastery of Zena Marqos (Debra Besrat), are the foundations of a large rectangular building of uncertain date discovered by Stanislaw Chojnacki in the 1960s. He described it in "Day Giyorgis," pp. 43–52.

9. During the last hour we spent in the *eqabet* we came upon a large, comparatively well-preserved icon divided into twelve panels illustrating episodes in Christ's life. Professor Chojnacki initially judged it to be a previously unknown work of the famous Venetian, Nicolo Brancaleon, who lived in Ethiopia from about 1480 until the 1520s. Subsequent study of the inscriptions on back of this icon has revealed it to be the work of a presumed Ethiopian student of Brancaleon by the name of Afnin, hitherto unknown. The inscriptions include information about his genealogy, which indicates Afnin may have been of Agaw ancestry.

10. Bahru Zewde also countered the monks' reluctance to have their treasures photographed and registered for fear thieves might be alerted to them (definitely a problem for the churches and monasteries in Ethiopia) by reminding them that if things were indeed stolen, photographs could provide authorities attempting to recover them with firm identification.

11. We concluded later that our cool initial reception must have stemmed in part from the fact that the abbot and monks were preoccupied with preparations for the great annual feast of the Virgin.

12. Tamre Maryam is "The Miracles of the Virgin Mary," a popular Ethiopian theme; *harag* is the geometric and floral ornamentation on the top, and sometimes on the sides, of manuscript pages.

13. Some local people explained the name as Merto la Maryam, "the Best for Mary." The historian's explanation seems more likely.

14. During our 1993 visit, the *memhir* at Debra Worq scoffed at Mertule Maryam's claims to great antiquity, asserting that his monastery is much older.

15. Alvarez, *The Prester John of the Indies,* pp. 458–459.

16. Translated extracts are contained in Beckingham and Huntingford, *Some Records of Ethiopia,* pp. 102–107. Pero Pais (Paez) has a brief mention in his *Historia da Etiopia,* p. 93.

17. *Archaeologia,* vol. 32, London, 1847, pp. 38–57.

18. *Guida,* Consoziazione Turisticta Italiano, Milano, 1938, p. 375 (translated by author).

19. Rey, *In the Country of the Blue Nile,* p. 81.

20. Cheesman, *Lake Tana and the Blue Nile,* p. 268.

21. Spencer, "Travels in Gojjam: St. Luke Icons and Brancaleon Rediscovered," pp. 201–220.

22. Bell, "The Ruins of Mertule Maryam," pp. 125–129.

23. As cited by Tamrat, *Church and State in Ethiopia,* p. 288.

24. Ibid., p. 289.

25. Pankhurst, *The Ethiopian Royal Chronicles,* pp. 41–48.

26. Alvarez, *The Prester John of the Indies,* p. 459.

27. Ibid., p. 434. If Alvarez is reporting something he experienced personally, Eleni may have lived beyond 1520.

28. Pero de Covilhao left Portugal in 1487 and came to Ethiopia by way of India in 1490. He was still there in the early 1520s. Alvarez, *The Prester John of the Indies,* pp. 369–376, recounts his adventuresome life and high status in Ethiopia.

29. Pankhurst, *The Ethiopian Royal Chronicles,* pp. 94–97.

30. The largest stand of what appears to be undisturbed original cedar forest I have seen in the region is located in the upper Goncha Gorge above the monastery of Wafa Yesus. Immense cedars rise here to a height of at least 25 meters and some are a meter or more in diameter. This forest includes many other native trees and bushes and is said to harbor many wild animals. There are also small stands of old forest near the lake called Bahr Giyorgis between Eneseqol and the gorge.

31. *Gadla Filipos,* p. 175, as cited in Tamrat, *Church and State in Ethiopia,* p. 179.

32. As cited from a passage from Budge, *The Life and Miracles of Takla Haymanot,* in Tamrat, *Church and State in Ethiopia,* p. 179.

33. Although both maintain that their monasteries were originally founded by Abraha and Atsbaha, monks at Dima say their monastery was established as a *gadam* during the reign of Emperor 'Amda-Seyon (1314–1344). Those at Debra Worq claim their *gadam* status dates from the reign of Emperor Dawit I (1382–1411).

34. Unfortunately no work in this rapidly developing archaeological field has yet been done in Ethiopia, so there is no base data for comparison. There is ample ancient wood throughout Ethiopia, going back to Debra Damo and Axumite sites in the north, to tempt dendrochronologists to begin work.

35. D'Almeida states that Empress Eleni originally sent for workmen from Egypt and that "this could not have been done had they not been given very large payments and a great reward, for the work shows that they were masters of their craft" (Beckingham and Huntington, *Some Records,* as cited, p. 103). How were they paid and rewarded? Were coins used, silver, or gold?

5

◆

Did Jewish Influence Reach Ethiopia via the Nile?

Steven Kaplan

The question of how and when (and some would say, if) Jewish influences reached Ethiopia has been the subject of scholarly discussion for decades. Researchers interested in the provenance of the Hebraic-Israelite elements in Ethiopian Christianity and in the origins of the Beta Israel (Falasha) have offered a variety of explanations for their presence in Ethiopia. While some argue that southern Arabia is the most probable source of Jewish influences, others claim the materials at hand provide no evidence of direct contact and may merely be the proof of *imitatio Veteris Testamenti*.[1] Until recently, the possibility that Judaism or Jews reached Ethiopia from Egypt via the Nile has been supported by comparatively few scholars, among them Philoxene Luzzato, Louis Marcus, Abraham Epstein, and Itzhak Ben Zvi. (The distinguished Ethiopianist, Ignazio Guidi, at one time supported this view but later changed his mind.) In the past two decades, however, a number of authors, particularly those engaged in the study of the Beta Israel, have contended that the Nile was the most probable and important source for Jewish influences in Ethiopia.

In this chapter I examine the theory that Jewish influences reached Ethiopia via the Nile from several perspectives. The evidence for this theory will be presented and critiqued, and I will demonstrate that it is arguably the most problematic of all the explanations for the presence of Jewish elements in Ethiopia. Additionally I will clarify some of the theoretical and methodological underpinnings of the Nilotic theory, particularly among scholars interested in the "Falasha origins" question. Finally, these Israelocentric Nilotic theories will be compared with the far better-known Afrocentric ideas of scholars such as Cheikh Anta Diop and Martin Bernal.

EGYPT

The claim for Nilotic origins of Ethiopian Judaism(s) can be stated briefly as follows: Egypt, as is well known, was already in pre-exile times the site of a diaspora Jewish community. In the Second Temple period (536 B.C.–A.D. 70) this community thrived and represented one of the premier centers of Hellenistic Judaism. The Greek translation of the Hebrew Bible, the Septuagint, which served as the basis for the Ge'ez version, was the product of Egyptian, particularly Alexandrian, Jewry. Given the geographic proximity of Egypt to Ethiopia, it seems reasonable to suggest that Jews following the path of the Nile could have made their way to its sources in Ethiopia. Significantly, perhaps, the traditional areas of Beta Israel settlement were in regions near the sources of the Blue Nile. Certain cultural phenomena would also appear to link Egyptian Jewry to the Beta Israel. Of particular interest in this respect is the Jewish military garrison that existed between the seventh and fifth centuries B.C. on the island of Elephantine, near present-day Aswan. The religious practice of this Egyptian community was in several ways similar to that of the Beta Israel, most notably its inclusion of a sacrificial cult conducted by priests. Finally, it should also be noted that some of the Beta Israel's own traditions mention Egypt as their country of origin.

At least with regard to some of its minor points, the Egyptian theory can be shown to be based on misunderstandings. Thus, for example, the fact that the Ge'ez version of the Old Testament is based primarily on a Greek original is of limited significance once it is recalled that it is not the Greek but rather the Aramaic and Hebrew borrowings that appear to reveal a distinctly Jewish element.[2] In a similar fashion, while the hypothesis of a Nile route for Jewish influences would appear at first glance to explain the Beta Israel's presence in the Lake Tana region, it does not account for the introduction of Judaic-Israelite characteristics into early Ethiopian (Aksumite) Christian culture. Is this to be seen as the product of a different stream of Judaism, or are we to believe that Jewish elements reached Aksum from the Lake Tana region?

ELEPHANTINE

Of even greater concern than the general claim of Egyptian influence are the questions that must be raised concerning the alleged ties between Elephantine and Ethiopia, which lie at the heart of most arguments for an Egyptian source for Ethiopian Hebraisms, including, most recently, those of David Kessler and Graham Hancock.[3] The Jewish community of Elephantine was established sometime in the seventh century B.C. and survived for approximately 250 years. The site it occupied, an island in the Nile at the first cataract, the traditional southern border of Egypt, was of considerable strategic importance throughout its history. The Elephantine garrison came to the attention of scholars at the beginning of the twentieth century with the discovery and subsequent publication of a large collection of Aramaic papyri, which detailed the essentials of the community's life.[4] Unfortunately, no external sources on the Jews of Elephantine have been discovered to date, and our knowledge of the community's history and religious life remains incomplete.

Because there is no direct evidence of an ancient connection between the Jews of Elephantine and those of Ethiopia, proponents of this theory have relied on the indirect evidence of geographical proximity and shared religious practice to support their case. With regard to the former, relatively little attempt has been made to develop a detailed migration theory. Even the most diehard diffusionists have recognized that cultural parallels do not themselves prove contact, hence the silence of scholars on this matter is more than a little troubling. Although we would certainly not claim that either the 800-mile overland journey from Aswan to Aksum or the far longer journey via the Nile to the Lake Tana region is an impossible endeavor, we would welcome further discussion of the precise route, timing, and motive.

In this context, it is particularly distressing to note the tendency of some authors to minimize the difficulties they confront not by a more detailed explication of their theories but by the geographical equivalent of a sleight of hand. Elephantine island is, as we have noted, located near Aswan. To speak of it as being located on the border of Egypt and the (modern) Sudan is both inaccurate by almost 200 miles and misleading.[5] In a similar fashion, while it is certainly correct to locate Elephantine on the border of what the ancients called "Ethiopia," that is, the area south of Egypt, too casual a use of this term is merely confusing. Thus, while it is true that some residents of Elephantine knew an "Ethiopian" language and that certain garrisons fled to Ethiopia, neither report should be taken to refer to Aksum or Ethiopia in its present connotation.[6] To treat such sources as if they refer to the Aksumite kingdom of Ethiopia without elaboration and justification is somewhat akin to treating all ancient and medieval references to India as unambiguously pointing to the Asian subcontinent.

Turning to the claim that the Beta Israel and the Jews of Elephantine shared a religious culture, here, too, considerable difficulties can be shown to exist. To begin with, it is not at all clear how one can demonstrate a historical link between a little-known group that disappeared long before the Christian Era and a community whose religious system can only be documented beginning in the fifteenth century. (We shall return to this point at the end of the chapter, when we consider the view of history that characterizes these works.) Leaving these historical difficulties aside for the moment, it must be admitted that an Elephantine could explain some features of Beta Israel religious life. The Elephantine and Beta Israel communities are almost unique among Jewish groups in their practice of sacrificial ritual outside the land of Israel. Even here, however, it must be admitted that important differences also exist. While the Jews of Elephantine performed their sacrifices in a temple, the Beta Israel performed theirs in the open air.[7] While both, therefore, used the term *masgid* to describe sacred places, the Beta Israel's was a prayer house, the Jews of Elephantine's a site of sacrifices.

These similarities must be viewed with some caution. Indeed, one of the things that all of the authors who support a Nilotic matrix for the arrival of Jewish influences to Ethiopia have in common is their willingness to draw far-reaching conclusions on the basis of scant evidence. In several instances a single fact taken in isolation is called upon to support a complete chronological framework. Hancock, for example, writes: "Since the Falashas themselves still practised sacrifice in Ethiopia. . . . their ancestors must have converted to Judaism at a time when it was still acceptable for those far away from the centralized national sanctuary to practise local sacrifice. This would suggest that the conversion took place before King Josiah's ban."[8] He is silent as to how they acquired the Torah (whose importance he admits), much less later apocryphal works. He similarly views the fact that they do not celebrate Hanukah but is silent as to how they came to possess Maccabbees among their religious books. (One of the more amusing moments in a book full of overblown prose is Hancock's "discovery" that "the Feast of the Dedication of the Temple was properly known as Hanukkah.")[9]

In fact, when a careful comparison is made between the religious life of the two communities, differences can be shown to outweigh similarities. The attitudes toward the Sabbath presented by the two communities are, for example, a study in contrast. Although the Elephantine papyri contain no explicit mention of Sabbath observance in that community, it should probably be accepted that the Jews of Elephantine were aware of and commemorated the day.[10] If, however, as some experts contend, this day was "honored more in the breach than in the observance [at Elephantine]"[11] it is hard to see how this community could have been the source of Ethiopian Christian devotion today, much less the Beta Israel's extremely strict celebration.[12] Moreover, the Beta Israel's rules concerning the Sabbath, as well as many other features of their religious life, were strongly influenced by the *Book of Jubilees,* a work composed in the middle of the second century B.C., long after the Elephantine community had ceased to exist.[13]

Nor is this the only major difference between the two communities. The Aramaic texts found at Elephantine are in a dialect quite different from that of the loanwords in Ge'ez.[14] Supporters of the Elephantine connection to the Beta Israel have, moreover, discreetly ignored the clear evidence that the Jews of the military garrison were not strict monotheists. While there can be little question that Yahu (Yahweh or YHWH), the God of heaven, was the primary focus of religious attention for the Jewish garrison, proof also exists that other gods were rendered homage as well. Particularly striking in this context is the decision of the Elephantine community's leader, Jedaniah b. Gemariah, to distribute a portion of the moneys collected for YHWH to the deities Anathbethel and Eshembethel.[15] Needless to say, neither of these gods nor any gods like them (unless we wish to argue for a precursor of Christian Trinitarianism) are found among the Jewish influences that reached Ethiopia.

Finally, a word must be said about the religious literature of Elephantine. No copy of the Pentateuch was found at this community, nor is it likely they possessed one. It is hardly likely they would have appealed to Jerusalem for help in rebuilding their temple, as they had been aware of the Deuteronomic prohibition of sacrifice outside Jerusalem. It is difficult, therefore, to see how the Jews of Elephantine who almost certainly did not possess a complete Pentateuch much less a Bible can be depicted as the religious forebears of the Orit-, or Torah-centered, Beta Israel. The situation with regard to later biblical books as well as such apocryphal works as *Enoch* and *Jubilees* is even more striking. None of these works could have reached Ethiopia through the Elephantine community.

In summary, nothing in the recently published literature provides any reason to dissent from Edward Ullendorff's succinct summary published almost three decades ago: "Such aspects of Elephantine religious life as emerge in the papyri are in sharp contrast to the entire cast of religious expression among the Falashas in particular and the Judaizing trends of the Abyssinian Church in general."[16]

MEROË

Until comparatively recently, proponents of a Nilotic origin for Ethiopian Judaisms paid little attention to the Nubian kingdoms of Napata and Meroë. The lack of any consensus that Judaism had influenced these kingdoms apparently removed them from the theories of most writers. In recent years, however, several authors, most notably the British Jewish community leader and philanthropist David Kessler, have sought to place this region at the center of the debate on Falasha origins.

Kessler argues that, contrary to the generally held scholarly view, the queen of Sheba came not from an ancient southern Arabian kingdom or even as Ethiopian legend would have it from Aksum, but rather from the ancient Kush.[17] This, he notes, is the opinion of the first-century A.D. Jewish historian Josephus Flavius, and it can also be supported by a variety of other sources. Indeed, as other scholars have noted, the products brought to Jerusalem by the queen could easily be claimed to support an African rather than an Arabian locale for the queen. By moving the queen (in Kessler's view she is actually a queen mother of the Nubian king) to this African kingdom, he apparently hopes to solve some of the geographical difficulties alluded to above.

Several crucial difficulties, however, can be shown to exist with this theory. First and foremost, serious questions must be raised as to what Kushitic kingdom the queen could possibly have come from. The kingdom, which had its first capital at Napata and later was centered to the south at Meroë, only substantially established itself in the ninth century. Prior to this period, there is little evidence that the Kushitic dynasty had even made an impact on Egypt and could thus have scarcely engaged in more wide-ranging diplomatic activities.[18] Yet, even the rise of Napata commenced approximately a century and a half after the time of Solomon. It is therefore difficult to accept Kessler's claim that "it is possible that she [the queen of Sheba] belonged to the royal family of Meroë,"[19] even if we understand Meroë in its broadest sense, that is, the Napatan (later Mero(tic) kingdom of Kush.

Kessler is, of course, not totally unaware of these chronological difficulties and offers a solution: the queen actually came in the time of King Hezekiah![20] Kessler's suggestion is rather typical of another of the most troubling trends among supporters of the Nilotic theory. In the search for a solution that fits the author's already-formulated hypothesis, a wholesale rewriting of history is undertaken. New difficulties that arise as a consequence are, of course, ignored. In this particular case, Kessler, in an attempt to preserve the queen's "Meroëtic" origins, argues that a later author seeking to add glory and importance to his narrative transported the queen from the court of Hezekiah to that of Solomon. This is, he notes, merely one more example of the common phenomenon whereby famous events are attached to famous names. What he does not explain is why the same author, rather than identifying the queen with the well-known kingdom of Kush, names her as the mysterious queen of Sheba. Would not a biblical author seeking to link famous events with famous names identify the queen with a famous kingdom? Are we to assume that the biblical author chose to preserve this event by misidentifying both the protagonists and misdating it by more than two and a half centuries? Kessler would apparently answer in the affirmative, although it is not always clear how seriously he himself takes this argument. He writes, "Whether the queen's journey took place in the tenth century or the eighth is less important than the event itself."[21] Certainly the difference is crucial if he wishes to argue for the queen's Meroëtic origins!

A further question must, of course, be raised regarding this narrative. Even if we were to concede, for the sake of argument, that the queen of Sheba may have come from Nubia, of what relevance is this to the problem of the Jewish influences on Aksumite Ethiopia? Neither biblical version of the Sheba story claims that she accepted the religion of King Solomon. Indeed, the idea that the queen's visit resulted in a religious revolution in her kingdom appears only in the *Kebra Nagast*. Here and elsewhere Kessler's attitude toward this work is perplexing. Where it appears to support his arguments, he treats this late and legendary work with exaggerated seriousness as to its historical value. Elsewhere he chooses to ignore that the *Kebra Nagast*'s basic premise—that the queen came from Aksum or that her son brought the Ark of the Covenant—does not support his theories. Consider, for example, Kessler's statement, that "seen through the eyes of an Ethiopian-Christian or Jew—the notion that the queen of Sheba was a Sabaen, who returned to Arabia after visiting Solomon, would destroy the whole foundation on which his history was built and would deprive the *Kebra Nagast* of its authority."[22] The result (not that this is a concern of a historian) would of course be no less destructive if "Sabaen" and "Arabia" were replaced by "Nubian" and "Meroë." For seen through the eyes of an Ethiopian Christian or Jew, the notion that the queen of Sheba was a Nubian, who returned to Meroë after visiting Solomon, would also destroy the whole foundation on which his history was built and would deprive the *Kebra Nagast* of its authority. Surely, this hardly counts as a conclusive argument in support of his theory. Indeed, using this logic, the historian of Christianity would have little choice but to accept that Jesus was in fact the Son of God, for to do otherwise would destroy the whole foundation on which Christian history was based and would deprive the New Testament of its authority. As we shall discuss in somewhat greater detail below, this willingness to pay lip service to local myths, when convenient for the author's arguments, and grant them a historical status most scholars would refuse them, is another of the striking characteristics of the Nilotic theory.

Thus, whatever one's opinion of Kessler's success in proving that the queen who visited Solomon (Hezekiah) was the queen or queen mother of Meroë, the episode appears to be of little significance in explaining the source of Jewish influences in Ethiopia. It is not even clear that he has demonstrated how (or if) Jewish influences reached Nubia.

Even if we were to accept for the sake of argument Kessler's suggestion that Jewish influences reached Nubia in the time of Hezekiah (eighth century B.C.), there is no reason to assume that it survived there for centuries. This theory finds no support in the mass of archaeological evidence uncovered in ancient Nubia, where the excavation of numerous royal tombs, cities, and temples has failed to uncover a single Judaized ruler.

Nor do any of the biblical references (Old or New Testament) offer any in-dication that Jews ruled in Kush.

For his part, Kessler seems to put great stock in the New Testament story (Acts 8) of the Ethiopian eunuch who visited Jerusalem and was con-verted by St. Phillip to Christianity. Although this story is often cited as a legendary account of how Christianity reached Ethiopia, Kessler views it as yet further evidence of Ethiopian (i.e., Meroëtic) Judaism. The eunuch, he argues, was himself a Jew. But the structure of his argument is reveal-ing. At first he is suitably cautious: "It has been suggested that he [the eu-nuch] might have longed to the class of 'God-fearers,' Gentile adherents of Judaism who did not or could not have become actual proselytes." A mere thirteen lines later, he has moved on: "It is clear that while he [the eunuch] left his home an adherent to Judaism [the qualifications and hesitations have dropped away], he returned as a Christian convert. It is unlikely that he lived in religious isolation or that he was not part of a larger Jewish community."[23] Not only have the doubts been wiped away, but the eunuch is no longer an individual semiconvert but a member of a large commu-nity. Although the intervening lines have not provided any new evidence, they have neatly succeeded in eliminating the 800 or more years that sep-arate Hezekiah and the suggested arrival of Jewish influences in Ethiopia.

METHODOLOGICAL AND THEORETICAL CONSIDERATIONS

The limits of this chapter do not permit me to fully explore all the falla-cies and weak points of the Nilotic theory. It should be noted, however, that none of the versions of this theory have garnered much support from the scientific community at large. It is doubtful if the authors in question would be much troubled by this. Kessler and Hancock both revel in their position as outsiders, although one suspects that the former at least would have appreciated a more favorable reception from the Ethiopianist community.

It is their "outsider" status that perhaps best explains some of the methodological curiosities found in their works. Scholars of African his-tory who read these works cannot help but feel that they have been thrown into something of a time warp, for supporters of the Nilotic theory can be said to have embraced wholeheartedly two of the cardinal elements of long-discredited European depictions of Africa: (1) diffusionism—African civilizations are best understood in terms of external influences, and (2) ahistoricity—there is little or no history of Africans but only that of out-siders in Africa. Indeed, they can in many ways been seen to be echoing Hugh Trevor-Roper's notorious dictum, "Perhaps in the future there will be some African history to teach. But at present there is none: there is only the history of Europeans [and we might add Israelites] in Africa. The rest is largely . . . darkness. And darkness is not the subject of history."[24]

Kessler and Hancock, perhaps unwittingly, join Trevor-Roper in viewing African (in their case Ethiopian) history as primarily the result of outside influences. Kessler, for example, is an unabashed diffusionist, writing, "We must also recognize that there is a tendency to underrate the significance of the impact of ancient Egypt and of Nubia and Meroe, which lay within Egypt's cultural and religious sphere on the development of the Horn of Africa. The importance of the Nile Valley and the Red Sea as channels of communication and, in general, the nature of the spread of ideas from one centre of civilization to another, deserve greater attention." Yet, despite Kessler's call for great attention to "the spread of ideas from one centre . . . to another," what interests him is not the interaction between two centers of civilization, but rather the influence of what he clearly views as a non-African civilization on an African people. Ethiopian influences upon the wider world garner nary a mention in his work. Even the admittedly African kingdoms of Nubia are of interest to him only insofar as they were conduits of an external influence—Judaism—to Ethiopia.[25]

Hancock, for his part, seems oblivious to the richness of the Ethiopian past and views the arrival of the Ark of the Covenant as the definitive event in Ethiopian cultural history. Indeed, so great was its impact in his view that later influences, even the coming of Christianity, were absorbed only externally and on the surface. Writing on Ethiopian Christian ritual he notes, "*Despite a thin and superficial Christian veneer,* the central role of the *tabotat* [arks] in the ceremonies that I had witnessed . . . were all phenomena lifted straight out of the most distant and recondite past" (emphasis added).[26]

Hancock's final statement, "lifted straight out of the most distant and recondite past," leads us directly to his ahistorical depiction of Ethiopia. Writing elsewhere about Ethiopian Christian practice he notes, "With a shiver of excitement I realized that there was nothing in the scene unfolding around me—absolutely nothing at all—that belonged to the twentieth century A.D. I might just as easily have been a witness to the arcane rituals of the tenth century B.C."[27] Kessler, for his part, has little trouble convincing himself that Beta Israel ritual (with the possible exception of monasticism) can be traced from Second Temple Judaism in an unbroken sequence from their first arrival in the highlands of Ethiopia.

The ahistorical nature of Ethiopian religious life is of importance to these scholars not merely for its dramatic value but also as a crucial methodological tool in their expositions. It is this assumption of static unchanging archaic form of practice that permits these scholars to transform *similarities* between Ethiopian practice and that of Qumran, Alexandria, and Elephantine into *influences*.[28] Only if it is assumed that either Ethiopian Christian practice or Beta Israel practice or both, as they existed only a few decades ago, have remained unchanged for thousands of years are we justified in viewing similarities between modern customs and those dating two millennia earlier or more as clear proof of continuous cultural influence.

Despite the Trevor-Roperian features of the Nilotic theory, it has often received a surprisingly positive reception from members of different Ethiopian communities. Indeed, far from being dismissed as Europocentric/Judaeocentric depictions of the Ethiopian past, the books in question have frequently been welcomed and discussed with enthusiasm. One need not look far for an explanation of this situation. Nilotic theorists draw heavily on popular folk models, traditions, and myths in constructing their works. Indeed, while never wholeheartedly accepting these popular views, they pay them due homage. Thus, they offer the reader a rare opportunity to partake of two worlds: to hold on to cherished national or ethnic myths while also making claims to academic-scientific credibility.

Although both Kessler and Hancock (and particularly the former) would probably reject the comparison, these Judaeocentric approaches to Ethiopian cultural history have more than a little in common with the Afrocentrism of such writers as Cheikh Anta Diop and most recently Martin Bernal.[29] Bernal and Diop also enjoy their role as academic outsiders, adopt highly diffusionist perspectives, and believe that the importance of Egypt as a center of civilization has been underestimated. (Indeed, Kessler concludes his volume by suggesting that Jewish influences reached West Africa and Central Africa via the Ethiopia-Meroë axis.) Diop and Bernal, like Kessler, see those scholars who in the present and past have adopted views other than their own as causing harm to the peoples in question, to the quest for historical truth, and as being motivated by other than pure scientific motives.[30] Finally, all four authors base much of their reconstruction on what most scholars would consider to be dubious linguistic evidence or mythological material and place a paramount emphasis on origins in the definition of a people's identity.

In this context, therefore, it is appropriate to Mary R. Lefkowitz, one of Bernal's harshest critics, to apply her words to Nilotic theorists: "Even if a myth helps people to gain confidence, it will also teach them simultaneously that facts can be manufactured or misreported to serve a political [or humanitarian] purpose; that origins are the only measure of value . . . [and] that the true knowledge of customs, language, and literature is unimportant for understanding the nature of a culture."[31]

In the final analysis, recent supporters of the view that Jewish influences reached Ethiopia via the Nile have contributed little that is new to the debate on this subject. Nor have they attempted to contend with or refute the numerous objections raised to this theory in the past. They have succeeded, however, in reminding us that popular mythic views of history have a life of their own and rarely rely on scientific support for either their survival or revival.

POSTSCRIPT: THE BETA ISRAEL (FALASHA) AND THE LAKE TANA REGION

Although Hancock and Kessler have succeeded in capturing the imagination of much of the public, recent research by scholars far better versed in the complexities of Ethiopian history has produced a picture radically different and far more complex than that suggested by Nilotic theorists.[32] Although there is clear evidence of Jewish influences on Ethiopian culture, it does not appear to predate the first centuries of the Common Era, nor is there any reason to conclude that Egypt was the primary cradle for such influences. The Red Sea and the Judaized communities of southern Arabia remain the most probable sources for early Jewish elements in Ethiopian culture.

In a similar fashion there does not appear to be any basis for depicting the Beta Israel as the direct descendants of those who brought Judaism to Ethiopia. From a cultural perspective there appears to be little question that the Beta Israel must be understood as the product of processes that took place in the regions around Lake Tana between the fourteenth and sixteenth centuries. During this period a number of inchoate groups of *ayhud* living around the source of the Nile coalesced into the people known as the "Falasha."[33] Their emergence as a distinctive people was the result of a variety of political, economic, and ideological factors. The rise of the so-called Solomonic dynasty in the last decades of the thirteenth century and its subsequent expansion throughout the Ethiopian highlands placed the *ayhud* of the Lake Tana region, as well as many other hitherto autonomous groups, under unprecedented pressure.[34] From the early fourteenth century onward, a gradual process of disenfranchisement took place that eventually deprived many of the Beta Israel of their rights to own inheritable land. Denied this crucial economic asset, they pursued a number of strategies to retain their economic viability. While some doubtless identified themselves with the dominant Christian landholders, others either departed for peripheral areas where competition for land was limited, or accepted the reduced status of tenant farmers. In both the latter cases, they probably began to supplement their income by pursuing crafts such as smithing, pottery, and weaving. Thus, the vague religious and regional bases for their identification were supplemented and further defined by an occupational-economic distinction.[35]

At the same time, revolutionary changes in their religious ideology, practice, and institutions resulted in the development of a far more clearly defined and articulated religious system. Both the Beta Israel's oral traditions and the testimony of their literature offer strong evidence that crucial components in their religious system developed no earlier than the fourteenth or fifteenth century. Beta Israel accounts of their history trace virtually all major elements of their religion to the influence of the originally Christian monks, Abba Sabra and Sagga Amlak. Monasticism, purity laws, holidays, literary works, and the prayer liturgy are just a few of the features credited to these cultural heroes. While doubtless a somewhat idealized and condensed view of their role, it finds support in other sources.[36]

Although the reconstruction briefly outlined above has in recent years enjoyed broad acceptance in scholarly circles, its wider impact and penetration of public awareness have been limited. By *de*-mythologizing rather than *re*-mythologizing the Ethiopian past, its proponents have offered little to capture the public fancy. They have, however, offered a reconstruction that is historical, based on primary sources rather than speculation, and that places Ethiopia at the center of Ethiopian history.

NOTES

1. For a survey of the vast literature on this subject see Kaplan, *The Beta Israel,* pp. 27–32.

2. Ullendorff, *Ethiopia and the Bible,* pp. 120–125; Polotsky, "Aramaic, Syriac, Ge'ez," pp. 1–10.

3. Kessler, *The Falashas,* pp. 41–47; Hancock, *The Sign and the Seal,* pp. 424–446. See also Waldman, *The Jews of Ethiopia,* p. 10. Luzzato, Marcus, and Epstein all wrote prior to the discovery of the Elephantine papyri.

4. Porten, *Archives from Elephantine;* Vincent, *La Religion des judéo-arméens d'Elephantine;* Cowley, *Aramaic Papyri of the Fifth Century B.C.*

5. Waldman, *The Jews of Ethiopia,* p. 10.

6. Baron, *The Social and Religious History of the Jewish People,* p. 588. It should also be noted that neither of these reports can be demonstrated to refer to the Jewish garrison.

7. Lifchitz, "Un sacrifice chez les Falachas, Juifs d'Abyssinie," pp. 16–123.

8. Hancock, *The Sign and the Seal,* p. 407.

9. Ibid., p. 134.

10. Porten, *Archives from Elephantine,* pp. 126–128.

11. Ibid., p. 10. It is strange to find Kessler, p. 42, quoting this passage with approval given his claim that Elephantine practice was "remarkably reminiscent" of that of the Beta Israel.

12. Leslau, *Falasha Anthology,* p. xxxii: "The day celebrated in the strictest manner is the Sabbath."

13. On the dating of Jubilees see Vanderkam, *Textual and Historical Studies in the Book of Jubilees,* pp. 207–285. On the decline of the Elephantine garrison, see Porten, *Archives from Elephantine,* pp. 296–301.

14. Personal communication, Professor Edward Ullendorff, August 1990.

15. Porten, *Archives from Elephantine,* p. 163.

16. Ullendorff, *Ethiopia and the Bible,* pp. 16–17.

17. Kessler, *The Falashas,* pp. 24–57. The possibility that the queen was of African origin has also been raised by Isaac and Felder, "Reflections on the Origins of Ethiopian Civilization," pp. 71–83. No attempt, however, is made in their paper to associate the queen with either Judaic influences in Ethiopia or more specifically the Beta Israel.

18. Adams, *Nubia: A Corridor to Africa,* 249–259.

19. Kessler, *The Falashas,* p. 40.

20. Ibid., pp. 34–47.

21. Ibid., p. 37.

22. Ibid.

23. Ibid., pp. 49, 50.

24. The statement was originally made during a series of lectures at the University of Sussex transmitted by BBC Television. For an illuminating discussion see Fuglestead, "The Trevor-Roper Trap or the Imperialism of History, an Essay," pp. 309–326.

25. Kessler, *The Falashas,* p. xvi. For a telling critique of such diffusionist approaches to the study of religion see Sharpe, *Comparative Religion: A History,* p. 174: "The ease with which historical links could occasionally be demonstrated was an open invitation to certain enthusiastic scholars to extend these chains of evidence by means of free hypothesis, and to suggest, on inadequate evidence, that all civilization—or in this case, religion—had originated in some temporarily fashionable corner of the world." See also Blaut, *The Colonizer's Model of the World: Geographical Diffusionism and Eurocentric History.*

26. Hancock, *The Sign and the Seal,* pp. 267–268.

27. Ibid., pp. 263, 267–268.

28. See Kaplan, "The Origins of the Beta Israel: Five Methodological Cautions," pp. 41–47, for a more detailed discussion of this point.

29. Diop, *The African Origin of Civilization: Myth or Reality;* Bernal, *Black Athena.*

30. Kessler, *The Falashas,* p. xx: "I have found myself under a strong obligation to enter this argument because I deemed it necessary to try to mitigate the damage which could be done to the Falashas' reputation and the cause of historical truth as well as to their own pride in the origins. . . . An obligation surely rests on those who have regard for Ethiopian Jewish studies to proclaim the historical truth as we see it."

31. Lefkowitz, "Ancient History, Modern Myths," p. 22.

32. Abbink, "The Enigma of Beta Isra'el Ethnogenesis: An Ethnohistorical Study," pp. 397–450; Shelemay, *Music;* Kaplan, *Beta Israel.*

33. *Ayhud* literally means "Jews" but is generally used to refer to Christian heretics and other political or religious deviants. *Falasha* appears to be derived from either the Ge'ez *falasawi* (a landless person) or *falasyan* (a monk). See Kaplan, *Beta Israel,* pp. 65–73.

34. For a masterful survey of this period see Tamrat, *Church and State in Ethiopia.*

35. Quirin, *The Evolution of the Ethiopian Jews.*

36. Ibid., pp. 65–72; Shelemay, *Music;* Kaplan, *Beta Israel.*

6

♦

Arab Geographers, the Nile, and the History of Bilad al-Sudan

Nehemia Levtzion

Dedicated to the memory of the late J. F. P. Hopkins
of Cambridge University, with whom I edited
Corpus of Early Arabic Sources for West African History,
in which the Nile features so prominently

The sources of the Nile were a riddle for humanity until the middle of the nineteenth century. This chapter investigates what the Arab geographers knew or theorized concerning the Nile, its sources, and its course. We meet information about the Nile in texts that deal with sub-Saharan Africa, known in the sources as *Bilad al-Sudan*. This part of Africa was better known to the Arabs than the lands south of Egypt.

The Arab geographers adopted Ptolemy's theory of astronomical geography about the sources of the Nile in the *Jabal al-Qamar* (Mountains of the Moon). *Surat al-Ard* of al-Khuwarizmi (died sometime after 846) is an adaptation to Arabic of Ptolemy's *Geography*. But al-Khuwarizmi was able to add names of places (like 'Alwa, Zaghawa, Fezzan, and Dunqula) that represent the new geographical knowledge of the Arabs:

> There are two round lakes. Into the first pour five rivers from the Mountain of the Moon. Five rivers also issue from the Mountain of the Moon into the second lake. [All these rivers finally unite in a single lake called the Little Lake.] From the Little Lake issues a great river which is the Nil of Egypt. It passes through the land of the Sudan, and 'Alwa and Zaghawa and Fezzan and the Nuba, and passes through Dunqula, the city of Nuba.[1]

In the tenth and eleventh centuries the knowledge of the Arabs about the countries south of the Sahara expanded, based on the direct observation of military commanders, travelers, and traders.

Ibn al-Faqih, writing shortly after 903, begins with Ptolemy's theory: "Some people say that the Nil issues beyond the equator from two lakes. . . . It flows around the land of the Habasha, and then it passes between Bahr al-Qulzum and the desert, to flow on and to pour itself at Dimyat into the Mediterranean." But he soon adds information based on direct observation: "Abu'l-Khattab [d. 761] related that al-Mushtari b. al-Aswad said: 'I have raided the land of Anbiya twenty times from al-Sus al-Aqsa, and I have seen there the Nil. Between the river and the salty sea is a dune of sand and the Nil emerges from beneath it.'"[2]

The raids of Abu'l-Khattab were from Morocco to the Sahara, and the evidence suggests that as early as the middle of the eighth century, the Arabs had some idea about a system of rivers south of the Sahara, which they identified as the Nile.

Writing in 1067, a work of descriptive geography, based on information gathered from travelers and traders, al-Bakri refers to the major river of West Africa as the Nile. The town of Takrur, which was located in Futa Toro, in present-day Senegal, was "situated on the Nil."[3] In Sila, close to Takrur, "in the Nil, where it adjoins their country, an animal is found living in the water, which resembles the elephant in the size of its body as well as its snout and tusks." This was undoubtedly a hippopotamus, which as al-Bakri described, "goes to pasture on land, but then seeks its abode in the Nil."[4] The Nile described in those two references was undoubtedly the Senegal River as it approached the Atlantic Ocean.

Al-Bakri's informants were acquainted with the routes from Ghana to the sources of the gold in the south. From the town of Yarisna, on the Nile, African merchants exported gold to other countries. On the opposite side of the Nile were the two kingdoms of Do and Malal.[5] These were undoubtedly Malinke principalities, predecessors of Mali, and the Nile in question was undoubtedly the upper reaches of the Niger River, where the Bure goldfields seem to have been opened about that time. It should be noted, however, that the Upper Senegal and the Upper Niger Rivers are not very far apart, close enough to confuse them as being one river. When al-Bakri referred again to the Nile, it was in his description of the bend of the Niger River, at Tiraqqa, which must have been not far from where Timbuktu developed later:

> At a place called Ra's al-Ma' you meet the Nil coming out of the land of the Sudan. One of its banks is inhabited by tribes of Muslim Berbers, called Madasa, and opposite them, on the other bank, live pagan Sudan. Then you go from there six stages along the Nil to the town of Tiraqqa.

. . . From Tiraqqa the Nil turns towards the south into the land of the Sudan.[6]

Al-Bakri seems to have had quite an accurate idea of the course of the Niger at that point, in its flow to the northeast to the farthest point of penetration into the Sahara, the land of the nomad Berbers, where it turned to the southeast back into the land of the Sudan.

Al-Idrisi, writing in 1145, goes back to Ptolemy's theory, first presented by al-Khuwarizmi. Arguments concerning the reliability of the information provided al-Bakri and al-Idrisi touched on one of the more important issues in the history of *Bilad al-Sudan,* namely the location of the capital of Ghana. According to al-Bakri, the capital was in the Sahel, far away from any river. Its people obtained water from wells.[7] Al-Idrisi, on the other hand, located Ghana astride the Nile.[8] Historians suggested that the capital of Ghana was relocated, perhaps as a result of the Almoravids intervention during the period in between the writing of al-Bakri and al-Idrisi.

But our argument is that al-Idrisi's location of Ghana on the Nile was simply a geographical aberration, a result of his adherence to the theory of Ptolemy. Al-Idrisi followed Ptolemy in assuming that all of the southern lands are in an arid torrid zone, where life depended completely on the river. Here is al-Idrisi's description of the town of Bilaq in the land of the Nuba: "There is no rain at all in the town of Bilaq, nor in all the other regions of the Sudan. . . . They have no rain or mercy from God nor succor other than the inundation of the Nil, on which they rely for agriculture."[9]

No town could have therefore existed away from the river, and al-Idrisi placed all the towns of *Bilad al-Sudan,* including the capital of Ghana, on the Nile. The Nile of al-Idrisi was indeed a very strange river that meandered in order to pass through all the towns of the region. Al-Idrisi imagined Ghana as situated on a river surrounded by a terrible desert. He described the route from Ghana to Mali as "being over dunes and deep sands where there is no water."[10] As we know well, this route was in plain savannah country, which a traveler like Ibn Battuta found safe and easy.

Al-Idrisi followed al-Khuwarizmi in the account of the sources of the Nile in Jabal al-Qamar, from where a number of springs come in and out of a series of lakes. Al-Idrisi had new information concerning the last lake:

> This lake is just beyond the equator, and touching it. In the lowest part of this lake in which the rivers collect, a mountain protrudes, splitting the main part of the lake into two, and extending from the lake to the northeast. One of the branches of the Nil flows along this mountain on the western side. This is the Nil of *Bilad al-Sudan,* on which most of the towns are situated. The second branch of the Nil comes out of the lake on

the eastern rift of the mountain, and flows to the north, through the country of the Nuba and the country of Egypt.[11]

Al-Idrisi produced an answer to the existence of two "Niles," which split in the lake, one—"the Nil of Egypt"—that flows to the north, and the other—"the Nil of *Bilad al-Sudan,* on which most of their towns are situated." Ibn Saʿid, writing sometime after 1269, added that the Nile flows past Ghana and Takrur into the Atlantic Ocean.[12]

Ibn Saʿid named the great lake where the Nile splits as Lake Kuri. An elaborated Ptolemy's theory is being collated with concrete evidence from an informant, a certain Ibn Fatima who traveled extensively in Africa. In connection with Lake Kuri, Ibn Saʿid quoted Ibn Fatima as saying: "I have never met anyone who has seen its southern side. It is navigated only by the people of Kanim and their neighbors, such as we encountered on the northern side."[13] Ibn Saʿid's Lake Kuri was therefore Lake Chad, on the northeastern corner of which was Kanim.

Ibn Saʿid fitted another piece of concrete evidence into the elaborated theory when he described not two but three "Niles" coming out of his Lake Kuri. In addition to the Nile of Egypt and the Nile of Ghana he also recorded the "Nil of Maqdishu."[14] Writing half a century after Ibn Saʿid and relying on him, though without acknowledgment, al-Dimashqi (d. 1327) was more specific concerning a river that "flows towards the east then bends towards the south and is the river of Maqdishu of the Zanj," which pours itself into "the Southern Sea."[15] *Zanj* is the term used by the Arabs for the black people of East Africa, and the "Southern Sea" is the designation of the Indian Ocean. Hence, the third river was undoubtedly the Juba River of Somalia.

Al-Dimashqi departed from earlier geographers by reserving the name Nile for the true Nile only, saying, "the river of the Nuba, otherwise called the Nil."[16] He referred to the two other "Niles" as "rivers" only. But the Nile that cuts across *Bilad al-Sudan* "resembles the Nil in its rise and fall and the manner of the tilling of its lands."[17]

The Nile of *Bilad al-Sudan* was in fact a creation of the Arab geographers, who gathered pieces of information from traders and travelers and put them together. They made one long river out of several rivers that flow in the region immediately south of the Sahara, between the Atlantic Ocean and the Nile itself. These rivers are the Senegal, the Niger, the Shari, Bahr al-Arab, and Bahr al-Ghazal. Some of these rivers flow from west to east and others from east to west. Al-Idrisi, and all those who followed him, made the long river flow from east to west, perhaps because they were aware that a river poured itself into the Atlantic Ocean.

But Ibn Battuta made the river flow in the other direction, from west to east. The reason was that Ibn Battuta, who visited *Bilad al-Sudan* in

1352 and 1353, sailed on the Niger River from Timbuktu to Gao and was able to ascertain its direction. From Gao he believed that the Nile continues to flow to the same direction, until it descends to "the Country of the Nuba, who are Christians, then to Dunqula. . . . Then it descends to the cataracts, which are the last district of the Sudan (meaning of the blacks) and the beginning of the district of Aswan of Upper Egypt."[18]

Ibn Battuta still considered the major river of *Bilad al-Sudan* to be part of the Nile system. Those who made this river flow from east to west had to make the two or three Niles split in a lake. But, for Ibn Battuta, who believed that the river continued in the direction that he saw, namely from west to east, the two Niles became one. The origin of the Egyptian Nile, according to Ibn Battuta, was therefore somewhere south of ancient Mali.

No more information on the Nile came from West Africa after the fourteenth century. Thus, our exploration of the Nile came to an end, together with the examination of a fascinating venture in following the Arabs' discovery of *Bilad al-Sudan*, a collation of theory, myth, and eyewitness evidence.

NOTES

1. Abu Ja'far Muhammad b. Musa al-Khuwarizmi, *Surat al-ard,* edited by Hans von Mzik, Vienna, 1926, pp. 106–107, also in N. Levtzion and J. F. P. Hopkins, *Corpus of Early Arabic Sources for West African History,* Cambridge, 1981, p. 9 (referred to in the following notes as *Corpus*).

2. Abu Bakr Ahmad b. Muhammad al-Hamadhani Ibn al-Faqih, *Mukhtasar kitab al-buldan,* edited by M. J. de Goeje, Leiden, 1885, p. 64, also in *Corpus,* p. 27.

3. Abu 'Ubayd 'Abd Allah b. 'Abd al-'Aziz al-Bakri, *Kitab al-masalik wa'l-mamalik,* edited by Baron MacGuckin de Slane, Leiden, 1911, p. 172, also in *Corpus,* p. 77.

4. Ibid., p. 173, also in *Corpus,* p. 78.

5. Ibid., pp. 177–178, also in *Corpus,* p. 82.

6. Ibid., pp. 180–181, also in *Corpus,* pp. 84–85.

7. Ibid., p. 175, also in *Corpus,* p. 80.

8. Abu 'Abd Allah Muhammad b. Muhammad al-Sharif al-Idrisi, *Nuzhat al-mushtaq fi ikhtiraq al-afaq,* edited by R. Dozy and M. J. de Goeje, Leiden, 1866, p. 6, also in *Corpus,* p. 109.

9. Ibid., p. 20, also in *Corpus,* p. 115.

10. Ibid., p. 6, also in *Corpus,* p. 109.

11. Ibid., p. 15, also in *Corpus,* p. 115.

12. Ali b. Musa Ibn Sa'id al-Maghribi, *Kitab bast al-ard fi'l-tul wa'l-'ard,* edited by J. Vernet Gines, Tetuan, 1958, p. 23, also in *Corpus,* 184.

13. Ibid., p. 27, also in *Corpus,* p. 187.

14. Ibid., pp. 27–28, also in *Corpus,* pp. 187–188.

15. Shams al-Din Abu 'Abd Allah Muhammad b. 'Ali Talib al-Ansari al-Dimashqi, *Nukhbat al-dahr fi 'aja'ib al-barr wa'l-bahr,* edited by M. A. F. Mehren, St. Petersburg, 1866, p. 89, also in *Corpus,* p. 206.

16. Ibid., p. 89, also in *Corpus,* p. 206.

17. Ibid., p. 110, also in *Corpus,* p. 207.

18. Shams al-Din Abu 'Abd Allah Muhammad Ibn Battuta, *Tuhfat al-nuzzar fi ghara'ib al-amsar wa-'ja'ib al-asfar,* edited by Defremery and Sanguinetti, Paris, 1858, pp. 395–396, also in *Corpus,* pp. 287–288.

Part 2

The Nile
as Seen from a Distance

7

◆

Up the River
or Down the River?
An Afrocentrist Dilemma

Yaacov Shavit

The nature of the Nile Valley and the Nile River's function as a unifying factor for Egypt, Sudan, and the rest of Africa are a major subject in the Afrocentric world view and historiography.[1] The writings of the Afrocentric pan-Negroid school, especially those of the prominent Sengalese scholar Cheikh Anta Diop and his disciples, reveal, in my view, the inner dilemma of the Afrocentric view and its historical reconstruction.[2] The argument over who has seniority in the Nile Valley—Nubia or Egypt—is a subject in itself, which I will not address here. Our question is why was it necessary to choose at all? If "Africa" is described as a racial and cultural unity, of which Egypt is an indivisible part,[3] why is it important to ask who has seniority—Egypt, Nubia, or equatorial Africa and its many nations?

My aim here is not to touch on the question of Africa's cultural homogeneity. My sole intention is to suppose that the classical view that the river Nile was responsible for the uniqueness of ancient Egypt as a physical and cultural entity, different in nature from the rest of Africa.

THE ADORATION OF THE NILE

Hail to thee, O Nile, that issues from the earth
   and comes to keep Egypt alive! . . .
He that waters the meadows which He created . . .
He that makes to drink the desert . . .
He who makes barley and brings emmer into being . . .
He who brings grass into being for the cattle . . .

He who makes every beloved tree to grow . . .
O, Nile, verdant art thou, who makes man and cattle to live.[4]

The ancient Egyptians considered the flow of the Nile River from south to north to be the "normal" natural course of any river. A victory stele was erected for Thutmose I (1504–1492 B.C.) at Tombos, just north of the third cataract, in which the king boasts of his northern frontier at the Euphrates "that inverted (or: circling) water which goes downstream in going upstream (or that circling water which flows north [= downstream] in flowing south). This curious designation reflects Egyptian amazement at a river which, unlike the Nile, flows towards the south."[5]

But what was most important to the ancient Egyptians were the functions of the Nile as the cultivator of Egypt, primarily its northern region (Lower Egypt). The ancient Egyptian name for this land, Kmt, "the black one," emphasized the singular nature of Lower Egypt compared to other regions and the major contribution of the Nile in creating and preserving this singularity.[6] The myth of the resurrection of the god Osiris is deeply rooted in the Nile, the natural force that fertilized the land of Egypt. It is Osiris who built canals with floodgates and regulators to prevent the Nile from overflowing the neighboring countryside and turning it into a marsh.[7] "Osiris was regarded as the power of the moon, which produced the Nile-flood and therefore all the fertility in Egypt."[8] *The Book of Making the Spirit of Osiris* (or *The Spirit Burial*), for example, says: "Hail, Osiris. . . . Hàp[y] (the Nile) appeareth by the command of thy mouth. Making men and women to live on the fluxes which come from thy members, making every field to flourish."[9]

The significance of the river is manifested in the cosmogony of Pharaoh Akhenaten (Amenhotep IV) of Amarna (1353–1335 B.C.), in "The Great Hymn to the Aten":

You made Hapy (hʿpy) (the Nile God) in dat (the Netherworld).
You bring him [as flood waters] when you will,
To nourish the people.
You made a heavenly Hapy [i.e. rain] descend for them.[10]

According to this cosmogonical picture, there is one Nile in heaven that brings rain to strange nations, and another Nile on earth that issues from the underworld for Egypt alone.[11] Indeed, all the various cosmogonical systems in ancient Egypt shared the perception of overwhelming importance ascribed to the Nile and its annual flooding.[12] The Nile occupied an important position in Egyptian culture; it influenced the development of mathematics, geography, and the calendar; Egyptian geometry advanced due to the practice of land measurement "because the overflow of the Nile caused the boundary of each person's land to disappear."[13] "The most important event in Egyptian life was the annual flooding of the Nile, the inundation period, which coincided closely with the helical rising of Sirius the Dog, the brightest star in the earth's hemisphere just before dawn."[14] Many wall paintings reveal the different functions of the Nile in religion, fishing, and trade.[15] In no other African religion had a river such status and function in its myths of creation.[16]

Classical writers from Herodotus to Diodorus Siculus and Strabo, as well as Jewish writers from Philo of Alexandria to the sages, carried on this tradition, recognizing and praising the Nile's contribution to Egypt's unique nature. When Herodotus wrote the famous words "Egypt is the gift of the Nile," he was referring to the thick mud and black soil of the Delta brought by the river from Ethiopia, stressing the uniqueness of Lower Egypt. "What is Egypt but a river valley, which the water floods?" Strabo asks rhetorically (1.2.25). "Egypt is a land rich in plains, with deep soil,"[17] wrote Philo of Alexandria, "very productive of all that human nature needs, and particularly of corn. For the river of this country, in the height of summer, when other streams, whether winter torrents or spring-fed, are said to dwindle, rises and overflows, and its flood makes a lake of the fields which need no rain but every year bear a plenty of crop of good produce of every kind" (Philo, De vita Mosis, 1.5–6 and see also 114–118).[18]

According to Karl Butzer, the roots of Egypt's agricultural system "must be sought in both Africa and Asia, from among a wide array of economic traditions."[19] Domesticated animals, for example, gradually expanded into Egypt from Asia. However, Egypt's agriculture and system of food production, which finally appeared in northern Egypt shortly before 5000 B.C., were indigenous in character.

Thus we find that all of the ancient and classical sources shared the view that the Nile was the major factor in the creation and flourishing of ancient Egyptian civilization and the main force behind its distinct and unique character—a view shared by modern historians. I too am focusing on the river, following the classical sources and emphasizing its dominant role in shaping Egyptian culture (and, in part, the Kushite culture as well), very different from the inner-African cultures that supposedly had contacts other than trading various kinds of goods such as gold, slaves, and ivory.

Yet none of all these sources, be they of ancient Egypt, classical antiquity, or the Hellenistic-Roman period, mentions anything about the Nile as a water route between the Nile Valley (Nubia and Egypt) and inner Africa, nor do any Egyptian records in our possession describe the Nile as Egypt's route to sub-Saharan equatorial Africa. Egyptian records and ship logs reveal the importance of the Nile in unifing Egypt; the Egyptian kings (and their Ptolemaic successors) made regular river trips from temple to temple, but nothing is said about frequent trips up the river from Upper Egypt to Sudan—the gateway to inner Africa. The main function of the river was the unification of Upper and Lower Egypt: "It was the Nile, and traffic upon it, that was in time to permit the creation of a great Egyptian kingdom."[20]

The Nile could hardly replace the desert caravan routes through the Sahara because the southern part of the Nile provides neither good water nor land routes. Not only were travelers forced to bypass the six cataracts between central Sudan and southern Egypt,[21] they also had to bypass the river valley. As a result the Middle Nile was actually a backwater, even though light boats (made of papyrus), used for fishing and transporting goods, could be easily carried from one place to another over land, thus bypassing the cataracts. Stronger and larger boats and ships, carrying heavy commodities, sailed primarily to and from the sea on the northern part of the river.[22] Early in the sixth dynasty (2291–2323 B.C.) the governor of Upper Egypt, Weni, excavated five canals to overcome part of the natural obstacles,[23] and in the eighth year of Sesostris III (1870 B.C.), the period in which Lower Nubia was subjugated, a canal 150 cubits long, 20 cubits wide, and 15 cubits deep had been constructed at the cataract at Aswan.[24]

If this is so, then the Nile, as a means of communication, barely served as a connecting link between Egypt and the Sudan, while the Lower Nile permitted contact and interaction between Lower and Upper Egypt and Lower and Upper Nubia, serving as a major factor in the unification and centralization of the land and its kingdom.[25] One had to leave the water route and later return to the river several times, and afterward continue over land farther south through Sudan to the interior of Africa. There was no easy way into the heart of Africa from the Nile Valley. The Egyptians used donkeys on caravan routes to carry on the long-distance trade with the south. But there is no mention of donkeys making their way into the heart of Africa, and the journey there and back, off the track of desert roads, must have been based entirely on porters.[26]

Egypt could also use the sea route to Punt (Somali) and from there reach the inner continent. Several autobiographical accounts exist of organized expeditions to the south: the Weny expedition to Nubia and farther south during the sixth dynasty; and the sixth-dynasty Harkhuf expedition, which traveled to Punt through Hammamat and the Red Sea.[27]

It was not the Nile, provider of water and alluvial soil, creator of the natural environment for the genesis and evolution of a unique civilization, that served as a route and corridor between equatorial Africa, the Nile Valley, and the Mediterranean. It was not the river as a water route that created a long and intensive movement of migration, cultural diffusion, and cultural transmission between the Nile Valley and Africa. It was not the the movement up and down the river that was responsible for Africa's place under the sun as the cradle of Egyptian civilization, or Egypt's place as the birthplace of African (and world) civilization. The river's role was performed inside the Nile Valley alone, up to the cataracts and not beyond. The traffic on the Nile permitted the creation of the Egyptian kingdom and offered the only natural and convenient route from village to village; as we saw, the very concept of travel was expressed by sailing upstream and downstream.[28]

Because the matter concerning us is Egypt's connection with Africa, contact did not have to be based on the Nile as a transit route. Hence the question of "up the river or down the river" need not focus on the role of the river as a route of transportation but on the very nature of the contacts between the Nile Valley and equatorial Africa. This issue can also be discussed without entering into the role played by the Nile in creating these contacts. The question of up or down is therefore metaphorical; the real question is "from north to south" or "from south to north"; whether it took place through the Nile or through other possible routes, what concerns us are two different phenomena of migration and diffusion between Africa and Egypt: first, the gradual and very long prehistorical (predynastical) phenomenon; and second, the diffusion between tribes and organized nations with a defined identity, which were able to control both migration and diffusion during the historical (dynastical) period.

Between Migration and Transmission

If there were ongoing contacts between Egypt and Africa, what were they like and what influence did they wield? My discussion will focus on clarifying the underlying ideology usually given to this question and its implications. Who was the benefactor (donor) and who was the beneficiary (receiver) in the relationship between the Nile Valley and tropical Africa south of the Sahara?

The Afrocentric view is that the Nile, in John Henrik Clarke's words, "played a major role in the relationship of Egypt with the nations in southeast Africa. During the early history of Africa, the Nile was a great cultural highway on which elements of civilization came into and out of inner Africa."[29] Or, as Molefi Kete Asante, the leading African scholar, wrote: "Cataracts aside, the ancient Nubian and Egyptians never considered the rocks in the river impregnable boundaries that prevented social, political, and military interrelation and interventions."[30]

At this point it is important, first, to distinguish between relationships during the prehistorical period and the historical period, and between

Egypt and Nubia's relationship and that of Egypt and equatorial Africa. Second, in dealing with contacts between Egypt and sub-Saharan (equatorial) Africa, we should distinguish between two different periods: the long period before 3000 B.C., and the period after. We should also distinguish between human migration and the diffusion of cultural traits in general, and within these two long spans of time in particular during these two time periods. The differences between various forms of immigration or cultural diffusion should be examined because there is a fundamental difference between the movement of populations in the prehistorical period and migratory movements between settled and politically organized regions. There is also a difference between the diffusion of cultural elements in the prehistorical period and diffusion involving developed cultures. There is a difference between a large-scale nomadic movement, takeover, and settlement on one hand, and cultural changes resulting from the slow infiltration of small groups, trade relations, and the like on the other.

This is an important fact in our case because the chances of influential contacts between the Egyptian Nile Valley, the Sahara, and "Africa" south of the Sahara and along the upper reaches of the Nile were better between 5000 and 3000 B.C. than in later periods.[31] East Africa was the cradle of humanity, and the peopling of the Nile Valley was a result of waves of migration from the south. As mentioned earlier, the Nile Valley provided a unique environment for the development of an agricultural society, dependent upon domesticated crops and animals, basically different from the African societies in the equatorial rain forest.[32]

These waves of migration suggest that there may have been a transmission of cultural elements and goods between the north and south. Perhaps a common cultural substratum existed during the prehistorical period as well. If this is true, the question is whether discrete cultures developed from that substratum and then fragmented, or whether it was sufficiently vigorous and strong to remain active even after the various cultures split off and went their own ways.

Nevertheless, following the prehistorical period, almost all significant contact between Egypt and most of sub-Saharan Africa via the Sahara came to an end,[33] mainly as a result of climatic changes in the Sahara region, which had become arid, and as a result of Egypt's rapid development. Some scholars believe that the Sahara region could not continue to serve as a route between Egypt and Africa, whereas others believe that even after 3000 B.C., a "rich trade was carried on for all the coveted commodities of Africa, for ivory and ebony, for ostrich feathers and eggs, for leopard skins and cattle and slaves, and gold."[34] On the basis of his findings in Knossos, Sir Arthur Evans even reached the conclusion that some African products may have found their way into Crete by way of the Nile Valley and Egypt, or by overland routes across the Sahara from the interior via Nubia.[35] Some of these commodities were brought to Egypt and the Mediterranean.[36] According to this view, prior to the introduction of the camel to Africa,[37] "donkey-drawn and possibly horse-drawn carts and even chariots crossed the western and central Sahara between North Africa and the regions of the Niger River, throughout a long period before the middle of the first millennium B.C. Another useful route lay between the Middle Nile and the western region around Lake Chad, passing across Africa by way of Kordofon, Darfur and Zangawa."[38] The Nile never replaced the desert routes; even if we accept the view that favored continuous trade contacts, it is quite clear that only limited Egyptian commodities reached Africa, and that only a very few Egyptian commodities reached the interior of Africa through the Nile Valley.

As mentioned earlier, the question of the nature of the Nile Valley civilization—the nature of the relationship between its two parts, Egypt and Nubia, and the nature of the relationship between them and the African interior—has gained a new ideological dimension in recent years. Those African and African American scholars who invested so much effort into establishing the theory that Egypt and the Nile Valley were an integral part of Africa must inevitably claim that it was the river and the river valley that played an important part in creating this unity and uniformity.[39]

From an Afrocentric point of view, however, it is not nearly enough to find the traces of intensive trade contacts between the interior of Africa, Nubia, and Egypt, or even a limited cultural exchange. Its aim is to claim far greater, more intensive, continuous, and influential biological and cultural contacts during the prehistorical periods. Thus, Afrocentrist writers argue that these contacts occurred during the predynastic period (before the third millennium) and continued during the historical dynastic periods; that they were based on deep cultural affinities and resemblances based on common racial backgrounds. In other words, they were based on a substratum of racial and cultural unity and uniformity, thus creating another cultural unity and uniformity.

It seems that Afrocentrists emphasize this point—the continuity of interdependence during the historical (dynastic) period, based on the common substratum—because they are fully aware that the phenomena of human migration and cultural diffusion in prehistorical periods are fundamentally different in nature from cultural diffusion in historical periods, just as they are fully aware that this fundamental difference is much more evident when one party in the relationship, the Egyptians, was a highly advanced civilization, while the peoples of interior Africa were far less culturally advanced. In other words, I believe the Afrocentrists fully realize that even if Egypt and Africa shared the same material culture during the Neolithic period, Egypt developed so rapidly that it became very different from the interior cultures, as well as from Nubia and Sudan.[40] In contrast to the Nile Valley, agriculture in Western and Central Africa spread very slowly, while the use of iron dates from 700 B.C. to 400 B.C.[41]

This Afrocentric view can be regarded as an inverted intellectual response to Western diffusionist theories that claimed that African culture developed through the outside influences of the white or Hamitic race and that so-called African backwardness resulted from Africa's long isolation from the Near East and the Mediterranean basin. In one famous example, Gordon Childe claimed that Egypt advanced as a result of a migration of large numbers of people into the river valley oasis during the last Ice Age who settled in the Nile Valley and did not migrate to the south, resulting in Africa's isolation.[42] The early Egyptians came as conquerors from outside Africa (Asia) and advanced through Lower Egypt southward.[43] Until the beginning of the twentieth century, European literature rarely considered the possibility of ties and contacts between Egypt and sub-Saharan Africa. From this point of view, the only acceptable theory is that there were mutual influences between Kush and Egypt.[44]

Their urgent need to respond in kind led the Afrocentrists to adopt a hyperprehistorical and historical diffusionist paradigm and to stress the importance of the racial factor. This factor, some of them assume, was responsible for the common human traits that, according to this view, were (and are) long-lasting and stronger than any other cultural development, evolution, and context. In their view, African cultural evolution was free of any outside African influences. Instead, Africa is perceived as the source and origin of human evolution. The goal of the Afrocentric theory and worldview was to turn the picture of African isolation and backwardness upside down. African American scholars replaced the European diffusionist paradigm with a hyper-African or Egyptian paradigm, in which Africa and Egypt became the cradle of a homogeneous black race that spread its culture and knowledge throughout the world, from China to the pre-Columbian civilization.[45] They were preceded by a few European scholars, such as G. Elliot Smith and Charles G. Seligman, who drew parallels between ancient Egyptian and African cultures and believed they discerned a basic resemblance between Egyptian and African customs that, in their view, arose from a common African substratum.[46] Smith's Egyptocentric (heliocentric) diffusionism claimed that Egypt—black Egypt—was the single source of human culture,[47] and that an ebb and flow of migrants from the south came to Nubia and Egypt, bringing with them the concepts and patterns of divine kingship, cosmology, language, and more. Africans and African traits were transmitted to Nubia and Egypt from the south, whereas the predynastic age was characterized by the migration of blacks into Egypt, not only from Nubia but from the inner regions of Africa as well. This flow continued during the dynastic period. However, these

Western scholars stopped at this particular point: an African substratum existed, expressed mainly in popular religion, but Africa was never able to attain the high achievements of Egypt.

It is no wonder that only part of this theory has been adopted by African and African American scholars, convinced as they are that Egypt, Nubia, and Africa sprang from a common racial stock or substratum, shared the same philosophical concepts and customs, and that the Egyptian language belongs to the family of African languages. For the Afrocentrists, this view or theory became a scientific truth, an ideological faith, a political stand, a historical revelation and redemption.[48]

EGYPT, THE NILE, AND AFRICA

I do not wish to enter the debate about the racial origins or racial traits of the ancient Egyptian population.[49] Even some Afrocentrists agree that in the course of hundreds of years, the population of the Nile Valley must have undergone physiogenetic changes as a result of living in a physical environment that differed from the one in equatorial Africa. Diop himself wrote that the man born in Africa was "necessarily dark-skinned due to the considerable force of ultraviolet radiation to the equatorial belt. As he moved toward the more temperate climes, this man gradually lost his pigmentation by process of selection and adaptation."[50] A more reasonable argument is that the Egyptian population underwent changes as a result of non-African migration. A geographically defined population, as was the Egyptian population, "can undergo significant genetic change with a small percentage of steady assimilation of 'foreign' genes."[51] As a result "the people of the Nile Valley present a continuum, from the lighter northern Egyptians to the browner Upper Egyptians, to the still browner Nubians and Kushites and to the ultra-dark brown Nilotic peoples."[52]

But let us assume, for the sake of argument, that Africa and the Nile Valley indeed shared a common biological and cultural substratum. Does this mean, as Afrocentric writings claim, that Egypt was African in its way of writing, in its culture, and in its way of thinking? Is there any connection between a common "racial" origin, and culture and civilization? Even if we are able to point to some biological and cultural similarities, the question still remains: Was this a result of the common biological substratum, of common cultural roots, resulting from similar responses to the natural environment, or a result of continuous cultural contacts between the Nile Valley and the sub-Saharan savanna? Here we may argue that if one stresses the racial substratum, there is no need to claim continuous contacts and influences, since those who belong to the same race will respond in similar patterns and create a similar human culture. And if, indeed, we accept the theory of both a common biological substratum and continuous contact between Egypt and Africa, one may wonder how the vast differences separating the civilization and culture of ancient Egypt from that of Nubia, and even more so, from that of Africa, may be explained.

Afrocentrists often refer to Africa as a homogeneous entity, whereas, as Wyat MacGraffey observes, "the influence of Egypt on Africa, and vice versa, must be studied in terms of plurality of discrete, autonomous groups instead of the undifferentiated Negroes and Hamites of the traditional approach."[53] From a historical point of view we should try to trace the influence of Egypt not on the whole of Africa but on specific African nations and regions. However, if we find a similiarity between Egyptian culture and one of the cultures south of the Sahara, we must ask why this similarity is found in that particular culture and not in other African cultures. Moreover, even if we assume that there is a common linguistic stratum, the claim that modern research (of the nineteenth and twentieth centuries) in oral traditions of the Western African peoples reveals that they contain living, active sediments of an ancient Egyptian tradition that vanished more than 2,000 years ago (!) actually asserts that the said African societies have remained static, without undergoing any cultural real change for thousands of years. In this manner, a hyperdiffusionist hypothesis becomes the theory that a certain society functioned as a receiver during a particular period, and then remained in a frozen state.

Thus, from a geographical-regional perspective, we are dealing with two separate issues: one refers to the nature of the ties between Egypt and Nubia within the Nile Valley; the other to the nature of the links between Egypt (and Nubia) and the interior. Because space is limited, I shall deal only with the second issue: the relationship between Egypt and Africa. All Afrocentrists believe that humankind originated around the region of the Great Lakes and that the peopling of the Nile Valley (and other parts of the world) must have taken place in a succession of waves.[54] W. E. Burghardt Du Bois, for example, wrote: "The Negroid came as hunters and fishermen. Probably they came up from Nubia. They began to settle down and till the soil. . . . They had copper and varied tools of flint capable of working timber."[55] In his view, the origin of the indigenous Egyptian is African, and as a result the African people who moved or pushed northward along the Nile brought the basic elements of their culture with them until Egypt "passed from the wings to the center stage in the unfolding human drama of northeastern Africa."[56] If, however, this is so, what happened after the end of the prehistorical and predynastic period?

On this point, Afrocentrists take two different tracks that bear historical as well as ideological significance.

THE "UP THE RIVER THEORY": FROM NORTH TO SOUTH

According to Diop and his disciples, black Egyptian civilization originated in Upper Egypt from the Paleolithic period onward,[57] and the different inhabitants of the African interior originated from this southern Egyptian stock and derived their culture from Egypt, namely, up the river.[58]

I believe that Diop adopted this paradigm because it was evident to him that even if a common Stone Age African substratum existed, the Nile Valley civilization advanced more rapidly than other African civilizations. Since Diop could not be satisfied with the basic Stone Age traits, and since ancient Egypt was a literate culture while African cultures were oral cultures, he was inclined to assume that it was Egypt that influenced Africa (an influence which became possible because Egypt and Africa shared the same racial and mental equipment!). For us, wrote Diop, "The turn to Egypt in all domains is a necessary condition for reconciling African civilization with history . . . in order to renovate African culture. . . . In a reconceived and renewed African culture, Egypt will play the same role that Greco-Latin antiquity plays in Western culture."[59] According to this view, Egyptian cultural influences spread for thousands of kilometers in the direction of sub-Saharan Africa.[60]

In his many publications, including his contribution to the UNESCO International Scientific Committee for the Drafting of a General History of Africa, Diop claimed that Africa was inhabited by people from the Nile Valley. He also said that "in all likelihood, after the drying of the Sahara (7000 B.C.), Black mankind first lived in bunches in the Nile basin before swarming out in successive spurts toward the interior of the continent,"[61] and that the Yoruba are of Egyptian origin. According to Diop, the nations of the Kara from southern Sudan and Upper Oubangui, the Kare-kare from northeastern Nigeria, the Yoruba of southeastern Nigeria, the Fulani, the Poular, the Serer, the Zulu, and others, all originated in the Nile Valley. These Negro people left the Nile Valley because of overpopulation and a series of odd crises.

The fundamental changes resulted from the different ecological conditions they met when they penetrated deeper into the continent and their adaptation to the different ecological conditions. Thus, they abandoned the technical equipment and scientific knowledge they had brought with them, assets that were not needed in their new environment. Diop claims that with economic resources assured by nature, without the need for perpetual inventions, the Negro became progressively indifferent to material progress.[62] Although the Negro was the first to discover iron, he found no use for it. Asa G. Hilliard III is one of many African American writers who adopted this theory, claiming that "indigenous Africans were driven from

Egypt by various invasions occurring after the 12th dynastic period circa 1783 B.C., settling in other parts of Africa including West Africa."[63]

Diop was neither the first nor the only scholar to develop this theory. Archdeacon Lucas, T. E. Bowdic,[64] E. L. R. Meyerowitz,[65] and others asserted that there were strong cultural and linguistic ties between the Yoruba, the Ashantees, and the Egyptians as a result of diffusion processes from Egypt south to the lands of the Yoruba and Ashantee, as well as to other West African peoples. These statements, writes Peter L. Shinnie in his contribution to Harris's *The Legacy of Egypt,* "have been repeated time and time again without any further authority. Apart from the inherent improbability of cultural and artistic traits surviving in recognizable form over such a period of time, it is difficult to see how any objective study could find anything distinctively Egyptian in the cultures of the people described."[66] Following this line of thought, Dana M. Clark suggests similarities between the Egyptians' and the Dagons' (Mali) perception of "Man, God and Nature,"[67] whereas according to Yoruba traditions, "enthusiastically propounded by some Yoruba historians,"[68] they were influenced by ideas from the Nile Valley, perhaps transmitting via Meroë. Even if we accept the possibility that certain techniques and forms of government were influenced by the Sudanic state, writes Robert S. Smith, "these possibilities far from justify the acceptance of the Egyptian theory, while other parts of the argument, especially the supposed resemblance in language, between ancient Egyptian and Yoruba, can be dismissed."[69]

One may wonder why these Egyptian immigrants never thought of using their technological heritage to shape their environment; to use, for example, iron tools (which were transmitted to the main body of Africa primarily through North Africa),[70] irrigation systems, and the like. Indeed, iron-pointed spears were a great social and political innovation in Africa, but the use of iron was limited and very backward compared to the Nile Valley civilization. And how do we explain the theory that while they maintained their basic social organizations and cosmology in the savanna and the rain forest, all their other cultural, social, and political achievements were so unlike the Egyptian origin?

As mentioned earlier, scholars do not exclude the possibility of mutual contacts. Shinnie, for example, does not rule out the possibility of Egyptian influence on Africa, or vice versa, and agrees that there exist "here and there faint traces of common culture or of influence of the one on the other. Through the haze of centuries of separation there is the suggestion that there were exchanges, some in the realm of ideas and institutions, some in the realm of material objects." But, he sums up, it is very hard to tell which way these ideas or objects traveled,[71] or when. Even if we assume that the idea of the divine pharaonic monarchy, rule by a god, is founded on a broad African *soubassement* (base) as claimed by E. L. R.

Meyerowitz,[72] this idea underwent fundamental changes in Egypt, not to mention changes in its functions; the Egyptian king was "closely tied from the outset to the fertility of the Nile and the soil of Egypt. He personally guaranteed this fertility."[73] Nevertheless, the crucial question is the degree of importance of the components transmitted from Egypt to Africa, in shaping the nature of the various cultures in Africa, or in affecting the dynamics of their changes. The cultural elements that moved from north to south during the period in question, according to the "up the river" theory, were not the sort that could shape the nature of African society or influence its dynamics.

Diop and his school conclude that Upper Egypt (Nubia and Sudan) was the birthplace and cradle of humanity. From there, people and culture migrated to the south (inner Africa) and the north (Lower Egypt and beyond). But during the historical period it was Egypt (Upper and Lower), a far more advanced civilization, that transmitted its high culture to Africa.

THE "DOWN THE RIVER" THEORY:
FROM SOUTH TO NORTH

The second theory claims that ever since the prehistoric period, the movement of human migration, cultural diffusion, and transmission went from the south (the Great Lakes and inner Africa) to the north—down the river—and that the movement of Negroes from the south to the north along the Nile Valley and the Sahara Desert brought with it the African language, myths, cosmogony, and skill. This view was held by quite a few European scholars. For example, English Egyptologist E. A. Wallis Budge, in *Osiris and the Egyptian Resurrection,* asserted that Africans and African traits arrived in Nubia and Egypt from the south, and that the predynastic age was characterized by migration to Egypt by black people from sub-Saharan Africa in a stream that continued during the dynastic period. The indigenous Egyptian beliefs in a god creator of the world and in his resurrection and immortality are African in origin.[74]

Thus, according to this view, Africa was the first and genuine source of migration and cultural diffusion; it was from Africa that Nubia and Egypt received almost everything that enabled them to rise. This school of thought holds that Egyptian civilization is millennia older than is usually believed, and that the Sphinx represents "prima facie evidence of the existence of a full-fledged, flourishing Nile Valley civilization no later than 7,000 years ago, quite possibly as old as 9,000 years!" The conclusion is that high Egyptian culture evolved from a confluence of migration and influences coming down the Nile from the Great Lakes, merging with those moving eastward out of the Sahara.[75] This cultural influence was a result not only of Stone Age diffusion, but also of Bronze Age and Iron Age diffusion and transmission.[76]

The ideological implications are quite clear. If we accept the first view that cultural diffusion during the historical period went down, not up, the river, this gives cultural priority to black Egypt, and, thus, in the opinion of many Afrocentric writers, seems to undermine the originality and greatness of the African culture. Even if Afrocentrists regard Egypt as a land of black people, from the ideological point of view they still prefer to give priority to pure Africans and genuine Africa. If Africa was the fountain of Egyptian cultural achievements, and these great achievements grew out of a genuine African culture, then it is Africa that gains the status of the primordial civilization.

The other point of view states that if Egypt is considered the source of African culture, then Africa gains from having been inspired by this great civilization. If Africa was influenced by Egypt, it could not have been a backward continent. Thus, black Africans can and must lay exclusive claim to the cultural heritage of the Egyptian civilization.[77] Basil Davidson, I believe, is aware of the difficulties inherent in this theory. Thus, even though he refers to classical authors who wrote that pharaonic culture had derived from inner Africa, and he writes that inner Africa was the cultural begetter of the ancient Egyptians, his African source is not equatorial Africa but the cultures of the then green Sahara of the fifth millennium B.C. and earlier.[78]

This idea was recently repeated by Miriam Ma'at-Ka-Re Monges, in her book *Kush—The Jewel of Nubia: Reconsidering the Root System of African Civilization*.[79] This book, like most others, is not based on an original study, but rather on a summary of existing literature, collected in such a way that it reflects her premeditated decision to reject books that do not concur with her opinion and to praise those books that support it (Diop in particular[80]). For the most part, her book focuses on the connection between Nubia and Egypt. Both, according to the authors, are closely connected to eastern Africa and tropical Africa. She ignores Diop's views on Egypt's influences during the historic period and prefers to focus on Africa's alleged influence on Egypt (and Nubia). Monges rejects the findings and conclusions of scholars such as Graham Connah,[81] William Y. Adams,[82] and others who admit that Africa south of the Sahara supplied Nubia and Egypt with gold, ivory, and slaves, while various concepts such as that of divine kingship were diffused from north to south. Her view is that residents of the Nile Valley were of indigenous African ancestry, who brought with them important elements of their culture from south to north, or down the river—elements that became the foundation of Egyptian culture. She also feels it necessary to argue that despite Egypt's progress, its culture was not necessarily superior to other African civilizations.[83]

In addition to these two extreme views, there is another moderate, and more accepted, view, according to which "correlations of linguistic and archaeological data suggest a westward migration of Nilo-Saharan speakers at approximately 3000 B.C."[84] Here Africa is not considered a homogeneous racial-cultural entity, and diffusion and acculturation are regarded as complex and dynamic phenomena.

As we have already argued, there is a basic difference between a common substratum of two different civilizations and a similarity between two different civilizations. To speak of a racial substratum of equatorial Africa and Egypt that created a common culture (or even common collective personality) is to accept a black version of the myth of an Aryan (Indo-European) race and to presume that Indians, Persians, and Germans are a homogeneous cultural-human entity. Common racial origin does not inevitably produce a common culture. Thus, even if we accept the view that Egypt was an integral part of Africa, this partnership could have been a result of prehistorical background or of common racial features, but not based on intensive and prolonged contacts (as was the case with Egypt and the Nubian riverland, and desert dwellers in Upper and Lower Nubia). Nevertheless, the fact remains that different human entities emerged and developed from the real or alleged common substratum.

Let us accept, for argument's sake, the theory that common racial origins create a common worldview, symbols, and social organization in the early stages of the evolution of human society. This does not mean, however, that different cultures cannot, in later periods, emerge from the same racial source and substratum. If this is so, the population that sprang from the assumed common African stock underwent physiogenetic and more important cultural changes. The claim of constant migration and diffusion from Africa to Egypt or vice versa is baseless, but if indeed this constant and continuous migration and diffusion took place, one may wonder what caused the fundamental differences between the cultures of interior Africa and the Egyptian-Nubian civilization.

The historical fact remains that if Africans were descendants of the Egyptians, or vice versa, they underwent cultural separation from their original culture; even if we accept the radical view that "the ancient Egyptians retained for more than 3000 years their essential African outlook in terms of myths, symbolism, and ethos throughout the history of the country" until the arrival of the Greeks,[85] we still cannot deny that their culture diverted from its origins. Moreover, popular and high Egyptian culture was transmitted to Hindu-European Greeks or to Semitic people, and not to their racial partners, the black Africans.

Was this a result of cultural isolation or of the unique genius of the Egyptians? According to Davidson, "Much of the greatest numbers of tropical Africans lived in former times, as many live today, in villages or scattered homesteads, having few material possessions, knowing nothing or little of the written word, enjoying the present as a gift from the golden age of their ancestors, and not much caring for a different future. Yet their technological simplicity was no guide to their social and cultural achievement. In truth they had tamed a continent."[86] Davidson also rejects the notion of diffusion from one "common fund" and what one may define as "parallelomania." Here, then, a processual approach is taken.[87] The internal progress of African societies is seen not as a mere result of outside influences but as a result of internal dynamics.

It is quite clear that Diop and his disciples are fully aware of the problem and attempt to overcome it. We have already noted that in Diop's view, it was Egypt that played the role of the cradle of black Africans. He based his theory on etymological data, including a discussion on totemism, circumcision, kinship, cosmology, social organization, and matriarchy. Yet, like all African American writers, he cannot deny the notion that the Nile Valley constitutes an independent cultural record. He also must accept that a deep and wide cultural chasm separates Africa and Egypt. Egypt "brought the African genius to its highest and finest expression. Inner Africa was the mother, the great Nile the father, and Egypt the brilliant son and fulfiller."[88] If this is so, then it is necessary to explain what gave the son the driving force and ability to ascend higher than his mother.

In his efforts to explain the fundamental cultural differences between Egypt and Africa, Diop offers a solution: the assertion that there was no need for Egyptian material civilization in the African environment and that the tropical climate caused them to lose interest in technological innovations. "With economic resources assured by means that did not require perpetual inventions, the Negro became progressively indifferent to material progress," he writes.[89] Cut off from the Nile Valley and the Mediterranean, the people of Africa settled in a geographical environment requiring a minimum effort of adjustment, and became oriented toward the development of their social, political, and moral organization, rather than toward speculative scientific research. Can we really accept the view that in this tropical setting, humans were freed from the need to adjust to nature, or had no incentive to change it according to their own needs? The Afrocentric view tends to describe this human condition as an ideal and harmonious coexistence with nature. The fact is that the different peoples of equatorial Africa adapted themselves to the limitations or the possibilities of the land in different ways, which resulted in pronounced regional differences.

Afrocentrists also portray Africa as the home of an ideal civilization that emerged as a harmonious balance of nature and environment—the same ideal environment as in Egypt. Kete Asante, for example, compares Africa to the Nile Valley, claiming:

> The central physical phenomenon of Egypt is the great river, the Nile. It played a vital role in the creation of Kemetic philosophy, agriculture, technology, and religion. . . . Much like other Africans in riverine areas of the continent the Egyptians viewed the world with security, stability and optimism. The world did not seem harsh and ferocious, cruel and menacing to the Egyptians. To a large extent the geography of Egypt provided the people with a pleasant isolation except to the south. There were no harbors in the Delta, deserts east and west, and so openness to the south through the cataracts allowed Ethiopians and Nubians to interact with the Egyptians. . . . The Egyptians retained their essential African outlook in terms of myths, symbolisms, and ethos throughout the history of the country.[90]

Needless to say, this is an unhistorical and imaginary description of ancient Egyptian society, which ignores its close interrelations with the Near East, the Aegean, and even inner Asia. It is misleading to compare the economic resources of the Nile Valley with those of tropical Africa, or to argue that Egypt was not indifferent to material progress. Yet, can we accept his statement that Egypt's social and moral order in Egypt had attained a level of perfection?

While Kete Asante unifies Africa and the Nile Valley, Diop accepts the notion that the obviously deep cultural changes between Africa and Egypt were the result of the different ways by which different people, even those belonging to the same racial stock, responded to their environment or developed their collective genius.

Thus, we may conclude that from an ideological, Afrocentrist point of view, hyperdiffusionism may be perceived as the right response to European racial hyperdiffusionism; at the same time, however, it presents a very grave challenge to Afrocentrism itself: If all the Negroes share the same mental qualities, why, according to Afrocentric theory itself, did all the black peoples need Egypt to serve as their source of high culture, and were unable to invent and develop their own cultures along the same lines of progress without the help of diffused traits from the Nile Valley? This hyperdiffusionism frees ancient Africa from its image of a dependent culture—dependent on Europe—but instead portrays it as dependent on ancient Egyptian culture. This dependence is not considered an expression of inferiority because the ancient Egyptians are perceived as belonging to the Negro race.

Nevertheless, this awareness of the profound gap separating Egyptian and African cultures gave rise to three speculative paradigms: (1) the claim that the Africans' uniqueness is manifested in their distinct phenomenology, philosophy, ethics, and collective psychology, and not in their creative skills in science, technology, and so on;[91] (2) the claim that Africans in tropical Africa were able to develop their own science and technology; and

(3) the claim that Egyptian achievements in these fields belong to the entire Negro race.

Therefore, in their geographical lore, East Africa—the Great Lakes, Sudan, and Upper Egypt—are considered the heart and cradle of Africa, and as a result, their historical lore was forced to spin a web of migrations and cultural contacts between this heart, inner Africa, and Egypt in order to describe Africa as a cultural unity based not only on race but also on mutual cultural transmissions first from south to north and later from north to south.

THE WONDER THAT WAS EGYPT

At this point we must return to the Nile and the Nile Valley and to the common perceptions about them.

Some Afrocentrists often accept the climatic theory and the influence of environment on creative genius and social and political order. According to Diop, the black skin color of the first human beings was a result of the warm and humid climate that secreted a black pigment. Thus, even if the racial origin of the Egyptian population in predynastic Egypt was Negro, their color underwent changes throughout the years. The color of the Egyptians has become lighter down through the years, like that of the West Indian Negroes, but, he argues, the Egyptians never stopped being Negroes.[92] Not only was the climate of the Nile Valley different from the climate of the African hinterland, but, according to Herodotus, the Nile Valley and the river had different features and functions compared to the other great African rivers. The Nile necessitated the creation of an organized social and political order able to produce large surpluses of food, consequently resulting in a stratified society, a segment of which was urban and highly developed. Crops had been grown in the Nile Valley since 7000 B.C.: barley unknown to Africa, emmer wheat and flax, and later, palm trees, dates, papyrus, and others. The Nile also played a key role in religion and ritual. The horse and chariot, which could not reach Africa, also influenced the shaping of the state and political society. The plow and the pump, as well as other irrigation techniques, were not used in Africa's fields. There were no temples or libraries in Africa, no scribes and books, no science like that in Egypt. All the elements of culture that Afrocentrists claim are common to Africa and Egypt only serve to underscore the number of disparate elements, as well as a number of elements in Egyptian culture that are absent in African cultures.

And is it not a historical irony that, according to the Afrocentrist view, it was Greece that inherited the wisdom of Egypt, spawning literature, philosophy, and science, while Africa was left behind? That would mean that the Sinai desert and the Mediterranean Sea have played a far more important role as routes of cultural transmission than the river Nile.

The paradox here, in my view, lies in the fact that while the Afrocentrist (or pan-Negroid) theory believes that by claiming Africans and Egyptians belong to the same race, they are providing the black African people with a new historical and cultural past and future and are, in fact, replacing an old white racial theory with a new black racial theory, in response to white racism. Furthermore, since many of them accept the historical fact that a deep gap separated Egyptian cultural achievements from African cultural achievements during the dynastic periods, they themselves undermine the basic foundation of their racial theory and its racial-cultural message of redemption.

We may conclude that if the ecology of the valley shaped the nature of Egyptian culture, it was stronger than the primordial common substratum. In other words, even when we accept the influence of a real or alleged common substratum and the existence of several similarities, we, as well as most of the Afrocentrists, cannot avoid accepting the ancient view, echoed by Du Bois, that "to the Nile Egypt owes all the special peculiarities which distinguish it from Africa." Even though he tries to stress the unity of Negro history and culture from the Mountains of the Moon to the Mediterranean, he is forced to admit that this culture blossomed along the lower Nile ("but was never severed from the Great Lakes and Inner Africa"). Even though he argues that Egyptian religion "came naturally from the primitive animism of the African forest," he admits that "gradually. . . . The Egyptians became a separate inbred people with characteristics quite different from their neighbors," and that the "primitive animism" progressed to a more "advanced" religion.[93]

Civilization is an assemblage of styles and patterns of life consisting of a form of government, laws, literature, social organization, a mode of production and economy, religious beliefs, and organization.[94] All of these create and formulate a complete pattern of life. I believe this to be the primary reason why Afrocentrists with a modern orientation cannot accept the Western notion that they lack any cultural heritage (except for popular religion, etc.), but at the same time are not ready to reject a Western cultural heritage, as some radical Afrocentrists do, and find refuge in the notion of unique spiritual traits (i.e., a unique phenomenology). Their solution is to make Egypt part of African culture and thus appropriate it, without any need to claim that this culture originated in Africa or that Africa was part of it. From this point of departure, there is no need at all to deny the uniqueness of the Nile Valley, nor is there any need to propose a hyperdiffusionist paradigm—be it a diffusion that moves up the river or down the river. Herodotus himself asserts that not only is the Egyptian climate peculiar to that country, and that the Nile is different in its behavior from other rivers elsewhere, but the Egyptians themselves in their manners and customs seem to have reversed the ordinary practices of humankind,[95] thus stressing the unique nature of Egyptian civilization that separates it from the rest of the world, including Africa.

The debate I have surveyed here is an important expression of the search for an ancient past as a part of the endeavor to forge a new identity. It is doubtful, however, whether a reconstruction—even one that is historically reliable—can serve this goal. In truth, this leads to the conclusion that cultural diffusion (i.e., the dissemination and borrowing of culture) is an integral and essential part of the history of culture, and that racial commonality does not create cultural communality, not to mention political commonality.

In his poem, "The Negro Speaks of Rivers" (1921), the African American poet Langston Hughes wrote:

> I built my hut near the Congo and it lulled me to sleep.
> I looked upon the Nile and raised the Pyramids above it.

Hughes, I presume, was unaware that with these lines he was clearly pointing not to a common basis but to fundamental differences—the differences symbolized by a hut on one hand, and a pyramid on the other.

We may conclude that the main function of the Nile and the Nile Valley was not a route or corridor—up- or downstream—between Egypt and inner Africa, creating and preserving racial and cultural interrelations and even unity—but a river that provided Egypt with a distinct environmental setting for the emergence and development of an integrated, advanced, and unique civilization; a civilization that developed and flourished on both sides of the river and that was, from its inception, fully aware of its uniqueness. This was a civilization that may have been accessible to the south, to Africa, but maintained a deep and fruitful cultural relationship with neighboring cultures in the Mediterranean basin and in the ancient Near East instead.

NOTES

1. See Levine, "Bernal and the Athenians in the Multicultural World of the Ancient Mediterranean," p. 20. On Afrocentrism, pan-Negroism, and Egyptocentricism see Howe, *Afrocentrism: Mythical Pasts and Imagined Homes;* Moses, *Afrotropia: The Roots of African American Popular History;* and Shavit, *History in Black* (forthcoming).

2. See van Sertima, *Great African Thinkers;* and Fauvelle, *L'Afrique de Cheikh Anta Diop.*

3. See, for one example, the statement by Kete Asante: "The Egyptians retained their essential African outlook in terms of myths, symbolism, and ethos

throughout the history of the country" (Kete Asante, *Kemet, Afrocentricity and Knowledge,* p. 52).

4. Pritchard, *Ancient Eastern Texts Relating to the Old Testament,* p. 372. See the translation in Lichtheim, *Ancient Egyptian Literature,* pp. 205–210: "Hail to you, Hapy: / Sprung from earth, / Come to nourish Egypt!" See also the "Hymn to the Nile" ("Nilhymanus") in Helck, *Kleine Ägyptische Texte: Der Text des "Nilhymnus,"* p. 11. On the Nile in Egyptian theology, see in Morenz, *Egyptian Religion,* p. 150. He writes: "What the author of the Hymn to the Nile apparently had in mind was the fact that the Nile did not have a cult image or receive daily service, but that sacrifice was made to it as a festival on the occasion of the flood (h'py). Heitsch, p. 126. A love poem dedicated to the Nile that floods its banks, from the Roman era, says, among other things: "My betrothed, do not tarry, yours . . . / Embrace your bride, / bearer of sheaves of corn, / With wave-enveloping flowers, / Take pleasure in your wedding songs. / Path that shakes earth to Egypt . . . / Flows exuberantly [. . .]." See Heitsch, *Die Dicterfragmente der Römischen Kaizerzeit,* p. 126. In Aeschylus's play, *Supliants,* the Danaids praise the Nile (lines 516, 854–857), and in W. Kranz's view, Aeschylus was familiar with ancient Egyptian hymns to Hapy Walther Kranz, *Stasimon: Untersuchungen zu Form und Gehalt der griechischen Tragödie,* p. 101.

5. Hallo and Simpson, *The Ancient Near East: A History,* p. 261. In ancient Egyptian, many words concerned with movements were determined by the idea of sailing: to travel south is to get upstream, and to travel north is to go downstream, even when referring to traveling outside Egypt (Kees, *Ancient Egypt,* p. 96).

6. Morenz, *Egyptian Religion,* p. 46. On the environmental changes in the Nile basin and their influence, see Krzyzaniak, Robusiewicz, and Alexander, *Environmental Change and Human Culture in the Nile Basin and Northern Africa Until the Second Millennium B.C.*

7. Budge, *Osiris and the Egyptian Resurrection,* vol. 1, pp. 11, 19.

8. Ibid., p. 385. Budge suggested that the conception of Osiris was of purely African origin (p. 17).

9. Ibid., vol. 2, p. 51. Borghonst notes that from the New Kingdom onward, "those who were drowned in the Nile were thought to become 'saint' by coming into immediate contact with the primeval waters (Nun), represented on earth by the River Nile" (see Borghonst, "Magical Practices Among the Villagers," p. 122).

10. Clagett, *Ancient Egyptian Science/A Source Book,* vol. 1, tome 2, p. 579.

11. Morenz, *Egyptian Religion,* p. 46.

12. Clagett, *Ancient Egyptian Science,* vol. 1, tome 1, pp. 265–266. Statues of the River god were painted green and red; the first was supposed to represent the color of the river in June, when it is a bright green, before the inundation.

13. Cohen and Drabkin, *A Source Book in Greek Science,* p. 34. James Breasted writes: "Thus a genial and generous, but exacting soil, demanded for its cultivation the development of a high degree of skill in the manipulation of the life-giving waters, and at a very early day the men of the Nile valley had attained a surprising command of the complicated problems involved in the proper utilization of the river" (Breasted, *A History of the Ancient Egyptians,* p. 9).

14. Gillings, *Mathematics in the Time of the Pharaohs,* p. 235. On the three Egyptian calendars, see pp. 265–266.

15. See one example of many, the painting of a state ship of Viceroy Huy who gets ready to sail for Nubia, *From the Tomb of Huy,* about 1360 B.C., in Wilkinson and Hill, *Egyptian Wall Paintings,* p. 51. See the biblical perception of the Nile and its different functions in Isaiah 19:4–10.

16. One should, of course, distinguish between the role and perceptions of a river that flows through a rain forest and a river (such as the Upper Niger) that flows through desert land. In the Edo cosmogony, for example, water is considered "the primordial substance that once covered the world and from the center of which land first emerged" (Ben-Amos, "The Promise of Greatness," p. 119). See "Flute Poem in Praise of River Deities" from Ghana: "River Adutwum, in you we bathe, and from you we quench / Our thirst. / From you we take the water to wash our clothes. / Asante Kotoko, our children and our grandchildren, / But for you what we have done?" (in Curlander, *A Treasure of African Folklore*, pp. 1–7).

17. Indeed, as one moves to the north, the climate becomes progressively more arid, and the importance of the river is enhanced until it is the only life-sustaining feature. As to the role of the Nile in the history and kingdoms of Kush, it should be noted that Kush extended into a number of diverse climatic zones which offered vastly different potentials for agricultural activities. Some degree of homogeneity in the lifestyle of the peoples inhabiting its banks, however, was provided by the river Nile which traversed these zones. See Welsby, *The Kingdom of Kush*, p. 153. In his *Geography* (1.2.23), the geographer Strabo comments that "even if this is not true of the whole of Egypt, it is certainly true of the part embraced by the Delta, which is called Lower Egypt" (p. 153). Diodorus Siculus wrote that, according to Egyptian accounts: "When in the beginning the universe came into being, men first came into existence in Egypt, both because of the favourable climate of the land and because of the nature of the Nile. For this stream, since it produced much life and provided a spontaneous supply of food, easily supported whatever living things have been engendered" (1.10.1) (trans. C. H. Oldfather, *The Loeb Classical Library*, vol. 1 [1981 edition], pp. 34–35). In Plato's *Timaeus* the Egyptian priests tell Solon that the Nile is the savior of Egypt in various ways because whereas other dry places suffer destruction as a result of dry weather, the Nile "saves us also at such times from this calamity by rising high" (D.11–12). Egypt has no floods that bring destruction: "Neither then nor at any other time does the water pour down over our fields from above, on the contrary it all tends naturally to well up from below" / (E.18–21) (trans. R. G. Bury, *The Loeb Classical Library*, vol. 2 [revised and reprinted, 1952], pp. 34–35). In *Ethiopica* (An Ethiopian Romance), written in the second or third century A.D., Helodorus refers to sacred books about the Nile, "which only priests may read and understand, telling how the Nile spreads over its banks like a sea and fertilizes the filth it floods. That is why its water is sweet to the taste: it is supplied by clouds in the sky" (trans. Moses Hadas, *Ethiopica*, Ann Arbor: University of Michigan Press, 1957, p. 58). In *De Rerum Natura* (On the Nature of Things), the Roman poet Lucretius describes the flow of the Nile: "The Nile towards summer-time swells and overflows on the fields, the only river in the whole land of Egypt. This river is wont to irrigate Egypt through the middle heats" (6.712) (trans. W. H. Rouse, *The Loeb Classical Library* [1959 edition], pp. 494–495).

In *Metamorphoses* the Roman poet Ovid repeats this theme (1.422–424). These are primarily descriptions that mainly fit the situation in Lower Egypt, as life in the southern rain belt of Egypt has never relied exclusively on the Nile. The truth is that the flooding of the Nile was not regular but rather prone to long- and short-term trends. Egypt, both the delta plain and the river valley, experienced floods on one hand and drought on the other. This is also the reason for the importance of the irrigation system of the flood plain (see Butzer, *Early Hydraulic Civilization in Egypt*). Nevertheless, the phrase coined by Herodotus was expanded and became a common topos of both parts of Egypt, both Upper and Lower, as one

physical unit; see Volney, *Voyage en Syrie et en Egypte,* pp. 18–34. This view became the conventional wisdom. Hegel, for example, wrote that the Nile Valley was
adapted to become a mighty center of independent civilization and has a singular
and unique nature as a geographical region in Africa (Hegel, *The Philosophy of
History,* pp. 207–210). At the same time, however, he accepted Diodorus's view
that the Egyptians received their culture from Nubia (Meroë).

  18. Trans. F. H. Colson, *The Loeb Classical Library,* Vol. 6 (1994 edition), pp.
279, 333–335. This description follows Genesis 13:10, which described Egypt as
the garden of the Lord, and Herodotus ("now, indeed, there are no men, neither in
the rest of Egypt, nor in the whole world, who gain from the soil with so little
labour") (Herodotus, 2.14, trans. A. D. Godley, *The Loeb Classical Library* [1960
printing, p. 291]), but undermines the biblical story about the seven years of
drought!
  Jewish exegeses repeat this topos to explain how this basic difference between
Egypt and Palestine makes a decisive impact on the worldview of each people:
"The land of Egypt—only if you work over it with mattock and spade and give up
sleep for it [will yield], if you do not, it will yield nothing. The land of Israel is not
like that—its inhabitants sleep on their beds while God sends down rain for them"
(Finkelstein, 77). This is the explanation offered by the Jewish sages for the sub-
limity of the Land of Israel—a country blessed by God—compared to the land of
Egypt. Yet this saying obviously implies, intentionally or not, that Egypt's prosperity and its surplus of food were not only the result of a "gift" granted by nature
but were based on the social and political organization required, and created, to
control the use of the water and the soil.
  19. Butzer, *Early Hydraulic Civilization in Egypt,* p. 11.
  20. Redford, *Pharaonic King-Lists,* pp. 115–118, 204. See also Janseen, *The
Ancient Egyptian Ships Logs.*
  21. "The six cataracts upstream Aswan prevented navigation, and the Nile
seemed to lose itself inextricably in the marches of the Sudanese lowland at a latitude of some 8-N, making it impossible to track the river to its sources" (Hugon,
The Exploration of Africa, p. 42).
  22. Wilkinson, *The Ancient Egyptians, Their Life and Customs,* vol. 2, pp.
119–132. "The nile itself was characterized by more vigorous summer flood with
the competence to carry massive loads of gravel from Nubia to Cairo" (Butzer,
Early Hydraulic Civilization in Egypt, p. 13).
  23. Lichtheim, *Ancient Egyptian Literature,* p. 21.
  24. Kees, *Ancient Egypt,* pp. 100–101. Herodotus wrote that at some point the
travelers had to leave the river "for forty days, because sharp rocks . . . make the
river impracticable for boats" (2.29); according to Diodorus, it took ten days to sail
the Nile from Alexandria to Ethiopia (3.34.7). According to Ibn Khaldun: "Boats
cannot get through. Cargoes from the Sudanese boats are taken off and carried on
pack animals to Assuan at the entrance to Upper Egypt. In the same way, the cargoes of the boats from the cataracts to Assuan is a twelve day's journey" (Ibn
Khaldun, *The Muqaddimah,* p. 121). Welsby writes: "In the reach from Abu Hamed
to el Debba, where the direction of the current and the prevailing winds coincide,
movement upstream is virtually impossible for vessels under sail. Elsewhere boats
were able to float downstream with the current or sail upstream before the north
wind which blows virtually all the year round" (Welsby, *The Kingdom of Kush,* p.
171). The Nile served a water route for 750 miles, from the red granite outcropping
at Aswan northward to the Mediterranean and back. See Budge, *The Nile,* pp.
45–49, and Kees, *Ancient Egypt,* pp. 96–141. The Nile continued to serve as the

highway of Egypt beyond Cairo until the railway was laid and steam power introduced ("Cook's Nile Service," from 1869). Travelers during this period could sail on private *dhahabiyya* up the river from Cairo to Aswan and back, a voyage of 590 miles. See the selection from travelers' books in Pick, *Egypt: A Traveler's Anthology,* pp. 116–145.

25. O'Connor, *Ancient Nubia,* p. 12.

26. There is no evidence of trans-Saharan trade from Egypt to southwest Africa.

27. Lichtheim, *Ancient Egyptian Literature,* p. 21. Harkuf sent a great altar of alabaster downstream in a barge that he built for it. On Harkhuf see Lichtheim, pp. 23–27. Punt was described as a land full of treasures, and the lands east of it were perceived as marvelous land and fabulous realm in Egyptian travelers' tales. See Maspero, *History of Egypt,* pp. 224–226, 365–368. However, it is hard to accept his view that "the Nile afforded an easy means of access to those who wished to penetrate into the heart of Africa" (p. 221).

28. Landstrom, *Ships of the Pharaohs,* p. 11.

29. Clarke, "Cheikh Anta Diop and the New Concept of African History," pp. 115–116.

30. Kete Asante, *Kemet, Afrocentricity and Knowledge,* p. 33.

31. Egypt was part of the Sahara Desert before it began to get humid (since 7000 B.C.) and then dried up (around 2000 B.C.), and it was its link with the rest of the continent. See Nougera, *How African Was Egypt?*

32. Many scholars believe that this development was due to diffusion from the East. See Newman, *The Peopling of Africa,* p. 42.

33. O'Connor, "Ancient Egypt and Black Africa—Early Contacts," p. 2.

34. Steindorff and Seele, *When Egypt Ruled the East,* p. 97.

35. Hanseberry, *African History Notebook,* Vol. 2, p. 39.

36. O'Connor, "Ancient Egypt and Black Africa—Early Contacts," p. 2.

37. First in the eastern horn of Africa. The camel arrived in Egypt in Roman times. See Bulliet, *The Camel and the Wheel.*

38. Davidson, *African Civilization Revisited,* p. 13.

39. Many scholars, however, emphasize the impact of internal factors on the developments of African societies in Central Africa. And see the different and contradicting views expressed in the essays in Celenko, *Egypt in Africa.*

40. According to George Murdock, Egypt, Nubia, and Sudan shared a common culture during the Stone Age up until c. 3000 B.C. The agricultural advances in the Lower Nile Valley brought about a cultural spurt that separated it and formed the basis for the early dynastic age (Murdock, *Africa: Its Peoples and Their Cultural History*).

41. Newman, *The Peopling of Africa,* pp. 104–157; van der Merwe, "The Advent of Iron in Africa," pp. 453–506. Afrocentrists often claim that metallurgy was discovered first in Africa, basing this idea on "scientific news" such as an article from February 6, 1970, in the *New York Times,* announcing that South African archaeologists had discovered an iron mine in Swaziland that revealed that iron smelting dates back at least 43,000 years in Africa (Clark, "Similarities Between Egyptian and Dagon Perception of Man, God and Nature," pp. 121–122.

42. Trigger, "Egypt and Early Civilizations," p. 26. This was the conventional wisdom among many scholars. The logical conclusion from the identification of the ancient Egyptians as "non-Africans" in origin was that every cultural evolution southward to Egypt was a result of diffusion or transmission from the Nile Valley. See Holl, "West Africa: Colonialism and Nationalism," pp. 229–301.

43. See Wilkinson, *The Ancient Egyptians, Their Life and Customs,* vol. 1, pp. 302–303.

44. Adams, "The Kingdom and Civilization of Kush in Northeast Africa," pp. 775–789.

45. De Barros, "Changing Paradigms," pp. 150–172. For a hyperdiffusionist approach, see Kraus, *Human Development from an African Ancestry.*

46. Seligman, *The Pagan Tribes of the Nilotic Sudan.*

47. Smith, *Migration of Early Culture.*

48. Diop, "Origin of the Ancient Egyptians," pp. 27–57. See also van Sertima, *Egypt Revisited,* pp. 9–37.

49. See Berry and Berry, "Origins and Relationship of the Ancient Egyptians," pp. 199–208. They write that "Egyptian skull samples are not very distinct from the Nubian samples . . . (however they are more distinct from the Ashanti series . . . and the Near Eastern series)"; Yorca, "Black Athena," pp. 62–100; O'Connor, "Ancient Egypt and Black Africa—Early Contacts"; Macgraffey, "Concept of Race in the Historiography of Northeast Africa," pp. 1–17. For an Afrocentric view, see Crawford, "The Racial Identity of Ancient Egyptian Populations," pp. 35–44.

50. Diop, "Africa: Cradle of Humanity," p. 21.

51. Keita, "The Geographical Origins and Population Relationship of Early Ancient Egyptians," p. 24.

52. Yorca, "Were the Ancient Egyptians Black or White?" p. 58. See also Trigger, "Nubian, Negro, Nilotic?" pp. 27–35.

53. Macgaffey, "Concept of Race in the Historiography of Northwest Africa," p. 17.

54. See the summary in Finch, "Nile Genesis," pp. 35–54.

55. Du Bois, "Egypt," p. 100.

56. See Ehret, "Ancient Egyptian as an African Languge," pp. 25–27.

57. Diop, *The African Origin of Civilization,* pp. 85–98.

58. Ibid., pp. 179–201.

59. Diop, *Civilization or Barbarism,* p. 3.

60. Diop, *The African Origins of Civilization,* p. 254.

61. Diop, *Precolonial Black Africa,* p. 213; Diop, *The African Origin of Civilization,* pp. 134–178.

62. See Holl, "African History," pp. 200–204; Diop, *Precolonial Black Africa,* pp. 212–234.

63. Hilliard, "The Meaning of KMT History," p. 13.

64. Bowdich, *An Essay on the Superstitions, Customs, and Arts Common to the Ancient Egyptians, Abyssinians, and Ashantees.* See also Massey, *Book of the Beginning,* pp. 598–674.

65. Meyrowitz, *The Divine Kingship in Ghana and Ancient Egypt.*

66. Shinnie, "The Legacy to Africa," pp. 436–437.

67. Clark, "Similarities Between Egyptian and Dagon Perceptions of Man, God and Nature," pp. 119–130. And see Baines, "Origins of Egyptian Kingship," pp. 95–156. He stresses the unique nature of the dual kingship of ancient Egypt, which is a result of the physical contrast of the Nile Valley and the delta.

68. Lucas, *The Religion of the Yoruba.*

69. Smith, *Kingdoms of the Yoruba,* p. 10.

70. Davidson, *African Civilization Revisited,* p. 13.

71. Shinnie, *The Legacy to Africa,* p. 438.

72. See Meyerowitz, *Divine Kingship in Ghana and Ancient Egypt,* and Nouguera, *How African Was Egypt?* pp. 123–201.

73. Redford, *Pharaonic King-Lists,* p. 24.

74. Budge, *Osiris and the Egyptian Resurrection,* pp. 348–349. See also the entire chapter, pp. 348–383. Also see the articles in van Sertima, *Egypt Child of Africa.* According to this view, African nations in various part of the continent knew the secret of iron-toll production and astronomical mathematics, and even possessed proto-script. This view was adopted by the modern Egyptian scholar Salama Musa in his book *Hadanat Misr fi Ifriqiya,* under the influence of Elliot Smith.

75. Finch, "Nile Genesis," pp. 35–54.

76. See, for example, Ben-Jochannan, *Africa—Mother of Western Civilization,* pp. 292–303. However, he stresses primarily the deep links of the Nile Valley (down to Zimbabwe) and the Great Lakes.

77. Diop, *The African Origin of Civilization,* p. 249.

78. Davidson, "The Ancient World and Africa," pp. 324–325.

79. Monges, *Kush—The Jewel of Nubia.*

80. See Monges, "Homage to the Elders," in *Kush—The Jewel of Nubia,* pp. 52–60.

81. Connah, *African Civilizations—Pre-colonial Cities and States in Tropical Africa.*

82. Adams, *Nubia—Corridor to Africa.*

83. Ibid., p. 39.

84. Macgaffey, "Concept of Race in the Historiography of Northeast Africa," p. 17.

85. Kete Asante, *Kemet, Afrocentricity and Knowledge,* pp. 50–53.

86. Davidson, *The African Genius,* pp. 27–28.

87. See Renfrew, *Archaeology and Language,* pp. 120–144.

88. Finch, "The Works of Gevnal Massey," p. 401.

89. Diop, *The African Origin of Civilization,* p. 23. And see Holl, "West Africa: Colonialism and Nationalism," p. 203.

90. Kete Asante, *Kemet, Afrocentricity and Knowledge,* pp. 50–53.

91. African and African American writers try to prove that some branches of technological skills and scientific innovations originated in Africa or were known in it prior to their development in Egypt or independent of it. See van Sertima, *Blacks in Science.*

92. Diop, *The African Origin of Civilization,* p. 249.

93. Du Bois, "Egypt," pp. 98–114.

94. Singer, *When a Great Tradition Modernizes,* p. 252.

95. Herodotus, *The Histories,* p. 142.

8

◆

Renaissance Geographical Literature and the Nile

Benjamin Arbel

Nearly one and a half centuries ago, Jacob Burckhardt published his famous book, *The Civilization of the Renaissance in Italy*. Part 4 of this book, entitled "The Discovery of the World and of Man," opens with the following phrase: "Freed from the countless bonds which elsewhere in Europe checked progress, having reached a high degree of individual development and been schooled by the teaching of antiquity, the Italian mind now turned to the discovery of the outward universe, and to the representation of it in speech and form."[1] In this chapter I do not pretend to go into the long discussion on Burckhardt's view of Renaissance culture. My purpose is more limited: by presenting the changing attitude to the Nile in the geographical literature of the Renaissance, I should like to point out that, beyond the idealistic and provocative phrasing, Burckhardt's basic idea concerning the discovery of the world is still valid.

The image of the Nile in the medieval West can be viewed as a later phase in a long tradition, beginning in ancient Egypt and later reflected in Greek, Hellenistic, and Roman cultures. The sacred character of the river was related to its periodical flows and to the mystery of its sources. But above all, a very unrealistic and rather incoherent world picture had been at the base of many myths related to the river. The questions of the sources of the Nile and the reasons for its annual inundations occupied the attention of several important Greek and Roman writers. Herodotus, for example, devoted much attention to these questions. As he was unable to obtain any information from the Egyptians concerning the Nile's inundations and its sources, and had discarded all hypotheses concerning the Nile's inundations, he suggested a theory of his own. During the winter, the sun was driven out of its usual course by storms; consequently, the Nile, not deriving

105

any of its bulk from rains, ran at that season with a smaller amount of water. Herodotus ascended its course up to Elephantine and made inquiries concerning the parts beyond. He suggested that the Nile was of equal length with the Danube River, but he was finally forced to conclude that the sources of the Nile were unknown to all men.[2] These questions were not clarified in later centuries. Alexander the Great is said to have believed, when reaching the Ganges River, that it was one of the Nile's tributaries.[3] Strabo lived in Egypt and also traveled up the Nile, but his estimate of the size of Africa was less than a third of its real dimensions.[4] Pliny's description of the inner and southern regions of Africa and his presentation of its form have been described by a modern scholar as "a mass of inextricable confusion."[5] Ptolemy, in his *Geography,* traced the course of the Nile from the Mountains of the Moon (*Lunae montes*), the great basin of its sources and its eastern tributary.[6] Thus, no coherent picture of the sources of the Nile was transmitted from antiquity to later generations.

Medieval travelers and writers who were, of course, just as impressed by the Nile, considered the big river and the phenomena related to it as a wondrous expression of divine creation. The Nile was associated with one of the rivers of the earthly paradise, generally the Gihon,[7] which, like the Euphrates, the Hiddekel, and the Pison, was believed to run underground before emerging at a different place.[8] Practically all European travelers to the Levant did not go farther down the Nile than Cairo, and the information they provide on the river is often imaginary and stereotyped. For example, the thirteenth-century chronicler Jean de Joinville dedicated to the Nile a passage in his *Life of Saint Louis,* in which he recorded the event of the so-called crusade of Damietta. The Nile, according to this author, "is different from all other rivers; for as these others flow down towards the sea, more and more brooks and rivulets flow into them; but no other streams of any kind fall into this river which, as it happens, runs down one unbroken channel into Egypt, and then divides into seven branches that spread throughout the land." After describing the inundation of the Nile, he writes: "Nobody knows how these inundations occur, unless it be by God's will." He adds that "when morning comes, the Egyptians find in their nets cast into the river products such as ginger, rhubarb, aloes and cinnamon." "It is said," he reports, "that these things come from the earthly paradise; for in that heavenly place the wind blows down trees just as it does the dry wood in the forests of our own land; and the dry wood from the trees in paradise that thus falls into the river is sold to us by merchants in this country." Alongside these fantasies, de Joinville reports of an attempt by the Mamluks to reach the sources of the Nile. According to him, an expedition sent by the sultan for this end reported on its return that "after they had gone a considerable distance up the river they had come to a great mass of rocks, so high and sheer that no one could get by. From these rocks the river fell streaming down, and up above, on the top of the mountain, there seemed to be a marvelous profusion of trees. They also said that they had seen a number of strange and savage creatures of different species, such as lions, serpents, and elephants, that came and looked at them from the banks of the river as they were going upstream."[9] Thus, a description that probably had some real foundation is used to confirm the association of the Nile with the unreachable earthly paradise. William of Boldensele, a powerful German nobleman and Dominican who visited Egypt in the course of his pilgrimage to the Holy Land in 1332–1333, expressed a commonly accepted opinion when writing that the Nile was the Gihon of the Scriptures, if not the Gihon and the Pison combined into one stream.[10] Ludolph Sudheim, who traveled in the East between 1336 and 1341, refers to a subterranean course of the Upper Nile in certain regions. Like many other travelers, he was fascinated by the crocodiles. According to him, the Templars, by judicious tooth extraction, had converted these fearful animals into beasts of burden.[11]

The mystery of the Nile and its sources was an ideal topic for writers who were eager to supply their readership with delightful stories. For example, the Spanish traveler Pero Tafur writes about a story reported to him in 1436 by the Italian traveler Nicolo de' Conti: it concerns a mission allegedly organized by Prester John (by then identified as the Christian monarch of Abyssinia) to discover the sources of the Nile. According to this story, to ensure success of the expedition, it was necessary to produce a race of men who could live on fish. The African monarch collected a group of babies, deprived them of milk, and brought them up on raw fish. When fully grown, they were sent on the projected expedition. Reaching the Mountains of the Moon, they saw the Nile pouring out high up out of a hole in the rock. Yet, some scouts who were sent up to investigate refused to return, while others who did were unwilling to say what they had seen.[12]

These are typical examples of themes mingling religious traditions and fantastic descriptions, which characterize a great part of this kind of literature during the later Middle Ages.

The image of the Nile underwent a gradual but radical transformation during the Renaissance. This was a result of several interrelated developments, none of which can be dealt with in detail here. The first and most important was the gradual emergence of a secular culture, especially in urban Italy. The second was the rediscovery of works of classical antiquity in general, and more specifically several works of geographical and historical interest, such as Ptolemy's *Geography* and the works of Strabo, Herodotus, and Diodoros, all of whom had much to say about Egypt and the Nile (though not always correctly). These were thoroughly studied, translated, and widely diffused during the Renaissance. The voyages of this Age of Exploration widened the European horizons and consolidated knowledge about the configuration of the earth in general and of the African continent in particular. The accounts written by travelers and explorers helped to develop a new critical attitude toward the venerated works of classical authors, who during earlier phases of the Renaissance had been treated as infallible authorities. Particularly, repeated and continuous contacts with Ethiopians in Europe, in the Levant, and in Ethiopia itself led to a growing interest in the only Christian kingdom in Africa and to everything related to it, including the Nile.

European missionaries and merchants seem to have reached Ethiopia already in the fourteenth century.[13] But it was especially during the fifteenth century that mutual contacts of various kinds intensified. Several sources attest to the presence of European missionaries and adventurers in Ethiopia during the fifteenth century.[14] For example, Pietro Rombulo from Messina spent three years in Egypt before passing to Ethiopia, where he lived for thirty-seven years with his Ethiopian wife and eight children. In 1450, when on an embassy on behalf of King Zar'a-Ya'qob to the king of Naples and the Pope, he met Pietro Ranzano, another Sicilian, who recorded a few elements from Rombulo's diary.[15] A Venetian merchant, Gregorio, or Hieronimo Bicini, is said to have settled in Ethiopia, where he is believed to have served as secretary to the emperor in the late fifteenth century.[16] A Venetian painter, Francesco Brancaleone, was reported by James Bruce to have been active in the Ethiopian court during the reign of Ba'eda Maryam (1468–1478).[17]

European potentates developed an interest in the Christian emperors in faraway Africa who could serve as allies against Muslim powers in the Levant. The once legendary Prester John, a figure placed in earlier centuries in the Far East, became identified with a flesh-and-blood monarch, who was expected to collaborate with Western Christendom.[18] Toward the end of the fifteenth century, Portuguese efforts to reach the Indian Ocean were also accompanied by attempts to establish friendly relations with Ethiopia. The two Portuguese envoys, Afonso de Paiva and Pero de Covilhã, sent to Ethiopia in the 1480s, never returned from their mission, but Father Francisco Alvarez, who spent about six years in Ethiopia between 1520 and 1526 as a member of an official Portuguese delegation headed by Rodrigo de Lima, returned to Europe and was able to publish in Lisbon in 1540 a detailed account of his Ethiopian experience.[19]

During the same period, and more significantly from our point of view, the presence of Ethiopians in Italy and the Mediterranean became a regular phenomenon. An Ethiopian delegation, the first to appear in Europe, came to Europe at the beginning of the fourteenth century to ask for assistance against the Muslims.[20] Ethiopian monks from Jerusalem were sent by their king to the Council of Florence (1439), and subsequently Ethiopian pilgrims, mainly from Jerusalem, occasionally went to Rome, where a small church, Santo Stefano Maggiore, later Santo Stefano degli Abissini, was placed at their disposal in 1479.[21] By the end of the fifteenth century there were small Ethiopian communities in Cyprus (where they had been established in the middle of the previous century), Venice, Rome, and perhaps also in Florence.[22]

It should be noted, however, that the rediscovery of Ptolemy's *Geography* at the beginning of the fifteenth century, and its later publication in print from 1475 onward, though contributing to a more secular approach to geographical matters, must have also augmented the confusion concerning the configuration and size of the African continent and the course of the Nile. Paradoxically, this happened just when modern cartographers and writers were starting to present the contours of Africa in a more realistic manner. The authority attributed to classical knowledge deterred cartographers of the early Renaissance from rejecting Ptolemy's world picture on the basis of contemporary experience. The ensuing confusion was to influence the presentation of the Nile for over a century. No wonder, therefore, that Anselmo Adorno, who traveled to the East in 1470–1471, though distinguishing between India and Ethiopia, could still write that the Nile, which he identified with the biblical Gihon, originated in India and flowed through Ethiopia into Egypt.[23] Likewise, the influence of traditional Christian concepts and the tendency to satisfy the European readership with fantastic tales did not vanish in the Renaissance. Not surprisingly, the association of the Nile with the earthly paradise is found in Ariosto's *Orlando Furioso*, published for the first time in 1516, where fantasy and reality are firmly interwoven.[24] But the survival of the traditional world picture is also reflected in geographical works and in the writings of some sixteenth-century travelers to the East. The Franciscan friar Suriano, whose travel account was published in 1524, writes that the sources of the Nile were in the earthly paradise, adding that the river passed through Ethiopia over a bed of pure gold.[25] Sebastian Münster's *Cosmography,* published in Basel in 1554, includes a chapter on the dragons of India and Ethiopia.[26] As late as the 1580s, Johann Michael Heberer still associated the Nile with the earthly paradise.[27]

But besides such traditional accounts, there was an increasing number of others in which secular curiosity was combined with a more critical spirit in dealing with everything related to the river, including its sources, its course, the life around it, the archeological remains scattered along it, its flora and fauna, and any other aspect worthy of notice. Consequently, the Nile gradually changed its character in the eyes of educated Europeans:

from a wondrous phenomenon, drawing its waters from the earthly paradise, it became an object of scientific investigation, including a critical analysis of all available written material and research expeditions. This process was nourished by travel literature, which provided more and more material to the educated public in Europe, and also reflected the results of this process, by an ever-growing secular approach to the river and its civilizations.

Descriptions of travels to the Levant carried out by Europeans during the fifteenth and sixteenth centuries are numerous. Authors of travel accounts came from many countries; they represent a wide spectrum of Renaissance society, including churchmen and laymen, soldiers and humanists, merchants and physicians, noblemen and burghers. Their accounts were generally written in the modern vernacular languages, which meant that their readership was not restricted to the scholarly world. Indeed, travel literature was a very popular genre in Renaissance culture, particularly after the introduction of the printing press around the middle of the fifteenth century. Travel accounts were reprinted time and again, were translated into different languages, and enjoyed a wide diffusion. It should also be noted that despite the growing interest in newly discovered lands, descriptions of travels to the Muslim Levant continued to attract much interest, at least until the end of the sixteenth century.[28]

The new spirit of the age is reflected in the motivation of travelers, often explicitly formulated in their works. The famous traveler Ciriaco of Ancona, for instance, made at least two visits to Egypt, motivated, as he himself wrote, by his "great desire to see the world." His main interest lay in the monuments of classical antiquity, but he seems to be among the first who was also attracted by the marvels of pharaonic times, copying hieroglyphic inscriptions and sending them to his humanist friends in Italy.[29] Ludovico di Varthema, who traveled in the East between 1503 and 1508, wrote that his purpose was "to see different people and different customs" and "to learn new things in every way."[30] Other travelers were attracted to the Levant by professional motivations: for example, Pierre Gilles (1547), Pierre Belon (1547), Leonard Rauwolf (1573), and Prospero Alpino (1582–1584), all of them physicians, were mainly interested in the flora and fauna and in the medical practice of the Levant but did not leave out anything worthy of notice when putting pen to paper.[31] An anonymous Venetian traveler of the late sixteenth century accomplished a trip of about 3,000 kilometers from Cairo to southern Egypt and Nubia out of sheer archaeological interest.[32]

As a result of this cultural change, Africa in general and Egypt, Ethiopia, and the Nile in particular became subjects worthy of independent scholarly treatment. As early as 1483, Polo Trevisan, a Venetian who spent many years in the Levant, wrote a book on the Nile and Ethiopia. Though unfortunately lost, the subject of the book points to the growing interest in the river as well as in Ethiopia. Another Venetian, Alessandro Zorzi (b. before 1470), who was apparently greatly interested in various enterprises of European explorations, assembled a collection of itineraries, mostly of Ethiopian monks who traveled northward.[33] The growing interest in Egypt was probably also related to the development of an Egyptian vogue among artists and scholars of late fifteenth- and sixteenth-century Italy.[34]

An important contribution to the knowledge of Africa and especially that of the Nile is that of Hasan ben Muhammad al-Wazzan al-Zayyati, better known in the West as Leo Africanus. Born in Granada and a resident in Fez, he was a learned Muslim who had been captured by corsairs in the course of a maritime journey near the Tunisian coast and subsequently brought to Rome, where he was converted to Christianity by Pope Leo X. Before returning to the Maghreb and to his original faith, he lived in papal Rome for about ten years, where he also composed, or translated from the Arabic, his *Description of Africa*. This work is a unique contribution to the Europeans' lore of Africa, combining learned knowledge with the author's personal travel experience. It is interesting to encounter in this work a critical spirit similar to that which characterized some Italian scholars of the same age, an attitude also reflected in his treatment of the Nile. He does not seem to take too seriously a statement found in the work of the tenth-century Arab geographer Mas'udi, who wrote that in the mountains around the sources of the Nile there were wild human beings who ran around like goats and lived in the desert eating herbs like wild beasts. Following this citation, Leo wrote: "Had I cited everything written by our historians on the Nile it would rather seem like telling fairy tales, and would be tiresome to read." He seems to have more confidence in the statements of "many Ethiopians" living in the plains "like the Arabs," a few of whom, when searching for their lost camels who tended to wander away when in heat, went upstream for about 500 miles, where they often saw small lakes and big tributaries.[35]

Portuguese contacts with Ethiopia and the Upper Nile Valley started sometime before the circumnavigation of Africa by Portuguese ships, but these contacts were often kept secret and therefore, during their early stages, did not have a wide impact on Renaissance culture. Even after 1541, when a rescue expedition, led by Christopher da Gama, initiated a new age of Portuguese presence in Ethiopia, information on the remote Christian kingdom hardly trickled to wider European circles.[36] It is only by the middle of the sixteenth century, when some Portuguese accounts of Ethiopia were published in print, that the hitherto unknown aspects of Ethiopian reality reached the educated public in Europe.[37]

The year 1550 marks an important stage in Europe's acquaintance with Africa and the Nile. In that year the Venetian scholar Giovanni Battista Ramusio published the first volume of his collection of travel accounts, *Navigazioni e viaggi,* accompanied by maps made by the famous cartographer Iacopo Gastaldi.[38] Ramusio represents Venetian geographical interests at their best. A renowned humanist,[39] he was also deeply involved in public affairs, serving as secretary of the Venetian Senate and later of the all-powerful Council of Ten. His friends included famous scholars, such as Girolamo Francastoro, the important Paduan astronomer and physician; the famous printers Manuzio and Giunti; Cardinal Pietro Bembo; and Iacopo Gastaldi, the official cartographer of the Venetian Republic. Another interesting figure in his milieu was Filippo Membre, official interpreter of the republic and one of its chief intermediaries with the world of the Orient.[40] Ramusio also corresponded with scholars in other countries, such as Gonzalo Fernandez de Oviedo, the famous historian of the West Indies.[41] He was considered an expert in Levantine affairs, and among other assignments, he was charged by the Venetian authorities to interview David Ha-Reuveni, the mysterious Jewish messenger from the East, during his stay in Venice in 1530. From our point of view it is worth noting that Ha-Reuveni told Ramusio that he had descended the Nile when passing from Ethiopia to Egypt. He also told Ramusio that the Nile was to be identified with the biblical Pison.[42]

Ramusio's collaboration with people such as Francastoro and Gastaldi and his systematic arrangement of travel accounts, both ancient and modern, enabled him to combine the results of humanistic scholarship with contemporary travel experience, presenting for the first time to the large European public the new world picture emerging from the intensive activity in the field during the first half of the sixteenth century. His collection of travels, though not the first that appeared in print, is undoubtedly the best and most systematic that had ever appeared in Europe. Though a scholarly enterprise, it was intended to be read by a wide audience.[43] It is written in the Florentine dialect, which was then becoming the modern literary language of all Italians, also understood by many foreigners. Interestingly, the first of the three folio volumes of this pioneering work was dedicated to Africa. Beside the first printed edition of Leo Africanus's work, it included, among other texts, the report of Francisco Alvarez,[44] two short essays on the periodic inundations of the Nile (presented as an exchange of letters between Ramusio and Francastoro), and Gastaldi's new map showing the course of the Nile.

Though it was already published some ten years previously in Portuguese, the publication by Ramusio of Alvarez's *Voyage in Ethiopia* was an event of some significance, since it caused the information on Ethiopia, which until then had been mainly the domain of Portuguese official circles, to be widely diffused.[45] Alvarez's account has a relatively short passage on the sources of the Nile, which is not based on his personal experience but relies on what he heard from other Portuguese who had been there. The sources of the Nile, according to this account, were in the kingdom of Goyame. The river was said to originate in two big lakes, forming some islands in its upper course. Alvarez also noted that the inundations of the Nile were caused by heavy rains in Ethiopia starting in mid-June and continuing till mid-September.[46] Ramusio, in his short introduction to Alvarez's treatise, though stressing the great value of this account, expressed his regret that Alvarez did not visit personally the sources of the Nile, its upper course and the first cataract. Had he done so, and had he used an astrolabe, which, according to Ramusio, all Portuguese sailors used, he could have measured the latitude of these places. "Who knows," adds Ramusio, "perhaps one of Italy's princes will be convinced by reading this book, to send a worthy person to visit these regions and make such measurements so as to establish the exact location of the sources and cataracts, and to describe them in greater detail."[47]

The periodic inundations of the Nile are discussed in two short treatises by Ramusio and Francastoro, which are included in the same collection. It should be noted that, during the sixteenth century, the relation between rainfall and rivers was not yet taken for granted as it is today.[48] Ramusio and Francastoro agree that the only plausible explanation could be heavy rains during certain periods in Ethiopia. Francastoro is actually more interested in the causes of these rains. In any case, these treatises reflect a genuine belief in the progress of human knowledge and in the superiority of the writers' own age compared to earlier ones. Ramusio examines all the available explanations of the periodical inundations of the Nile that he could find in the works of ancient authors, systematically discarding nearly all of them for various reasons.[49] In particular he does not seem to have much respect for writers who did not take into consideration the experience of people who had personally seen and described the phenomenon.[50] In his concluding remarks, explaining why he addressed his essay to Francastoro, he writes that the latter dared to present the movements of the sky "and many other beautiful parts of philosophy," contradicting the opinions of ancient writers; he calls upon him to act likewise with regard to what they had written on the globe, which, as was already clear, was inhabited all over, with no part of it, either in the seas or on land, devoid of people or animals. Francastoro affirms in his treaty that thanks to the reconnaissance of the earth by his own contemporaries, earlier scholars seem like little children.[51] Both Ramusio and Francastoro did not even bother to mention the earthly paradise or the traditional biblical rivers, and their treatises do not have anything to say about wonders unfathomable to humans. Though containing a few errors, their research is characterized by a clear conviction that study and experience are the only tools to understand such phenomena, and that only by combining the two can one reach satisfactory results.

A clear reflection of the changes described above can be found in the development of Renaissance cartography and particularly in the depiction of the Nile and the adjacent regions in maps of that period. We have seen that as late as 1554, Sebastian Münster's *Cosmography* still presented Ethiopia as a land inhabited by dragons. But in reality an important change had already been well under way by then. If most fifteenth-century maps still associated the Nile with the earthly paradise, and on the other hand were strongly influenced by the cartographical tradition associated with Ptolemy's *Geography,* by the middle of the sixteenth century, the Nile became a river like any other big river. Even if its sources and exact flow were still partly unknown, their cartographical depiction depended less on religious and mythical concepts and more on knowledge accumulated by Renaissance travelers and discoverers. The map known as "Egyptus Novelo," dated before 1454, has been described by a modern scholar as "a remarkably good approximation of the real geography of Abyssinia of which it is the first map."[52] Fra Mauro's map of Africa (1460), though still typically medieval, and also influenced by Ptolemy, incorporated information derived from travelers, missionaries, and Ethiopian monks.[53] Crawford has remarked that the Abyssinian river system, as depicted in this map, is remarkably correct in its essentials, though many details are still in the realm of fantasy.[54] The data accumulated during subsequent decades were used in Giacomo Gastaldi's "Disegno della geografia moderna de tutta la parte dell'Africa" (Venice, 1564), an important event in the history of African geography. This map, together with another that accompanied Filippo Pigafetta's book on the kingdom of Congo (Rome, 1591), served as a basis for several other important maps of Africa that were to be published subsequently by leading cartographers, such as Ortelius, De Jode, and Mercator.

Another important step forward was made during the first three decades of the following century and was related to the activities of Jesuit missionaries in Ethiopia.[55] In particular, the chapter on the Nile included in Pero Paez's important *History of Ethiopia* is a model of critical approach to the subject.[56] Paez (d. 1622), who came to Ethiopia in 1603, even if not the first European to reach the sources of the Blue Nile, is the first to have left a detailed and scholarly description of the upper parts of the river, which he visited in 1618.[57] The only residue of traditional opinions in this chapter is a brief reference to the association of the Nile with the biblical Gihon, which Paez attributes to "ancient writers and *nearly* all modern ones.[58] Most significantly, he has nothing to say about his own opinion on this point and seems to be much more interested in the physical, historical, and anthropological aspects related to those parts of the river visited by him. He has no inhibition in criticizing ancient and modern authors who had written on the subject. All theories that do not link the Nile's inundations to the heavy seasonal rains in Ethiopia are described by

him as "fables and mere fantasies."[59] Some of his contemporaries who
wrote about the Nile are also sharply criticized. Among other things, he re-
pudiates the claim, repeated by several Renaissance writers, that the Mamluk and Ottoman sultans paid tribute to the negus in order to prevent the
total inundation of Egypt by the Nile. Paez checked the veracity of this
story by questioning the emperor himself, who, according to Paez, was
rather amused to learn about it.[60] Paez's precious geographical information
was used by the Venetian cartographer Vincenzo Coronelli (1650–1718),
probably the last representative of Venice's prestigious cartographical tradition, who included a map of Africa in his *Atlante Veneto* (first edition,
Venice, 1690).[61] The map of Abyssinia, dated 1662, which accompanies
Almeida's *History of Abyssinia,* summarizes the information obtained by
Portuguese missionaries up to their expulsion in 1632. In this map, the
upper course of the Abbay is shown correctly, along with several of its
tributaries. According to O. G. S. Crawford, it reveals an intimate and
fairly accurate knowledge of Abyssinian topography.[62]

Considering that the Muslim Levant had been the subject of Western
visits and descriptions long before the Renaissance, descriptions of travels to this region are a most suitable means to follow transformations in
Western world perceptions. The depiction of the Nile in this literature reflects not only a new attitude to travel but also the widening geographical
horizon of the Renaissance world, and particularly a change toward a more
secular attitude to the universe, based on human capacity to understand
natural phenomena once conceived as unfathomable wonders. In fact, the
attitude to the Nile may serve as a typical example of the development of
the world perception in Renaissance culture. Secularization of knowledge
was achieved by transforming the rediscovered world of classical antiquity
into a cultural model. This had also a negative effect, by attributing too
much authority to the erroneous world picture found in Ptolemy's *Geography* and other ancient texts. Subsequently, however, increasing reliance
on the results of European reconnaissance in the Age of Exploration led
to growing criticism toward the once authoritative ancient writers. For
scholars such as Ramusio, Francastoro, and Paez, the ultimate authority in
establishing learned knowledge became experience, accompanied by a
critical approach to available sources.

In this context it is also noteworthy that neither the travel literature
nor scholars, such as Ramusio, Francastoro, and Gastaldi, who used it,
make any reference to the hermetic tradition, to which recent Renaissance
scholarship has attributed such a great importance. It should be remembered that this tradition was closely associated with ancient Egyptian culture. The hieroglyphs, for example, were believed to contain the secrets of
divine truths, and were subject to speculations concerning their hidden

meaning.[63] The absence of any hint of this cultural trend in the travel literature and in the scholarly works related to Egypt and the Nile may indicate that the impact of the hermetic tradition on Renaissance culture was probably not as all embracing as several modern historians would have us believe.

Finally, as a marginal note, it is also appropriate to refer briefly to the value of Renaissance travel literature as a source for the history of the Nile Valley and the Levant. During recent generations, for various reasons, Orientalists have been reluctant to use Western sources in general and travel accounts in particular for the study of Oriental societies. Yet, in the light of the cultural transformations treated in this chapter, this reservation is hardly justifiable. The travel accounts of the Renaissance are not merely a reflection of Western attitudes. They contain much valuable information on the countries visited, which often has no parallel in Oriental sources, especially on subjects that were too obvious to be pointed out by local writers, as, for instance, Belon's description of various types of boats on the Nile and on the manner of swimming in the river,[64] or Johann Wild's observations on children in villages along the Nile.[65] If used systematically and with care, this rich and fascinating material may open new vistas in the study of these regions in the period parallel to the Renaissance in the West.[66]

NOTES

1. Burckhardt, *The Civilization of the Renaissance in Italy,* p. 171.

2. Herodotus (2.19–34). See also Lloyd, *Herodotus Book II, Commentary 1–98,* pp. 91–93, 98.

3. Berger, *Geschichte der wissenschaftlichen Erdkunde der Griechen,* pp. 75–76.

4. Bunbury, *A History of Ancient Geography,* p. 328.

5. Ibid., pp. 430–432.

6. Sitran Gasparini, "L'Egitto nella rappresentazione cartografica," p. 17. For some remarks on the Mountains of the Moon, see Crawford, "Some Medieval Theories About the Nile," p. 18.

7. According to Bernard Hamilton, this association is already found in Josephus, *Jewish Antiquities,* I, 39 (Hamilton, "Continental Drift," p. 239, n. 15).

8. Wright, *The Geographical Lore of the Time of the Crusades,* pp. 298–299.

9. Joinville, *Chronicles of the Crusades,* pp. 211–213.

10. Beazley, *The Dawn of Modern Geography,* p. 10. In the King James Bible, the land of Kush, associated in Genesis with the river Gihon, is translated as "Ethiopia," whereas the Pison is associated with land of Havila, where gold comes from.

11. Ibid., pp. 399–401.

12. Referred to by M. Letts in his remarks to Crawford, "Some Medieval Theories," p. 24.

13. Crawford, "Some Medieval Theories," pp. 7–8.

14. Crawford, *Ethiopian Itineraries,* pp. 20–21.

15. Figliuolo, "Europa, Oriente, Mediterraneo nell'opera dell'umanista palermitano Pietro Ranzano," p. 340. It is not clear whether Pietro from Naples, whose
personal description of Ethiopia and the Nile was recorded by a French traveler at
Pera in 1432, is to be identified with Pietro Rombulo. See La Broquière, *Le Voyage
d'Outremer,* pp. 142–148; and Trasselli, "Un Italiano in Etiopia nel XV secolo,"
pp. 173–202.

16. Crawford, *Ethiopian Itineraries,* pp. 21–22.

17. Bruce, *Travels to Discover the Source of the Nile,* pp. 69, 87–88, 90.

18. Crawford, "Some Medieval Theories," p. 8.

19. Diffie and Winius, *Foundations of the Portuguese Empire 1415–1580,* pp.
163–164; Ramusio, *Navigazioni e viaggi,* vol. 2, p. 77.

20. Beckingham and Huntingford, "An Ethiopian Embassy to Europe," pp.
337–346.

21. Marrassini, "Insieme contro Maometto. Europa ed Etiopia dal Medioevo
all'età moderna," pp. 31–33; Hamilton, "Eastern Churches and Western Scholarship," pp. 234–235. From these contacts originated the Ethiopic psalter printed in
Rome in 1513 by Johannes Potken, to which was appended the Ethiopic alphabet
and an explanation on the formation of Ethiopic syllables.

22. Hamilton, "Continental Drift," p. 253.

23. Adorno, *Itinéraire d'Anselme Adorno en Terre Sainte (1470–1471),* pp.
178–183. It should be noted that medieval writers often used the name Ethiopia to
denote the entire trans-Saharan region.

24. Ariosto, *Orlando Furioso,* pp. 101–128.

25. Campbell, *The Witness and the Other World,* p. 134.

26. Suriano, *Treatise on the Holy Land,* p. 193.

27. Heberer, *Voyages en Egypte de Michael Heberer von Bretten,* p. 39.

28. Atkinson, *Les Nouveaux horizons de la Renaissance française,* pp. 10–11.

29. Voigt, *Die Wiederbelebung des classischen Altertums oder das erste
Jahrhundert des Humanismus,* pp. 270, 276. Voigt suggests that Ciriaco's second
visit to Egypt took place in 1434.

30. Varthema, *The Travels etc.,* p. 221.

31. On Pierre Belon and Pierre Gilles, see Belon, *Le Voyage en Egypte de
Pierre Belon du mons 1547,* pp. i–xxxvi, and "The French Embassy of D'Aramon
to the Porte," pp. 27–39; and Paviot, "Autour de l'ambassade de d'Aramon: Erudits et voyageurs au Levant 1547–1553," pp. 381–392; and Musto, introduction to
Giles, *The Antiquities of Constantinople,* pp. xvi–xx. On Prospero Alpino, see Lucchetta, "I viaggiatori," pp. 60–64. On Rauwolf, see Henze, "Leonhart Rauwolff,"
pp. v–xxxiii.

32. "Mi son mosso non per util nissuno, ma solo per vedere tante superbe fab-
rice, chiese, statue, collossi, aguglie e colonne, e anco il loco dove si cavano dite
colone e aguglie"—cited in Lucchetta, "I viaggiatori," p. 64. See also Chevalier,
"Le Voyage archéologique au XVIe siècle," pp. 357–380.

33. For these itineraries and for Zorzi, see Crawford, *Ethiopian Itineraries,*
pp. 23–27.

34. Iverson, *The Myth of Egypt and Its Hieroglyphs in European Tradition,* pp.
59–75; Castelli, *I geroglifici;* Calvesi, *Il mito dell'Egitto nel Rinascimento;*
Grafton, "The Ancient City Restored," pp. 118–123.

35. Ramusio, *Navigazioni e viaggi,* vol. 1, pp. 437–438.

36. On the presence of Westerners in sixteenth- and early seventeenth-century
Ethiopia, see Conti Rossini, "Le sorgenti del Nilo azzurro e Giovanni Gabriel," pp.
38–47.

37. Tamrat, "Ethiopia, the Red Sea, and the Horn," pp. 180–182.

38. Three volumes were published: the first in 1550, the third in 1556, and the second in 1559, two years after Ramusio's death. On Gastaldi, see Karrow, *Mapmakers of the Sixteenth Century and Their Maps,* pp. 216–249.

39. Between 1530 and 1542 Ramusio was acting librarian of Bessarion's collection, one of the most important collections of Greek codices in the West (the official librarian, Cardinal Bembo, was generally absent) (Milanesi, "Introduction" to Ramusio, *Navigazioni e viaggi,* vol. 1, p. xvi).

40. Fabris, "Note sul mappamondo cordiforme di Haci Ahmed di Tunisi," pp. 8–10.

41. Milanesi, "Introduction" to Ramusio, *Navigazioni e viaggi,* vol. 1, p. xix.

42. Ibid., p. xv. On Ramusio, see also Lucchetta, "Viaggiatori e racconti di viaggi nel Cinquecento," pp. 482–489.

43. See the letter written by the Florentine merchant Filippo Sassetti, admirer of Ramusio, and particularly of his essay on the Nile, Milanesi, "Introduction" to Ramusio, *Navigazioni e viaggi,* vol. 1, pp. xxxiii–xxxiv.

44. Ibid., p. xx.

45. Ramusio's edition also served the Antwerp editor Plantin in publishing a French translation of Alvarez's work in 1558 (Pankhurst, *Ethiopia. A Cultural History,* p. 314).

46. Ramusio, *Navigazioni e viaggi,* vol. 2, p. 359.

47. Ibid., p. 80.

48. See the observations of E. G. R. Taylor in Crawford, "Some Medieval Theories," p. 26.

49. "Quando la certezza della esperienza distrugge la probabilità delle ragioni, si debbe ben laudare lo ingegno dell'uomo, ma non già si debbe dar fede a quelle cose che da lui sono dette" (Ramusio, *Navigazioni e viaggi,* vol. 2, p. 401).

50. Ibid., pp. 401–402.

51. Ibid., p. 407, note.

52. Crawford, "Some Medieval Theories," p. 9.

53. Ullendorff, *The Ethiopians,* p. 3.

54. Ibid., pp. 13, 16.

55. Conti Rossini, *Etiopia e genti di Etiopia,* pp. 5–7.

56. Beccari, *Notizia e saggi,* pp. 273–291.

57. Giovanni Gabriel, a descendant of a Venetian soldier in Christopher Da Gama's expedition, seems to have visited the place in 1588 (Conti Rossini, "Giovanni Gabriel," p. 39). James Bruce, who reached those parts toward the end of the eighteenth century, claimed that Paez had never actually been there, a claim that has meanwhile been proven as baseless. See Beccari, *Notizia e saggi*, pp. 269–271, and Ullendorff, *The Ethiopians,* p. 14.

58. Beccari, *Notizia e saggi,* p. 274.

59. Ibid., p. 283–285.

60. Ibid., p. 290. For this belief, see, for instance, Ariosto, *Orlando Furioso,* canto 33, p. 106: "And the Egyptian Sultan, it is said, / Pays tribute and is subject to the king, / Who could divert into another bed the river Nile, and thus disaster bring / on Cairo, and on all that region spread / the blight of famine and great suffering. / Senapo by his subjects he is named; / As Prester John among us he is framed."

61. Sitran Gasparini, "L'Egitto nella rappresentazione cartografica," pp. 17–42.

62. Crawford, "Some Medieval Theories," pp. 19–20.

63. Iversen, *The Myth of Egypt,* pp. 59–89.

64. Belon, *Le Voyage en Egypte de Pierre Belon du Mons 1547,* pp. 101a–101b.

65. Wild, *Voyages en Egypte,* pp. 154–155.

66. For a demonstration of the use of these sources for the urban history of Levantine port towns, see Arbel, "The Port Towns of the Levant in the Sixteenth Century Travel Literature."

9

The Legend of
the Blue Nile in Europe

Emery van Donzel

For at least 600 years, perhaps even a millennium, Arab, Ethiopian, and European sources mention that the Ethiopians were able, or thought to be able, to block off the Blue Nile, or divert its course, so as to starve Egypt and bring Islam to its knees. This idea, qualified here as a legend, has played an important role in the relations between Christianity in Ethiopia and Islam in Egypt in the first place. Later, when the Western powers had begun to send out their discoverers, conquerors, and missionaries, the legend played its part in Western concepts about the way in which Islam in Egypt could be subdued.

The origin of the legend is perhaps to be found in Egypt in the second half of the eleventh century, when the country was hit by several consecutive, severe famines, caused by internal political strife that led to social unrest and neglect of the irrigation systems. The legend most probably was not caused by a low level of the Nile. On the contrary, the level of the water seems to have been quite normal during that period. In later times, these famines were supposed to be related to the Ethiopian power over the water of the Nile. In Egypt, the Christian kingdom was felt as a constant threat to Islam because it dominated the Nile; in Ethiopia, the so-called mastery over the river was seen as a means of the Ethiopian kings to assist the Copts, their co-religionists, against their Muslim overlords. The legend thus became a political and religious issue between Muslim Egypt and Christian Ethiopia.

The oldest Arab source to mention the legend probably is the *Kitab al-Jawahir al-buhur,* a legendary history of Egypt, written by Ibn Wasif Shah al-Misri, who died in 1202–1203.[1] The oldest Ethiopian source known so far, in which the legend is found, seems to be the fourteenth-century manuscript of the *Gadl* of King Lalibala.[2] This chapter, which owes much to the works of Enrico Cerulli and Taddesse Tamrat, deals with the European sources only.

The legend was known in Europe by the end of the thirteenth century. When European interest in the Crusades, notwithstanding Dante and Petrarca,[3] came to an end with the fall of St Jean d'Acre (Akko) in 1291, European strategists nevertheless continued to develop plans against Egypt, and the idea of starving Egypt out by diverting the Nile was part of these plans.[4] In 1317 Guillaume Adam, a Dominican friar who for many months had been waiting on the island of Socotra to enter Ethiopia, submitted plans to Cardinal Raymundus Guillelmi de Fargis "de modo Saracenos extirpandi."[5]

The oldest written European source is Jacob of Verona's report of his journey to Palestine in 1335. It contains a reference to the tradition about the power of the Ethiopian sovereign over the Nile.[6] In December 1338 Pope Benedict XII sent the Franciscan friar Giovanni da Marignolli (John of Marignola) with three other legates to the Mongol court in Cambalec (Peking). After fifteen years he returned to Avignon, then the papal city. In the recollections of his Asiatic travels Giovanni writes that the river Gyon (Nile) flowed around the land of Abyssinia and that it was believed to descend to Egypt through a crack in a place called Abasty, probably a clerical error for "Abascy," Marco Polo's "Abasci," and Arabic "Habasha." The land, according to Giovanni, was inhabited by the Christians of the Apostle Matthew, and the sultan of Egypt paid them tribute because it was in their power to cut off the water of that river.[7]

In 1384 Simone Sigoli, accompanied by some other Florentines, visited Egypt, the Sinai, and Palestine. He too wrote that the sultan of Egypt paid tribute to Prester John because the latter had control of certain sluices in the river Nile. These were opened a little, but if the Prester chose to open them widely, Cairo, Alexandria, and the whole of Egypt would be drowned. Fearing this, the sultan every year sent a ball of gold with a crown on top of it and 3,000 gold bezants.[8] Still in the seventeenth century Milton was to write that in his days the people of Egypt believed that there was a sluice in the Nile, which the Abyssinians began to open on June 12, widening the passage every day somewhat more until September 14, during the rainy season. But, Milton adds, the Egyptians were not aware of the real reason why the Nile rose, and nobody seemed to have seen the sluice.

In 1403 Guillebert, seigneur de Lannoy,[9] traveled from Hainaut to Palestine and Egypt. He left again on a secret mission from 1421 to 1423 to study the possibilities of a crusade for the liberation of Jerusalem. He writes that the (Mamluk) sultan of Egypt was not able to divert the bed (*le cruschon,* or "little jug") of the Nile and that Prester John could give it another course but refrained from doing so because otherwise the many Christians in Egypt might then die of hunger.

In 1432, some forty years after Sigoli's report, Pietro the Napolitan, of Spanish origin, visited Ethiopia just after the death of Negus Yishaq (1413–1430). He was a member of an embassy sent by Jean de France, Duke of Berry, a leading patron of the arts. He stayed for two years in the country and married an Ethiopian woman. On his way back he met, in Pera, the well-known European quarter of Istanbul—then still known in the West as Constantinople—the Frenchman Bertrandon de la Brocquière, a courtier of Philip the Good, Duke of Burgundy.[10] In the report of his journey, Pietro writes that Prester John, if he wished to do so, very well could divert the river Nile in another direction. But Pietro had not seen the great river either.

In the same century, the story of the Nile had become part of the popular literature of Ethiopia.[11] It was logical for the Ethiopian priests and pilgrims to emphasize the power of their king; and the West, afraid of Islam, was all too much inclined to believe those stories. The legend of Prester John is a case in point. A reflex of such credulity is found in the letter sent in 1450 by Alfonso V the Magnanimous of Aragon (1416–1458) to King Zar'a Ya'qob (1434–1468). The Portuguese king requested his Ethiopian counterpart to be solicitous in diverting the waters that flowed to Cairo.[12]

A new element in the legend was introduced by Guerin Meschino.[13] The Saracens ("Sarraini"), he writes, paid a substantial tribute to Prester John in order not to lose the waters of the Nile. He also relates that he had visited the gate of the river and had asked whether the sluices where the water passed through could be locked. The local people answered that in that case the water would flow to the mountains of the Red Sea. Guerin Meschino uses the word *cataratta,* which may be rendered as the English *sluice,* but also with *cataract.* It is possible that Guerin Meschino saw the Alato cataract near the place where the Abbay leaves Lake Tana.

An important document, which probably contributed much to the spread of the legend, is the letter that Jean de Lastic, Grand Master of the Knights of St. John at Rhodes, sent on July 3, 1448, to King Charles VII of France (1422–1461).[14] He writes that some Indian (i.e., Ethiopian) priests had arrived at Rhodes, reporting that Prester John had won a great victory over the Saracens. The Prester had warned the ruler of Egypt (Sultan Jaqmaq, 1438–1453) that, unless he desisted from persecuting the Christians, he would "snatch away" the entire river Nile and give it another course.

Not only pilgrims and travelers who heard about the legend reported on it. During the Renaissance, it was also known to the men of letters. In his *Orlando Furioso,* Ludovico Ariosto (1474–1533) describes Orlando's desperate love for Angelica. The setting of the poem is the struggle between Saracens and Christians around Paris, the story being part of the Carolingian cycles. Ariosto himself led a miserable life as a humble servant of Cardinal Hippolytus d'Este. Poetry was an escape for him. He "loved to travel over the world, but only on maps and with his phantasy."[15] In doing this, he made use of what was common knowledge in his days. At a certain point, his hero Astolfo flies along the Nile in a southern direction. On his right-hand side, he has "Tlemsen algerina" and on his left "altra tremisenne" (Christian Nubia). He then reaches "Senapo, imperator della Etiopia." Already back in 1339 Angelino Dalorto had explained the word *Senapo* as "Servus Crucis" (Servant of the Cross), and in the "Libro del Conoscimento," written between 1348 and 1375 by Francescano di Castiglia, the Abyssinian ruler had been called "Abdelselib," in Arabic "'Abd al-salib" (Servant of the Cross). This title is the Arabic equivalent of Ethiopic Gabra Masqal (Servant of the Cross), the baptismal name of Negus 'Amda Seyon I (1314–1344). Cerulli remarks that around 1350 Genovese merchants had traveled to Dongola, thus opening the road to Abyssinia through the Nile Valley.[16] The first historically identifiable contacts with Abyssinia, however, had been established in the beginning of the fifteenth century, not by the Genovese and along the Nile Valley but by the Venetians via Suakin and the Red Sea. It is remarkable that Ariosto's hero Astolfo follows the road opened by the Genovese and not that of the Venetians.

> Si dice che il Soldan re dell'Egitto
> A quel Re da tributo e sta suggetto
> Perch'e in poter di lui dal cammin dritto
> Levare il Nilo e dargli altro ricetto;
> E per questo lasciar subito afflitto
> Di fame il Cairo e tutto quel distretto.

> [It is said that the sultan, king of Egypt,
> Pays tribute to that king and is subject to him
> Because it is in his power to deduct from its straight path
> The Nile, and to give it another receptacle;
> And in doing so to leave at once afflicted
> Through famine, Cairo and all that region.]

These lines by Ludovico Ariosto represent the ideas about the Nile current in Europe at the time, and they must have contributed to the spread of the legend.

The same version is to be found in an account of a journey made by Jehan Thenaud, guardian of the monastery of the Cordeliers (Franciscans) in Angoulême. He left his town in July 1511 and returned in May 1512. The king of the "Abassins or Ethiopes whom we call in corrupted language 'le prebstre Jehan,' is rather ('assez') feared by the sultan since Jehan can diminish the waters of the Nile and thus render the greater part of Egypt infertile."[17]

So far no European seems to have set eyes on the Blue Nile. Yet its legend began to play a part in Portuguese foreign policy. After the conquest of Goa and Malacca in 1510–1511, Afonso d'Albuquerque, the organizer of the Portuguese hegemony in the Orient, turned toward the Red Sea. He wanted to take the spice trade away from Egypt and deliver a deadly blow to Islam by diverting the course of the Nile and thus starving Egypt out. It was said that only a small mountain had to be tunneled in order to lead the water to the Red Sea. According to Afonso's son Braz, his father had written several times to King Manuel I of Portugal (1495–1521) that field-workers should be sent from Madeira "who are very skilful in splitting rocks and in building canals for the irrigation of the sugar plantations on their island."[18]

In seventeenth-century Europe, marked by Reformation and counter-Reformation, the reports on the Nile provided by the Roman Catholic missionaries were rejected by scholars such as Job Ludolf for reasons that had nothing to do with the Nile but everything with religious controversies.

The Roman Catholic Padre Pero Paez probably was the first European to see the sources of the Blue Nile, which happened on April 21, 1618. He writes: "I was very happy to see with my own eyes what in earlier times King Cyrus and his son Cambyses, Alexander the Great and the famous Julius Caesar had so ardently wished to see."[19] Paez's account was made known in Europe by the German Jesuit Athanasius Kircher from Fulda (d. 1680) in his *Oedipus Aegyptiacus*.[20] The Dutch scholar Isaac Vossius, following Kircher, wrote a booklet called *De Nilo* and a *Dissertation touchant l'origine du Nil*.[21]

The sources of the Blue Nile are also described by another Jesuit, Jeronimo Lobo, in his *Itinerario*. This work was translated into French by M. Le Grand and into English by Samuel Johnson.[22] Lobo's description of the sources of the Blue Nile is probably borrowed from Paez.

Manoel de Almeida, another Jesuit, was a keen observer and an indefatigable explorer. His sound knowledge of Abyssinia's geography made him a sober and realistic critic of Albuquerque's high-strung projects. Everywhere, he writes, the Nile was at least 100 miles distant from the Red Sea, and the mountains were so high that the Alps and Pyrenees were but hills in comparison.

Yet the reports by Paez, Lobo, and d'Almeida were unacceptable to Job Ludolf. In the eyes of the fervent Protestant, the Roman Catholic missionaries were untrustworthy, even in matters that had nothing to do with religion. Ludolf very often refers to the Jesuit Balthasar Tellez, who had published a shortened version of d'Almeida's work, but attacks him wherever he can. Although Ludolf had never set foot on Ethiopian soil, he neverthe-less posed as an expert and judge in geographical matters. In his rather heavy Latin he writes: "Nunc sequitur questio non minus mira quam mo-mentosa. Num Rex Habessinorum Nilum divertere possit ne in Aegyptum fluat?" (There now follows a question no less curious than momentous. Is it in the power of the king of the Abyssinians to divert the Nile so that it does not flow to Egypt?") For Ludolf the answer is affirmative, "for only one single mount stands in the way; it would be possible to dig a canal next to it." The argumentation for this view is astonishing indeed: "It is not probable that such a man [Albuquerque] would write such unreal ('vana') things to his king, or that he would have requested the execution of such great works without serious reasons, to no other purpose than to expose himself, and his king, to mockery for proposing aimless efforts."[23] Ludolf was probably the first to ask whether the story had a basis in reality, but his answer is very unsatisfactory: the story is true because a great man wrote about it to his king.

Ludolf must have read the sober and realistic remarks of the French traveler Jean de Thevenot (d. 1667), who writes that it was not true that the sultan of Istanbul paid the Abyssinian king so that he would permit the river Nile to follow its natural course, because the sultan believed the King could not divert the river.[24] In 1658 Thevenot had met in Alexandria a cer-tain Hajj Michael Abu Yusuf, who had told him that he was on his way to Istanbul as envoy of the Abyssinian king.[25] It was through Thevenot's in-termediary that Ludolf in 1683 had been able to meet an Armenian mer-chant in Paris.[26] He even quotes Thevenot's information about Michael in his *Historia*.[27] Yet, he does not seem to have taken into account Thevenot's information on the Nile.

On the other hand, Ludolf quotes the Spanish Dominican Urreta, al-though he despises him. According to him the Pope had written to Negus Minas (1559–1563) that he should divert the Nile and disregard the tribute of 300,000 *sequins* (Venetian gold coins) that the negus received from the Turks to keep the Nile open. At the request of Ernst Duke of Saxony, Wansleb, a pupil of Ludolf, had made investigations about the Nile.[28] At first he wrote that the Europeans in Egypt considered the whole story as Abyssinian brag-ging. Later, in 1677, he said that he had found a letter of an Abyssinian king in which the latter threatened the sultan that he would divert the Nile.

In the early eighteenth century, the European discussions about the Nile were revived in France. In 1703 Louis XIV sent Le Noir du Roule, the French vice consul in Damietta, to King Iyasu I (1682–1706) to estab-lish trade relations and to resume the missionary activities. But the Fran-ciscans, the Jesuits, and the Coptic patriarch were opposed to du Roule's mission. The patriarch even spread the rumor that the Frenchman was a magician who was going to Ethiopia to change the course of the Nile. King Takla Haymanot (1706–1708) wrote to the sultan in Egypt that he very well could repay him for the fact that the sultan had arrested his envoy Murat, the Syrian: "The Nile would be sufficient to punish you, since God hath put into our power his [sic] fountain, his outlet and his increase, and that we can dispose of the same to do you harm."[29]

The French physician and traveler François Bernier, who died in 1688, and thus was a contemporary of Ludolf, gives a realistic description of the Nile. The inundations of Egypt, he writes, were caused by the rains in Ethiopia, and from this the kings of the country derived the right of exacting tribute from Egypt. When the Christians in Egypt were oppressed, the Ethiopian monarch thought of turning the course of the river toward the Red Sea. However, Bernier adds, "the project appeared so gigantic, if not impracticable, that the attempt was never made to carry it into execution."[30]

But the legend did not die out. James Bruce told his readers that King Lalibala, if he had persevered, might have completed his purpose of turning the current of the Nile into the Red Sea, as would have Alexander the Great and, perhaps, Louis (Lewis) XIV.[31] But Bruce's judgment on the possibility was negative: "In my time, no sensible man in Abyssinia believed that such a thing was possible, and few that it had ever been attempted." The legend, however, did not disappear, not even when the river became an object of scientific investigation. In the 1840s, the English geographer Charles Tilstone Beke mapped about 180,000 square kilometers of Ethiopia and ascertained the approximate course of the Blue Nile. In 1848 he published an article in French that was meant to be a rehabilitation of Pero Paez and Jeronimo Lobo and as such was directed against James Bruce, who so desperately had claimed to be the discoverer of the sources of the Nile.[32] It is remarkable that Beke, who published several works on the river,[33] seriously reflected on the possible change of the Nile's course. In 1851 he sent a copy of his *Memoir on the Possibility of Diverting the Waters of the Nile so as to Prevent the Irrigation of Egypt* to Lord Palmerston, secretary of state for foreign affairs.[34]

Some thirty years later, another well-known English explorer seemed to share Beke's view on the Nile. On October 9, 1888, Sir Samuel White Baker who, together with John Hanning Speke, had established the sources of the Nile,[35] wrote a letter to *The Times* in which he attributed the exceptionally low state of the Nile to some "unexplained interference with the river." He adds: "I have seen a spot, about 230 miles from the mouth of the Atbara, where the river might be deflected without difficulty, and be forced to an eastern course towards the Red Sea."[36]

NOTES

1. Wüstenfeld, "Die älteste Ägyptische Geschichte nach den Zauber und Wundererzählungen der Araber," pp. 326–340. A manuscript of this text was kept in the

Asiatic Museum in St. Petersburg (see "Aus den Briefen des Dr. Chwolsohn," p. 408); Brockelmann, *Geschichte der Arabischen Literatur,* p. 409; Supplement 1, p. 574.

2. Perruchon, *La Vie de Lalibala, roi d'Ethiopie,* pp. xx–xxviii. Na'akuto La'ab, Lalibala's successor, is said to have diverted the bed of the river Takkaze during three years and seven months (see Conti Rossini, *Storia d'Etiopia,* p. 310, and *Gli atti di re Na'akuto La'ab,* p. 110; and Cerulli, *Etiopi in Palestina,* p. 118, who reproduces an illustration from a nineteenth-century manuscript showing Na'akuto La'ab blockading the Nile).

3. Dante Alighieri, *Divina Commedia* (Paradiso), pp. ix, 137–138; Petrarca, *Trionfo della Fama,* vol. 2, pp. 141–146.

4. Hayton (Hethum), "La Flor des Estoires de la Terre d'Orient," pp. 232, 241, 247; Blochet, "Neuf chapitres du 'Songe du viel Pélerin,'" vol. 4, pp. 373–374, vol. 5, pp. 144–145; Cerulli, *Etiopi in Palestina,* vol. 1, pp. 20–26, 92–99, 155–161; D. Newbold, quoted in Tamrat, *Church and State in Ethiopia 1270–1527,* p. 252, n. 1.

5. Kohler, "Documents relatifs à Guillaume Adam," pp. 16–17.

6. Röhricht, "Le Pèlerinage du moine augustin Jacques de Vérone (1335)," pp. 155–302.

7. Sir Henry Yule, *Cathay and the Way Thither,* 1866, pp. 3, 177ff.

8. Sigali, "Viaggio al Monte Sinai," p. 202.

9. Potvin, *Oeuvres de Ghillibert de Lannoy voyageur, diplomate et moraliste, recueillies et publiees par Ch. Potvin, avec des notes geographiques et une carte par J. C. Houzeau,* Louvain, 1878.

10. Schefer, "Le Voyage d'Outremer de Bertrandon de la Brocquière," p. 148; La Roncière, "La Découverte," vol. 2, pp. 110–111.

11. Guidi, "Due nuovi manoscritti della Cronaca Abbreviata di Abissinia," pp. 360–361.

12. Creone, "La politica orientale di Alfonso d'Aragone," pp. 40–88.

13. Cerulli, "Il volo di Astolfo," pp. 19–38.

14. Marquis de Lastic, quoted in Tamrat, *Church and State,* p. 264, n. 1; La Roncière, "La Découverte," vol. 2, p. 119.

15. Momigliano, *Storia della Letteratura Italiana,* p. 151.

16. Cerulli, "Il volo di Astolfo."

17. Cerulli, *Etiopi in Palestina,* vol. 1, p. 355; Schefer, "Le Voyage d'Outremer," pp. 5, 99.

18. Maffei, *Historiarum Indicarum libri xvi,* p. 233; De Birch, *The Commentaries of the Great Afonso Dalbuquerque.*

19. Kammerer, *La Mer Rouge,* p. 36; Beccari, *Rerum Aethiopicarum Scriptores,* vol. 1, p. 273ff., vol. 2, p. 255. According to Ullendorff, *The Ethiopians,* p. 14, Conti Rossini established with a fair degree of probability that the sources of the Nile were visited even earlier by Giovanni Gabriel, son of an Italian father and an Abyssinian mother.

20. Kircher, *Oedipus Aegyptiacus,* vol. 1, pp. 50–59.

21. Vossius, *De Nilo et aliorum fluminum origine,* and *Dissertation touchant l'origine du Nil.*

22. Johnson, *A Voyage to Abyssinia by Father Jerome Lobo,* pp. 206–219. In "Dissertation III on the Nile," Le Grand writes: "We do not pretend that a canal cannot be dug from the Nile to the Red-Sea, but that the Abyssins cannot do it" (pp. 218–219).

23. Ludolf, *Historia Aethiopica,* L. 1, c. 8, pp. 76–102; and *Ad suam historiam Aethiopicam Commentarius,* pp. 130–132.

24. Thevenot, *Voyages de M. de Thevenot,* vol. 2, p. 767.

25. See on him van Donzel, *Foreign Relations of Ethiopia 1642–1700,* pp. 12ff; Thevenot, *Voyage de M. de Thevenot,* vol. 2, p. 754.

26. De Birch, *Commentarius of the Great Afonso Dalbuquereque,* p. 265; cp. van Donzel, *Foreign Relations,* p. 177.

27. Ludolf, *Historia Aethiopica,* L. 2, c. 16.

28. Paulus, "J. M. Wansleb bisher ungedruckte Beschreibung von Aegypten," vol. 3, p. 162.

29. Bruce's translation, quoted in Jones and Monroe, *A History of Ethiopia,* p. 117.

30. Bernier, *Travels,* pp. 448–449.

31. Bruce, *Travels to Discover the Source of the Nile,* vol. 3, pp. 712–725.

32. Beke, "Mémoire en rehabilitation des P. P. Paez et Jer. Lobo."

33. Beke, *An Essay on the Nile and Its Tributaries,* and *The Sources of the Nile.*

34. Quoted in Bernier, *Travels,* p. 449, n. 1.

35. Baker, *The Nile Tributaries of Abyssinia.*

36. Quoted in Bernier, *Travels,* p. 449, n. 1.

10

◆

The "Gondar Utopia"

Joachim Warmbold

Novels by German authors about Africa or, at least, with an African back-drop are scarce. The first publication—rather a travelog than a novel—written in German by a German about Africa was Otto Friedrich von der Gröben's *Brandenburgische Schifffahrt nach Guinea* (The Brandenburg Voyage to Guinea), published in 1694, a detailed fact and fiction account of the founding of Groß-Friedrichsburg Castle on the Gold Coast in 1683 by representatives of the Great Elector of Brandenburg.[1] The same subject was then being treated in a novel entitled *Berlin und West-Afrika*, by a certain Heinrich Smidt, published in 1847.[2] Only German colonial rule in Togo, Cameroon, German East Africa, and German southwest Africa, beginning in 1884, set off a veritable flood of *Kolonialliteratur* that, not very differently from the colonial literature of other European countries, depicted Africa and Africans in a rather unfavorable light.[3] With the loss of Germany's colonies after World War I, finalized in the Treaty of Versailles, this literature did not come to an end, though; on the contrary, it flourished and was deliberately promoted during the Third Reich by the Nazis, who considered the subject of Germans in Africa a superb opportunity to propagate their racist views.[4]

Of course, apart from these fictional publications there were scholarly ones by a number of German explorers as well as missionaries, such as Heinrich Barth, Gerhard Rohlfs, Eduard Schnitzer (alias Mehmet Emin Pasha), Gustav Nachtigal, Georg Schweinfurth, Hermann von Wissmann, Leo Frobenius, Johann Ludwig Krapf, and Johannes Rebmann.[5] There were, from the very beginning, translations from Latin, Dutch, English, and French into German of voyages and expeditions to and through Africa by foreign travelers and explorers.[6]

Still, in the seventeenth, eighteenth, and early nineteenth centuries Africa was at best known as a "dark," inhospitable continent. A considerable number of adventurers had to pay for their curiosity with death or lifelong illnesses. The ever negatively slanted reports were completely unsuited to make West, Central, and East Africa acceptable as backgrounds for fictional exotic literature. A Robinson Crusoe in Africa would seem unthinkable, for even if he had not succumbed in the shortest time to malaria, he would doubtless have sought in vain for a loyal Friday amongst the "negroes." While North and South America; the Near, Middle, and Far East; as well as the Pacific Islands proved perfectly suitable for pirate adventures and Robinsonades, enriched with "noble savages," Africa and its peoples remained excluded from the big literary adventure vogue.

Thus, any exception to the rule is most noteworthy. The book I am going to discuss is such an exception. But before I shall turn to the text itself, I would like to take a brief look at its author.

Adolph Franz Friedrich Ludwig von Knigge was born in 1752 on his parents' estate at Bredenbeck, near Hannover, in northern Germany. He was raised and educated at various German courts. As one will remember, Germany as such did not exist in those days; it consisted of a territory split into dozens of independently and autocratically governed states and miniature states, whose rulers, in the vast majority of cases, tried to imitate the glory and splendor of the French royal court. Disgusted with the excesses of absolutism, Knigge gave up his aristocratic title *Freiherr,* the German equivalent of *baron,* and deliberately, and provocatively, called himself "der freie Herr Knigge" (the free Mr. Knigge). Barely twenty years old, Knigge joined the Freemasons, and a little later the so-called Illuminatenorden, a secret society promoting the teachings and ideas of the Enlightenment. From 1791 onward he took up an administrative post in the city of Bremen, which, being a free hanseatic city, provided considerably more freedom than the court of Hesse-Cassel, where he had worked before. Knigge became an ardent defender of the French Revolution and a much feared critic of the ruling aristocracy and its suppressive politics. He published extensively and died in 1796 in Bremen.

Many of Knigge's publications were banned, censored, confiscated, or even falsified, and for a long time the author was deliberately ignored by German literary historians. Only recently have scholars in Germany and abroad shown a new interest in Knigge and his works.[7]

Let me now turn to Knigge's exemplary "Ethiopian" novel. Its complete title reads: *Benjamin Noldmann's Geschichte der Aufklärung in Abyssinien oder Nachricht von seinem und seines Vetters Aufenthalte an dem Hofe des grossen Negus, oder Priesters Johannes* (Benjamin Noldmann's History of the enlightenment in Abyssinia or news of his and his cousin's stay at the court of the great negus, or Priest John). The text was published in 1791, its first edition without the author's name for fear of reprisals by the censor. Yet a second edition, by a different publisher, which appeared in the same year, did mention Knigge's name, and on its title page was printed the rather amusing addition, no doubt aimed at the critics at court: "Mit kaiserl. Abyssinischem allergnädigsten Privilegio" [With the most benevolent imperial Abyssinian authorization].[8] The novel was published in two volumes with 262 and 300 pages, respectively. It is divided into a preface and five main parts and is adorned with six engravings depicting scenes from the text.

I shall now present a brief summary of the five main parts of the novel.

Part 1 describes Benjamin Noldmann's adventurous voyage via England; Madeira; the Canary Islands; Morocco; various West, Central, and East African kingdoms; and, finally, along the Nile, to Abyssinia. Noldmann, a lawyer from Goslar, a little town in the Harz Mountains between Hannover and Göttingen, had received an invitation from the royal court in Gondar to join his cousin, Joseph Wurmbrand, who held the post of minister of state in Gondar. Wurmbrand had reached Abyssinia a few years earlier, also after a series of startling adventures, and is cooperating with the king, "das Aufklärungswesen in Abyssinien mit großem Eifer nach Europäischer Weise zu treiben" [in order to introduce the system of Enlightenment in Abyssinia with great eagerness and according to the European way].[9]

In Part 2 we encounter Noldmann at the court of Gondar. He has been promoted to "Baalomaal und Oberster der Leibgarde" [gentleman of the chamber and colonel of the body guard]; he is studying the social, cultural, and political situation in Abyssinia and its neighboring countries; he is actively involved in developing plans for an enlightened system of government, together with the king and his cousin Wurmbrand. An essential part of the plan is an extensive educational tour of the crown prince of Abyssinia to Germany, following the footsteps of "Czaar Peter der Große von Rußland." Noldmann is requested to accompany the crown prince on this tour, and, after its completion, return to Abyssinia with some "Stück [sic!] Deutscher Gelehrter, Philosophen, Pädagogen, Fabrikanten, Dichter, Mahler, Bildhauer, Tonkünstler u.s.w." [pieces (sic!) of German scholars, philosophers, educators, manufacturers, poets, painters, sculptors, composers, etc.].[10]

Unfortunately, however, as we read in Part 3, the grand educational tour of the crown prince and Noldmann turns out to be a total failure. With the exception of a two-week-long stay in Hamburg, a free city and state, where the prince's "schwarzes Gesicht" [black face] "kaum Aufsehen erregen wird" [will hardly cause a sensation],[11] and where the republican spirit could be sensed everywhere, bad examples abound. The miserable political situation our travelers encounter in various German states and the decadence and corruption at German courts turn the prince into a decadent, physically and mentally corrupted, power-lusting tyrant, and as such he returns—with Noldmann—to Abyssinia five years later.

At Gondar, meanwhile—and this is the content of Part 4—the king and Wurmbrand have failed with their efforts to introduce an enlightened system of government, the German specialists all proved to be a complete disappointment, and, to make things worse, shortly after the return of the crown prince and Noldmann, the old king dies. The crown prince seizes power and, well equipped with all his newly acquired vices made in Germany, establishes an appalling regime of terror and suppression. However, his rule is soon being challenged by a popular revolution in the neighboring state of Nubia, where the people overthrow a similarly despotic monarch. War breaks out between Abyssinia and Nubia. The revolutionaries from Nubia win the war, unite with the Abyssinian people; "unser alberner Negus" [our silly Negus] flees, and, already weakened "durch viehische Ausschweifungen" [by beastly debauchery],[12] dies shortly after, in 1787.

After the tyrant's death, his younger brother takes over. He is an enlightened, good monarch; he calls for a national collegium with twenty-four deputies, two from each of the twelve provinces, and presents his draft of a republican constitution, which is unanimously accepted by the representatives. These events as well as a detailed draft of the constitution can be found in the last and final Part 5 of the novel. Noldmann, his cousin Wurmbrand, and all the other German specialists are sent home by the king, as, according to the new constitution, foreigners are not tolerated anymore in the newly formed government. The two cousins are the only survivors of the voyage back home; they resettle in Goslar, and Noldmann, as the I-narrator, decides to make their adventures public.

Jörg-Dieter Kogel, one of the eminent Knigge scholars,[13] is, of course, absolutely right when stressing that the fictional space Knigge is creating for his readers (by fictional space I mean the descriptions of exotic countries, the travels, the adventures), that all this is a perfectly attractive bait to catch the readers' interest, a well-designed vehicle for transmitting revolutionary messages. And Kogel is equally correct in stating that Knigge's satirical descriptions of corrupt and decadent monarchs, of the latter's despicable exploitation of the people, and of the disastrous effects of well-meant, but badly founded educational processes—like the crown prince's tour through Germany—that all this is in fact Knigge's criticism of the German situation, a criticism he would not have been able to publish openly had it been taken out of its fictional space, had it been clearly marked as criticism of absolute rule in Germany instead of being described as criticism of utopian African courts in general, and the utopian court at

Gondar in particular. And, finally, Kogel is perfectly right when pointing out the many similarities between elements in Knigge's oeuvre and that of Jean-Jacques Rousseau's *Du Contrat Social ou Principes du Droit Politiques,*[14] between Knigge's Abyssinian novel and Montesquieu's *Lettres Persanes,*[15] between Knigge's social utopias and those described in Fénelon's *Les Aventures de Télémaque,*[16] Morelly's *Code de la Nature ou le véritable esprit des lois,*[17] and Albrecht von Haller's *Usong. Eine morgenländische Geschichte.*[18]

Interestingly enough, though, neither Kogel nor any of the other scholars dealing with Knigge ever felt any need to ask the seemingly obvious question: Why did the author choose Africa as a setting for his utopian ideas? Why Abyssinia? Why take the reader to Gondar, and not, as so many of his contemporaries preferred, to a fantasy island, or the Orient, or any of the other standard settings? Could it be that Knigge was familiar with Hiob Ludolf's *Historia Aethiopica,*[19] or did he have other sources of inspiration? Had he possibly met personally with one or several of the "Mohren" (Moors), as Africans were called in those days, at the various German courts he was familiar with? It is an established fact that Mohren were considered a fashionable addition to courts and rich households in Knigge's time, that they were imported, bought, and used as porters, servants, musicians, and we even know of an exceptional case where a certain Anton Wilhelm Amo, who had been working at the court of Wolfenbüttel, was allowed to study at the University of Halle and became a professor of philosophy at Jena University between 1739 and 1747.[20] In short: as valuable as any research about Knigge's sources of philosophical and political inspiration may be, the African question should definitely not be overlooked, or simply left unanswered.[21]

Knigge's *Geschichte der Aufklärung in Abyssinien* (and with this I am returning to Kogel) is a clear product of "Zweckliteratur,"[22] of *littérature engagée,* written out of truly felt support and admiration for the French Revolution, an attempt at combining the historical experience of the French people from 1789 with his (Knigge's) personal hopes for a revolutionary process on German soil.

Being a German revolutionary, however, Knigge does not completely subscribe to the French recipe. As we have seen, any attempt at introducing the principles of Enlightenment from above, at the monarch's initiative, must fail: the old king, although willing to try—with Wurmbrand's help—a few reforms, is at the same time afraid of granting the essential element of freedom to his people. The negus enthusiastically supports Wurmbrand's idea of "Wissenschaften und Künste in seinem Lande blühen zu machen" [making the sciences and the arts blossom in his country] but simultaneously introduces "eine Bücher-Censur" [book censorship]. Not at the rulers' initiative, well meant as it may be, will real, positive changes occur, as Knigge laconically writes: "Man bekehrt die Despoten und ihre Kinder nicht" [one cannot convert despots and their children]. No, real change will only be brought upon by a popular uprising, like the Nubian—and later Abyssinian—revolution. "Fürchterliche Grausamkeiten und Ungerechtigkeiten" [terrible cruelties and injustices] in connection with such an uprising must, according to Knigge, be accepted. "An wem liegt denn die Schuld" [who is to blame], he writes, "wenn abscheuliche Mißbräuche, verzweiflungsvolle Mittel unvermeidlich machen?" [when disgusting abuses make desperate means unavoidable].[23]

Yet—and this is the specific German element in Knigge's philosophy, I am afraid—after the revolution, after all the violence and bloodshed, a strong, even authoritarian leadership will be necessary to secure a stable, enlightened system of government. This is why in our text a postrevolutionary, enlightened, and therefore "guter Prinz" [good prince] is introduced, almost like a deus ex machina, the brother of the evil former crown prince, a new monarch who has quietly and diligently learned his lesson, without being in power yet and thus being positively predisposed, and who is willing to share his power with "Deputierten" in a "National-Versammlung" [national assembly].[24] All in all, as we can see, Knigge's Gondar utopia has its limits: revolution, yes, but no unrestricted power to the people. Enlightenment, yes, but under enlightened aristocratic guidance. Still, with all its limitations with regard to its ultimate political consequences, Knigge's novel is a true masterpiece of enlightened, and revolutionary, literature written and published in Germany.

One might even say—and this takes me back to the opening of the chapter: Knigge's *Geschichte der Aufklärung in Abyssinien* is the first and, unfortunately, only publication by a German author projecting an—and I deliberately use this term now—*enlightened* image of Africa. True, Gondar, Abyssinia, Africa, are depicted as "exotic," but Knigge's exoticism does not involve a distinct eurocentric perspective, something that, a mere hundred years later, has become the norm. Corrupt African monarchs are not any more corrupt, despicable, or ridiculous than the ones the reader, Noldmann, and the crown prince encounter in Germany. Nubians and Abyssinians are not any different in their sufferings under absolute rule from Germans. Africans are, as shameful as this may sound, still normal human beings, no savages, no black devils, no underdeveloped poor souls, or whatever other stereotypes one might quote from colonial or even contemporary German "Afrikaliteratur." Paradoxically, Knigge's novel at times seems like a perfect example of anticolonial or even postcolonial literature with its descriptions of despots supported by European advisers and experts, with its presentation of European political and social models that fail in the African context, and, most unique indeed, with its emphasis on African superiority. Since, as we must not forget, it is only in Africa, in Nubia and Abyssinia, that a revolution leads to a new, enlightened political system, Germany in Knigge's novel remains under the rule of numerous tyrants. Only because of the new Abyssinian constitution, drafted by an enlightened Abyssinian king and his equally enlightened national collegium and presented to the German readers by Noldmann/Knigge, is there hope for a change in Germany, too. Thus the myth of "darkest Africa," which badly needs European Enlightenment, is happily turned around by Knigge: for him it is "darkest Germany" in dire need of African Enlightenment.

Knigge's *Geschichte der Aufklärung in Abyssinien* has a lot more to offer to the modern reader than one might expect from a 200-year-old publication. It offers a stunningly different perspective guiding the readers' eyes not up but down the Nile toward Germany and Europe, a unique, an enlightened, a utopian view in German literature about Africa.

NOTES

1. Von der Gröben, *Brandenburgischen Schifffahrt nach Guinea.*
2. Smidt, *Berlin und West-Afrika.*
3. Warmbold, *Germania in Africa;* see especially pp. 49–96.
4. Ibid.; see especially pp. 97–129.
5. For bibliographical data see, for example, Heine and van der Heyden, *Studien zur Geschichte,* and Warmbold, *Germania in Africa.*
6. For bibliographical data see, for example, Atkinson, *The Extraordinary Voyage in French Literature Before 1700;* Mercier, *L'Afrique Noire dans la littérature Française;* Hamann, *Der Eintritt der südlichen Hemisphäre in die europäische Geschichte;* and Bitterli, *Die Entdeckung des schwarzen Afrikaners.*
7. The latest edition of Knigge's works is Adolph von Knigge, *Ausgewählte Werke in zehn Bänden* translated by Wolfgang Fenner; the latest bibliographical data can be found in Arnold, *Adolph Freiherr Knigge.*
8. I am using the reprint of the "Erstausgabe," Knigge, *Benjamin Noldmanns Geschichte der Aufklärung in Abyssinien,* vols. 1 and 2. Hereafter, page number indications are given with vols. 1 and 2, for first and second volume of the original, respectively.
9. Ibid., vol. 1, p. 182.
10. Ibid., vol. 1, pp. 182, 258, 261.
11. Ibid., vol. 2, p. 9.
12. Ibid., vol. 2, pp. 154, 159.
13. Kogel, *Knigges ungewöhnliche Empfehlungen.*
14. First published in 1762.
15. First published in 1721.
16. First published in 1699.
17. First published 1755–1760.
18. First published in 1771. For a detailed discussion of the various influences on Knigge, see Kogel, *Knigges ungewöhnliche Empfehlungen,* pp. 17–31.
19. First published in Frankfurt, 1681–1694, 4 vols.

20. See, for example, Brentjes, *Anton Wilhelm Amo,* and Sadji, *Der Neger-mythos am Ende des 18.*

21. Veronika Six from Hamburg pointed out to me that she was presently doing research about Knigges's possible sources of information and inspiration for his Abyssinian novel. She is planning to publish the results of her research soon, and therefore it would be somewhat unfair to report here on the discussion we had.

22. Kogel, *Knigges ungewöhnliche Empfehlungen,* p. 32.

23. Knigge, *Geschichte der Aufklärung in Abyssinien,* vol. 2, pp. 111, 123, 150.

24. Ibid., vol. 2, pp. 167, 168, 239.

11

♦

The Nile as a Gateway for Missionary Activity in Abyssinia

Uoldelul Chelati Dirar

Missionary expansion in Africa has been studied intensively and extensively. Scholars have examined carefully the main social, cultural, political, and of course, religious consequences of this phenomenon. However, despite this impressive research, little attention has been paid to the role played by the environment and more generally by the geographical context as a facilitating or disabling factor in the missionary scramble for Africa. This is quite surprising because the environment was the first major problem with which missionary activities in Africa had to cope. In fact for a long time, environment, as a result of both climatic conditions and tropical diseases, restricted missionary activities to the coast of Africa and, more significantly, strongly influenced most of the famous missionary plans for the evangelization of Africa. Recent progress in both missionary and African studies requires a more comprehensive approach incorporating an analysis of the entirety of the relationship between society, environment, and missionary expansion.[1] This chapter discusses the role played by the Nile in the spreading of missionary societies in nineteenth-century Ethiopia.

There has always been a close and constant connection between geography and missions. Missionaries, as a consequence, but also as a necessity of their pioneering travel, were among the first to draw maps of Africa, to give extensive descriptions of African societies, and to draft grammar of African languages as well. Of course we have come a long way since the first maps simply described Africa as divided between "Etiopia" and the land of *hic sunt leones,* otherwise of barbarians and foolishness; but the analysis of this evolution would lead us too far from the topic of this chapter. What I would like to underline, as we will examine later, is that, though in a rough and sometimes inconsistent way, missionaries never stopped accumulating data and storing them away for future (if not for immediate) use.

Information, collected by assembling Greek and Roman literature, official reports, memoirs of travelers, and also fantastic stories, combined to sketch a blurred image of Africa but one able to kindle the keen interest of traders, explorers, and (why not?) politicians. At this level we can safely speak about an interaction between myth and geography.[2] Anyway what must be stressed here is that since the first maps and planispheres were drawn, the Nile was the element that most caught the rapt attention of European geographers.[3] Although outlined in a very fanciful way, the course of the Nile was depicted as a gateway to a fabulous region inhabited by black peoples who were affluent with gold, ivory, and spices. And it could not have been different, as long as the Nile, with its yearly flood and dregs of fecund humus, epitomized the idea of wealth and opulence.

In this composite process of knowledge and imagination, what about Ethiopia? Although often perceived as a synonym for the whole of Africa, Ethiopia has been one of the preferred objects of both geographical and missionary regard. There is also great evidence of the diffusion of an image of Ethiopia (though a mythical one) in European literature since the Middle Ages.[4] Such references give a clear idea of the familiarity of European culture with the "idea" of Ethiopia, and at the same time they raise questions about the reasons for that particular interest. First of all to feed this particular interest were the fabulous descriptions of treasures and lush landscape that filled the reports of travelers as well as the Greek and Roman descriptions. However, for people of faith the main reason for such interest was the recurrent description of the ancient Christian roots of Ethiopia firmly surviving in a continent generally perceived as drifted away by a dozing paganism and a fanatic Islam. Another factor that maintained the interest in Ethiopia alive was the regular flow of Ethiopian pilgrims to the Holy Land, some of whom prolonged their journey to Rome.[5] Those pilgrims in Jerusalem had the invaluable opportunity of getting in touch with people from all over the Christian world, receiving information from them about the troubled theological debate and about the main social and political changes in the East and in the West. At the same time Ethiopian pilgrims, particularly those who went to Rome, acted as spreaders of news about the general situation of Ethiopia.[6] In this sense the famous institute known as Santo Stefano Maggiore dei Mori in Rome, which operated more or less uninterrupted from the end of the fifteenth century to the end of the nineteenth, had a pivotal role in the definition of the Catholic image of Ethiopia and in delineating missionary strategies toward this country.[7]

This complex and extremely lively network of relationships and of cultural exchanges contributed significantly to the development of three important myths that had long conditioned the European approach toward Ethiopia and the development of the Ethiopian national identity as well. I am referring here to the myth of the Prete Janni (Prester or Priest John), the myth of Ethiopia as a Christian island, and to the myth of Semitic Ethiopia. All those myths are strictly connected and must be regarded as the expression of Europe's interest toward Ethiopia, but also in the long term as expression of the European wish of using exoticism as an instrument of knowledge. Otherwise, borrowing with due caution the analytical concepts offered by Edward Said's analysis of Orientalism, exoticism could also be described as a way of affirming, or perpetuating, European and Christian domination by forcing different cultures into insulated paradigms.

As long as it operated, the myth of Prete Janni was a powerful bait for the travelers and missionaries keen to revive the greatness of the Christendom. In fact the quest for Prete Janni gathered an astonishing amount of mental and material resources and by so doing made way for a long and fascinating history of contacts between Abyssinia and Europe.[8]

Closely connected to this was the mythical image of Ethiopia as a Christian island in a troubled sea of paganism and Islam. I am not going to repeat the history of that well-known image, but I would like to emphasize the importance that this image had in the planning of both Catholic and Protestant missionary strategies.[9]

Finally, connected with the previous myth we must consider the myth of the Semitic specificity of Ethiopia. Risen mainly as a product of the linguistic studies of orientalists and missionaries, the myth of Semitic Ethiopia empowered missionaries and later colonial pretensions over this country on the basis of the supposed superiority of Semitic roots over sub-Saharan Africa. By the way, it is interesting to see how those assumptions found part of their legitimacy by emphasizing the pre-existing Ethiopian national epic of the Solomonic tradition but were also embodied in twentieth-century Ethiopia's "nationalism."[10]

It is with that background that at the beginning of the nineteenth century arose a renewed interest of missionaries toward Ethiopia. What made particular this new wave of missionary activities was both the composition and the reasons of the protagonists. On the one hand, in western Europe the Christian Church was not anymore a monolithic reality; doctrinal debates and conflicts had split the Church, and now, besides Roman Catholics, there were also Protestant missionaries eager to shepherd flocks of pagans and heretics toward the true light of the Gospel. On the other hand, the reasons of missionary expansion had also changed. During the eighteenth century, because of the diffusion of rationalist theories and of the political changes put in motion by the French Revolution, Christendom in Europe had experienced a deep crisis that had seriously endangered its spiritual and material leadership.

As a consequence, missionary expansion was seen as the only way to put new oxygen into a wheezing Church. Apart from theology the main differences between Catholics and Protestants were the premises of their missionary strategies. Catholics looked at the integral conversion of pagan and heretic peoples because they thought, by so doing, they would inject fresh blood into the anemic body of Christian Europe. Behind that theory there was the idea that African peoples, because of their seclusion from corrupted and degenerated Europe, had lived in a state of eternal and un-contaminated childhood and when educated to the values of the Bible would regenerate the Christendom.[11] On the other side Protestants also looked at Africa and Asia as continents from which new life was expected to come, but, with a slight difference. Instead of a direct and total conversion they preferred to put in motion an intense theological debate. The purpose of that debate, mainly in the case of the so-called Oriental Churches, was the starting of an internal awakening whose consequences, in the long term, would have been fruitful for all Christendom. From a theological perspective, the basis of that awakening was to be the renunciation of external ritual in favor of a more internal and "rational" worship.

It is into this composite and often unpredictable framework that should be fitted the analysis of the role of the Nile in the missionary expansion of the nineteenth century. A first consideration to be made is that the Nile, although not always explicitly, played an important role in the first missionaries' steps in Ethiopia. The first and most obvious reason for that is that the Nile appeared to be the easiest and most direct route to both Ethiopia and equatorial Africa. But reality was completely different, and often the Nile disclosed an unpredicted range of pitfalls that ruthlessly decimated or simply hindered the missionary flock, frustrating the rush of the first half of the nineteenth century. Nevertheless, though the Nile ceased to be considered a real gateway to missionary penetration in Abyssinia, it started to become a mythological gateway. In this second role, the Nile as a myth became an ideological weapon functional to the missionary scramble for Africa (not only for Abyssinia). At this level the differences between mythological and ideological levels were particularly dim. What can be said, for sake of clarity, is that, before the nineteenth-century missionary and colonial interest in Africa, the Nile was more an "idea," suggesting the possible existence of mysterious people living on its banks in far and inaccessible countries, rather than a geographically defined entity.

In the nineteenth century, in spite of an increasing amount of geographical knowledge and also after the discovery of the sources of the Nile, this river still retained its mythological dimension of a gateway toward Africa, becoming an important aspect of missionary ideologies. Strange as it might seem there is an interesting parallelism between the role played by the Nile and the Niger, the two most important and, at that time, most mysterious African rivers in the missionary and colonial partition of Africa. In fact both were seen as the key for European penetration into the "dark core" of Africa and as the best way to achieve the spreading of the Gospel and the eradication of the plague of the slave trade. A first important episode to be reported is the organized, though initially fruitless, way the Church Missionary Society, strongly supported by the British government, organized three expeditions on the Niger.[12] The aim of those expeditions was to explore the course of the river, establishing the basis for the study of the languages spoken there and the subsequent starting of a diffused missionary activity. Behind this ambitious project there was the idea that the Niger, unknown as it must have been, was indeed the best way to penetrate the interior of Africa in order to fight the slave trade and by so doing to soothe one of the plagues of the black continent. In the word of one of the outstanding promoters of this expedition: "I can form no conception of a stronger argument in favour of carrying thither civilization and Christianity, than the existence of the Slave Trade itself, as it is found at this day,"[13] and after, "It is the Bible and the plough that must regenerate Africa."[14]

Something very similar happened in respect to the Nile during the same period. Before the nineteenth century many European travelers had used this river as one of the ways to access Ethiopia, and most of them were missionaries.[15] What kindled a new and more intense interest toward the Nile were the discussed memoirs of the Scottish traveler James Bruce of Kinnard. In fact his description of Ethiopian societies and traditions as well as his claim to have discovered the sources of the Nile significantly influenced any successive travel, and for a long time his work was seen as obligatory references.

The importance of Bruce's memoirs seems to be in his vivid account of Christian and pagan Ethiopia, which renewed the old interest of missionary agencies. In the new diffused atmosphere of revivalism of those years, Ethiopia and the Nile became a turning point for missionary strategies. There is strong evidence in the archival and missionary literature of the nineteenth century of a perception of Ethiopia and the Nile as gateways toward Africa. This pattern was clearly expressed by the German missionary J. L. Krapf when he said, "As the Romanist missionary said, 'Give us China and Asia is Ours' so may we say 'Give us Gallas and Central Africa is ours.'"[16] Also, more explicit was the Roman Catholic missionary Guglielmo Massaja when, writing about Daniele Comboni's *Piano per la rigenerazione dell'Africa,* said that it was a good plan but applied in the wrong area. In fact he thought that Ethiopia would have been the best place from which to start a general conversion of Africa. It is a document that, though quite long, needs to be quoted extensively:

"The plan of Daniele Comboni has to be reduced to the eastern part of Africa, this inhabited by Semitic races more capable of being educated and the only part that has a future, for three reasons: (1) Ethiopia is the best zone, partly Christian party pagan, and the richest and healthiest in Africa. (2) It is cultivated and held by a nation of religion capable of re-uniting millions of Christians. (3) Because it is located in the middle of Islam and it is so near to Mecca that it will be an operation, perhaps the only one, that may stop the progress of Islam. The Ethiopian Christians, who constitute less than a third of these peoples, waged war for twelve centuries against Islam. In so doing they managed to save their faith and save all those regions to the south. If Ethiopia could do so with only three or four million inhabitants, why will it not be done by all those countries together, united by the same Christian relgion?[17]

This letter has the value of a manifesto of missionary ideology; moreover, we can find assembled some of the main stereotypes of the new strategy toward Ethiopia and Africa in general: the idea of the superiority of the Semitic element over the rest of sub-Saharan Africa; the image of Ethiopia as a Christian Island in perennial fight against Islam; and eventually Ethiopia as lighthouse and basis for a further missionary expansion.

It is interesting to observe that in this optimistic period of evangelical expansion, but also some years later, Ethiopia tended to be viewed as a wonderland where everybody could find what they wanted. Priests of the Lazarist order wanted to convert heretic Christians, and they found them in the borderland between Tigray, Akkala Guzay, and Karan and in some way contributed in laying the basis for Eritrean nationalism. In the same way, the London Society for Promoting Christianity amongst the Jews found its de-sired object in the Falashas, as did Joseph Halevy some years after on behalf of the *Alliance Israelite Universelle*.[18] The same happened to the Oromo people who were the object of desire for many different missionary soci-eties, although the only one that could work there with a certain degree of intensity was the order of Cappuccini, led by the famous Cardinal Massaja.

Indeed the history of missionary penetration amongst the Oromo is a fascinating one and can be regarded as a paradigm of the process of imag-ination of identities in colonial and precolonial Africa.[19] Missionary atti-tudes toward Oromo swung between a mere acceptance of Ethiopian stereotypes—which described Oromo as an outsider people with a low de-gree of social and cultural cohesiveness—and an assertive policy of rede-finition of Oromo identities. The latter attitude emerged as a dual policy. On a theoretical perspective, Oromo as a "backward" and "savage" peo-ple were appointed as the key for the conversion of Ethiopia and through Ethiopia for the whole of the African continent. At the same time, mis-sionaries put in motion their traditional praxis consisting of intensive translations of the Bible and other religious material in the Oromo language, the grammatical pattern of which was first codified by them in those years.[20]

From this new perspective it is interesting to see the sudden change of tone in missionary reports. As soon as Oromo became a privileged target of proselytism, they lost the attributes of ruthless and wild cruelty usually employed to depict them. They suddenly became a dull and sluggish people to be patronized and protected from the violence of the Christian Orthodox of the highlands and from the slave trade. So, again, the old missionary and colonial obsession of eradicating the slave trade connected European activities in the region of the Nile with what was happening in West Africa and on the banks of the Niger. Later on, in 1869, the Nile too, though in a more secular and violent way, would have its own expedition against the merchant of flesh that infested its banks in those years,[21] but it was to be mainly a military expedition.[22]

So far we have examined the function of the Nile as a gateway for nineteenth-century missionary strategies, but it would be too simplistic to confine the analysis to this aspect. In fact another important characteristic of the Nile was that of being an impressive hindrance, frustrating the attempted expansion toward Ethiopia. This is its most dramatic aspect, because it implied the death, often tragic, of many missionaries.[23]

One reason for the high mortality rate was the climatic conditions. Malaria and other tropical diseases killed many European missionaries and were factors that indirectly influenced Comboni's *Piano per la rigenerazione dell'Africa*.[24] In fact, behind the idea of utilizing Africans as missionaries instead of Europeans, there was not only the thought that Africans would be better accepted because of their knowledge of the social and cultural environment but also the thought that Africans would better tolerate the harsh climatic conditions of the region.

Another reason reported by missionary sources about the difficulty in entering Ethiopia by the Nile was connected with politics and particularly with the feeling of bitter resentment engendered in the populations that used to live on the southern banks of the Nile. As a consequence of the ruthless and bloody ransacking effected by Turks and Egyptians, those peoples tended to identify all white travelers with agents of the Turks and for that reason sought to take their revenge on them.

Eventually the most banal but nevertheless forbidding reason that periodically transformed the Nile into an obstacle was the regular period of drought that for some months transmuted the river into a muddy stream, restraining the travelers coming from Egypt to the dreadful climate of Khartum.

At the end, the last perspective from which we can analyze the Nile in relation to missionary activities in northeastern Africa and particularly in Ethiopia is that of the Nile as an outlet. Particularly for what concerned the missionary stations among the Oromo people living south of Goggiam, the Nile—during the rainy season that made it unfordable—became a sort of natural and self-patrolled border that protected people and missionaries from the raids of the Ethiopian Imperial army or from the pillaging of the local lords.[25] From the same perspective there is a recurrent tendency of the missionaries, mainly Catholic, to consider the borderland around Matamma and the Sudanese branch of the Blue Nile as a harbor. There they could find shelter during the unpredictable war or persecution that missionaries experienced in the first years of their activity in Ethiopia. The idea of a network of missionary stations scattered on the border of the Ethiopian empire is a recurrent one in this period, but the most clearly expressed is that proposed by the Italian Lazarist Giuseppe Sapeto. In a report forwarded to the board of Propaganda Fide Sapeto, he suggested building up missionary stations on the Red Sea and in the Sannar, proposing to use them as safe haven for missionaries and the converted. In this way, once a storm had passed, the frustrating and hard burden of restarting the work in the field would be avoided. A second aim of the project was the possibility of utilizing those bases as hostels for the pilgrims directed to Jerusalem.[26]

From the same perspective, because of one of the strange coincidences of history, Matamma and the Nile tended to be also the sad road to exile for many of the most famous missionaries.[27] A last but marginal aspect is that of the Nile as *lieu de perdition* (symbol of the loss of moral integrity and of faith) in the missionary purpose. From this point of view the Nile could be seen as a metaphor of the dark heart of Africa. That is an aspect of missionary pitfalls, mainly on the Catholic side, that has not received due attention yet. In the context of this discussion I would like to underline only that from missionary sources there emerges a blundered idea of the Nile as a place where missionaries could lose their interior equilibrium as expressed in renouncing celibacy or in the temptation of commerce and the achievement of material rather than spiritual wealth.[28] Finally, both on the Protestant and Catholic sides there are recurrent warnings against the bait of science. This could refer to the desire to discover the source of the river,[29] as well as to the "excessive attention to the study of languages.[30]

After this long sketch of the multiple and often contrasting features of the Nile during the missionary period spreading over Africa there is a question to be answered that could eventually lead to a provisional conclusion. The question, which mainly referred to the Catholic side of the missionaries, is: Why is there such a sharp contrast between the mythological idea of the Nile carried by missionaries and the wide and often very detailed geographical and social knowledge that the main missionary organizations, such as Propaganda Fide, used to have? During the centuries, the archives of Propaganda Fide, as well as most of the archives of many other congregations, collected an impressive amount of historical, anthropological, linguistic, and of course also geographical materials. Those materials, integrated with the regular exchanges with the Ethiopian pilgrims who used to visit Jerusalem and Rome, should have enabled the missionaries to have a clearer idea of the places that they were going to visit. On the contrary we notice a general lack of communication between the high hierarchies of the ecclesiastic establishment and the missionaries in the field. In other words, the wide knowledge collected at the center failed to become a common heritage of the new generations of missionaries in the field.

This is not the place for an extensive evaluation of such a complex matter. However, I would like to prospect some general hypotheses. The first evidence to be pointed out is that the missionary milieu was troubled by deep conflicts and rivalries. Those conflicts were not only between Catholics and Protestants but also between the different religious orders and missionary *congregationes.* Internal rivalries and a sort of missionary "scramble for Africa" could be one of the possible reasons behind this lack of communication.

Another possible reason often undervalued in the studies on missionary activities could be founded in the high budgets with which priests and ministers had to deal. A shortage of funds was often the main reason that influenced the choice of the itineraries. In fact, it must be remembered that missionaries, particularly the Catholics, suffered a chronic lack of money. That problem often hampered missionary plans. This would be increasingly true after the colonial partition of Africa, when, for example, colonial administrations used to offer free passages to missionaries on boats.[31]

No less important was the role played by the background of missionaries in the field. Often they had very short training and serious difficulties in understanding and making operational the instructions that came from the high hierarchies.

Last but not least, there is an interesting and, at the moment, little explored aspect of missionary activity that could disclose new insights. I am referring here to the role played by Africans in the development of the European image of Africa. Whatever the concern for missionary activities in Ethiopia, it would be interesting to see how deeply the European image of Abyssinia and, of course, the Nile was affected by the information given by Ethiopian monks and pilgrims during their travel to the Holy Land and Europe. I think that in the long term this kind of approach could lead to a more balanced comprehension of African history and of the history of the relationships between Africa and Europe. It is important to also adopt in missionary studies a perspective that focuses attention on the assertive role of Africans in both colonial and missionary history.

NOTES

1. For an interesting review of the main scholarly works on missionology and African Church history, see Spindler, "Writing African Church History 1969–1989, pp. 70–87; and Melloni, "Facteurs involutifs et lignes de développement, pp. 283–310.

2. See Conti Rossini, "Leggende giudaiche del IX secolo," pp. 160–190, and "Il 'Libro del Conoscimiento,'" pp. 656–679.

3. See Lefevre, "L'Etiopia nella stampa del primo Cinquecento," pp. 345–369, and "Geografica I," pp. 215–233; Crawford, *Ethiopian Itineraries;* and Conti Rossini, "Geografica I," pp. 167–199.

4. Cerulli, "Il volo di Astolfo," pp. 19–38; Conti Rossini, "Il 'Libro del Conoscimiento,'" pp. 656–679.

5. On the history of Ethiopian pilgrims to Jerusalem, the most important work is still Cerulli, *Etiopi in Palestina,* vol. 2.

6. Lefevre, "Roma e la Comunità etiopica," pp. 71–86; Lefevre, "Note su alcuni pellegrini etiopi," pp. 16–26; Lefevre, "Presenze etiopi in Italia," pp. 5–26.

7. On the history of this institution the most important contribution remains Leonessa's, *S. Stefano Maggiore o degli Abissini.*

8. An important example of the strength of this myth in the history of European attraction toward Ethiopia is Alvarez, *The Prester John of the Indies.*

9. Last but not least this myth has played a central role in the development of Ethiopian national identity and by so doing has also strongly influenced Ethiopia's foreign policy. On this topic see Iyob, *The Eritrean Struggle for Independence,* and Sorenson, *Imagining Ethiopia.*

10. On the complex process of development of the Solomonic epic in the nineteenth and twentieth centuries see Crummey, "Imperial Legitimacy," pp. 13–43; and Levine, "Menilek and Oedipus," pp. 11–23.

11. It is interesting to see that in this way the Roman Catholics utilized, though from a different perspective, the rationalistic myth of the *bon sauvage.*

12. The first was in 1841, the second in the 1854, and the last in 1857. Of the last expedition there is an interesting journal written by two outstanding Nigerian missionaries, Rev. Samuel Crowther and Rev. John Christopher Taylor. It permits a fascinating inside regard of the expedition viewed with African, though converted, eyes (see Crowther and Taylor, *The Gospel on the Bank of the Niger*).

13. T. F. Buxton, *The African Slave Trade and Its Remedy,* p. 512.

14. C. Buxton, *Memoirs of Sir Thomas Fowell Buxton,* p. 451.

15. Some of the most important were Remedius Prutkij and Michelangelo Pacelli da Tricarico, whose memoirs constitute a precious source for both missionary and Ethiopian history (see Prutsky, *Prutsky's Travels in Ethiopia and Other Countries,* and Stella, *Il viaggio in Etiopia di Michelangelo Pacelli*).

16. Krapf, *Travels, Researches, and Missionary Labours,* p. 24.

17. "Letter of G. Massaja to Card. Alessandro Barnabo," in Massaja, *Lettere,* p. 208, translated here by the author. The original text is as follows:

Il piano di D. Daniele Comboni dovrebbe ridursi alla parte più orientale dell'Affrica, quella che è abitata da razze semitiche più capaci di educazione, e quasi l'unica parte che presenti un avvenire in grande per queste tre ragioni: 1. L'Etiopia è zona migliore, parte cristiana parte pagana la più ricca e più salubre di tutta l'Affrica. 2. Perchè coltivata e concentrata in nazione della religione può riunire molti milioni di cristiani.

3. Perchè luogo situato proprio al centro di tutto l'islamismo e tutto vicino alla Mecca sarebbe un operazione, forse l'unica che potrebbe arrestare i progressi dell'islamismo medesimo. L'Abissinia cristiana, che non fa il terzo di tutte quelle popolazioni, conta dodeci secoli di guerra contro l'islamismo. Con ciò ha potuto salvare la sua fede e salvare tutti gli alti piani a sud di essa. Se l'Abissinia ha potuto fare questo con soli tre o quattro milioni di abitanti, cosa non farebbero tutti quei paesi insieme uniti dalla medesima religione cristiana?

18. See Kaplan, "The Beta Israel (Falasha) Encounter with Protestant Missionaries, 1860–1905," pp. 27–42; also very interesting though mainly connected with fascist policy toward Jews and Beta Israel is Trevisan-Semi, *Allo specchio dei Falascia.*

19. I am using the word *imagination* here in the sense given by T. Ranger in his recent revision of the category of "tradition" that he had previously elaborated upon in the famous Hobsbawm and Ranger, *The Invention of Tradition;* see Ranger, "The Invention of Tradition Revisited," pp. 129–172.

20. Arens, *Evangelical Pioneers in Ethiopia,* pp. 383–387, and Massaja, *I miei trentacinque.*

21. Noting slave trade in Sudan and Ethiopia. See Abdussamad Ahmad, "Ethiopian Slave Exports."

22. Some of the most interesting reports of this expedition are to be found in S. Baker, *Ismailiya,* and A. Baker, *Morning Star.*

23. On this aspect of missionary experience, see Gaffuri, *Africa o morte.*

24. This plan, though proclaimed as particularly innovative, seems to be mainly the best-known expression of a common feeling amongst the missionaries in the field. In this sense there was no difference between Catholics and Protestants and very similar projects were proposed quite simultaneously in different regions. In the case of Nigeria, see Ajayi, *Christian Missions in Nigeria,* pp. 8–16, and Ayandele, *The Missionary Impact on Modern Nigeria,* pp. 20–25. Something similar happened also in Algeria with Cardinal Lavigerie's schemes. For the vicariate of Abyssinia with De Jacobis see APF, "P. Etienne to Propaganda Fide," p. 214, and "Poussou to Fransoni," p. 451. For the "Vicariate of the Gallas," see Massaja, *Lettere,* vol. 1, pp. 43–46, 352–358.

25. Massaja, *Lettere,* vol. 2, p. 53.

26. APF, "Sapeto to Propaganda Fide," pp. 233–240.

27. It was by this route that Massaja, Krapf, and many others left Ethiopia. Nevertheless, though little attention has been paid to the Catholic bishop Tobia Gheresghier, he was one of the first illustrious missionaries to leave the country through this way and was forced to retreat from Ethiopia in 1792 (APF, "Tobia Gheresghier to the Pope," p. 496).

28. Regarding commerce, one aspect of missionary failures, an interesting episode is referred to in Massaja with reference to the Catholic missionary Angelo Vinco (see Massaja, *Lettere,* pp. 347–352).

29. "Suggestion of the Committee to the Missionaries," *Proceedings of the Church Missionary Society* 29, p. 138.

30. APF, "Istruzioni fatte in Sinodo da Mons. G. Massaja," pp. 308–340; see also Massaja, *I miei 35 anni di missione,* pp. 124–125.

31. For example in 1851 the French foreign ministry ordered that all missionaries directed to the Horn of Africa and the Red Sea were to be offered free access to French vessels (APF, "Brenier to Havett," p. 352).

Part 3

◆

Old Waters,
Modern Identities

12

◆

The Father of Rivers: The Nile in Ethiopian Literature

Bairu Tafla

The Nile, the sea, and Islam were perhaps the most significant factors that played a role for a thousand or more years in the foreign relations of Ethiopia. A great deal has been researched and published about each of them, but the history of the Nile seems still far from being exhausted, as the themes of this and other volumes show.[1] The Nile has played, and will probably do so further, an important role in the history of Ethiopia. It has been one of the major historical factors that drew the attention of the country more toward the Middle East than toward the regions to the south of it. If we imagine the country in the form of a human being sitting on an elevated place, then Ethiopia has been unmistakably looking northwards, watching its neighbors flourish on its flooding rivers, and its enemies encroaching into its valleys. It was the magnetic Nile that intrigued explorers as early as the Roman times and as late as the twentieth century; it drew to its vast valley adventurers who sought gold, slaves, and gum arabicum, lured foreign missionaries to preach the Gospel to the numerous peoples of the grand valley, and attracted the colonialists to possess a major part of the region. It was precisely in this direction that most of the bloodiest battles of Ethiopia were fought in the period from 1840 to 1900. Conferences, consultations, and treaties that began in the aftermath are still momentous.[2] And who knows what exactly took place in the watershed of this mysterious river in earlier periods?

From the remote times, we have mainly legends left, at least for the upper course of the Nile, which nonetheless indicates that the Alexandrian metropolitan and the Nile were occasionally the objects of bargain between Ethiopia and Egypt. The legends also include the peoples, civilizations, and cultures that intermittently moved along the Nile throughout the

153

centuries. No wonder then that Emperor Haile Selassie emphasized in his speech during an official visit to the Republic of Sudan in January 1960 that, since history began to be recorded, the Nile contributed toward "the heritage of culture and economic similarities" of the neighboring countries.[3]

The aim of this chapter is not to describe the foreign relations of Ethiopia or the economic potentialities of the Nile or the politics ensuing from the complexity of the problems that the longest river in the world involves, but rather to assess the notion and the role of the Nile in Ethiopian literature in the widest sense of the term. It seems that this area has been scarcely treated, though the peoples' thoughts, beliefs, and imagination must also have played a part in the attitudes and policymaking of their leaders. It is an attempt at identifying and analyzing the various aspects of the popular notion of the greatest river, how this notion is articulated in the oral traditions, and to consider some of the perspectives of its intellectual expression. In this preliminary study, three components lend themselves easily to identification: the awe-inspiring nature of the Nile, the formidable obstacle that the river poses, and the treacherous character of the stream.

Before considering the vicissitudes of these points, it is necessary to straighten up a few points. A conclusive study of such a topic requires thorough research, which in turn presupposes accessing full information on the subject. Unfortunately, not all the oral traditions have been collected and archived nor have all novels and other works in Ethiopian languages been available abroad. Hence, this chapter remains preliminary in character, and any statement made is liable to change in the face of new evidence or the reconsideration of a fresh interpretation.

THE ABBAY—A SYMBOL OF THE NATION

Ethiopia is full of torrential rivers, some of which are comparable to the Blue Nile. But the Abbay (known as the Blue Nile on the Ethiopian highlands[4]) is no doubt the most popular. So far, other rivers have indeed been more useful in economic aspects,[5] but none could rival the Abbay in reputation on the national level.

It is difficult to establish beyond doubt whether it always enjoyed the same nationwide popularity in the past. A few developments since the mid-twentieth century have certainly contributed to the enhancement of its prestige. An all-weather road has been constructed across the province of Gojjam, traversing the Abbay at a few points. Its beautiful waterfall and the associated Lake Tana together with its ancient monasteries have become an attraction for tourists, and their beautiful scenery has decorated postcards and magazines. A hydroelectric power station has been built at its waterfall, and a great deal of propaganda was made in the press on the potentialities of the Abbay. The waterfall panorama eventually became a symbol of the birr, the basic unit of the Ethiopian currency and, hence, a national symbol.

The river has been personified in praising poems and descriptive prose in the country with which it is occasionally paired. For example, a politically inspired song of recent years underscores the unity of the country by attributing honesty to almost all the remaining provinces and concludes by emphasizing the historical characteristics—the name of the country, the mighty Abbay, the diligence of the women, and the valor of the men:

> Yabulga lej yallawem abay
> Yamanz lej yallawem abay . . .
> Agarachen ityopeya wanzachen Abbay
> Setu qatchen fatay wandu tagaday.

> [The sons of Bulga know no deceit
> The sons of Manz know no deceit . . .
> Our country is Ethiopia, our river the Abbay
> The women are yarn-spinners and the men warriors.][6]

If the nationwide popularity of the river is connected with the economic and political needs of the period, to the riparian provinces, namely Bagemeder, Gojjam, Shawa, and Wallo, that is, mainly the Amharic-speaking people, the Nile has always been of a special significance. Both male and female children have been named after the mighty river,[7] which itself had no name in the proper sense of the word.[8] For this society, this particular river was unique, especially with regard to its size. It was simply *the river,* the father of rivers, as the Amharic lexicons put it, and was thus referred to.[9] The legends, the anonymous poems, proverbs, and anecdotes related to the Nile are a product of the intellect of that very people. Much of the modern creative literature in which the Nile plays a role has also been produced by the intellectuals of this particular society.

The Amharic as well as the bilingual dictionaries include a number of phrase entries or expressions whose equivalents or similarities are not to be found in the lexicons of the neighboring languages such as Tigrinya and Oromo.[10] The American lexicographer, Thomas Kane, who produced the most comprehensive two-volume English-Amharic dictionary, lists "Abbay masku" as "one who swims across the Blue Nile or one who frolics in it," while "Gush Abbay" refers to "turbid waters of the Nile in the rainy season."[11] Another well-known expression is "Abbayen batchelfa," which literally means "[emptying] the Blue Nile with a ladle,"[12] but which is applied to undertaking a considerable task with insufficient means.

A few well-known proverbs are also still in use in the language. The French Catholic missionary, J. Baeteman, records: "Abbay, anta ayyahañ kadarat, enem ayyahuh kagulbat,"[13] which literally can be translated as, "Nile, you have seen me at the breast and I have seen you at the knee," but which is often applied to the downfall of a rich or powerful and atrocious person in comparison to the rise and fall of the Nile's flow. Two ironic proverbs are: (1) "Abbay madarya yallaw, gend yezo yezoral"—"Though the Abbay is homeless, he carries around a tree trunk." This is often applied to an active but aimless person; and (2) "Yalatchen lej qemal balaw; yabbay lej weha tammaw"—"The son of the barber suffers from lice, the son of the Abbay suffers from thirst." This is usually applied to a person who has the means but pretends to be needy. A similar but less widely used proverb goes: "Tchatch-ata yalammada saw abbay dar qebaruñ yelal"[14]—"He who is used to clatter-ings requests to be buried at the bank of the Nile." An Ethiopian writer who in recent years compiled some 6,000 proverbs also records most of the above and adds one more of the ironic ones: "Abbayn yalayya mentchen ya-masagenal"—"One who has not seen the Nile praises a brook."[15]

THE ABBAY—A FORMIDABLE OBSTACLE

When Negus Menelik of Shawa heard that Negus Takla Haymanot of Goj-jam had sent an army contingent southward across the Abbay to claim new territories, the first question Menelik is said to have posed was, "What ter-ritorial rights does he have to the south of the Abbay?" In actual fact, Menelik did not at this particular time have control over the claimed terri-tories, either; he only had conceived a plan to conquer them. The underly-ing assumption was that his plan was more legitimate than that of his peer on the other side of the Abbay. The Abbay did not only form a natural boundary of Gojjam in the thinking of the period, but it also posed a for-midable obstacle in communication between the peoples of Gojjam and other regions. Almost all of the couplets and proverbs refer to this chal-lenge. For example, among the prominent ones are the following lines:

> Abbayen batankwa sishaggaru bay
> Bagre gabbahulesh abasayan lay.

> [Having seen others crossing the Abbay in a Tankwa[16]
> There I entered (for you) on foot to suffer greatly.]

> Kabbay Wadya mado zamad alaga malat
> wa blo maqrat naw wehaw yamollalat.

> [Refusing to find a relation beyond the Nile river
> One wails and fails, when the waters swell.]

Yamihon yehonal yamayhon ayhonem
and abbay simola saw ayashagerem
yafarra mashella mattashat ayqarem
yezagayal enji yassabnaw ayqarem.

[What can't happen, can't happen, what should happen will happen
When the Nile swells it lets none across
A ripened millet cannot remain uneaten
What we planned will happen even if it may be delayed.]

The barrier was not only the high waters of the Abbay as mentioned in the couplets, which is actually seasonal, but it also had a number of components more dangerous at times than the swift current of the river. When describing in a trilogy the changes the Ethiopian society experienced in this century, the famous Ethiopian writer, Haddis Alamayyahu, accounted vividly for the elements that constituted the danger. The setting he chose is the ravine between Dajan in Gojjam and Gohatseyon in Shawa, though the situation is equally applicable to any point of the river. The two towns are located on the edge of the escarpment overlooking the deep gorge and may not be more than 10 kilometers' distance from each other as the crow flies; but the chasm below them has to be negotiated with at least two hours' drive. Prior to the construction of the winding road and the bridge, the crossing took quite a different dimension that the novelist let his characters go through, which in actual fact might have been a real personal experience, as he is a native of Gojjam who undertook the journey in his youth some seventy years ago. As an illustration, I quote the gist of the passage[17] in my own translation:

Before a road was constructed through its deep ravine and a bridge spanned across its waters, the Abbay was a place that travelers heading from Gojjam to Addis Ababa or vice versa had to traverse. Until they arrived at Gohatseyon or Dajan they trembled and their hearts throbbed for fear as if a prophecy of disaster was told about them. The Abbay was not one death, but rather a place where a host of deaths settled, where a multitude of sufferings and affliction rested. There was none who could number those who met their deaths within a year being carried away by the current of the Abbay, eaten up by the crocodiles, murdered by outlaws, stung by serpents or infected by malaria, snatched away by beasts after having been beaten to the ground by bandits, as well as those who were stripped of their clothes or robbed of their wealth. All these could be enumerated only by the houses and families that this tribulation had befallen. More dreadful than the deaths and sufferings converging in the Abbay was the rumor. Some fabricated stories about the tribulation they suffered and how they came out of it through their might or skill or the help of God; and, to those who had not yet experienced it, the Abbay became as terrifying as hell when these stories spread by their inventors who exaggerated them a thousand times. Hence, when from the escarpment of Dajan the travelers, heading for Addis Ababa or beyond, view the Abbay stretching up and down in a terrifying majesty like the king of hell, covered by fog in the rainy season and by mist in the dry season, concealing in its depths the known and the unknown deaths and sufferings, their hearts throb for a while; soon they look above and across the fog or mist at Gohatseyon and get the feeling that the death and suffering would remain behind and never encounter them thereafter if they only reached there unscathed and, hence, they turn to planning and devising a way for reaching there safely. All their wishes, prayers, and preparations concentrate on reaching Gohatseyon as if it were the ultimate target of their journey. The journey beyond, be it as far as Addis Ababa or the borders of Ethiopia, will not count for the time being. That is something that comes after the arrival at Gohatseyon. Likewise, the feeling of the travelers heading for Gojjam from Addis Ababa or elsewhere and looking at the Abbay and beyond it at Dajan from the escarpment of Gohatseyon is similar to that of the travelers looking at the Abbay and Gohatseyon from Dajan. Thus, Gohatseyon and Dajan were starting points where traders and other travelers intending to cross the Abbay waited for further company so as to resist together whatever might be encountered, where they made preparations, where they armed themselves, where they prayed to God so that they might go across in safety, and where they made their wills. They were also places where those who crossed the Abbay safely would praise God, where those who suffered a mishap blamed God and their luck, where those attacked by outlaws or befallen by a malady would recuperate, and where those who died would be buried.

THE ABBAY—AN ABODE OF THE SPIRITS

Rivers, mountains, and seas are perhaps the most captivating natural objects of the human intellect, possibly on account of their permanent presence and formidable nature. The challenges they pose or the benefits they offer are a constant reminder of their significance to the societies that, by virtue of their location, have to do with them. The mightier these objects are, the livelier is the human fascination with them. At least in Ethiopia, the gigantic mountains and the mighty rivers were believed to be the abode of the spirits—both the good and the evil ones. Thus, these natural entities are by virtue of that very privilege endowed with special healing or influential attributes. Hence, going to Tis Abbay (the waterfall) around midday when the spirits would be active was discouraged. Though this is one of the few superstitions that have survived until our time, it appears that more spirituality was attached to the river in earlier times. When the Scottish traveler arrived at the source of the Blue Nile in November 1770, he was required to take off his shoes, as the place was holy. He observed altars at the venue and eventually described the impact of the river on the life of the inhabitants who cleansed themselves with the holy waters of the Gelgal Abbay (the Minor Nile) from visible dirt and invisible obscenity:

The Agows of Damot pay divine honour to the Nile; they worship the river, and thousands of cattle have been offered, and are still offered, to the spirit supposed to reside at its source. They are divided into clans, or tribes; and it is worthy of observation, that it is said there never was a feud, or hereditary animosity between any two of these clans; or, if the seeds of any such were sown, they did not vegetate longer than till the next general convocation of all the tribes, who meet annually at the source of the river, to which they sacrifice, calling it by the name of the *God of Peace.*[18]

These holy waters were believed not only to cleanse people from maladies and iniquities but were also regarded as having the power to relieve individuals from the fetters of an excommunication. The reminiscences of the famous Ethiopian church scholar, Alaqa Lamma Haylu, include a reference to a discussion between two prominent church scholars of the nineteenth century—Alaqa Kidana Wald of Shawa and Alaqa Yamesserach of Amara Saynt. The point of discussion was the practice of washing away a preemptive excommunication at the Abbay or in any other river for that matter. The practice emanated from the divisive circumstances of the eighteenth and nineteenth centuries prevailing over the Ethiopian Orthodox Church. There was only one Coptic metropolitan for the whole country despite the enormous size of the empire and the prevalent doctrinal or Christological dissensions. At the time the discussion of the two scholars of the second half of the nineteenth century took place, the metropolitan lived in Gondar. Priests and deacons from Shawa, Amara, Gojjam, and elsewhere went to him for ordination. He excommunicated them if they did not believe in the Hulat Ledat (two births) doctrine, which he maintained. For fear of being denied ordination, those from a sectarian group suppressed their belief during the ordination ceremony but washed the excommunication away at the Abbay, the Mofar Weha, or elsewhere on their way home and believed they were rinsed from the excommunication. The two scholars, we are told, were convinced that it really worked.[19] Amazing is, however, that they by implication believed that the rivers were so intelligent as to be able to discern between the blessing and the condemnation of the highest dignitary!

The reminiscences of Alaqa Lamma also entail a belief on how the spirits used persons in the 1880s to cross the Nile whenever that river was flooded. Alaqa Lamma describes how on their way to Dima Giyorgis, the famous center for monastic education, he and his student companions swam across the Abbay, fighting against attacking crocodiles. Worse than the riverine beasts were, however, the spirits and an epidemic, the usual associates, which took advantage of the traveling students. An epidemic had broken out in Gojjam before Lamma and his friends came to Dima.

The epidemic took its horse, the zar (a particular spirit), and tried to go across to Saynt, the region on the eastern side of the river. The river swelled and hampered it. According to some of the victims in Lamma's group who suffered from hallucinations, the epidemic left its zar and used the students as its horse to come back to Dima.[20] Lamma himself was only slightly ill and could not experience the riding spirit. With the spread of secular education and technology that undermine the awe-inspiring attributes of the Abbay, the spirits and their horses are now fading away. Unfortunately, the healing waters of the Nile are also likely to be defiled with the growth of industry.

HISTORIC ABBAY

Ethiopian historical sources are notoriously silent about routes of communication with the outside world. Countries of origin or the final destination of the envoys, traders, or missionaries are often mentioned, but not always which route they took. A few Ethiopian legends, however, depict the Abbay as a highway that was occasionally used by migrants and fugitives and implicitly by traders and envoys. Though the famous legend of the queen of Sheba does not connote the queen's preference to this route[21] (and indeed the region from where the Blue Nile springs was peripheral to the Aksumite kingdom), there are other legends that allege the use of this highway in earlier and later periods. The learned Alaqa Tayya Gabra Maryam, who compiled traditions of origin of the Ethiopian peoples in the early years of the twentieth century, recorded that, according to tradition, the Wayto people living around Lake Tana and along the banks of the Abbay originally came along the Nile on account of famine in Egypt and Sudan. They followed the river and ate all sorts of animals, a practice that has remained their custom. Similarly, the Shenash people are also said to have come along the Nile from Egypt on account of famine and civil war around 1800 B.C.[22]

Another legend that uses the Abbay as a route of migration and a means of communication with Egypt and the Sudan is that of King Lalibala, who ruled from around 1180 to 1220 and to whom the construction of the rock-hewn churches at Roha is attributed. The legend goes that the prince was chased out from the capital by a relation who seized power, so he went into exile to Gojjam, the region almost encircled by the Abbay and which apparently was not under the direct control of the Zagwa dynasty to which Lalibala belonged.[23] After spending some time there, Lalibala went down to Egypt and mobilized some 60,000 Christian fugitives whom he led along the Nile to Ethiopia. Reinforced by men from Gojjam, this force enabled the prince to regain his legitimate throne.[24]

Other legends allege that the Ethiopian rulers were aware of the river's importance to Egypt and, hence, they used it as a political instrument in the Middle Ages to get a Coptic metropolitan consecrated for Ethiopia or to ameliorate the lot of the Coptic Christians who from time to time suffered under the harsh rule of some sultans. The means of pressure was the threat to divert the Nile to the desert or the Red Sea and dry up Egypt.[25] Apparently, this threat was taken seriously in Egypt, as can be gathered from a legend also known in Egypt.

In the tenth century, the Coptic metropolitan of Ethiopia became a victim of a political rivalry within his diocese, and he was sent on exile where he died. The patriarch in Alexandria was unhappy about it and refused for a long time to consecrate another bishop for Ethiopia. This coincided with an occurrence of a dry spell of some years on the Ethiopian highlands, which inevitably brought the current of the Nile very low. This was interpreted in Egypt as the execution of the Ethiopian threat, and consequently the sultan intervened with the patriarch to consecrate a metropolitan for Ethiopia. By the time the new metropolitan arrived in his diocese, rains began to fall and the rivers swelled, a coincidence that probably confirmed the Egyptian belief in the seriousness of the threat of the Ethiopian rulers.

The threat is believed to have brought for Ethiopia a better result in the fourteenth century when Emperor Dawit (r. 1380–1410) allegedly relieved the Coptic Christians from persecution and he himself received a piece of the actual Holy Cross, which the Ethiopian Orthodox Church venerates and jealously preserves until this day.

ETHIOPIA'S IMAGE OF EGYPT AND THE EGYPTIANS

According to the "ancient" Ethiopian traditions, the Abbay was a river of two countries: Ethiopia, the source country, and Egypt, the main user of the water. Ethiopian oral traditions and written historical sources of the pre-nineteenth century recognize primarily one African state beside Ethiopia itself, namely Egypt, to which the country was linked by the Nile and the church,[26] and it was precisely these two links more than anything else that shaped the relations and image of both countries. Too little is said about the legendary kingdom of Damot in the south. The sultanates in the southeast, though a considerable challenge to the Christian kingdom of Ethiopia between the thirteenth and sixteenth centuries, were somehow regarded as minor political entities based on lost provinces that were at any rate to be retrieved sooner or later. The Sudan, too, was regarded to be more or less under the Ethiopian sphere of influence.

According to the legends that concern the remote times, northeast Africa as a whole is conceived as one unit inhabited by four peoples of the same stock—Saba, Noba, Balaw, and Kalaw—ruled by a dozen or more kings with silver and iron thrones at the head of which is the king of Ethiopia with a diamond and gold throne.[27] Hence, no reference is made to diverting the Nile to punish any state in the Sudan. In fact the point of diversion was assumed to be at Khartoum, the name of which is popularly derived from the Tigrinya verb *kartama* (to break, to cut).[28] Ezana's military expedition to Meroë and the intervention of the Nubian King George with the Egyptians on behalf of the Ethiopian sovereign in the tenth century have apparently sunk to oblivion; the military expeditions of Emperor Susenyos (r. 1607–1632) and that of Emperor Iyyasu I (r. 1680–1704) against Senaar are described by the royal chronicles in the same manner as those of the expeditions of the fourteenth and fifteenth centuries against the southeastern sultanates of Yefat, Fatagar, and others. Only Egypt and its associates—the Arabs and the Turks—were regarded as foreign and a great challenge to Ethiopian sovereignty at least since the sixteenth century. The challenge became a real threat in the second half of the nineteenth century, when Egypt, with the tacit blessing of the Turks and the European powers, tried to conquer Ethiopia.

Long before the Egyptian scheme, the Ethiopian view of Egypt was rather ambivalent. On the one hand, Egypt was a holy land next to Palestine in which the Holy Virgin, the Holy Child, and St. Joseph took refuge, and where the apostle St. Mark chose to have his "seat." Throughout the centuries, Ethiopian monks traveled to Egypt to live in seclusion in the Coptic monasteries founded by the ancient church fathers in the desert.[29] Alexandria in particular was regarded as a sacred city. When Emperor Yohannes IV declared at the Council of Borumeda in 1878 that his father was St. Mark and his mother Alexandria, he was only restating an old creed.[30] Until the mid-twentieth century, the Ethiopian Orthodox Church drew its metropolitans from the See of Alexandria and they were highly respected for the most part. Basically, the attitude of the believers has not changed significantly today in spite of the intermittent conflicts between the two churches.

On the other hand, there were quite a few formidable intricacies, primarily originating from the Egyptian side, which made the Ethiopians frown at the Egyptians. No tract seems to have been written to attack the Egyptians, but there are sufficient indications that the Copts (not to speak about the Muslims) were looked upon with mistrust and at times with contempt.[31] Among the reasons were the Coptic claim that only a Copt could be consecrated a metropolitan for Ethiopia, the inability or negligence of many of the metropolitans to live up to the dignity of their office, the intermittent appearance in Ethiopia of Egyptian pretenders and fraudulents, the violation of the rights of the Ethiopian Church by the Coptic monks at the Holy Sepulchre, and the influence of the sultans on the patriarchs and their representatives. The details of each exceed the scope of this chapter.

The fact that Egypt was under the control of outsiders, and Muslims at that, had obviously created a low opinion of the Copts in Ethiopian thinking, which was normally not expressed unless solicited by a serious provocation. Such a case was recorded by a foreigner who was in Gondar in the eighteenth century. The occasion was provided for in the 1770s, when a rebel attempted to overthrow the emperor during his absence from the capital, Gondar. Both the Coptic metropolitan and the highest Ethiopian dignitary, the Aqabe Sa'at, were involved. The coup aborted, and both dignitaries were arrested and brought to the Imperial court of justice presided over by the sovereign himself behind a curtain. The court obviously made a difference between the Ethiopian and the Egyptian defendants, though both were accused of the same treason. An officer spoke on behalf of the sovereign:

> The king requires of you to answer directly why you persuaded the Abuna to excommunicate him? the Abuna is a slave of the Turks, and has no king; you are born under a monarchy, why did you, who are his inferior in office, take upon yourself to advise him at all? or why, after having presumed to advise him, did you advise him wrongly, and abuse his ignorance in these matters?[32]

A similar remark was made by Empress Mannan in the 1840s when the turbulent Abuna Salama disputed with her faction and unduly offended her: "The metropolitan is a slave, for he is bought with money. Furthermore, the slave executes the wishes and orders of the lady of the house; but he has no say in anything." The *abun* responded in equally arrogant terms, which possibly reflected a latent Egyptian prejudice against Ethiopians: "My price as a slave you refer to is a thousand Talers; I am bought for a thousand Talers. But you would not be worth even ten Talers in my country."[33]

With the deterioration of the political relations between Ethiopia and Egypt that resulted in a bloody war of 1875–1876 and the growth of Ethiopian nationalism in the subsequent decades, Ethiopian criticism of the Copts became louder and harsher. A famous writer and government official criticized retrospectively Menilek's decision to staff the first modern government school with Egyptian instructors in the early years of the twentieth century and remarked that the Egyptians were at any rate a people who themselves needed instructors.[34] Some years thereafter, a work that incorporated the traditional teachings of a particular school within the Ethiopian Orthodox Church characterized the Egyptians as "lawbreakers who like Adam and Eve seek what is not due to them and who do not abide by the law given to them."[35]

The same work accuses them of falsifying the decision of the 318 church fathers who met at Nicaea in A.D. 325. Here the dispute was not whether Ethiopia had been legally placed under the See of Alexandria but rather that the Copts denied the Ethiopians the right to have a bishop from among their number. Another point the Ethiopians regarded as unjust was that the Copts even restricted the number of dignitaries to be sent to Ethiopia usually to one, and occasionally to a maximum of four, numbers that were obviously inadequate for the needs of the large empire. The Ethiopians had challenged these interdicts at least since the eleventh century, but they could not force the Copts to change their mind. Various attempts to switch their alliance to the Syrians or Armenians were also frustrated through the intrigues of the Egyptians.

What infuriated the Ethiopians in the late nineteenth century was the allegation that the four bishops who arrived in Ethiopia in 1882 after a protracted negotiation between the Ethiopian and the Egyptian governments had to take an oath before leaving Alexandria "not to consecrate under any circumstance an Ethiopian to the office of metropolitan or bishop," even if they were forced at the threat of death by the Ethiopian authorities.[36] This was followed in the subsequent decades by alleged incidents of Ethiopian clerics being badly treated at the hands of Coptic dignitaries in Alexandria, including the patriarch himself. In the 1910s and 1920s, the two Amharic newspapers occasionally carried overt criticisms while the government intensified their demand for the consecration of Ethiopian bishops.[37]

The problem was solved when the Copts agreed to ordain five Ethiopian bishops in 1929–1930 and a metropolitan in 1951. Finally, an Ethiopian patriarch was consecrated for the first and last time in Alexandria in 1959. However, lapses have occurred in the relations between the two sister churches in the 1970s when the Ethiopian Orthodox Church decided to elect and consecrate a new patriarch although the second patriarch, deposed by the Marxist regime, was still alive, and again in the 1990s when Patriarch Shenuda ordained bishops for Eritrea.[38]

If the church issue is thus solved and needs only a skillful diplomacy to maintain its old good relations, the question of the Nile is yet far from being settled. Gone are the days when a threat or a rumor to divert the river to the desert could prompt peace overtures. But the possibility of decreasing the flow of the river, not for punishment but for economic purposes, still endures and can bear crucially on the relations between the two countries. As long as Egypt was under the shadow of a foreign power, the negotiations of 1900–1903 and those of the 1920s regarding the Abbay were not accompanied by vile words of propaganda like those of the 1970s and 1980s. The period following World War II revived the old resentments. Ethiopia was perturbed in the 1940s and 1950s by Egypt's keen interest in regaining Eritrea as its old territory. Egypt's attempt to arouse Ethiopian Muslims and revolutionaries through propaganda was thwarted only by the astute diplomacy of Emperor Haile Selassie who visited Cairo in 1959. Nevertheless, in the same year Egypt concluded a treaty with the Republic of Sudan on the distribution of the Nile waters without consulting with Ethiopia, a case that was viewed by Ethiopia (and now by many other countries as well) as an obstacle for a better understanding.

THE ABBAY—AN INDICTEE

In the 1920s, an Ethiopian journalist allegedly commented sharply against the Egyptians in general and Abuna Matewos in particular following an Abbay incident. About thirty would-be priests and deacons from Bagemeder and Gojjam were carried away by the Nile current, with them also the amole (salt bars then used as a means of exchange) they had carried as a fee to the abun when traveling to the Ethiopian capital. The journalist reported the incident, consoled the relatives of the deceased, and concluded by saying that the metropolitan had in any case lost nothing, as the Nile carried the amole to Egypt on his behalf. Abuna Matewos was incensed and tried to complain about the journalist before the government, but his influence had long waned and he could do very little.[39] Such criticism of the Abbay was by no means unique in Ethiopia, though the general tendency under the last emperor was apparently to say as little about the Abbay as possible so as not to arouse Egyptian emotion.[40]

The new Ethiopian generation is obviously not satisfied with the symbolic pride entailed by the mighty river or the healing spirits abiding in it or the historic route that the Nile may have been. At least a part of the new generation seems to be convinced that the disadvantages of the Nile outweigh by far those benefits and is now demanding action against the treacherous river. The crime begins with erosion, as the Abbay wrenches away over half a million tons of fertile soil from the country.[41] The river has also dug itself deep into the bowels of the earth so as to look invincible and to make communication difficult. These and many other characteristics arouse vexation in the mind of the poets who retort with chastising words. The Abbay is visualized as a full-fledged person and is told his crimes straight in the face in plain words.

The lamentation of the new generation is understandable: drought and famine have taken a heavy toll on the Ethiopian population in recent years while the Abbay waters thundered unused down the precipice as always. This contradiction made many Ethiopians restless, and some began to compose challenging poems.

In 1985 a young poet resounded the gigantic plans of the Marxist regime and told the Abbay that his days were counted and that he would soon be harnessed to produce electricity and to water plantations. Above all, he could no longer snatch away people and properties nor would he be admonished by the superstitious and the cleric.[42] The dream was never fulfilled; there remained only bitterness and despair. An anonymous poem that appeared in the daily newspaper *Addis Zaman* in April 1990 charged the Abbay with treachery, theft, and robbery, all being evidenced by the amount of erosion the river caused.[43] The river was spoken to in this piece and elsewhere, as it was impossible to charge the relevant government organs for doing too little about it. This is in conformity with the traditional *qene* (sacred hymn) technique; but looking at the Abbay from the negative aspect was an innovation that probably was initiated by Haylu Gabra Yohannes.

This renowned poet who lives abroad had published a book only a year earlier precisely on the same theme. He entitled his monograph "Innatkin Belulgn," a pejorative Amharic expression that can at best be translated as "Insult him on my behalf," and repeatedly posed the rhetorical question, What use is there in bragging that one owns the Abbay?[44] In a monologue—for the Abbay never gets a chance to respond—the poet charges the Nile with insubordination, robbery, arrogance, desertion, betrayal of his own home country, and letting the poor Ethiopians die of hunger and thirst while he (the Nile) flows into the sea.

Unlike Addis Zaman's poet, however, Haylu was in a position to switch his focus intermittently from the criminal river to the thoughtless authorities who limited their project to constructing a road and failed to harness the unruly stream and make it useful. Thus, the poet expressed his wish, his anger, his criticism, and hopefully he is relieved of his passion; but the flow of the Nile, the erosion it causes, the country's limitation of resources, and the international entanglement in the question of the Nile will probably continue for a long time.

CONCLUSION

The Blue Nile transcends the concept of a river in the country of its origin. Its notion indeed varies in degree of consciousness and intensity on the national and regional levels; but it is in any case a deep-rooted element in the Ethiopian culture. As an awe-inspiring, mighty natural entity, it was venerated in the past; as a formidable barrier whose crossing could only be negotiated with difficulty, it has set a distinct sociopolitical boundary within the state; and, as the longest river in the world, it determined to a large extent the historical character of Ethiopia's foreign relations. In other words, the Nile was, and still is, an ever-present factor in the mind of the Ethiopian society, and as such its significance has won a prominent position at least in the official language. With the introduction of modernization into the country, a new dimension of a political and economic nature has inevitably cropped up in recent decades which has markedly enhanced the international significance of this renowned river.

NOTES

1. Like the Tel Aviv one, The Fifth Nile 2002 Conference, held in Addis Ababa on 24–28 February 1997, attracted quite a few experts from various fields and with interesting papers. The fact that the number of the countries concerned with the Nile rose from three to ten in recent decades is also indicative of the new aspects of the riverine question.

2. For texts and commentaries on the various treaties, see Hertslet, *The Map of Africa by Treaty,* pp. 431–436; Tilahun, *Egypt's Imperial Aspirations,* pp. 67–152; Lemma, "Ethiopia and Egypt," pp. 755–780; and the following two papers presented at The Fifth Nile 2002 Conference, Addis Ababa, 24–28 February 1997: Mekonnen, "A New Basis for a Viable Nile River Water Allocation Agreement," and Amare, "The Imperative Need for Negotiation on the Utilization of the Nile Waters."

3. Haile Selassie, *Fre kanafer* (Fruit of the lips), p. 2423.

4. In the twentieth century, the attribute *teqqur* (black) has been added to Abbay. Thomas Kane states that "blue" is perceived as "black" and that the term was used by intellectuals after the White Nile was generally known. He does not, however, clarify why the "intellectuals" could not apply the actual equivalent of blue (Kane, *Amharic-English Dictionary,* p. 1203).

5. The only couplet identified in the course of the research has been that of the late singer Asaffa Abata, which asserts that the Abbay was used for fishing:

> Asabalashaallahu abbay dar naw bete
> Doro maraqemma kawadet abbate.
> [I will feed you on fish; my abode is at the Nile
> As to chicken soup, where from should I fetch it?]

6. From the 1994 recording of Darbabaw Abunu's traditional songs made on behalf of the Ethiopian Research Council in Florida, U.S.A. The melody is traditional, but the poem could not be identified in earlier recordings. The first line repeats itself twenty times, changing only the name of the region, as exemplified in line 2, and touches upon all administrative units, excluding Eritrea, which was separated by this time.

7. The most popular names are Abbay, Abbaynah, and Abbaynash. The first spread even as far north as Tegray and Eritrea, where the Takazze is more popular. It is interesting to note, however, that no person with the name Takazze could be identified in the course of the research. In the southern regions, particularly in the Oromo-inhabited areas, the names of other rivers such as the Awash, the Wabi, the Didessa, the Baro, and the Gilo are popular, and persons are named after them.

8. Two other rivers share the same fate of being called simply "the river": the Takazze in the north, which is known as Gash-Satit at its lower course; and the Djama in Shawa, which is referred to as the Adabay at its lower course. See Mika'el, *Ya'amarena mazgaba qalat,* p. 597; and Wald, *Addis yamarena mazgaba qalat bakahnatenna,* p. 518. Whether all the so-called names of rivers in actual fact signify river or stream in archaic or extinct languages has yet to be determined by linguists.

9. The Ethiopian lexicographers assert that the river was so referred to as a result of its having many tributaries that it gathers together like a father does with his children. See Kefle, *Mashafa sawesew wages wamazgaba qalat haddis nebabu bage'ez fechchew bamareña,* p. 195; and Wald, *Addis yamarena mazgaba qalat bakahnatenna,* pp. 75, 255. Alternate names for the same river are the biblical Gihon and Epheson (Genesis 2:11). The original appellation, however, seems to

have been the Ge'ez adjective "Abbawi" (fatherly), mentioned at the earliest in the chronicle of Ba'eda Maryam, 1468–1478, the mobile sovereign who seems to have been the first among his like to traverse the Abbay (Perruchon, *Les Chroniques de Zar'a Ya'qob,* p. 169). The chronicle of Amda Tseyon, 1314–1344, does not mention the river by name, though the title of the ruler of the region and an army contingent of Gojjam are listed. Later records show that "Abbawi" was in use at least until the end of the eighteenth century. Bruce made an attempt to find out the African name for the river and wrote: "It is not to be wondered, that, in the long course the Nile makes from its source to the sea, it should have acquired a different name in every territory, where a different language was spoken; but there is one thing remarkable, that though the name in sound and in letters is really different, yet the signification is the same, and has an obvious reference to the dog-star. Among the Agows . . . it is called Gzeir, Geefa, Seir; the first of these names signifying God; it is also called Abba, or Ab, Father; and by many other terms which I cannot write in the language of that nation, whilst, with a fervent and unfeigned devotion, under these, or such like appellations, they pray to the Nile, or spirit residing in that river" (Bruce, *Travels,* vol. 3, pp. 654–657).

10. The Takazze, the largest river of the Aksumite kingdom, recurs in Tigrinya expressions, in the same way the Nile does in Amharic, whereas the Abbay is of less significance in Oromo in comparison to the Gibe, the Didesa, and the Baro in the south (see Cerulli, *Folk-Literature,* under their respective entries).

11. Kane, *Amharic-English Dictionary,* p. 1203.

12. Ibid.

13. Baeteman, *Dictionnaire Amarigna-Français,* p. 586. See also Mahtama-Selassie, *Yabbatochqers,* p. 75.

14. Mahtama-Selassie, *Yabbatochqers.*

15. Warqu, *Messaleyawi annagagar,* pp. 106, 150.

16. A small, light boat made of reeds or the like. Actually, this refers to a means of transport that was, and still is, used mainly on Lake Tana.

17. Alamayyahu, *Feqer eska maqaber,* p. 531.

18. Bruce, *Travels,* vol. 3, pp. 597–602, 633.

19. Lamma, *Matshafa tezzeta za'alaqa lamma haylu walda tarik,* pp. 125 ff.

20. Ibid., p. 83.

21. Tegegne attempts to set the whole Aksum tradition in Gojjam, but he fails to make the queen travel down the Nile toward Jerusalem (see Tegegne, *"Gojjam" the Stigma,* pp. 21 ff).

22. Maryam, *Ya'ityopeya hezb tarik,* pp. 16 ff.

23. The legend has many versions. See Makweriya, *Ya'ityopeya tarik,* p. 432; and Institute of Archeology, *Ya'atse lalibala gadl,* pp. 41 ff. The latter source is not sure where the Prince went and suggests Harar or Egypt as possibilities.

24. Tafla, "Atsma Giyorgis and His Work," p. 205.

25. Emperor Zar'a Ya'qob is alleged to have once said that "it was within his power to divert its course. He desisted from doing it, only for the fear of God, and in consideration of the human sufferings that would result from it." Both Egyptians and Europeans of the Middle Ages presumed that the Ethiopian sovereigns could divert the Nile (Tamrat, *Church and State in Ethiopia,* pp. 256, 262).

26. For the history of the relations between Ethiopia and Egypt, see Reinisch, *Ein Blick auf Aegypten und Abessinien;* Wiet, "Les Relations Égypto-Abyssines sous les sultans Mamlouks," pp. 115–140; Doresse, "L'Ethiopie et le patriarcat copte," pp. 7–15; Meinardus, "A Brief History of the Abunate of the Ethiopian Church," pp. 39–65; Meinardus, "Ethiopian Monks in Egypt," pp. 61–70; and Seyberlich,

"Beziehungen und Abhang igkeibverhaltnisse," pp. 253–258.

27. Mondon-Vidailhet, "Une tradition Ethiopienne," and Beyene, *Fesseha Giyorgis*—storia d'Etiopia, pp. 5–7.

28. Tafla, "Atsma Giyorgis and His Work," p. 205.

29. Meinardus, *Monks and Monasteries of the Egyptian Deserts,* pp. 147, 159. The reverse, though rare, seems also to have been true. The Christian fugitives who came to the Aksumite kingdom and who introduced monasticism in the late fifth and early sixth centuries were Copts, Syrians, and Greeks who had lived in Egypt for at least some time. One of the later saints, Abuna Gabra Manfas Qeddus, was also believed to have come from Egypt.

30. De Coppet, *Chronique du regne de Ménélik II,* p. 149.

31. Apart from the metropolitan, no Egyptian has apparently won a significant office or position in Ethiopia comparable to that held by individual Europeans. Even the metropolitan's power was very limited when it came to administration. His authority lay primarily in spiritual matters, particularly the ordination of priests and deacons. Next to the emperor, the most powerful person in church administration was an Ethiopian cleric—the Nebura'ed of Aksum, the Aqabe Sa'at of Hayq, the Etchage of Dabra Libanos, or any other dignitaries who won Imperial favor. The Ethiopian Church scholar and lexicographer, Alaqa Kidana Wald, describes vividly the relationship between the two dignitaries: "There is a paradox in Ethiopia's attitude toward the Coptic metropolitan. On the one hand, Ethiopia accepted a foreign metropolitan whose language she did not understand and he equally did not understand her language, instead of electing one from among her own clergy in accordance with the decisions of the Council of Nicaea. On the other hand, she did not want to give up her honour and her authority. Hence, she appointed an *Etchage* who for all practical purposes was a bishop. In the absence of a bishop, he undertook the activities of the metropolitan. Both sat to the right and left of the Emperor, the *Etchage* sat to the left. Whenever the metropolitan was no longer there, the *Etchage* sat to the right of the Emperor. As the metropolitan was dumb and hornless [speechless and powerless] who could neither teach, nor judge nor comment at the court of justice, it was the *Etchage* who did all these. He was in charge of the Fetha Nagast" (Wald, *Addis yamarena mazgaba qalat bakahnatenna,* p. 457).

32. Bruce, *Travels,* vol. 4 (1771), p. 76.

33. Mondon-Vidailhet, *Chronique de Théodoros II,* pp. 9 ff.

34. Baykadane, "Ate Menilekenna Ityopeya" (Emperor Menelik and Ethiopia), p. 345.

35. Kefle, "Haymanota Abaw—la foi des péres anciens. I: Texte Éthiopien," p. 121, and also pp. 127–130.

36. Ibid., pp. 123 ff.

37. Habla-Selassie, *Ya'amarena yabeta krestyan mazgaba qalat.*

38. Lesinski, "Zwischen Mutter- und Schwesterkirche," pp. 18–22.

39. From the reminiscences of Qes Badema Yalaw (then the most senior pastor of the Makana Yasus Evangelical Church), interviewed in Addis Ababa in 1966. The newspaper was said to be the "A'emero," a complete collection of which could not be located in the course of the present research.

40. The monarch himself did not give a speech at the time he laid the foundation stone of the hydroelectric power plant on 13 May 1959, and the speech of Ato Sayfu Mahtama-Selassie, who was then in charge of the Electric Power Authority, was carefully calculated to emphasize the country's need for energy (see Ministry of Information, *Ya'abbay weha lemat majammarya masarat,* pp. 62 ff.).

41. Mulatu, "Teqqur abbay," pp. 32–35.

42. The Ethiopians were aware of the erosion caused by the Nile and other rivers at least in the Menilek period. Foreigners, who had vested interest in the Nile, urged them to do something about it. The German envoy to the Ethiopian court, Friedrich Rosen, has, as his brother notes, impressed the Ethiopians in 1905 when he drew their attention to the disadvantages of deforestation and erosions: "Wherever you go, you burn down the forests. Hence, the rains wrest your rich soil from the plateaus and the Nile carries it down to Egypt. There the farmers become rich, because you do not know how to preserve your wealth. There the population grows, and you are obliged to abandon your settlements every ten years to move elsewhere lest you will starve. The Egyptians flourish at your expense!" (Rosen, *Eine deutsche Gesandtschaft in Abessinien,* p. 225).

43. *Addis Zaman* (Ethiopia), 19 April 1990.

44. GabreYohannes, *Innatkin Belulgn,* pp. 78 ff. Note that the above transliteration is that of the author himself who has entitled his book in both Amharic and English.

13

◆

Brothers Along the Nile:
Egyptian Concepts of
Race and Ethnicity, 1895–1910

Eve Troutt Powell

In 1901 and 1902, a British anthropometrist and ethnographer named Charles Myers began his exploration into the racial identity of Egyptians. Later, he acknowledged the support of Major-General F. R. Wingate, sirdar of the Egyptian army and governor-general of Sudan for "the supply of subjects." These subjects were all fellahin conscripts in the British-led Egyptian army, and the anthropometrist described his evaluations thusly:

> I here give a complete list of the measurements which I made during my anthropometric investigations in Egypt. It comprises height when 1) sitting, 2) standing, 3) kneeling; height above the ground of 4) ear-hole, 5) chin, 6) acromion, 7) elbow, 8) wrist, 9) great trochanter, 10) knee, 11) ankle; 12) maximum breadth and 13) length of head; 14) upper and 15) total length of face, 16) bimalar, 17) bizygomatic, 18) bi-auricular and 19) bigonial breadth; 20) width of mouth.[1]

The subjects of this quote, subject to the pushing and pulling fingers and measuring tools of the British researcher, were all soldiers in the Egyptian army. How had the soldiers of Egypt come to this? Could the racial origins of the Nile Valley be so easily measured?

Myers was not the first foreigner to try to pin down the size, shape, and origins of Egyptians; Egypt had endured over a century of this kind of racializing scrutiny since the scientists and artists of Napoleon's expedition in 1798 had both measured and sketched prototypes from all walks of urban and rural life for their masterwork *Description de l'Egypte*. Ever since the French occupation, in fact, Egyptian rulers in search of ways to bring their country towards greater parity with Western Europe had often hired Europeans to come to Egypt and analyze the weaknesses and strengths of their subjects. Interestingly, Egyptian scholars, writers, and theologians trained in London or Paris in the middle of the nineteenth century often returned home with new ways of seeing their homeland, and wrote or translated their own analyses of what kept Egyptians from being like Europeans. But although it was not the first, Charles Myers's study occurred at a crucial point in Egyptian history. While Egyptians of certain classes, like the unfortunate soldiers, were being exposed to the stares and instruments of foreign scientists, politically minded Egyptians of great education and wealth were turning similar eyes to the Sudanese.

Egypt had conquered the Sudan in 1821 and governed much of it until about 1885, when the Mahdi and his forces destroyed the last vestige of Egyptian authority in Khartoum. Shortly before Egypt lost the Sudan, it was itself occupied by the British in 1882. But even under occupation, after the Sudan was lost in 1885, Egyptian nationalists began a campaign to the British authorities for the eventual return of the Sudan to Egypt. Sudan remained under the Mahdi's and then his successor's control, however, until 1898, when General Herbert Kitchener led the Egyptian army to victory over the remaining forces of the Mahdiyya. In 1899, under the auspices of Kitchener and Lord Cromer, the governor-general of Egypt, the Sudan began a new existence as "The Anglo-Egyptian Condominium."

Egyptian authority was only nominal, however, and Egyptian nationalists were deeply enraged over this dishonoring of claims to the Sudan they considered historical, geographic, and religious. But British figures like General Wingate and Lord Cromer found their arguments unconvincing, and, as Charles Myers's acknowledgment illustrates, supported the efforts of anthropologists who were conducting research projects into the racial homogeneity of the Egyptians and thus their racial distinction from the Sudanese. This situation thus reinforces the quiet but profound drama of researchers turning the barracks of the Egyptian soldiers into a laboratory, and the soldiers themselves into specimens. Myers's article reinforced the conditions of their capture, rendering them forever splayed like powerless butterflies.

As Timothy Mitchell has shown, leading Egyptian thinkers like Sheikh Rifa'a al-Tahtawi, Ahmad Fathi Zaghlul, and Qasim Amin had for many years accepted "scientific" gradations of humankind borrowed from the West.[2] But by the turn of the century, some were also manipulating such paralyzing science into a powerful response to the measurements of race created by British anthropologists and used by colonial authorities. These thinkers, most notably Ahmad Lutfi al-Sayyid, promoted an alternative to the idea that the Sudanese and the Egyptians were racially distinct peoples, a theory that contradicted Egyptian claims to the geography and culture of the Sudan. The alternative was the concept that the Egyptians and the Sudanese were one people, and it developed into a political ideal and a slogan that redefined Egyptian ambitions for hegemony over the Nile Valley. This concept was, in fact, a colonialism that could exist between "brothers." The soldiers of Upper Egypt would thus still have a real job to perform.

MUSTAFA KAMIL AND THE
EXTENSION OF THE NILE'S "BODY"

In 1898, as it became clearer that the British were about to embark on the reconquest of Sudan from the forces of the Mahdi, Mustafa Kamil, the leader of the Egyptian Nationalist Party, mourned the impending "castration" of his nation. Almost like a eunuch, Egypt was about to lose its most sensitive appendage. He lamented this in vivid language in an article published in the French newspaper *Le Clair,* written after the retaking of the Sudanese city of Atbara: "There is no doubt that Egyptian blood and money was sacrificed in order to conquer the Sudan [*fath al-Sudan*], which gave Egyptians the first right in its administration and in mastering its resources."[3] But the British, in their eternal greed for Sudan, were seizing the harvest sown by Egyptians and would leave the Egyptians nothing; worse, they would make the Egyptians as helpless and "feminine" as the Sudanese. Egyptian soldiers had trekked through the killing heat of the Sudan, toiling and fighting, and proving victorious, only to hear it said that "the Egyptian is not humane enough, not worthy enough, of governing."[4] Now the British had wielded their most damaging weapon:

> The Sudan, as is clear to the reader, is a piece of Egypt, and has been stripped from her with no legal right, because the Egyptian khedivial government has not the least right to give up even a foot of her land or allow someone else to possess it. With this to be considered, the Sudan is still Egyptian property and the British do not have the right to any claims to it. It returned to khedivial authority after almost twenty years of the dervishes' upheaval and even if British soldiers participated with us in the reconquest, we did not need their help. Our army, even less than our whole army, would have been enough to accomplish this result.[5]

Kamil's words—territories, or sections, "stripped" and "detached" from the mainland by the British and Egyptian "possession" and "ownership" of the Sudan—stirred powerful images for his public. His sense of his audience, whether French or Egyptian, and the emotions that they shared against the British enabled him to deconstruct the words used to describe imperialism and to delineate two meanings for the same word, one a natural linkage between the Sudan and Egypt, the other a cold, calculated strategy of greed on the part of Great Britain.

For Kamil, Egypt and the Sudan were irrevocably linked by the bonds of Islam. Only co-religionists could communicate with or understand the Sudanese. Given both Egypt's physical proximity to the Sudan and the shared culture and spiritual background of the two regions, only Egyptians could in truth *know* the Sudanese, and on the strength of this knowledge, be their lawful and benevolent guardians. With his references to corporeal organs and members, Kamil thus extended a metaphor long to his target audience (an elite and educated class capable of moral and political leadership) that Egypt represented a "body" or a "body politic."[6]

But a question haunted Kamil: If the Sudan was really Egypt's possession, how did the Egyptians lose it? Mustafa Kamil placed the responsibility for this first on the British when he spoke in Alexandria in 1896: "Why did the Sudanese keep on determinedly rebelling against Egypt? Why would they not accept any agreement with us? No one can deny that the British presence in Egypt made the Sudanese behave that way."[7] But another quality in the Sudanese propelled them into the Mahdiyya against the Egyptians (and Mustafa Kamil never denies that the Mahdists rebelled against an Egyptian, and not Ottoman, authority)—and this quality is "native fanaticism."

> In reality, the Muslims of the Sudan are very rigid and fanatical; they would never and will never accept that any but Muslims rule them. In order to win them over, it is not necessary to use force, rather, we will call to them in the name of Islam. In the name of the Khedive and of the Sultan we will send a religious delegation to them consisting of several ulama. It would be enough to stanch the fire of revolution in them and bring them to our side for us to enter their territory carrying the holy Qur'an in one hand and the flag of the prophet in the other.[8]

As a culture, Egypt was therefore uniquely imbued with the capacity to bridge this untamed religious energy and Western European society. Kamil continued, "Is there any other country in the world as suited by religious liberalism (*al-muhid*) and absolute moderation to be the medium between civilized Europe and fanatical Africa if not Egypt?"[9] And this unique though combustible blend of qualities should have properly distanced Egypt and the Sudan from the rest of the continent's vulnerability to the European scramble for Africa.

> Egypt does not resemble other African countries, which can be seized simply by treaties between the Powers. Egypt is a different place. Behind the Egyptian question is actually a very dangerous and very important issue. Behind the Egyptian question there is the White Nile question and the African question and the Christian question and the Muslim question.[10]

Two years after that speech, however, Great Britain had seized Omdurman, and Egypt had become (willing or not) a significant part of the African question.

TAKING EGYPT'S FULL MEASUREMENT

With the reconquest of the Sudan, and in the context of the popular Mustafa Kamil's speeches, the British found a stronger imperative for charting and categorizing its inhabitants. The new political map required clear knowledge of who belonged where, and British anthropologists approached the question between Egypt and Africa as a racial puzzle. Their conclusions, even their guesswork, carried great weight in the discussion of race and identity in the Nile Valley, relying on science rather than indigenous conceptions of belonging. Colonial authority was the final proof, making the anthropological theories a reality.

Myers's work was published in a three-part series of articles in the *Journal of the Royal Anthropological Institute* entitled "Contributions to Egyptian Anthropometry," from 1904 to 1906. In the second of the series, "The Comparative Anthropometry of the Most Ancient and Modern Inhabitants," he measured the skulls of ancient Egyptians and compared the measurements to anthropometric data culled from troops in the Egyptian army. He also recorded the birthplaces of their parents, which he claimed enabled him to study the measure of the soldiers according to their origins. These were fellahin conscripts of Kena and Girga, modern people who lived on the same ground as their ancient Nahada ancestors had. Myers concluded that "there is no essential difference between the head dimensions of the prehistoric and those of the modern population of this region of upper Egypt." And from that evaluation came this conclusion: "It is evident that the homogeneity of the Egyptians of this district is the same today as it was 7000 years ago."[11]

On one level, Myers's assertions of a continual homogeneity among Upper Egyptians contributed to the anthropological debate over the origins of ancient Egyptian civilization, and thus genetically connected modern Egyptians to the glories of their ancestors. This kind of assertion might have made many Egyptian nationalists proud. But on a much more significant level, his confirmation of a genetic homogeneity among Egyptians of this area separated them from the other dwellers of the Nile Valley, the Sudanese. And Myers posited this theory of racial distinctiveness almost immediately after the Anglo-Egyptian conquest, under circumstances that could only be produced under a colonial administration. As mentioned earlier, without the help of General Wingate, Myers might not have had such obedient subjects for study. Wingate had long been involved with the British administration of Egypt and had almost single-handedly waged a propaganda campaign for the British conquest of the Sudan in the years following Charles Gordon's death in Khartoum. Wingate wielded a great deal of power as governor-general of the Sudan, and was eager to see that kind of power remain in British, and never Egyptian, hands. And so he lent out soldiers to Myers, who had these young conscripts measured standing, sitting, kneeling, breathing, opening their mouths to have their teeth measured, holding their arms out straight to gauge the span, in order to make concrete the relationship of these young men to the land and not to regions further south.

The anthropological idea of racial distinction between the Egyptians and the Sudanese reinforced official British policies about the structure of government in the Nile Valley. Lord Cromer, consul general of Egypt, echoed the concepts of Myers in his annual report on Egypt and the Sudan of 1905, when he denied the feasibility of having Egyptians come south to serve as functionaries in the building of a bureaucratic infrastructure in the reconquered Sudan. In the first case, he said, Egypt was itself in too great a need of these functionaries to send aid to the Sudan. In the second place, those Egyptians with the requisite competence would only serve in the Sudan at inflated salaries. And finally, "in the places where their services would be most needed, the climate is not at all suitable for *the Egyptian race* [italics mine]."[12] With a gaze like that of Myers on the bodies of the soldiers, Cromer insisted Egyptians were biologically unsuited for authority in Sudan, and thus, over the Sudanese.

SUDANESE CHARACTERISTICS

There were Egyptians who internalized this kind of scrutiny on themselves and their culture, as Muhammad 'Umar did in his well-known book *The Present State of the Egyptians, or, The Causes of Their Retrogression* (1902). The Egyptian army was the arena for other approaches to surveillance of social culture as well. In 1900, a Lebanese intelligence officer named Na'um Shuqayr was assigned to document the variety of contemporary life in the Sudan. The book he published in 1903, *Ta'rikh al-Sudan al-qadim wa'l-hadith wa-jughrafiyatuhu* (The history of ancient and modern Sudan and its geography), provided an ethnographic account of every Sudanese tribe, along with their customs, their physical characteristics, their religious practices, and, whenever possible, legends they told about themselves. Shuqayr carefully traced the genealogies of every tribe, and he organized the population of the Sudan into distinct racial and tribal groups: black, *shibh al-sud* (Negroid), the Beja, the Nuba, and the Arabs.

Na'um Shuqayr's text is a fascinating canvas of opinion, a census of facts and popular ideas about the Sudanese. Unlike the studies of Myers, in which the subjects were silent and pliable, Shuqayr's subjects were neither bending nor sitting on order, and thus his text relies a great deal on both European and Egyptian perceptions about the racial and cultural identities of the Sudanese. While it offered a wealth of information about the history and the lives of the Sudanese in this book, and in addition to the facts, *Tarikh al-Sudan* relied strongly on popular understandings of Sudanese racial identity then current in both Egypt and in Europe, here is where I find the book most revealing. In the chapters devoted to the inhabitants of the Sudan, "their origins, their tribes and their habitats," Shuqayr says of the Banqo, a branch of the Dinka, that they are "in the opinion of Schweinfurth, the famous German explorer, the most developed intellectually of all of the black tribes."[13] In the section of the book entitled "The Morals of the Sudanese, Their Customs and Superstitions," he described the Arab tribes of the Sudan as having the well-known moral standards (*al-awsaf al-khulqiyyah*) as Arabs have had in every place and through all times."[14] But other tribes in Shuqayr's accounting have not maintained the morals once so powerful among their ancestors, most infamously the Barabra, a tribe Shuqayr described as a racially mixed group, descended from relationships among the original Nuba, Arabs, and Turks. Unfortunately, as the author saw it, "they have lost the more splendid traits that distinguished their ancestors, so that you do not see in them Nubian courage, nor the chivalry of the Arab, nor the sagacity of the Turk; rather they are the ultimate in cowardice, dishonesty, laziness, ignorance and malice to an extreme extent."[15] And then this wonderful glimpse into current stereotypes: "Those among them who came to Egypt as servants made themselves famous by their cleanliness and their reliability, while those who penetrated deeper into the Sudan were known for their cunning and their deceit, as already mentioned."[16]

Shuqayr thus asked his readers to visualize his Barabra subjects in contexts more familiar than the Sudan. He placed them in Egyptian homes, as domestic servants. The three sets of ancestors whose interrelationship created the Barabra—Turks, Arabs, and Nubians—are broken down into essentials, and out of their miscegenation comes disorder: of racial identity, of features, of morals, and of authority. The racial pieces of the Barabra are reordered, in Shuqayr's analysis, in Egypt, where as domestic servants these same Barabra take on more noble characteristics and are distinguishable from their relatives much farther south in the Sudan for their cleanliness and dependability. It is important to note here that in Egypt at this time, the tribal distinctions of Sudanese and Nubian people were often overlooked. Although there is a region of the Sudan called Berber, for example, there developed a singular identity: *al-barbari* (or the Nubian) that encompassed dark-skinned Nile Valley residents, whether they were Nubian or Sudanese, and whose color, customs, and accents Egyptian writers sketched out in numerous essays, dialogues, and stories. In the nineteenth century, the native homelands of Nubians extended from Upper Egypt to northern Sudan, in the Wadi Halfa-Dongola region.[17] Shuqayr's account of the Barabra fits easily within this framework.

Shuqayr's text is most revealing in its relationship to its audience. The book was written originally in Arabic and was quickly published in Beirut and Cairo. It was intended for Arabic readers. Yet, while it is clear that he expected his Egyptian readers to understand his meanings about the Barabra working in Egypt, as opposed to their counterparts in the Sudan, the ultimate arbiters of racial distinction continued to be, for Shuqayr, European explorers in Africa, explicitly the Germans Schweinfurth and Junker. At the end of his presentation on the morals and customs of the black tribes of the Sudan, he wrote, "And whoever desires more details should refer to the books of European explorers who went to those territories and came to know their circumstances and published long books about them."[18] Shuqayr's work acknowledges two authorities over the Sudanese: Egyptian and European. But his final analysis grants the power of racial identification to the Europeans.

DE-RACING EGYPT AND THE SUDAN

By 1910, however, Egyptian nationalists could not afford parcelling the physical and racial attributes that these other viewpoints offered. Nor could Egyptian nationalists afford to rely on European constructions of race and identity in the Nile Valley. Accepting racial differences among the peoples of the Nile Valley now meant acquiescing to the potent categorizations of the British colonial administration; worse, meant losing the Sudan possibly forever. Ahmad Lutfi al-Sayyid, the famous educator, newspaper editor, and nationalist, saw this danger and encouraged a new approach to the campaign for the Sudan. At first, he saw no reason why Egypt should not claim Sudan as a colony and wrote, in his newspaper *Al-Jarida,* in 1910:

> The Sudan is Egypt's by right of conquest. She is a part of Egypt, and her not being separated is vital to Egypt's life, due to her holding the source of the Nile and being her neighbor. We loathed giving her up, then she was reconquered, this time with the participation of the English. During all of that we were submissive to the contract of the Condominium and the triumphant power [England]. That administration is void before public opinion and the law. The arrangement of the Condominium alters nothing of the correct concept that all Egyptians hold dear, and that is colonizing [*ista'mar*] the Sudan is the right of Egyptians, and no one else, just as the subsidizing of the Sudan is the duty of Egyptians, and no one else. Egyptians look at the Sudanese as brothers, as a part of their community, so it's their responsibility to look out for their brothers' welfare.[19]

Several months later, Ahmad Lutfi al-Sayyid deepened the discussion with his original ideas about how the sharing of culture created family ties between the inhabitants of the Nile Valley. The Egyptians had experienced everything that the Sudanese had suffered, and this shared past bound their cultures together. By linking them together, Lutfi al-Sayyid redefined the word "imperialism" for Egyptian society. Only foreigners could colonize.

> It is a mistake to consider the Sudan an Egyptian colony. The Sudan is rather a part of what makes up Egypt; she completes Egypt. There is Lower Egypt and the Sudan is Upper Egypt. Every Sudanese bears the same responsibilities to the nation of Egypt as every native Egyptian. When Sudanese people mention the tyranny of some Egyptian rulers, Egyptians can also relate the despotism of their own rulers. Egypt at times suffered autocrats throughout the entire nation. If it was within a governor's power in Sudan to hang a Sudanese, it was also within the power of the Mudir of Dakhiliyya or Sharqiyya to hang an Egyptian.

Lutfi al-Sayyid "bitterly disapproved" of class distinctions that Egyptians made among themselves. The sharing of such historical and political experience should have made any right-minded Egyptian forget the artificial prejudice that he acknowledged was harbored by many against the Sudanese. After all, there are those

> among the sons of Lower Egypt who continue to view the Sa'idi [villager from Upper Egypt] with a prejudiced eye [bi-nadhrati al-makhsusah], but that viewpoint cannot remove the Sa'idi from his equality with the British. Likewise, those who view the Sudanese with shortsightedness do not remove the Sudanese from their equality with Egyptians in all rights and duties.[20]

And so, racial equality resurrects the formerly limp bodies of the oppressed Egyptians and Sudanese.

These were new concepts in the development of Egyptian nationalist thought and the issue of the Sudan. Lutfi al-Sayyid's vision elevated the Sudanese from the stereotypes of wild fanatics or savages to co-citizens. His ideas also raised them from the stereotypes of buffoonish servants so prevalent in Egyptian popular culture into co-nationalists.[21] A more conscious awareness of past history and the path of politics united the Egyptians and the Sudanese, and in this way, Lutfi al-Sayyid asked both groups to mentally re-create their sense of community and their place in the world. For the sake of keeping the Nile Valley in one symbolic peace, and for the sake of family peace, Lutfi al-Sayyid chose to diminish the importance of the Mahdiyya. The discord was over, and "every Egyptian on the one hand and every Sudanese on the other must consider each other as immediate brothers, or as cousins [ibn 'amm], all from one mother, within the borders of one country."[22] With the revolt of the Mahdiyya extinguished, normal family relations could once again be resumed. But the implied easiness and informality of this relationship cannot disguise who runs the family.

Lutfi al-Sayyid never seemed to have imagined the Sudanese running the unified country of Egypt/Sudan. And their fourteen years of autonomy remained a blot to be airbrushed away, out of common memory.

When he encouraged both Egyptians and Sudanese to regard each other as brothers and to disregard the borders that separated the two countries, Lutfi al-Sayyid asked his readers to create for themselves a new ethnographic identity, a new geography, and to imagine an alternative reality with the sheer force of hope and rhetoric. He invited his readers toward rethinking their cultural and racial identities from deep within themselves. Ironically, the Sudanese, the brothers, are never quoted, never asked, never named individually. Raised to equality with the Egyptians, the Sudanese in Lutfi al-Sayyid's account are rendered practically invisible. Even their distinctiveness in Egypt, as noted by Shuqayr, is removed from them. And they thus are hidden by the bodies of Egyptians, even the passive bodies of the soldiers so carefully measured by Myers, the Egyptians standing, sitting, and kneeling in the name of science.

Once you problematize cultural constructions of race, where do you go? Where do these questions lead us, particularly in the case of Egyptian nationalism at the end of the nineteenth and in the beginning of the twentieth century, beleaguered a movement as it was? I am not raising these issues in order to accuse great figures like Ahmad Lutfi al-Sayyid of being racist, worthy of politically correct scorn—one cannot help but appreciate the intellectual power of this Egyptian hero when reading his articles. I believe that although Lutfi al-Sayyid and other nationalists manipulated constructions of race as a defense against the British restructuring and reordering of Egyptian society, this was a desperate self-defense. Still, they were not always able to see how their own refiguring of the Sudanese, whether in stereotypical images or by making them "faux" Egyptians, resembled the straitjacketed roles into which British officials were trying to fit them.

NOTES

1. Myers, "The Anthropometry of the Modern Mahommedans," p. 237.
2. Mitchell, *Colonising Egypt*, pp. 95–127.
3. Kamil, *Al-Maqalat*, p. 298.
4. Ibid., p. 299.
5. Ibid., p. 299.
6. Mitchell, *Colonising Egypt*, pp. 155–156.
7. Kamil, *Al-Khutub*, p. 115, from speech given 3 March 1896 at the High Chamber of the 'Abbas Theater.
8. Ibid., p. 115.

9. Ibid., p. 116.

10. Ibid., p. 123.

11. Myers, "Contributions to Egyptian Anthropometry II," pp. 83–84.

12. *Rapport de Lord Cromer sur L'Egypte, et le Soudan pour L'annee 1904,* Imprimerie National, Cairo, 1905, p. 186.

13. Shuqayr, *Ta'rikh al-Sudan al-qadim wal-hadith wa jughrafiyatuhu,* p. 55.

14. Ibid., p. 245.

15. Ibid., p. 237.

16. Ibid., pp. 237–238.

17. I thank Professor John Voll of Georgetown University for these insights.

18. Shuqayr, *Ta'rikh al-Sudan al-qadim wal-hadith wa jughrafiyatuhu,* p. 232.

19. al-Sayyid, *Al-Jarida,* 24 July 1910.

20. Ibid., 22 October 1910.

21. For a sense of the popular stereotypes of Nubians and Sudanese in Egyptian literature, see Troutt Powell, "Egyptians in Blackface: Nationalism and the Representation of the Sudan in Egypt, 1919," pp. 27–45.

22. Ibid.

14

Egypt, Ethiopia, and
"The Abyssinian Crisis,"
1935–1936

Haggai Erlich

Ethiopia and Egypt have been connected from antiquity by the Nile issue, by church affiliation, and by Red Sea strategy. Their common history is ancient, one of the more diverse cases of international relations that, at certain historic junctures, has produced chapters of mutual cooperation and understanding, as well as conflict. These chapters were always of formative importance to both parties. The Ethio-Egyptian war of 1875–1876 and its outcome, for example, were very much a determining factor in modern Ethiopian history. Emperor Yohannes's victory at the battle of Gura in March 1876 reaffirmed for a short while Tigrean hegemony in the country (until 1889) and led to the establishment of imperial control over Eritrea. In the long run it paved the way for a chain of military victories culminating in the Adwa 1896 victory over Italy, thus ensuring the survival of Ethiopia's sovereignty throughout most of the twentieth century.[1] Egypt's defeat at Gura was equally central to modern Egyptian history. Without Eritrea and a railway from Massawa to Khartoum, it became nearly impossible to effectively control Sudan. Gura led directly to the loss of Ismail's African empire and indirectly to the subsequent occupation of Egypt itself by Britain. Moreover, his personal observation of Egypt's humiliating defeat at the hands of Ethiopia triggered Colonel Ahmad 'Urabi's protest movement, which was to herald the emergence of modern Egyptian nationalism. The purpose of this chapter is not to factually reconstruct another chapter of the Ethio-Egyptian story but rather to identify some of the mutual images and concepts, and determine how they influenced matters during a major historical event.

ETHIOPIAN EXPECTATIONS

The year 1935, the time of the Abyssinian crisis, was far less dramatic than 1876 in terms of direct Ethio-Egyptian bilateral contacts. Ethiopia could expect little aid from Egypt in the face of Benito Mussolini's aggression. Egypt had long since lost its independence and could render no diplomatic or material help of concrete significance. A few Ethiopian emissaries were sent to Cairo in 1935 in a vain attempt to make contact with the Sanusis resistance movement of Libya in order to direct anti-Italian riots there. The British completely controlled Egypt's strategic assets, including the Suez Canal, on which the entire fascist enterprise rested. In fact, the Egyptians were in no position to discuss even the future of their own lifeline—the Nile waters. The Lake Tana Dam issue had long been a British-Ethiopian affair from which the Egyptian governments and public had been deliberately excluded.[2] From the beginning of the century the British had hoped to revolutionize the Nile irrigation system by building a dam at Lake Tana in Ethiopia, turning it into a major water reservoir. Such a project, of course, was to be under British imperial control; its implementation, no matter how executed, would, in effect, mean tearing western Ethiopia from the Addis Ababa government, bringing it under British rule. Because this was unthinkable to the Ethiopians, they conducted futile and prolonged negotiations, frustrating British policymakers. (The British continued to toy with the Tana Dam idea until 1954.[3]) When Ras Tafari, the future Haile Selassie, visited Cairo in 1924, he witnessed firsthand how the British kept the Egyptians in the dark. Indeed, British correspondence regarding the Nile and the Lake Tana project reveals an amazingly paternalistic British approach toward Egypt. Only in the early 1930s did the British allow Egyptian policymakers to have a partial glimpse of the British-Ethiopian negotiations picture, primarily because the Egyptian government had to pay for some relevant surveys. In 1935 Mussolini threatened to capture the source of the Blue Nile and the Lake Tana area, alarming the Egyptian politicians and the public.[4] All they could do, however, was rely on their British occupiers who, after Mussolini had occupied Ethiopia, reached an understanding with him in which he would not interfere with the flow of the Nile without their consent. This understanding was officially sealed in 1938.

During the period between the two world wars, Egypt, its political weakness so clearly exposed, still remained important to Ethiopia in cultural and religious terms. By 1935, however, Egypt's image had undergone significant changes. Prior to Britain's occupation of Egypt in 1882, the country had been perceived by Ethiopians primarily in terms of a Christian-Islamic conflict. Emperors Tewodros (r. 1855–1868) and Yohannes IV (r. 1872–1889), still influenced by medieval traumas (the "Ahmad Gragn syndrome"),[5] even depicted the modernizing Egyptians of the time as

Muslim holy warriors. Tewodros dismissed Khedive Sa'id's friendly gestures, even arresting the Egyptian Coptic patriarch sent by Cairo to his
court on a goodwill mission. Yohannes IV, clashing with Khedive Isma'il's
invading armies on the battlefield, disastrously failed to see the Egyptian
ruler, "an impatient Europeanizer," in terms other than that of a religious
enemy.[6] But after Egypt lost its political independence, Ethiopian suspi-
cions dwindled. Emperor Menelik I (r. 1889–1913) and his successors
were undisturbed when young Muslim Ethiopians flocked to the *riwaq al-
jabartiyya* (the Ethiopian Muslim wing of the al-Azhar Islamic University)
in Cairo. This atmosphere of greatly reduced Christian-Islamic tension culminated in 1935 when Haile Selassie, faced with Mussolini's anti-Christ-
ian Ethiopian-Islamic propaganda, did his best to appease Ethiopia's Islamic communities. He was aided by the leadership of the Egyptian
al-Azhar *madrasa,* which, in February 1935, sent two Azharite shaikhs
from Cairo to Addis Ababa to open a *madrasa* in the Ethiopian capital and
help rally support around the emperor.[7]

Paradoxically, things went less well in the Egyptian Christian context.
From the fourth century A.D., the Ethiopian Church was dependent on the
Coptic patriarchate of Egypt. The *abun* (Ethiopia's archbishop) was an
Egyptian appointed by Alexandria, a fact of pivotal importance in the region's long history. When Haile Sellassie began building his power base
(from 1916 to 1930 he was still Ras Tafari) he also aimed at enhancing
centralization by emancipating and nationalizing the Ethiopian Church. He
wanted the Egyptians to agree to the appointment of an Ethiopian *abun.*
He also began a campaign for the return of the keys of the Jerusalem
monastery of Deir al-Sultan, which had been taken over by the Copts from
their fellow Ethiopian monks in 1834.[8] Ras Tafari's combined effort culminated in his 1924 trip to Cairo. Much to his frustration, the Egyptian
government was unhelpful, and the Coptic establishment refused to compromise on either issue.[9] In 1926 a new Egyptian *abun* was appointed to
Ethiopia who, in 1929, consecrated five Ethiopian bishops, slightly im-
proving the situation. However, further negotiations came to nothing. Indeed, in 1935 the leadership of the Egyptian Coptic Church (unlike Coptic intelligentsia and modern politicians) failed to serve as a rallying point
in mobilizing sympathy for Ethiopia. Moreover, Mussolini's occupation
only aggravated relations in the Christian aspect. In late 1937 Abuna Qer-
ilos returned to Egypt and the Italians declared the Ethiopian Church autocephalous by appointing one bishop as a metropolitan. This arrangement
was annulled by Haile Selassie upon his return to Ethiopia in 1941.
Egypt's negative response to the 1937 emancipation of their church had
made its mark on the collective Ethiopian consciousness.

Egypt was important to Ethiopia's modernization in areas other than
church affairs. Egypt was perceived by many educated Ethiopians as the

corridor to Europe and European culture. Practically all Ethiopians who ventured to Europe passed through Egypt, marveling at its own modernization. Ras Tafari visited Cairo in 1924 en route to Paris, Rome, and London, and wrote that he conceived the Egyptian capital to be part of Europe's modern beauty.[10] In 1929 an Egyptian consulate was opened in Addis Ababa; during Haile Selassie's coronation ceremony in 1930, a high-ranking Egyptian delegation represented King Fuad along with other Western dignitaries and delegates. Modern education was of major importance in this context. The first modern school in Addis Ababa had been established in 1908, run and staffed by Egyptian Coptic schoolmasters. Ras Tafari opened the second school upon his return and continued to rely on Egyptian educators. Ethiopian youngsters were sent to study in Egypt's secondary and high schools.

The Ethiopian most identified with Egyptian ties was most likely Blata (Doctor) Heruy Walda-Selassie (died 1938). A prominent writer and historian, Heruy became Haile Selassie's chief adviser on foreign affairs. Heruy wrote extensively about his various tours in Europe and Asia, combining his religious concepts with his curiosity and admiration for everything modern. His special interest in Egypt helped him become the chief negotiator in church relations, the Deir al-Sultan issue, and modern educational affairs. His own two sons studied in Victoria College in Alexandria. It is quite apparent that Heruy was the go-between on the Nile issue, and that during his many visits to Cairo, he told his Egyptian hosts whatever the Ethiopian emperor wanted them to know on the Tana negotiations with the British. During the Abyssinian crisis in 1935, Heruy served as Haile Selassie's foreign minister.

Heruy Walda-Selassie's vision of Egypt, therefore, is most interesting. He published three books on his tours to the Lower Nile country. The first was issued following his 1923 tour to Jerusalem and Egypt,[11] and the second was his diary on the 1924 tour, in which he accompanied Ras Tafari to Egypt and Europe. The book, *Happiness and Honor,* was indeed a very optimistic account of Ethiopian-Egyptian relations.[12] During this year, his master, Tafari, made a major breakthrough as Ethiopia's promising modernizing prince; during this same year, Egypt enjoyed the "peoples' government," the first Wafdist cabinet under Sa'd Zaghlul. Heruy's 1924 descriptions of Egypt, both as a religious sister as well as a model of modernization, were vivid and admiring. Meetings with King Fuad, Prime Minister Zaghlul, and members of the Coptic Church establishment were most cordial and promising. The 1924 visit was indeed the Ethio-Egyptian's finest hour in centuries, and Heruy's book reflected high expectations for modern cooperation between the two ancient and culturally connected neighbors. By 1933, however, when Heruy revisited Egypt in September, disillusionment had set in. The Egyptians had failed to respond to

Ethiopia's modern needs in terms of nationalizing its church, and the Ethiopians continued to keep their Nile cards close to their chest. Heruy's 1934 book, *Experiencing and Seeing It All,* is a description of his tour through Palestine, Egypt, Syria, and Greece.[13] He accompanied the emperor's wife to Jerusalem (Empress Menen was a keen promoter of Ethiopian religious rights in Jerusalem) and went to Egypt to make another effort at emancipating the Ethiopian Church and regaining Deir al-Sultan. Heruy met again with King Fuad, the Coptic patriarch, and twice with the foreign minister. He achieved nothing, and his description of the country this time is nearly dismissive. In fact, he saved his enthusiasm for his short visit to Tel Aviv a few days later.

EGYPT AND THE CRISIS

In 1935, the Ethiopians were too overwhelmed to expect anything of substance from Egypt. Egypt, however, was forthcoming. Cairo sent the Azharite *shaykhs,* which helped Haile Selassie rally the Muslim community. Yet this was not the only Egyptian source of aid. In late 1935, soon after the beginning of the Italian invasion, Egypt actually sent volunteers (mostly Ethiopians residing in Egypt), led by two ex–Ottoman generals and three Red Crescent medical teams, all of whom saw action on the Harar front.[14] These were meaningful symbolic gestures of solidarity, whose significance can better be appreciated in the Egyptian context.

Indeed, it is from the Egyptian perspective that the Abyssinian crisis can be described as perhaps the most revealing chapter in Ethiopian-Egyptian relations. For as Mussolini defied the entire system of international relations, the year 1935 became a major watershed in Egypt's history. Egypt's political public—the old guard of rivaling politicians and a new emerging generation of the educated middle class—long engaged in the struggle for liberation from the British, were now torn between various pressing dilemmas. An intensive public debate on the nature of fascism ensued.[15] Mussolini's aggression had a double impact. In challenging British and French regional supremacy, he opened new strategic options; in violently threatening an oriental neighbor, he recycled and magnified old fears. Mussolini also introduced new forms in the political system, accumulating national pride and strength, and his image galvanized curiosity in Egypt. The debate culminated in the year of the Abyssinian crisis and helped Egyptians to realize where they really stood on democracy and parliamentarianism. Recent studies convincingly show that the overwhelming majority of opinion makers in Egypt at that time despised fascist totalitarianism, and publicly defended political openness, a topic outside our present scope. Mussolini also represented a new and more violent form of

Western imperialist aggression. Faced with this aspect, Egypt naturally perceived Ethiopia as the negative mirror image, and Egyptian debate on this issue during 1935 was equally intensive. But while the discussion of Mussolini and fascism was somewhat external, having to do with strategic options and the nature of politics, the debate over Ethiopia delved into the very issue of identity. In hundreds of newspaper articles, pamphlets, and books published in Egypt that year, Ethiopia was discussed in terms of its legacies during the long regional relations; in terms of old Islamic perceptions; in terms of ancient and modern Egyptian ideas of Ethiopia; and in terms of the renewed concepts of emerging pan-Arabism. "Al-mas'ala al-habashiyya" was not merely a discussion of the other; it was also a reflection of different ideas and concepts regarding the Egyptian self.

Like any other analysis of identity in history, our discussion does not simplify matters. Islam, Egyptianism, and Arabism are all far from being one-dimensional definitions of the self and of the other. We must therefore summarize our observations of their complexities in shaping attitudes during that stormy crisis.

ISLAMIC PERCEPTIONS

Islam's primary perceptions of Ethiopia stem from a formative experience dating back to its very emergence. These perceptions remained essentially polarized, a good reflection of Islam's own versatility.[16]

In A.D. 616 the *najashi* (the negus king of Ethiopia) gave asylum to the first group of the Prophet's followers, saving them from their Meccan persecutors and perhaps even rescuing Muhammad himself. The *najashi* continued to support Muhammad, who in gratitude, ordered his believers to "leave the Ethiopians alone as long as they leave you alone." This message was interpreted as a recognition of Christian Ethiopia as the only real "land of neutrality" exempted from Jihad. The Islamic notion of Ethiopia as a "land of righteousness and justice" has often resurfaced throughout history. The Ethiopian model of religious affinity and brotherly tolerance today serves the case of moderate fundamentalist Muslims in the United States, Great Britain, and Israel in urging acceptance of a non-Islamic government. Even leaders of Hamas recognize Yasser Arafat's Palestinian Authority, arguing that the Prophet ordered his followers to live under the non-Muslim, yet righteous *najashi*.[17]

It has long been established that the 1930s saw "the return of Islam" in Egypt. Until recently, this return was interpreted as implying the abandonment of Western ideas of tolerance and liberalism by many intellectuals. Recent studies accept the notion of *return,* but tend to highlight liberal dimensions in this renewed Islamic orientation. Examination of the

Ethiopian case supports this trend. Most of Islamic-inspired expressions and actions in Egypt of 1935 were consonant with antifascist and pro-Ethiopian expressions made by Egypt's liberals. They all resorted to the medieval image of noble Ethiopia, emphasizing Islam's tolerance. Shaykh Muhammad Rashid Rida, the old and tiring leader of the *salafiyya* movement who died in December 1935, led the field. He also inspired his followers to real action. The Association of Young Muslims, guided by Rida since the 1920s, became Ethiopia's most energetic supporter. In early 1935 leaders of the association established a "Committee for the Defense of Ethiopia," later joined by other elements.[18] This committee, in which the Young Muslims remained prominent, sent the two Azharite *shaykhs* mentioned earlier to Addis Ababa and supervised the enlistment of volunteers. The committee also raised contributions for an "Ethiopian Fund" that financed transportation for the three Red Crescent medical teams to the battlefield.

Needless to say, the expression of solidarity with Egypt's oppressed Christian neighbor was also clear support for the interpretation of Islam as an open and liberal religion. In 1935, however, this was not the only voice of Islam in Egypt. A more militant and less flexible Islam was on the rise, which, as it reasserted itself, also dealt with the Ethiopian dimension.

The initial chapter of Islam's relations with Ethiopia, the Muhammad-*najashi* story, had also left the opposite image of the Christian state in Islam a most negative one. It was argued by all relevant Muslim historians that in A.D. 628 the *najashi* answered the call of his friend the Prophet and embraced Islam. However, he had to conceal this fact from the priests and generals. They and their people betrayed him, remaining loyal to their Christian heresy. Seen from this angle, Ethiopia was already a legal part of the "land of Islam," and the demise of the Muslim *najashi* was therefore Islam's first defeat. The legacy of "Islam al-najashi" has been adopted ever since by Muslims less tolerant of other cultures. In their literature, these militants have portrayed Ethiopia as the embodiment of heresy, barbarism, and evil, one of Islam's principal enemies. For example, some medieval traditions recycled an old, pre-Islamic episode to show that the infidel Ethiopians wanted to destroy the Ka'ba, and predicted they would succeed. The infidel Ethiopians would also invade and destroy Egypt prior to God's redemption of Islam.[19] Many Islamic rulers throughout the centuries have refused to negotiate with Ethiopia's emperors, declaring them illegitimate usurpers and declaring that Ethiopia had no right to exist unless its people reconverted to Islam. These militant Muslims interpreted the "leave the Abyssinians alone" prophetic message to mean that Ethiopia, prior to its Islamization, should be boycotted, sidelined, and ignored.

The most prominent manifestation of this Islamic anti-Ethiopian stand in Egypt, 1935, was the publication in November of a book called *Islam and Ethiopia.* Written by Yusuf Ahmad, a teacher and formerly an inspector in the government archeology department, and subsidized by the Italian legation, it was the harshest condemnation of Ethiopia and a clear call for its destruction in the name of Islam. Resorting to old traditions and using some elements of modern research, Yusuf Ahmad described Ethiopia's major sins toward Islam in general and toward Ethiopia's own Muslims in particular. He provided extremely unbalanced surveys of the Islamic policies of Emperors Tewodros, Yohannes, Menelik, and Haile Selassie, making every effort to depict Ethiopia as the worst enemy of Islam and deserving of a good lesson by Mussolini. Indeed, another book, *Italy and Her Colonies,* written in Cairo in 1936 by Shaykh Muhammad Num Bakr, ran along the same lines, describing Mussolini as a champion and savior of Islam in Libya, and wishing an equally enlightened occupation on Ethiopia.[20]

Yusuf Ahmad's book was widely read. In the months following its publication, newspapers such as *Al-Balagh* and *Ruz al-Yusuf* published entire chapters of it. A very favorable review appeared in the prestigious monthly magazine, *Al-Hilal.* In years to come, *Islam in Ethiopia* was to become the standard text on that country for Arabic readers in the Middle East. In this capacity it replaced *Voyage to Ethiopia* by Syrian author Sadiq al 'Azm, published in 1908, a book written in the spirit of Islamic openness and one that had advocated recognition of Christian Ethiopia as a respected neighbor.[21] In fact, radical Islamic literature produced in Egypt today still recycles large portions of Yusuf Ahmad's book preaching the same concept of Ethiopia's illegitimacy.

The immediate influence of radical Islamic perceptions of Ethiopia on public opinion in Egypt must be investigated further. In any case, Ethiopia had been conquered by the middle of 1936, and its struggle was no longer a major focus of interest. Other issues such as the outbreak of the Arab revolt in Palestine in April 1936 captured public attention. In the midst of all the excitement, the Muslim Brethren, previously an offshoot of the Association of Young Muslims, had begun gaining momentum in Cairo. It began preaching a more militant Islam, though still much more moderate as compared to later radicalism. From our point of view, however, the following episode is worth mentioning. When the Arab revolt in Palestine broke out, the leader of the Brethren, Shaykh Hasan al-Banna, turned to Prince 'Umar Tusun, the head of the Committee for the Defense of Ethiopia, and in the name of Islam demanded that the Ethiopian Fund be transferred to help fellow Muslims struggling in Palestine. He was refused. Tusun replied that the money was not only of Muslim origins. It had been donated by Egyptian Muslims, Christians, and Jews alike, and in the name of pluralism should remain in the service of the Ethiopian cause.[22]

CONCEPTS OF EGYPTIANISM

Prince Tusun's reply reflected a modern Egyptian concept of Ethiopia, a very positive dimension of pluralist Egyptianism to which we shall turn shortly. In 1935, the majority of modern Egyptian nationalists detested Mussolini and identified with Ethiopia. The Committee for the Defense of Ethiopia, which supervised the activities and gestures mentioned earlier, was a coalition of moderate Muslims, Coptic Church leadership, and liberal Egyptians. However, Egyptian nationalism, a modern identity that began to emerge in the late nineteenth century, was divided as regards Ethiopia.

On one hand, a favorable concept of Ethiopia had appeared, stemming from a variety of reasons, all central to the emerging modern Egyptian soul. First was the renewed definition of Egypt as the land of the Nile, which held Ethiopia to be relevant. Second was the growing sense of equality of the Egyptian Copts, whose Ethiopian connections need no reminder. Third was the entire regional concept rooted in the new, pluralist Egyptian self. Within this concept of a pluralist, diversified, yet united East, Ethiopia, considered oriental in its religions, culture, and languages, was perceived as a fully legitimate partner. As mentioned earlier, this spirit culminated during Ras Tafari's visit to Egypt in 1924. In that same year, perhaps the culmination of parliamentary Egyptianism (the "people's government" of Sa'd Zaghlul), the crown prince of Ethiopia, leader of an independent Afro-oriental state, was enthusiastically and warmly received in Egypt as a dignified brother.[23]

On the other hand, as in the case of Islam's dichotomy and not entirely divorced from it, Egyptianism had also developed a distinctly negative view of Ethiopia. It essentially stemmed from the ancient fears that Ethiopia would divert the waters of the Nile, fears that multiplied with the renewed conceptual and practical centrality of the river. Interwoven with these anxieties was the sense of anger and shame in the wake of the 1876 Gura defeat. Gura was the Egyptian army's first significant defeat since its re-establishment by Muhammad 'Ali, and its grave consequences were strongly felt during the formative period of emerging modern nationalism. The image of barbarous Ethiopia ambushing an army that had been sent to spread advanced civilization in Africa, and then maltreating Egyptian prisoners, was burned into Egypt's modern collective memory. The Gura story, Ethiopia's savage image and its foiling of Egypt's dream of unity along the Nile, was recycled and retold on many occasions. Modern Egyptians of more militant bent could hardly forgive Ethiopia. For example, Ethiopia's 1896 Adwa victory over the Italians was widely ignored by the Egyptian public. Egypt's only significant response was the publication of a book in Cairo in 1896 written by a retired army officer. Far from crediting the Ethiopians for their unique achievement, the book narrated the officer's Gura misfortunes of twenty years earlier and his maltreatment as a prisoner of war at the hands of the "primitive Ethiopians." Forty years later, during Ras Tafari's visit in 1924 to Cairo, another ex-officer published an article to the same effect.[24]

During the 1930s, a more militant Egyptian nationalism was on the rise. Many members of the new generation, some established thinkers and movements such as Young Egypt, came forward with a less pluralistic concept of Egyptianism, ready to abandon parliamentarianism in favor of military pride and authoritarian politics. Their flirtation with fascism and Mussolini is a subject of some controversy, but we shall confine ourselves to a short observation from the Ethiopian angle. In 1935, the overwhelming majority of Egyptian public opinion strongly disapproved of Mussolini's aggression. The Abyssinian question, at least for a while, exposed both the crude imperialism and racism inherent in fascism. Thinkers such as Salama Musa,[25] youth leaders such as Fathi Radwan,[26] and others were now ready to declare their solidarity with Ethiopia. Members of Young Egypt participated in related activities. In this respect, at least during the crisis, Egypt's nationalistic-militant wing was clearly in favor of Ethiopia's survival. They were not, however, ready to go beyond this declaration and showed no real curiosity toward Ethiopia itself, its culture or history.

The mainstream of Egyptian modern nationalism, however, was quite ready to cross this line and wholeheartedly identified with Ethiopia in 1935. Most opinion makers, as recent studies have shown, attacked Mussolini in defense of political openness. At the same time they also rediscovered Ethiopia, and for the same purpose.

The quantity of relevant literature produced in Egypt that year was enormous. "Al Masala al-habashiyya" (the Ethiopian Question), in both its Italian and Ethiopian dimensions, was the main issue and a most stormy one. Hundreds of newspaper articles dealt with Ethiopia as well as dozens of analytical pieces and quite a number of books. Many newspapers, notably *Al-Ahram,* ran daily columns, even appointing special correspondents to Addis Ababa. The leading opinion makers were Muhammad 'Abdallah 'Inan,[27] 'Abdallah Husayn,[28] Muhammad Hasan al-Zayyat,[29] and, primarily, Muhammad Lutfi Gum'a. The latter, the author of the famous "The Life of the East" (1932), was a very prominent advocate of the concept of Easternism; the idea that all Eastern peoples, facing the Western challenge, should enhance their cultural affinity and cooperate politically. His book, *The African Lion and the Italian Tiger,*[30] depicted Ethiopia as the symbol of the entire East, its leader in the areas of bravery and survival. He went on to review Ethiopia's history explaining in most sympathetic terms its development and victories. Like almost all the other authors mentioned here, he wrote that he felt the need to reintroduce Ethiopia to himself and to the Egyptian public. He described Ethiopia's land, Christianity, customs, and social diversity, and praised its leaders for their efforts at modernization. He also referred to the old Islamic concepts of Ethiopia as the land of righteousness. Published in November 1935, Gum'a's book was the mirror image, at the opposite pole of Ahmad Yusuf's radical Islamic book. Paradoxically, it was equally popular.

Needless to say, most modern Egyptians yearned for an Ethiopian victory. This time they did not ignore the 1896 Adwa victory, but rather expected its recurrence. For liberals like Muhammad Lutfi Gum'a, such an Ethiopian victory would have enhanced liberalism and parliamentarianism in Egypt. 'Inan (and many others) kept reminding the Italians of Adwa.[31] Yet, although Gum'a predicted the African lion would defeat the Italian tiger again, a new Adwa was not to occur. Rather, the history of Egypt, its immediate politics, and its own struggle to shape its identities was forced to develop under the shadow of Mussolini's success.

ARABISM AND ETHIOPIA

The year of the Abyssinian crisis was also most significant in the history of the Arab modern identity. Mussolini's defiance of the British and French, his militant nationalism, and fascism's emphasis on the spirit of youth were instrumental in triggering the wave of the younger generation in politics. In Egypt, Syria, Palestine, and Iraq, the Abyssinian crisis was a factor in inspiring the emergence of paramilitary youth organizations, as well as in the strengthening of pan-Arabism as an ideology of the "middle class." The consequences for the history of Egypt and the entire region were far-reaching,[32] though our discussion refers only to the Egyptian dimension during the formative crisis.

Arab identity in Egypt was, at that time, an emerging element, blended primarily in the integral Egyptianism of the kind mentioned above. In order to observe it in isolation, we must refer to Syrians and Iraqis residing, or influencing the debate, in Egypt. In so doing we encounter another dichotomy, reflecting an equally intensive debate over Ethiopia in Syria that year.

On one hand, again, Ethiopia found supporters. 'Abd al Rahman Shabandar, the Syrian Arab national hero of the 1925 anti-French revolt, and long exiled in Egypt, becomes an important figure in our history. He joined the Committee for the Defense of Ethiopia and, himself a physician, was active in organizing the Red Crescent medical aid. He published articles in the Egyptian press in which he stated that Ethiopia represented all

Eastern peoples and that he was ready to die for Ethiopia the way he was ready to die for Syria.[33] Another Syrian residing in Egypt, historian Amin Sa'id, published a series of pro-Ethiopian articles in the *Al-Muqattam* daily, a main platform for Egyptian liberals. He stated that the Arabs and Ethiopia had always, even in pre-Islamic days, been part of the Orient, that all Arabs should be committed to support their Ethiopian sister on the basis of Oriental bond.[34]

General Taha al-Hashimi, a sworn pan-Arab Iraqi, one of Iraq's important politicians and the chief of staff of the Iraqi army at the time, answered the call of the Egyptian journal *Al-Risala* to explain the military dimensions of the crisis, Egypt at that time having no generals of its own. He produced a series of six articles published in the last weeks of 1935. Their subject was the 1896 Adwa victory of Ethiopia over the invading Italians, and their message, in terms of Arab hopes and expectations, was clear.[35]

Stronger, however, was the voice of anti-Ethiopian Arabists. The Lebanese Christian, Bulus Mas'ad, resident of Cairo, journalist, and the author of various books on Arab history, published a book entitled *Ethiopia or Abyssinia.*[36] Like Yusuf Ahmad's book, it was also subsidized by the Italian legation in Cairo and was equally venomous. The difference was that he narrated Ethiopian history, depicting the country as barbarous and primitive, not in Islamic terms but in modern progressive ones. He recycled material supplied to him by fascist propaganda machinery on Ethiopia, describing the cruel house of slavery, a land in need of a civilizing Mussolini.

Much more important was the work by the Lebanese Druze, Amir Shakib Arslan. Arslan was by far the most important figure in the context of Mussolini's influence in the whole Middle Eastern arena. He undertook to spread the world of the Duce, and to exploit the Abyssinian crisis in order to inspire the younger generation in the Middle East to revolt against the French and the British. He hoped that such an uprising would enhance pan-Arabism, especially his brand, namely Arabism with a strong element of Islamic identity and solidarity. In the dozens of articles published in 1935, Arslan depicted Ethiopia as a historical enemy of Islam, an oppressor of its own Muslims, an enemy of Arab language and culture. A skilled historian, he combined the negative messages of radical Islam with the modern message of fascist propaganda.[37] Most of Arslan's work was published primarily in Syrian, Lebanese, and Palestinian papers; nevertheless, he had his share in the Egyptian press and was widely read in Egypt.

CONCLUSION: THE NILE PERSPECTIVE

We have discussed just one dimension of 1935, which was a watershed in the histories of the two countries. In the years following the end of World

War II, nearly all the concrete issues of the old Ethio-Egyptian agenda resurfaced and culminated, their intensity magnified by newly emerging factors. Egyptian scholars and educators supervised Ethiopia's effort in the early 1940s to rehabilitate the education system ruined by the fascists. Haile Selassie's campaign to emancipate the Ethiopian Church led to an agreement in 1959 with the Coptic patriarchate, in which the former was declared autocephalous. In the mid-1940s, Egypt, which had lost control over Eritrea's territory to Gura in 1876, renewed its claims. Its diplomatic effort at the UN was conducted in Egyptianist terms, but they were transformed beginning in the mid-1950s into modern Arab revolutionary concepts of ethnic nationalism and subversion. Later in the same decade, Israel entered the picture, and its alliance with Haile Selassie further complicated Ethio-Egyptian relations.[38] (In 1969, after the Six-Day War, Israel handed the keys of Deir al-Sultan over to the Ethiopians.) The 1963 establishment of the Organization of African Unity headquarters in Addis Ababa, and Haile Selassie's rising prominence in African diplomacy, added a conciliatory tone to his relations with Gamal Abdel Nasser. These, and many other related matters, intensified Ethio-Egyptian relations. The main factor, however, remained the Nile issue.

After the British, along with their Tana Dam idea, left Egypt, Nasser built the High Dam at Aswan. His message was clear. Egypt's source of life would remain in Egyptian hands. It would never again be the subject of negotiations, such as those between Ethiopia and the British in which the Egyptians themselves were ignored. In erecting the dam and in shaping the water policy behind it, however, Nasser ignored the Ethiopians. Indeed, Egypt's long-range water strategy seems to rest on the assumption that Ethiopia, contributing four-fifths of Lake Nasser's waters, will never receive any of it for itself. One can never really appreciate the Egyptian approach without perceiving it as a new, modified version of the old Islamic legacy of "leave the Abyssinians alone," in the sense of ignoring and sidelining Ethiopia. Indeed, without a familiarity with the rich reservoir of old mutual concepts, one cannot make sense of the contemporary Ethio-Egyptian dialogue regarding the Nile. The Egyptians, on their part, continue to waver between the various and contradictory Ethiopian images created during their own transformations. The hard-liners in the Nile-Ethiopian context recycle the memories of Gura, Eritrea's Arabism, and radical Islam's concepts of Ethiopia's illegitimacy. Indeed, radical Muslims in Cairo still resort to Yusuf Ahmad's book when producing their anti-Ethiopian literature. The Egyptian soft-liners, such as certain circles in the foreign ministry circles and sources behind the *Siyasa Duwaliyya* magazine, prefer to emphasize the historical legacies of religious and cultural brotherhood with Ethiopia, derived from the more pluralist concepts of Islam, Egyptianism, and Arabism discussed above. The Ethiopians, on their part, also conduct their present-day Nile policy, wavering between deep suspicion and a sense of affinity. The former stems from old recycled concepts of Islamic enmity and historic sensitivities about the church; the latter relies on a sense of ancient, Oriental neighborliness, and of diplomatic ties in Heruy Walda-Selassie's tradition. In forming their foreign policies, Egyptians and Ethiopians, like all peoples, continue to struggle with their own identities derived from concepts and messages of the past.

NOTES

This chapter is based on research conducted under the auspices of and with the help of grants by the Israel Science Foundation, founded by the Israel Academy for Science and Humanities and the U.S. Institute for Peace.

1. On the battle of Gura and consequences see Erlich, *Ras Alula and the Scramble for Africa,* Chapter 1.

2. On the Tana project and Ethio-British negotiations see Abdussamad Ahmad, "Gojjam." Also, McCann, "Ethiopia, Britain, and Negotiations for the Lake Tana Dam, 1922–1935," pp. 667–699. For British efforts to conceal their negotiations from the Egyptians see British Archives, Public Record Office, Foreign Office 371/9989, Allenby to MacDonald, 17 May 1924. Also, Foreign Office 401/35–38, "Lake Tana Reservoir Scheme: Negotiations Since 1924" by H. K. Grey, 20 February 1935.

3. See British Archives, Public Record Office, Foreign Office 371/108264, Bromley to Luce, 7 July 1954.

4. For British reports on Ethio-Egyptian relations of the period see files in British Archives, Public Record Office, Foreign Office 401/35–38, and in Foreign Office 371 series; for Italian material see Archivio Storico, Ministero Degli Affari Esteri, Rome, the series "Etiopia fondo la guerra," buste 6–170.

5. The sixteenth-century conquest and destruction of Ethiopia (1529–1543) by the Islamic holy war, led from the town of Harar by Imam Ahmad ibn Ibrahim "Gragn," left a traumatic memory in the Ethiopian collective soul. Gragn was inspired and aided by the Islamic-Ottoman revival in the Middle East, and managed to unite the Muslims of the Horn of Africa against the Christian state. In Erlich, *Ethiopia and the Middle East,* the term "Gragn syndrome" is coined to reflect Ethiopians' recurring fear that Middle Eastern connections may encourage such dangerous local Islamic reunification (see Chapter 3).

6. On Tewodros and Egypt see Erlich, *Ethiopia and the Middle East,* Chapter 4; on Yohannes and Egypt, Chapter 5; also see Erlich, *Ethiopia and the Challenge of Independence,* Chapter 2.

7. Details in Erlich, *Ethiopia and the Middle East,* Chapter 8.

8. On Church relations see, for a Coptic perspective, Meinardus, *Christian Egypt, Faith and Life,* appendix, and for an Ethiopian perspective see Amanu, "The Ethiopian Orthodox Church Becomes Autocephalous." On the Deir al-Sultan, for a Coptic perspective see Suriyal, *'Dir al-Sultan bi'al-Quds.* For an Ethiopian perspective see Gabra-Haywat, *Yader Sultan ba'irusalem.*

9. See Erlich, "Ethiopia and Egypt," pp. 64–83.

10. See Haile Selassie, *My Life and Ethiopia's Progress,* p. 84.

11. Walda-Selassie, *Yale'lat wayzaro Manan mangad ba'iruslemna bamisr.*

12. Walda-Selassie, *Dastana kibir.*

13. Walda-Selassie, *Ba'adame masinbat hulun lamayet.*

14. Details in Erlich, *Ethiopia and the Middle East,* Chapter 8.

15. Israel Gershoni has just completed an extensive study on this subject, *Light in the Shade.* I am grateful to Professor Gershoni for allowing me to see his manuscript. Some of the ideas and material that I have presented in this chapter have come from his authoritative study.

16. For a detailed discussion of the formative concepts of Ethiopia see Erlich, *Ethiopia and the Middle East,* Chapter 1.

17. See a detailed discussion in Erlich, *Ethiopia and the Middle East,* Chapter 1.

18. On the committee see Erlich, *Ethiopia and the Middle East,* Chapter 8, and more in Gershoni, *Light in the Shade,* Chapter 3.

19. See more in Ibn Hamadû, *Kitab al-fitan,* pp. 403–409, the chapter entitled "The Ethiopians' Invasions."

20. Bakr, *Italy in Her Colonies,* pp. 61–66, 74.

21. al-'Azm, *Rihlat al-habasha.*

22. Gershoni, *Light in the Shade,* chapter 3.

23. Erlich, "Ethiopia and Egypt—Ras Tafari in Cairo, 1924."

24. See Erlich, "Egypt and Adwa."

25. Musa, "Italy and Ethiopia," *Majallati,* 1 July 1935.

26. Fathi Radwan, second in the command of Young Egypt, published a book on Mussolini and his road to power (Cairo, 1937), in which he did not mention the Ethiopian crisis.

27. 'Inan, "The Conflict Between Ethiopia and Western Imperialism," *Al-Risala,* 24 December 1934, and "Egypt, the Waters of the Nile and the Ethiopian Affairs," *Al-Risala,* 7 January 1935.

28. Husayn, *The Ethiopian Question.*

29. Muhammad Hasan al-Zayyat, "The Ethiopian Question—The Question of the East and of Freedom," *Al-Risala,* 5 August 1935.

30. Gum'a, *The African Lion and the Italian Tiger.*

31. See for example 'Inan's article, "The Conflict Between Ethiopia and Western Imperialism."

32. For an elaboration on these issues, see Erlich, "Periphery and Youth." Also see Erlich, *The Middle East Between the World Wars.*

33. See quotation from Al-Qabas of 1 December 1935 in Erlich, *Ethiopia and the Middle East,* p. 113.

34. Sa'id, "Arab-Ethiopian Relations—Why the East Supports Ethiopia," *Al-Muqattam,* 25 April 1935.

35. Al-Hashimi, "The Battle of Adwa."

36. Mas'ad, *Ethiopia or Abyssinia in a Turning Point in Her History.*

37. See Erlich, *Ethiopia and the Middle East,* especially Chapter 9.

38. See Erlich, *The Struggle over Eritrea, 1962–1978.*

15

◆

Geographers and Nationalism in Egypt: Huzayyin and the Unity of the Nile Valley, 1945–1948

Israel Gershoni

Nationalism and territory are two closely related entities. Simple relations of mutual attraction and dependence exist between them. The national imagination has to define for itself a specific territory, a fatherland, in order to people it with the national community and to realize a national life in it. The territory, for its part, constitutes the home of the national community and creates a country for it. The relationship between nationalism and geography as a science and a distinct academic discipline is more complex. Generally, in creating what Anthony Smith calls "poetic spaces," nationalism utilizes archaeology, history, anthropology, and philology as a "scientific" means of shaping the national landscape.[1] The "new priesthood of the nation," to borrow another of Smith's phrases, will generally be historians, archaeologists, philologists, folklorists, and anthropologists in addition to poets, writers, sculptors, artists, and musicians. They serve as an intellectual avant-garde that creates, manages, and disseminates a new community memory and identity and obliterates the old.[2] However, geography and geographers sometimes also have an important role in "inventing" the national poetic spaces and time. Geographers can endow the geographical structure of the national territory with scientism and objectivity; they can define its geographical and historical boundaries and establish the reciprocal relations between the climatic and topographical milieu and the human community residing in that territory. In this way, they become active partners in constructing the new national imagination.

In more saliently territorial types of nationalism, like the case of the ethnic communities living on the banks of the Nile, the role of geographer seems even more critical. Here their task is to turn the climatic and geographical space developing around the central existence of a river into a national landscape and national experience. They will tend to recruit scientific geographical knowledge to create a territorial memory. They will locate the "community of memory" in place and time, and will depict the organic continuity of human life in the course of thousands of years within a stable geographical structure. Geographers will explain the existence of ethnic homogeneity in the natural reality of geographical unity based on the eternal cyclical rhythm of the river flow. They will organize the national museum so that the ethnic artifacts of ancient national existence will rest on geographical displays that represent a rigid and unchanging pattern of an environment and *ethnie* that took shape on the banks of the Nile and live in its shadow. They will show how a river has created a nation in its own image.

This double stance of a geographer who is both an academic scholar and a "national priest" typifies the lifework of Sulayman Huzayyin, one of Egypt's most able and well-known geographers of this century. Huzayyin, who was born in 1909, graduated in the first class of the geography department of the newly established Egyptian (Cairo) University in 1929. He earned his M.A. and Ph.D. in the 1930s in England at the geography departments of Liverpool and Manchester Universities. His area of specialization was historical geography, and the subject of his early research was the place of Egypt in the ancient world in prehistory. Huzayyin took a great interest in what he called the "prehistoric age" of the Nile Valley, referring to the Stone and Bronze Ages. He tried to reconstruct the history of the earliest human habitation in Egypt before the first foundations were laid for the development of the ancient pharaonic civilization, which he regarded as the inception of Egypt's real history. In his research, he relied on historical knowledge and the anthropological and archaeological theories that prevailed in Western academia in the 1920s and 1930s. He also participated in several anthropological projects and archaeological excavations conducted in Egypt in the 1930s under the supervision and academic direction of European archaeological teams. In that period, after returning from his studies in Europe, Huzayyin joined the geography department of the Cairo University, where he taught and conducted research from the end of the 1930s to the early 1940s. In 1942, with the founding of Alexandria University, he was appointed to head the new department of geography. Later, in the mid-1950s, Huzayyin was one of the founders of the University of Asyut. For a while he served as the rector of that university, the first to be established in Upper Egypt to provide university services to the population in the peripheral areas of the south. In this position, he made an important contribution in establishing the academic and scientific foundations of the new academic institution. At the end of the 1960s, he was appointed president of the Egyptian Geographical Society, an office that he holds to this day. During this period, under the regime of Gamal Abdel Nasser, he served in 1965–1966 as minister of culture.[3]

In the course of more than sixty years of extensive scholarly activity, Huzayyin published scores of scientific papers on historical geography in academic journals in Egypt and in the West. Recently, in the 1990s, three new books of his were published. They are, in a sense, a summary of his academic work and public service. Huzayyin emphasizes his geographical interests not only in Egypt but throughout the Arab world, *ard al-'Uruba* (the land of Arabism). In the books, Huzayyin also collected his scientific papers and journalistic articles, the result of seven decades of research endeavors. To these he added autobiographical reflections and memoirs that document his academic and public life.[4]

In his later memoirs, Huzayyin returns to the scenery of his childhood. We learn that he was born in Wadi Halfa, a provincial town located exactly on the border between Sudan and Egypt. Wadi Halfa was on the banks of the Nile, and Huzayyin nostalgically describes the experiences of a child growing up on the banks of the "Great River." The symbiosis between the flow of the river, the types of plants and animals that grew on its banks, and the rural human milieu nourished by them through simple, hard agricultural work created a unique pastoral ambiance. Huzayyin recalls the smell of the fish that were caught each day by the Nile fishermen and displayed for sale in the local fish market. He remembers the croaks of the "alligators in the river that so terrified the fishermen." In Huzayyin's eyes, there was perfect harmony between the water, the soil, and human life and work. In retrospect, he remarks that his birthplace left a deep imprint on him and in fact destined him to become a geographer. Wadi Halfa gave him the perspective for unique geographical observation: Egypt to the north and Sudan to the south organically connected by the Nile Valley and delimited by the deserts surrounding the valley on the east and the west.[5] It was here that Huzayyin learned that the border drawn by the British between Egypt and Sudan (in 1899, a decade before his birth) was an arbitrary "imperialistic boundary." It artificially cut into two unnatural parts that Huzayyin calls, "the one Nile nation." It severs the territorial unity of the Nile Valley and splits the national community that populates it. It destroys the harmony between earth and man, thus contravening geographical laws and historical realities. From this point onward, Huzayyin becomes obsessed with the permanent need to defend the natural unity of the Nile Valley. He was enraged by the imperialist sin that had challenged the organic wholeness of nature. He regarded himself as destined to restore the symbiotic unity of the river and its distinctive surroundings, as someone blending the unity of the landscape with the unity of the nation that developed in its bosom. Hence, as he himself testifies, the choice of geography as a profession was for him a natural one.[6]

But Huzayyin, throughout his long career, was far from being simply a recruited national geographer. For him, his identity as an academic and professional geographer faithful to scientific truth was no less important than his identity as an Egyptian patriot. "I work for science," he stated, "and for Egypt, and my loyalty is to science and Egypt." And science was always mentioned first.[7] His commitment to the academic profession is reflected in the simple fact that most of his publications appeared in professional journals restricted to experts in the field. His public activity was limited in scale. Huzayyin belonged to the generation of Egyptian pioneering geographers that wrought a revolution in the profession. Between 1935 and 1955, this generation expropriated the profession of geography from the control of foreign geographers (in particular Europeans) and in a process of nationalization and Egyptianization turned it into an indigenous Egyptian profession dominated by young Egyptian geographers. The members of this generation who studied geography in Europe created a professional Egyptian discipline of high academic quality. As the youngest member of this pioneering generation (his teachers, Mustafa Amir and Muhammad 'Awad Muhammad, were about a decade older than him), Huzayyin worked, first and foremost, to advance geography as an academic discipline that created a scientific discourse.[8] He fostered the research of "total geography" based on archaeology, geology, anthropology, ethnology, biology, cultural studies, and history. He admits that a wide variety of Western influences, including his teachers at the Egyptian University and later in England, shaped his academic approach. Geographers, anthropologists, and archaeologists, like H. Lorin, P. M. Roxby, O. Menghin, and H. G. Fleir, deeply affected his career as a geographer.

Huzayyin together with others of his generation tried, based on these influences, to forge an independent, more indigenous Egyptian approach to geography. In addition to its affinity to universal science, it was supposed to meet the unique academic needs of Egypt and to constitute a tool for gaining self-understanding.[9] Huzayyin defined his field of specialization as *al-jughrafiya al-hadariyya* (civilizatory geography) or sometimes as *al-jughrafiya al-ta'rikhiyya* (historical geography). He regarded the school of civilizatory geography as a subdiscipline within the broad science of geography, based on the method that "geography is a field that deals with both science and culture." The role of geographers is to reconstruct the totality of the natural geographical milieu along with human life and culture and to present them as one historical entity. They have to deal with the physical geography, the material civilization, and the spiritual and cultural structures. Here Huzayyin viewed himself as the successor of Ibn Khaldun, who had attempted to "interpret the historical phenomena in the context of both the natural and the human environment." Huzayyin regarded his civilizatory geography as a theoretical elaboration of Ibn Khaldun's *al-'umran* (civilization) theory. Indeed, Ibn Khaldun's *Al-Muqaddima*, in particular the chapters on the reciprocal relations and mutual feedback between natural and climatic structures and the social organization and political regime of human communities, was a constant inspiration for Huzayyin's geographical theories.[10]

However, Huzayyin was also a product of his time and place. In his early adulthood, he experienced, together with others of his generation, the immense impact of the 1919 revolution and the struggle for national liberation from British rule. He saw

> in our generation of students, the children of the 1919 revolution . . . the generation that took shape in the shadow of the national revolution and lived through an experience that was unknown to the preceding generation. [The revolution and its aftermath] were the forge that shaped this new generation in which two aspirations were meshed—the desire to pursue [university] studies and the wish to learn Egyptian history. . . . Indeed the revolution was the greatest single influence in molding this generation, its political culture and its inclination to become intensively involved in the national movement.[11]

In the 1930s and 1940s, in the face of growing social and cultural crises, domestic political clashes, and international upheavals, Huzayyin could not remain indifferent to the rapidly changing political environment. Indeed, national pressures did remove Huzayyin from the ivory tower and bring him into the public political discourse. The decolonization of the profession was linked to the political struggle for decolonization. In these instances, Huzayyin brought the balanced critical voice of the professional geographer to the national discourse. On one hand, he placed an empirical professional restraint on the nationalistic rhetoric. On the other, he paid a considerable price for his political involvement. He tended to be captivated by the national myths and to become the person who provided them with a scientific basis. Professional truth was then supplanted by the national truth. The academic geographer became, albeit temporarily and partially, a national priest.

Between 1945 and 1948, Huzayyin published a series of articles on geographical subjects in *Al-Katib al-Misri*. This was the first time the conscientious geographer wrote articles intended for broad public consumption. *Al-Katib al-Misri* was a new cultural journal that began to appear after the war. Its owners were the Jewish Harari brothers. Under the management and editorship of Taha Husayn, the journal promoted liberal, Western, and Egyptian nationalist orientations as well as programs of social reform and cultural modernization. Occasionally, it also devoted some attention to current political problems. Taha Husayn also succeeded in enlisting several of the most impressive liberal intellectuals of that time to publish articles in the periodical. Salama Musa, Mahmud 'Azmi, Muhammad Rif'at, Muhammad 'Abdallah 'Inan, 'Ali Adham, Sayyid Qutb, and the young Lewis 'Awad regularly expressed their views in *Al-Katib al-Misri*. The geographer Muhammad 'Awad Muhammad also wrote for the journal.[12] The period was in fact marked by widespread national ferment stemming from the Egyptian national demand to rescind the 1936 treaty. From nearly the entire spectrum of the political arena the call went out to rescind the clauses relating to the continued British control of Sudan and its separation from Egypt. The national struggle for independence and liberation was then focused on the struggle for the unity of the Nile Valley, for the unity of Egypt and Sudan, for the common Egyptian-Sudanese fight against imperialism, and for the evacuation of foreign control from the Nile Valley. The oppositionary forces, led by the Wafd and the Muslim Brothers in a coalition with the leftist movements and student and workers organizations, waged a militant national struggle.

In 1945–1947 the political strife took to the streets in mass demonstrations and violent riots against British rule and often against the Egyptian minority governments that were represented as collaborating with the British.[13] *Al-Katib al-Misri* adopted a moderate pro-Wafdist position. It attempted to mobilize public opinion for the sake of the "struggle for the unity and liberation of the Nile Valley."[14] Apparently the Wafdist Taha Husayn, who at the time was chancellor of the new Alexandria University (established at the initiative of the Wafd government), enlisted Huzayyin, head of the geography department, for the task of explaining the national goals. Not only was Huzayyin unable to refuse the request of his chancellor, but it seems he undertook the assignment with great professional and patriotic enthusiasm. In the series of articles he wrote, Huzayyin did not deny the immediate political pressures that motivated him to compose them. In fact, he explicitly admitted to them. The national context was clearly reflected in the academic text and explained its meaning. As a geographer, Huzayyin asserted, his entire aim is to impart the "geographical dimension" to the national discourse and the political struggle, in order to endow them with "scientific force" and to base them, as far as possible, on solid historical and geographical realities. He complained that the political discussion was ignoring "solid geographical facts." With a certain degree of naiveté, he believed that the issue of the unity of the Nile Valley could not be clarified and explained merely as part of politics without its underlying geographical dimension. The politicians will be making a big mistake, he stated, if they dismiss this important scientific dimension. Their policy will only gain credibility and validity if it includes a clarification of the natural geographical conditions of the Nile Valley that either constitute or refute its unity and wholeness. Huzayyin felt that he, as a professional geographer, was compelled to contribute a systematic clarification of the "historical geographical perspective" to the political discourse. To his mind, this was an essential means to endow national political claims with an objective historical-geographical basis.[15] Once he entered into the national discourse and enlisted in the national cause, Huzayyin was compelled to engage in a mode of patriotic discourse in which he had to validate and sanctify national myths. At the same time, however, this did not prevent him from criticizing these collective myths and moderating their political intensity.

In these early articles, Huzayyin presented a series of geographical and anthropological theories intended to form a scientific explanation for the physical and mental existence of Egypt and the Nile Valley. His intention was to establish an objective scientific basis for the unity of the Nile Valley that would substantiate the physical, mental, and cultural "natural linkage" between Egypt and Sudan. Due to the limited scope of this chapter, we will only relate here to five key theoretical elements.[16]

THE PHYSICAL STRUCTURE

Huzayyin utilizes the primary physical data of the process in which the Nile Valley was created as a key basis for his theoretical structure. *Al-wadi* (the valley) is portrayed as an extremely early creation of nature, and in Huzayyin's words as an "objective geographical truth."[17] The Nile River carved a unique topographical and climatic belt into an arid desert. The geographical autonomy of this belt's environment is complete because it was the Nile that created it from its waters: from the water itself and the silt it brought with it that shaped the features of the soil and the landscape of the valley. The flow of the Nile and its rhythm dictated the structure of the valley. Over tens of thousands of years they created a rigid and permanent pattern of landscape. The absolute dependence on the Nile ensured symmetry, stability, and continuity. The relative isolation created by the deserts surrounding the valley preserved its independence as a self-contained ecological entity. Huzayyin differentiates between the *wadi al-nil* (Nile Valley), *hawd al-nil* (the Nile basin), and *hadbat al-nil* (the Nile heights).[18] From a geographical standpoint, only the Nile Valley, which comprises the areas of Egypt and north and central Sudan, represents what Huzayyin calls *al-bia'h al-niliyya* (the Nile environment). It is only in the valley that identical topographical and ecological conditions exist, making it one integrative geographical unit. Here the effect of the Nile on the physical environment is exclusive and absolute. In contrast, the Nile basin, comprising the areas where the waters of the Nile collect, and the Nile heights, the source of the main flow of its water, the mountainous areas of south Sudan, Ethiopia, and Uganda, do not represent geographical unity for Huzayyin. They are also affected by other geographical factors, and the Nile has no all-determining influence on their formation and development.[19] Huzayyin's rejoinder to those who developed nationalistic theories of a Greater Egypt, which also takes in southern Sudan and parts of northern Ethiopia, was that "the natural geographical unity" only exists between Egyptians and Sudanese. He added that "as far as the Ethiopians are concerned, they do not depend on the Nile for their livelihood, water, irrigation and fishing or fertilization salts." Therefore, although they form part of the *abna al-hadba* (peoples of the high plateau), they are not a part of the *abna al-wadi* (peoples of the valley), who are exclusively the Egyptians and the Sudanese. Nor do the widespread trade, cultural, and religious relations that flourished between the peoples of the valley and the Ethiopians for thousands of years make them one nation from a geographical point of view: "They never led to political connections or to popular or national unity [*wahda sha'biyya aw qawmiyya*] because it was never necessitated by the natural conditions." Huzayyin tried to limit the "national space," to strip it of territorial myths of "lebensraum" and to base it on "geographical truth."[20] In the map he defined, only the Nile Valley created within itself a territorial and historical entity with a defined identity that unites the river and its physical environment, the flora and fauna, and the human community. It was only the unique structure of the valley that melded land, vegetation, and people into one organic entity that developed a singular social organization, political regime, and national existence. Only it constitutes the cradle for the growth of "the civilization of Egypt." In this approach, the valley is a singular creation of nature "which has no equal in any other geographical region on the globe."[21]

THE HUMAN STRUCTURE

The physical geography has reproduced itself in human geography. The clear-cut climatic and ecological personality of the Nile Valley has bred in its bosom a singular national personality. Huzayyin describes the historical development of what he defines as *ummat wadi al-nil* (a nation of the Nile Valley): the human community that emerged on the banks of the Nile and was imprinted with its character. In the course of thousands of years, waves of human immigration came to the land of the Nile from the south, from central Africa, from the west, from north Africa, and from the east, from the Fertile Crescent and from the Arabian Peninsula. In the process, varied human groups and cultures settled in the Nile Valley. Their total dependence on the Nile as the source of life and livelihood, fishing, and agricultural crops dictated uniform patterns of life and molded a multitude of peoples into one homogeneous community. The naturalness of the geographical unity created a natural social bond. A common existence in the framework of a similar lifestyle formed for this community a "common experience" expressed in "its behavior as a cohesive nation whose members rely on and protect one another and together create a perfect internal integration." In this way the community developed into one *'umma wahida* (unified nation), into a national body that commingles the Egyptians and the Sudanese into one organic entity.[22]

However, when Huzayyin considers the "ethnic unity" of the inhabitants of the Nile Valley from an academic point of view, he presents us with a more complex picture. His nationalist self to a certain degree yields to his academic self. He attempts to prove the existence of "blood ties, origin and kinship" between the inhabitants of the north (the Egyptians) and the inhabitants of the south (the Sudanese) based on the anthropological and ethnological theories that prevailed in European academic fashion at the time. Huzayyin was aware that science was incapable of "precisely defining race." He concurred with the doubts expressed by anthropologists and ethnologists regarding the reality of race and the possibility of reconstructing it as a pure biological entity. At the same time, he appropriated from Western anthropological and historical knowledge the premise that it is possible to try to prove the existence of ethnic and cultural common origins and to scientifically trace the uninterrupted existence of an ethnic community, particularly if it has developed in a defined geographical and climatic pattern. Under the influence of those Western ethnological theories, Huzayyin stated that the inhabitants of the Nile Valley are "Hamitic in origin." Groups of people of Hamitic origin had settled in the Nile Valley and spread in it from the dawn of history. They provided the human infrastructure for the rise of the pharaonic civilization. From that time, the Hamitic roots of the Nile Valley inhabitants continued to be a hegemonic element in the various human compositions that populated the valley throughout its long history. It was also that element that created the unity and ethnic oneness of the Egyptians and Sudanese. In the course of hundreds of generations, the Hamitic stock absorbed other elements: barbarians from the west, black African and Nubian elements from the south, and Semitic groups from the east and north. And in fact these immigrations of Semitic groups influenced, more than any others, the reshaping of the Nile Valley community. Despite the fact that the Hamitic ethnic hegemony remained, Huzayyin stresses the power of Semitism to imbue the "Nile Valley nation" with a more mixed, Hamitic-Semitic, character. Following the Islamic conquest—the Arabization and Islamization of Egypt and Sudan—this mix consolidated and determined the new ethnic character of this nation. However, according to Huzayyin's theory, the Arabic language and the Islamic religion only served to reinforce the ethnic cohesiveness of the inhabitants and further enhanced their ethnic homogeneity. The historical ethnic unity of thousands of years was substantiated and consolidated with the cultural, linguistic, and religious unity that had prevailed since the seventh century among the valley's inhabitants.[23]

In Huzayyin's view, the natural ethnic unity between the "two halves" of the Nile Valley has created an economic and social unity between its inhabitants, and this in turn has given rise to national and political unity. This national existence is thousands of years old. It began back in the prepharaonic period. It achieved its complete formation during the pharaonic eras and has continued to exist throughout all periods until the present day. Huzayyin emphasizes the element of ethnic origin in the national existence. For him, this is a dynamic element operating from "above to below" (from north to south) and "from below to above" (south to north) in a nearly equal manner. In other words, in his view, two processes of feedback are constantly in operation. At times the human immigration came from Lower Egypt and at others from southern Sudan. But they all submitted to the enormous natural power of the Nile Valley; they all merged in its ecological melting pot, and they were all fused into a nation living on its banks.[24]

THE CULTURAL STRUCTURE

A unique culture sprang up in the physical and human conditions of the Nile Valley. The necessity to oversee the water supply and to manage an orderly agricultural hydraulic system created a constant need for social solidarity and a strong and stable political government. This regime in its turn was in need of a culture that would provide it with legitimacy and organize human life in a symbolic system that would give meaning to the human experience. Huzayyin has a manifestly functionalist approach to culture. Culture has a defined role in interpreting and organizing the relationships between physical existence and mental existence in the Nile Valley: on the one hand, it gives meaning to man's ties to the place, and on the other, to the link between man and the divine creation. In this way, culture serves the ecological and social structure of the human community, explains it, and ensures its integrity, stability, and continuity.[25] In his attitude toward culture, Huzayyin also reveals himself to us as a consummately Egyptocentric geographer. What he defines as *al-madaniyya al-misriyya* or *hadarat misr* (the Egyptian civilization) or as *al-madaniyya al-niliyya* (the Nile civilization) is actually a North Egyptian cultural entity. Huzayyin views Egypt, in the northern part of the Nile Valley, as the main producer of this civilization. In the pre-pharaonic age, in the time of the pharaonic dynasties, in the Hellenistic, Christian, and Islamic eras— in all these periods, Lower or Upper Egypt supplied *thaqafa* (culture) to the Nile Valley. Or in his words, "Egypt was the route via which culture and civilization reached Sudan"; it bestowed on Sudan the "light of culture."[26] In this hegemonic Egyptian approach, Egyptian civilization is an autonomous Egyptian product of the northern Nile Valley, almost devoid of any southern African influences. It was bequeathed by Egypt to Sudan. Huzayyin claims that the Sudanese reception and assimilation of Egyptian culture was easy and natural. Just as the existence of Egyptian civilization was dependent on the sources of the Nile that came through Sudan from below to above, in turn Egypt supplied from above to below the cultural systems, the material and spiritual culture, the elite and the popular cultures. Thus, the geographical unity of the Nile Valley created *al-wahda al-thaqafiyya* (a cultural unity) between Egypt and Sudan that solidified and fortified *al-wahda al-jinsiyya* (the ethnic unity) between them.[27]

This hegemonic approach, suffused with a tinge of Egyptian patronage, was expressed in the way Huzayyin depicted Egypt's contribution to the opening of Sudan to the modern era. Muhammad 'Ali's large-scale modernization project in the first half of the nineteenth century took Egypt from the Middle Ages and ushered it into the modern era, introducing it to modern technology and culture. Beyond the structural, economic, and military reforms, Muhammad 'Ali engendered a cultural *al-nahda* (revival) in Egypt that strengthened the Westernizing cultural orientations in it and connected it with Europe. The stepped-up processes of development, modernization, and Westernization rapidly exerted their influence on Sudan. "The nature of things produced a constant deterministic force that compelled life to go according to the river [the Nile]. Thus the revival that took place in Egypt by necessity had to spread [with the forces of the river and the valley] to Sudan."[28] Muhammad 'Ali's military conquests in Sudan were presented by Huzayyin as a reunification of the "parts of the Valley" and the creation of *wahda* (unity) and *nahda* (renewal) in both Egypt and Sudan. This modernization was passed down from the north to the south. The nation was reunited within one political framework under the leadership of the Muhammad 'Ali dynasty. Thus, it was able as one body—Egypt and Sudan—to burst into the modern era. In this way, Muhammad 'Ali put an end to hundreds of years of "political decline and deterioration that the Mamluks had inflicted on Sudan even more than on Egypt itself."[29] He reestablished one country that politically and nationally reunited Egypt and Sudan, that "created a holy unity between the two parts of this vast homeland." In this way, the unity fostered a great "cultural awakening" throughout the land of the Nile. It generated processes of change, reform, and modernization that raised the "nation of the Nile Valley" to a new cultural level, that of a modern, progressing, and enlightened nation.[30]

THE HISTORICAL DEVELOPMENT

As a geographer, Huzayyin was sensitive to space and environment. However, he did not overlook time and history. He challenges the static and archaic paradigm of the national pharaonicist ideology, which assumes that the rigid and unchanging physical structure of the Nile Valley preserved the pharaonic core of the Egyptian nation. This nationalistic approach, according to Huzayyin, made an absurd reduction of time to place and created a mythic, stagnant, and ahistorical representation of a stultified and eternal national Egyptian existence. According to it, present-day Egyptians are "pharaonic" and "Egypt's present is a precise reflection of its ancient past."[31] Huzayyin challenges this pharaonist narrative about the national past. He suggests an alternative, dynamic paradigm for an understanding of the historical development of the changing Egyptian reality. He rejects the total reduction of human existence to the natural environment. In continuous and consecutive processes one can always discern breaks and discontinuities. In his view, the environment of the Nile Valley underwent profound changes and frequent upheavals in technological and intellectual spheres that altered the economic, mental, and cultural structure of the human community living in it. Added to these were social and political transformations that were clearly expressed in the changing nature of forms of government, of dominant elites, and of the regimes that ruled the land of the Nile. He poses a rhetorical question: Was the political system of the pharaohs and the elite that predominated in their time the same regime or elite that ruled during the Mamluk period or the modern era of Muhammad 'Ali's dynasty? Obviously, the political history of Egypt is one marked by a multiplicity of constant change and upheaval that gave rise to new rulers and new predominant elites.[32]

However, Huzayyin tries to illustrate the "innovative mentality" of the Egyptian community in the most important sphere of its life—agriculture, the cultivation of the land and the rural pattern of life. That is precisely where he sees that an attempt was made to depict the unvarying "eternal continuity" of the life of the fellahin and the agrarian communities. Huzayyin believes there can be no greater mistake than that. He describes at length the transformations that took place in agricultural crops in Egypt: from an ancient agriculture based on grain crops such as wheat and oats to crops of vegetables and fruits, beans, olive groves, and vineyards, and later to the adoption of industrial branches of agriculture such as long-staple cotton and sugarcane. All of these changes in land cultivation and the introduction of new crops could not have taken place without the introduction of a new engineering technology. The construction of irrigation basins, dams, and water pumps called for new engineering and hydraulic know-how and the organizational ability to apply that knowledge in the field. Moreover, these innovations called for the cooperation and consent of the growers—the fellahin who worked the land. They required the adoption of modes of thought and action on their part in order to absorb the new technologies into the agricultural economy. In other words, the revolutionary technological developments spurred significant mental changes. In Huzayyin's view, they prove "beyond any doubt" that claims such as "the Egyptians are conservatives who zealously guard an unchanging tradition" are groundless and ahistorical. They are also fraudulent when they are uttered by Egyptian nationalists trying to prove the uninterrupted and eternal existence of the Egyptian nation.[33]

In the cultural sphere Huzayyin finds additional evidence of what he views as the Egyptian readiness to adapt to change and to accept innovations. In this sphere, the Egyptians and the Sudanese on several occasions absorbed languages, religions, beliefs, customs, and symbolic systems that came to them from outside the Nile Valley. In the process of acclimatizing to the Nile environment, new cultures were indeed stamped with a distinctly Nilotic imprint. However, they also forced the local population to change, leading to new historical stages in the life of the people of the Nile Valley. The acceptance of Hellenism in the post-pharaonic period, the adaptation to the Roman and Byzantine cultures and patterns of government in the first centuries A.D., and above all, the reception of Islam evince the Egyptians' great adaptability to substantive cultural changes. The changes made in belief systems, laws, languages, customs, and traditions, and the ability to accept the new and relinquish or forget the old, or to "reinvent" it as a new tradition—all these attest to the Egyptian "openness" to cultural change. They refute the claim of "cultural conservatism."[34]

In fact, for Huzayyin the processes of the Islamization and Arabization of Egypt are the strongest historical proof of the innovative mentality of the Egyptians and the Sudanese and their openness to cultural reconstructions. He devoted a special effort to prove that the processes of reception of Islam and Arabic by the inhabitants of the Nile Valley wrought profound cultural changes in them. Moreover, the Egyptian civilization's acceptance of Islam and Arabism strengthened its ability to survive, imbued it with political and intellectual prowess, and enhanced its influence on the entire Near East. Here also, Huzayyin challenges the territorialist paradigm that endeavored to represent the "Egyptian personality" as one that is free of any Arabic and Islamic influences and to establish it on purely pharaonic foundations.[35] Once again Huzayyin denies the pharaonist theory that the "hard core" of the Egyptian personality has remained pharaonic and that external cultural forces have had no real influence on its evolution. The Islamic religion and the Arabic language and culture have become the key elements shaping the Egyptian personality and the life of the people of the Nile Valley. A cultural-symbolic negotiation is constantly being conducted between Islam and Arabism, on the one hand, and Egyptianism, on the other, and it has brought about enduring reciprocal influences between them. Egyptianism has been reshaped as an Islamic Arabic entity. Islam and Arabism, in turn, following their assimilation in the Nile

Valley, have been reshaped: under the strong impact of the environment, they have taken on a local Egyptian character that has made them into cultural forces that are "friendly" to the human Egyptian-Sudanese environment. [36] But here also Huzayyin remains Egyptocentric in his approach. He explains to his readers that the processes of Islamization and Arabization first took place in Egypt and only then moved on to the Sudan. "The Arabs [the Muslims] came through Egypt to paint Sudan with their Arabic color," he emphasizes.[37] The Muslim conquerors did not arrive directly in Sudan from the Arabian Peninsula. They spread there from Egypt, and only after the religion and language they brought with them had been assimilated into the Egypt pot and had taken on an Egyptian complexion were they passed on, in their new local form, to the inhabitants of Sudan. Again, it was northern Egypt that served as the source of the creation and dissemination of the Arab-Islamic culture to all the other parts of the homeland of the Nile Valley.[38]

In Huzayyin's view, the present Islamic-Arabic identity of the inhabitants of the Nile Valley is natural and authentic. Moreover, Islam and Arabism have reinforced the national unity between Egypt and Sudan. Both the linguistic and the religious unity have fortified the geographical and ethnic unity and reconstructed the Nile nation as an Arabic-Islamic nation. Huzayyin does not conceal from his readers the fact that the establishment of the Arab League in 1945, the growing involvement of Egypt in Arab affairs and Arab culture, and the intensification of the sense of Arabist identity among Egyptians and Sudanese formed the background of his scientific endeavor to stress the Arabic essence of the unity of the Nile Valley.[39]

THE POLITICAL CONCLUSION

For Huzayyin, the unity of the Nile Valley is a "natural given." The boundary line drawn by the imperialistic rule at the latitude of 22 degrees is an "unnatural boundary because it was drawn along an imaginary line." The attempt to establish an "administrative" or a "political" border between Egypt and Sudan is unwarranted and is bound to fail, because it violates what Huzayyin defines as the human and physical al-hudud al-hayawiyya (vital borders) that nature has created and preserved.[40] Hence, he believes that "the aspiration of the Egyptian-Sudanese nation to realize its united national sovereignty in a territory with genuine and trustworthy geographical boundaries" is justified and would abolish the artificial boundary of 1899.[41]

Huzayyin also formulates this national link in more practical terms— economic and strategic. The economy of Egypt "drinks" the waters of the Nile and is in need of its free supply. Without Sudan, which holds part of the Nile sources and constitutes the river's main drainage area, "Egypt has no life." Its need for unity with Sudan is therefore "essential and existential." In the strategic sphere, Egypt is dependent on Sudan as a security backyard to ensure Egypt's economic prosperity and its physical defense against threats to the sources of the Nile. The Sudanese territory is Egypt's natural strategic and economic space. "Egypt will never find a secure and tranquil life for herself without the Sudan," he makes clear.[42] Hence, the nullification of the artificial 1899 border is essential for the very assurance of the "natural" material and cultural life of Egypt. Huzayyin sums up this argument by stating that "the unity of the Nile Valley is nature's commandment" and a "geographical truth," but it is also an "existential necessity" for Egypt from the national, economic, political, cultural, and strategic points of view. As a geographer, he is obliged to promote the scientific truth of "the geographical unity of the Nile Valley"; as an Egyptian nationalist, he must make that truth the basis of political, economic, and security considerations.[43]

NOTES

I am grateful to Donald M. Reid for having provided me with valuable biographical information on Sulayman Huzayyin. The research for this study was supported by a grant from the (American-Israeli) Binational Science Foundation.

1. Smith, *The Ethnic Origins of Nations,* pp. 183–190.

2. Ibid., pp. 157–161. See also Zerubavel, *Recovered Roots,* pp. 3–36.

3. Huzayyin, *Mustaqbal al-Thaqafa,* pp. 415–528; D. M. Reid's personal interview with Sulayman Huzayyin on 13 October 1987 at the Geographical Society in Cairo; Reid, "The Egyptian Geographical Society," pp. 559–563. For Huzayyin's concept of "Egypt in prehistory" see his "Qablu an Yabda' al-Ta'rikh fi Misr," *Al-Katib al-Misri,* February 1948, pp. 52–61.

4. Huzayyin, *Hadarat Misr;* Huzayyin, *Mustaqbal al-Thaqafa;* Huzayyin, *Ard al-'Uruba.*

5. Huzayyin, *Mustaqbal al-Thaqafa,* pp. 415–418.

6. Ibid., pp. 416–441; Huzayyin, "Wahdat Wadi al-Nil wa-Muqawwamatuha al-Jughrafiyya wa-al-Ta'rikhiyya," *Al-Katib al-Misri,* February 1946, pp. 31–40.

7. Huzayyin's interview with Reid, Cairo, 13 October 1987. See also Sulayman Huzayyin, "Bayna al-'Ilm wa-al-Siyasa," *Al-Katib al-Misri,* April 1947, pp. 435–445.

8. Huzayyin, *Mustaqbal al-Thaqafa,* pp. 444–478; Reid, "The Egyptian Geographical Society," pp. 560–567.

9. Reid, "The Egyptian Geographical Society," pp. 556–562; Huzayyin, *Mustaqbal al-Thaqafa,* pp. 434–470. See also Huzayyin, "Al-Hind Bayna al-Wahda wa-al-Taqsim," *Al-Katib al-Misri,* October 1947, pp. 31–41.

10. Huzayyin, *Mustaqbal al-Thaqafa,* pp. 450–452, 455–457, 462–470.

11. Ibid., pp. 432–433.

12. See various issues of *Al-Katib al-Misri* in the period 1945–1947.

13. For a detailed treatment of the period see Berque, *Egypt: Imperialism and Revolution,* pp. 577–582; al-Rafi'i, *Fi A'qab al-Thawra al-Misriyya,* pp. 154–215; Erlich, *Students and University,* pp. 139–168; Quraishi, *Liberal Nationalism in*

Egypt, pp. 158–163; and Vatikiotis, *The Modern History of Egypt,* pp. 359–363. See also Harb, *Wahdat Wadi al-Nil,* whose pamphlet expressed the official position of the Young Men's Muslim Association. Harb served as president general of the YMMA. Also see al-Nuqrashi, *Qadiyyat Wadi al-Nil,* whose pamphlet is based on the official address by the Egyptian prime minister (al-Nuqrashi) at the UN Security Council on 5 August 1947.

14. See issues of *Al-Katib al-Misri* in the period 1946–1948.

15. Huzayyin, "Rawabit al-Tabi'a wa-al-Ta'rikh fi Wadi al-Nil," *Al-Katib al-Misri,* May 1947, pp. 653–663; Huzayyin, "Wahdat Wadi al-Nil," *Al-Katib al-Misri,* February 1946, pp. 31–33, 39–40.

16. Some of these articles and essays were later republished in Huzayyin, *Hadarat Misr,* pp. 143–192, 273–302.

17. Huzayyin, "Rawabit al-Tabi'a wa-al-Ta'rikh," pp. 653–655; Huzayyin, "Wahdat Wadi al-Nil," pp. 38–40.

18. Huzayyin, "Rawabit al-Tabi'a wa-al-Ta'rikh," pp. 653–659.

19. Ibid., pp. 653–663.

20. Ibid., pp. 655–656.

21. Ibid., pp. 653–663, quotation from p. 653. See also Huzayyin, "Rabitat al-Ma' fi Wadi al-Nil," *Al-Katib al-Misri,* January 1947, pp. 51–62.

22. Huzayyin, "Rabitat al-Jins wa-al-Thaqafa fi Wadi al-Nil," *Al-Katib al-Misri,* July 1947, pp. 228–242; quotation from Huzayyin, "Rawabit al-Tabi'a wa-al-Ta'rikh," p. 653.

23. Huzayyin, "Rabitat al-Jins wa-al-Thaqafa," pp. 228–242.

24. Ibid.; Huzayyin, "Wahdat Wadi al-Nil," pp. 33–40. See also Huzayyin, "Bayna al-Delta wa-al-Sa'id," *Al-Katib al-Misri,* March 1948, pp. 220–228.

25. Huzayyin, "Misr Halqat al-Ittisal al-Thaqafi bayna al-Sharq wa-al-Gharb," *Al-Katib al-Misri,* December 1945, pp. 369–384; Huzayyin, "Rabitat al-Jins wa-al-Thaqafa," pp. 232–242; Huzayyin, "Fayadan al-Nil wa-Atharuhu fi al-Hadara al-Misriyya," *Al-Katib al-Misri,* October 1946, pp. 45–56.

26. Huzayyin, "Rawabit al-Tabi'a wa-al-Ta'rikh," p. 660. See also pp. 659–662.

27. Huzayyin, "Rabitat al-Jins wa-al-Thaqafa," pp. 228–242; Huzayyin, "Rawabit al-Tabi'a wa-al-Ta'rikh," pp. 658–663.

28. Ibid., pp. 661–662, quotation from p. 661.

29. Ibid., p. 662.

30. Ibid.

31. For this approach, which was dominant in the nationalist ideology of the 1920s and still influential in the 1930s and 1940s, see Gershoni and Jankowski, *Egypt, Islam, and the Arabs,* pp. 130–227; Reid, "Nationalizing the Pharaonic Past," pp. 127–149.

32. Huzayyin, "Al-Misriyyun wa-al-Muhafaza 'ala al-Qadim," *Al-Katib al-Misri,* January 1947, pp. 624–637; Huzayyin, "Marhalatan fi Ta'rikh Misr al-'Amm," *Al-Katib al-Misri,* May 1948, pp. 529–538.

33. Huzayyin, "Al-Misriyyun wa-al-Muhafaza 'ala al-Qadim," pp. 626–632. Huzayyin, "Kayfa Nash'at al-Madaniyya fi Misr," *Al-Katib al-Misri,* December 1947, pp. 375–384. See also Huzayyin, "Nash'at al-Zira'a wa-Atharuha fi Ta'rikh al-Hadara," *Al-Katib al-Misri,* January 1948, pp. 589–598.

34. Huzayyin, "Al-Misriyyun wa-al-Muhafaza 'ala al-Qadim," pp. 632–637; Huzayyin, "Kayfa Nasha't al-Madaniyya fi Misr," pp. 375–384.

35. Huzayyin, "Al-Misriyyun wa-al-Muhafaza 'ala al-Qadim," pp. 633–636; Huzayyin, "Rawabit al-Tabi'a wa-al-Ta'rikh," pp. 660–661.

36. Huzayyin, "Misr Halqat al-Ittisal al-Thaqafi," pp. 372–384.

37. Huzayyin, "Rawabit al-Tabi'a wa-al-Ta'rikh," p. 660.

38. Ibid., pp. 660–661; Huzayyin, "Misr Halqat al-Ittisal al-Thaqafi," pp. 376–379; Huzayyin, "Rabitat al-Jins wa-al-Thaqafa," pp. 238–239.

39. Huzayyin, "Al-Jami'a al-'Arabiyya wa-Muqawwamatuha al-Jughrafiyya wa-al-Ta'rikhiyya," *Al-Katib al-Misri,* January 1946, pp. 529–542. See also his articles in *Al-Katib al-Misri,* March 1946, pp. 243–255, and April 1948, pp. 357–367; Huzayyin, *Ard al-'Uruba,* pp. 11–268; Huzayyin, *Mustaqbal al-Thaqafa,* pp. 59–84. Another representation of Huzayyin's dynamic conception of Egyptian history can be found in his series of essays on "War and Geography," published in *Al-Katib al-Misri.* See for example "Bayna al-Harb wa-al-Jughrafiyya: Al-Hurub al-'Alamiyya wa-Mawqi' Misr," April 1946, pp. 414–424; "Bayn al-Harb wa-al-Jughrafiyya: Al-Sharq al-Awsat wa-al-Harb," May 1946, pp. 586–600; "Bayna al-Harb wa-al-Jughrafiyya: Dawafi' al-Harb wa-Ahdafuha fi Auruba," July 1946, pp. 224–237; and "Bayna al-Harb wa-al-Jughrafiyya: Al-Khitat al-Kubra fi al-Harb al-'Alamiyya al-Akhira," August 1946, pp. 413–427.

40. Huzayyin, "Wahdat Wadi al-Nil," pp. 31–40.

41. Ibid., p. 32.

42. Ibid., pp. 32–39.

43. Ibid., pp. 31–40. See also Huzayyin, "Rabitat al-Ma' fi Wadi al-Nil," pp. 51–62.

Part 4

Contemporary Voices

16

◆

The Aswan High Dam and Revolutionary Symbolism in Egypt

Yoram Meital

This chapter examines the construction of the Aswan High Dam in the context of the revolutionary experience of the Egyptian regime and society in the wake of the military coup of July 23, 1952. This study forms part of a project whose aim is an integrative examination of the characteristic features of the postmonarchical revolutionary experience in Egypt; namely those processes by which the revolutionary regime and its supporters had tried, mainly during the formative years 1952–1967, to forge new symbols and values, and to disseminate them by diverse measures in public and private spheres. These efforts were targeted to present the new regime and its policy as evidence of the revolutionary change that took place in postmonarchical Egypt. The actions of the Free Officers attested to their conviction that the seizing of power had given them a real chance of transforming the political, economic, and social domains.

The aspiration of the new leaders of Egypt to cause sweeping changes was not grounded on a detailed program inspired by any solid ideological agenda. In the immediate postrevolutionary stage, the intentions of the leaders regarding a number of central issues were unclear. The Free Officers considered the status quo ante to have been the central cause of Egypt's ills. Their basic objective was to guarantee their hold on power in the long run and to take vigorous action to consolidate a new comprehensive reality in their country, with commitment to the July revolution as its dominant driving force. The first moves of the Free Officers were therefore intended to dramatically change the status quo, which had characterized the monarchic era, and to create a dramatic atmosphere of sweeping change. Their actions attested to their conviction that the seizing of power had given them a golden opportunity to transform the political, economic, and social spheres.

The central argument of this chapter is that under the impact of the construction of the High Dam, some of the main symbols of the revolution were finally consolidated; foremost among them was the connection between such national goals as social-economic development and the struggle against imperialism. This huge project was designed to serve as fundamental leverage for the regime's agricultural and industrial plans. However, the lack of internal financial resources and technological capability brought Egypt, in 1954–1955, to apply for Western aid. The initial reactions were positive, as the United States, Britain, and the World Bank expressed their willingness to support the project and to provide it with substantial financial aid. This goodwill on the part of the international community was reversed, however, following the strengthening of Egypt's image as a central leader of the anti-imperialist struggle. This image basically emerged from Cairo's objection to Western efforts to consolidate regional military pacts (such as the Baghdad Pact), along with its support for national liberation movements (like the Algerian Front de Libération Nationale). Some Western capitals followed the Egyptian activities within the Non-Alignment group of states with much concern. Egypt's recognition of the People's Republic of China on May 16, 1956, its growing contacts with the Soviet Union, and the increasing prestige of president Gamal Abdel Nasser, especially after the role he played in the Bandung Conference (March 18–24, 1955), only exacerbated existing Western anxiety.

It seems that the signing of the Egyptian-Czechoslovakian arms deal had a crucial effect on Egypt's image in many Western states, as well as in Israel. This arms deal was perceived in the West as an expression of a fundamental change in Cairo's foreign policy orientation. The deal, which was negotiated between Egypt and the Soviet Union during the summer of 1955 and announced in September 27, was immediately perceived as an event with enormous regional and international implications. Egypt emphasized the direct impact of the Israel Defense Forces' raid on Gaza in February 1955 as the main motivating cause of this arms deal. The thirty-eight Egyptian officers and soldiers who had been killed during the raid symbolized the poor condition of the Egyptian armed forces and ultimately injured the national pride of its revolutionary regime. In view of these circumstances, Egypt decided to intensify its efforts to seek modern arms abroad.[1] However, the political circumstances of the Cold War made the issue of an arms deal a complicated one. The United States, for one, opposed Egypt's request for modern arms, arguing that it ran against Washington's commitment for the restraint of the arms race in the Middle East. The arms that Britain was willing to sell Egypt were limited both in quantity and quality. The Egyptian leadership thus felt increasingly frustrated. At that time they considered on several occasions the possibility of approaching the Eastern bloc. They were well aware of the broad implication and risks that could entail such a move toward the Soviets. This can be learned, for example, from Egypt's foreign minister at the time, Mahmoud Fawzi, who noted in his memoirs, "When the Egyptians and the Americans were alone together, Nasser said, 'You know, I've had a lot to do with the Russians, and I don't like the Russians. I've had a lot to do with your people, and basically I like your people.'"[2] However, as hope for acquiring arms from Western sources declined, the sensitive decision to turn to the Eastern bloc was ultimately taken.

The United States and Britain feared that Egypt's reorientation toward the Eastern bloc could harm their efforts to secure their interests in the Middle East, specifically the efforts to circumscribe Soviet penetration of the region. Consequently, on July 19, 1956, Washington announced its withdrawal from its previous intention to provide some financial aid for the High Dam project. Similar announcements were soon made by Britain and the World Bank. This development reflected the fact that the United States and Britain, as well as Israel and France, reassessed their policies toward Egypt—and this had a direct effect on the evolution of the Suez crisis. From Nasser's perspective, Western reactions were bound to undermine some of his most vital policy issues (i.e., arms supply, social-economic development, and political maneuvers). First and foremost, however, he felt that the steps that had been taken by the West could jeopardize the position of Egypt as a sovereign and independent state. The Egyptian president thus reacted unequivocally and vigorously: he declared the nationalization of the Suez Canal. Hence, the Suez crisis was born, during which the concerned parties took some unpredicted steps that were destined to have substantial implications on the history of the Middle East.

The announcement of the cancellation of Western financial aid for the High Dam project reached Egypt only a few days before the fourth anniversary of the July revolution. After some discussions regarding the options left for Egypt, Nasser decided to go ahead with the idea of declaring the nationalization of the Suez Canal Company. According to Muhammad Hasanayn Haykal, at that point Nasser summarized his thoughts on the issue in a handwritten paper dated July 22, 1956. In this personal document he wrote that the nationalization of the Suez Canal would give Egypt the financial resources required to cover the costs that it needed for the construction of the High Dam. He described his decision as an act that would gain the support of all Egyptians who dreamed of the day when the canal would be under direct Egyptian rule. He thus considered the nationalization as a true expression of Egypt's full independence, including its freedom of political maneuvering. Nasser surmised that the vast majority of the Arabs would support his decision, and he considered this support a message for the West in general and the United States in particular.[3]

Nasser had carefully calculated his steps in that sensitive situation. He therefore decided to announce the nationalization of Suez Canal Company in his traditional speech on the occasion of King Faruq's exile. It was the first appearance in public of Egypt's president since Western aid for the High Dam had been canceled. Many had, therefore, expected Nasser to disclose his country's reaction during his speech in Alexandria on July 26. In this speech, Nasser described at length Egypt's national struggle for true independence and freedom. He reviewed the history of the Suez Canal, emphasizing that it had been planned all along to serve and secure the interests of Western imperialism. "We dug the Canal with our lives, our skulls, our bones, our blood," he told his audience, but

> instead of the Canal being dug for Egypt, Egypt became the property of the Canal. . . . It is no shame for one to be poor and to borrow in order to build up one's country; what is a shame is to suck the blood of a people and usurp their rights. . . . Does history repeat itself? On the contrary! We shall build the High Dam and we shall gain our usurped rights. . . . Therefore I have signed today, and the government has approved, a resolution for the nationalization of the Universal Company of the Suez Maritime Canal.[4]

Although many were aware of the growing tension between Egypt and the West, it seems that no one was prepared for such a dramatic statement. The symbolic linkage between the content of Nasser's announcement (i.e., the nationalization of the Suez Canal) and the venue in which it had been made (the anniversary of Faruq's exile) was pregnant with symbolic meanings for the Egyptian public. This linkage was fully exploited by Nasser, to the point that when he reached the last part of his speech he reiterated that "in the same way as Faruq left on 26 July 1952, the old Suez Canal Company also leaves us on the same day."[5] Hence, the Suez crisis was born, during which the concerned parties took some unpredicted steps that were destined to have substantial implications on the history of the Middle East.

Egypt's policy during this crisis, and especially Nasser's dramatic statements, had a significant impact on the forging of the revolution's symbols. At this stage Nasser appeared with his extraordinary abilities to express the deepest national sentiments of wide sectors and even to create the impression that Egypt's political agenda was determined by these sentiments. Using symbols and images, Nasser, like other spokesmen and many supporters of the regime, gave the struggle for the construction of the High Dam and the Suez crisis meanings that went far beyond the question of irrigation, agricultural and industrial development, or of military confrontation in the battlefield. Since the initial stages of the crisis Nasser tended to describe the causes of its outbreak, as well as Egypt's position on it, as part of Egypt's long national struggle for true independence and freedom, as well as a part of its struggle for the revolutionary regime's values. In a certain way, these tactics reflected a permanent effort to present the revolutionary ideas and policies as a practical concept available for use in the political, social, and cultural spheres. Thus, like many other monuments and events, the Aswan High Dam was used as a metaphor that encompassed most of the national and cultural challenges that Egypt and the rest of the Arab states had faced. These included the struggle for national liberation and the establishment of political and economic infrastructures.

Diverse measures were employed by the regime with the efforts to disseminate the symbolism of the construction of the High Dam in the public and the private spheres. These efforts were expressed in countless official sources, street and square names, as well as in stamps, postcards, and, of course, in school textbooks. The High Dam is described in these sources in the most positive way. A formal expression of this hegemonic narrative can be found in the following words from the national charter:

> The revolutionary solution to the problem of land in Egypt is by increasing the number of land-owners. Such was the aim of the laws of land reform issued in 1952 and 1962. This aim—besides the other aims of raising production—was one of the motive powers behind the great irrigation projects, whose powerful symbol is the Aswan High Dam, for the sake of which the people of Egypt have suffered all sort of armed, economic and psychological wars. This Dam has become the symbol of the will and determination of the people to fashion its life.[6]

However, a greater importance should be attributed to the intensive presence of almost the same arguments and symbols in nonofficial quarters. Since the mid-1950s the Aswan High Dam has been used in Egypt as a metaphor that encompassed most of the national and cultural challenges that Egypt had faced. These included the struggle for national liberation and the establishment of political and economic infrastructures. Such metaphorical uses were apparent in the spheres of modern arts, poetry, popular songs, novels, dramatic plays, and movies. The tremendous popularity of the most prominent creators in these spheres among wide sectors of the Egyptian public enhanced the importance of the content of their works. Since 1956, dozens of songs, musical works, plays, and films were produced, which incorporated the hegemonic narrative about the construction of the High Dam and reinforced the positive image of the July revolution among wide sectors of the Egyptian public.

As a result of this process, in official documents like the National Charter, as well as in statements and works of prominent intellectuals, artists, and public personalities (like Taha Husayn, Tawfiq al-Hakim, 'Abbas Mahmud, Yahya Haqqi, and Louis 'Awad), the Aswan High Dam was depicted as a legitimate historical, moral, and political action; and the struggle for the completion of this huge project was characterized as a fundamental struggle for the country's freedom and independence. It is worth mentioning that the policy taken by the regime toward the construction of the High Dam received the support of many distinguished intellectuals, despite the fact that some of them were known as critics of the revolutionary regime. For example, the renowned intellectual Tawfiq al-Hakim declared on several occasions his support for the High Dam project, and during the Suez war he was quoted as saying that if he was to be called, he would be prepared to hold arms and fight the invading forces.[7]

There are many examples of the Egyptian general public support for the High Dam. However, I think that one of the most interesting reflections of this broad support can be found in popular and patriotic songs of the time. A perfect example of this can be found in Umm Kulthum's song "Tahwil al-Nil" ("Transforming the Nile"), which was set to music by one of the greatest composers in Egypt, Muhammad 'Abd al-Wahab. This song hailed the construction of the High Dam and its contribution to Egypt and its population in the following idealistic and nostalgic lyrics:

> We had changed the stream of the Nile
> I salute this change;
> which may be a token of the change in our life
> and not only of the Nile River.
>
> Who, who would have believed,
> that the river which runs for millions of years
> its direction left and right
> we would change at our own will,
> and even install adjustments in it.
>
> the Dam is no more a fantasy
> but an unprecedented fact.
>
> I gaze with overwhelming joy
> at an all-enlightening future
> with flourishing factories,
> and the color of green covering the arid land.
> Life of tranquillity in abundance for all people
> and a pleasant journey to the top.[8]

Nevertheless, at the same time, criticism of the revolutionary regime and its policies including the construction of the High Dam was also evident. In this context several persons described the project as Damocles' sword, which endangered the very existence of Egypt, and which could one day strike the population in a destructive manner. Others described the High Dam as an example of the incorrect national priorities of the revolutionary regime that preferred a grandiose project with an uncertain future, instead of finding a solution to the much more urgent daily problems that dominated the social, economic, and political life. An expression of this thought can be found in the following words of the well-known critic Sabri Hafiz, who wrote: "The sixties was indeed a decade of confusion, a decade of numerous huge projects and the abolition of almost all political activities; massive industrialization and the absolute absence of freedom; the construction of the High Dam and the destruction of the spirit of opposition; the expansion of free education and the collective arrest of intellectuals."[9]

The most critical metaphoric use of the High Dam can be found in the writings of Sunallah Ibrahim. In his works Ibrahim sophistically made use of the High Dam as a metaphor in his critique on the revolutionary regime. Ibrahim argued that the revolution, much like the High Dam, could be "divided into two stages: an initial stage of simple, clear work that involved digging on a large scale, and a second more technical stage characterized by its specialization and complexity." For Ibrahim, these two stages in the physical project suggested parallels with the developments in the revolutionary project itself. In this regard, Ibrahim said:

> Have not revolutions and historical rebellions always passed through these two stages? In the beginning the goal is simple and clear and everything is either black or white, with or against. There is enthusiasm and faith in the future and the ability to change the course of history. Not a time for reflection and analysis. Then the revolution is accomplished and another stage with a slower rhythm begins: tasks are more complex, objectives are less clear, and shadows of gray begin to smear the whiteness and the blackness. This becomes the time for thinking. What about? The mistakes of the first stage and the possibilities of the future.[10]

CONCLUSION

During the revolutionary experience symbols and images were important factors in the struggle to win the sympathy and support of various sectors of Egyptian society for the new regime, its values and leadership. The struggle for the building of the Aswan High Dam, like several other national projects—the Tahrir and New Valley provinces, and the Helwan Iron and Steel complex—was appropriated by the revolutionary regime and its supporters as a central symbol in their efforts to construct Egypt's new values and policies. At the same time, the High Dam was used by others as a metaphor for their criticism of the revolutionary regime and its policies.

In many regards, the High Dam can be consider as *lieu de mémoire,* or site of memory, a definition that was brilliantly invited by Pierre Nora, who argued that the *lieu de mémoire* was characterized by "three senses of the word—material, symbolic, and functional"; three aspects that always coexist, and are created by a play of memory and history.[11] In addition, it is worth mentioning that the High Dam was a symbolic site of memory even before the dam was officially opened in July 1970; more than that, the attractiveness of the High Dam as a central site of memory of the July revolution did not disappear when the revolutionary experience in Egypt came to its end following the 1967 defeat. Current evidence for the durability of this process can be found in the film *Nasir 56*. Apart from the heated debate that erupted regarding the historical accuracy of the script, what is much more important for this chapter is that when it was decided to produce (with unprecedented investment) a sympathetic film on Nasser, it was decided almost naturally to concentrate on his policy during the first stage of the struggle for the construction of the High Dam and the Suez crisis, which erupted consequently.

NOTES

1. In extensive research conducted by Egypt's defense ministry, it is argued that following the Gaza raid, Cairo decided to invest many more efforts and resources in the purchase of arms (Jumhuriyyat Misr al-ʿArabiyya, *Harb al-ʿudwan al-thulathi* [The Tripartite War], pp. 11, 21). The causes that motivated Israel's decisionmakers during 1955–1956 are discussed in Tal, "Israel's Road to the 1956 War," pp. 59–81.

2. Fawzi, *Suez 1956*, p. 31.

3. Haykal, *Milafat al-suwis* (The Suez files), p. 459. It was claimed in some sources that several times before 1956 the idea of nationalization of the Canal had been discussed in Egypt. See Fawzi, *Suez 1956*, pp. 38–40; and Hamrush in *Mʿaraqat al-suwis*, pp. 9–10. For the perspective of those who were charged with the management of the canal after it was nationalized, see *Qanat al-suwis wal-ayam alatti hazat al-dunya* (The Suez Canal and the days that had shaken the world), Cairo, 1987.

4. *Al-Ahram*, 27 July 1956.

5. Ibid.

6. Al-Jumhuriyya al-ʿArabiyya al-Mutahida, *Mashru ʿal-mithaq—21 mayu sanat 1962*, p. 74.

7. See, for example, his article in Al-Ahram, 1 May 1962.

8. *Umm Kulthum—hayat w-aghani kawkab al-sharq*, Beirut, n.d., p. 161.

9. Hafiz, "The Egyptian Novel in the Sixties," p. 171.

10. As quoted in Mehrez, *Egyptian Writers Between History and Fiction*, p. 125. Mehrez emphasized that this unique writing reached its climax in the story of Najmat Aghustus (August's Star) in which Ibrahim "represents a complex structure that critically reflects on and rereads the stages of the revolutionary process as they consolidated themselves in the physical presence of the High Dam" (p. 126).

11. Nora, "Between Memory and History," pp. 7–25.

17

◆

The Nile in Egyptian-Sudanese Relations, 1956–1995

Gabriel Warburg

The June 26, 1995 assassination attempt on President Husni Mubarak's life in Addis Ababa triggered an acute crisis and a fierce war of words between Egypt and Sudan. The immediate issue was political Islam, which had been behind the assassination attempt. Egypt accused the Sudanese authorities of having trained the would-be assassins and of smuggling them across its border with Ethiopia.[1] However, as in many previous conflicts which have developed since Sudan achieved independence in 1956, the Nile waters and the Egyptian-Sudanese border soon featured high on the agenda. Hasan al-Turabi, leader of the National Islamic Front (NIF), who is believed to be the power behind the throne in Khartoum, threatened to cut off the Nile water supply to Egypt. The next clash occurred in the Halayib Triangle, on the Egyptian-Sudanese border, where in the first week of July military patrols from the two countries clashed and several Sudanese lost their lives.[2] Several years have passed since the assassination attempt took place, yet the conflict is far from being resolved. The UN Security Council has implemented sanctions against Sudan in response to its failure to hand over the suspected terrorists to Ethiopia, but to no avail. Egyptian-Sudanese relations are as bad as ever, as the deteriorating situation in Sudan and its tense relations with nearly all its neighbors continue to threaten the stability of the whole region. A leading Egyptian commentator observed recently that Egypt's relations with Sudan are no longer emotional, political, or historical as they were prior to Sudan's independence. Due to the scarcity of water on the one hand and the population explosion on the other, the stability of these relations has become a matter of survival. Sudan's instability as a nation-state and the fact that after more than forty years of independence it is still torn apart by ethnic, religious,

227

and sectarian conflicts suggest that Egypt cannot regard Sudan as a dependable neighbor. The well-known Egyptian commentator, Milad Hana, noted in a recent article that historically the slogan of those advocating unity was always the "Unity of the Nile Valley" and not the "Unity of Egypt and the Sudan," for the Nile was the bond uniting the two regions, not its people. This remains true today, regardless of the regimes ruling in Egypt and Sudan.[3] My following observations will therefore be limited to the Nile because of its paramount position in Egyptian-Sudanese relations, in comparison with the other conflicts mentioned above.

THE NILE IN EGYPTIAN-SUDANESE
RELATIONS BEFORE INDEPENDENCE

As a result of Egypt's rapid population growth on the one hand and the considerable diminution of the flow of the Nile waters in the 1980s on the other, water became a most sensitive factor in Egyptian politics. On November 5, 1987, the *London Times* predicted that Egypt, "the cradle of civilization," was drying up. It based this prediction on so-called scientific evidence, namely, that the rains feeding the Blue Nile—in the mountains of Ethiopia—were gradually shifting southward. The *New York Times* Cairo correspondent was even more pessimistic when he wrote on February 5, 1990, under the title "Now a Little Steam, Later, Maybe, a Water War," that some Egyptian officials had warned that water, not oil, could be the Middle East's next cause for war.

'Abd al-Tawwab 'Abd al-Hayy, an Egyptian journalist who in the 1980s traveled some 6,800 kilometers from the sources of the Nile in Burundi and Ethiopia to Alexandria, on the Mediterranean coast, came to the conclusion that unless Egypt reached an agreement with its southern neighbors—primarily Sudan—about the immediate projects needed for saving the Nile waters, a major catastrophe was imminent.[4] Egypt's population growth has become so rapid during the twentieth century that it has passed the 60 million mark in the second half of the 1990s. Other countries feeding on the Nile have also experienced population growth, though on a somewhat smaller scale. In Sudan the population increased from about 2 million in 1900 to some 30 million in 1995. Hence, the demands on the Nile waters have increased at such a rate that despite conservation projects and the High Dam at Aswan, an acute shortage of water was already evident in the 1980s. Because not a single tributary joins the Nile from Aswan to Alexandria—a distance of some 1,500 kilometers—future conservation projects cannot be executed by Egypt alone and depend on the goodwill and cooperation of its southern neighbors, primarily Ethiopia and Sudan. Egypt can decrease its wastage of water by applying economical irrigation methods and by putting an end to the profligate waste of water in Cairo and other cities. And yet, even if all that is executed, Egypt would still face acute water shortages in the foreseeable future.

The quest for the unity of the Nile Valley was a direct outcome of this reality and was of crucial importance to the rulers of Egypt long before it became the slogan of Egypt's nationalists toward the end of the nineteenth century. Following the Egyptian conquest of the Sudan in 1820–1821, during the reign of Muhammad 'Ali Pasha, it became a major issue. Egypt's agricultural projects, as well as the search for the sources of the Nile, drew Egypt's attention to the centrality of the Nile in its future development and convinced its rulers that Sudan would have to be ruled from Cairo within a united Nile Valley. Egyptian politicians and historians viewed this quest as a legitimate extension of their country's borders. They argued that Egypt had been forced by Great Britain to withdraw from Sudan in 1885, following the Mahdist revolt, because of British imperialist designs. Hence, it was Egypt's historical right to recover this lost territory.[5] It was imperialism that ushered in the so-called scramble for Africa in the 1880s, during which European powers arbitrarily carved up the black continent into colonies and areas of influence. Britain's aim was to maintain its supremacy in the Nile Valley, and hence it started its conquest of Sudan in 1896 and ultimately clashed with France in Fashoda (Kodok) on the Upper Nile, in 1898. In order to overcome European (primarily French) objections to its domination of the Nile, Britain adopted the "dual flag" policy, and the Anglo-Egyptian Condominium came into being. The history of Anglo-Egyptian relations between 1899 and 1956 cannot be understood without taking this into consideration. For Egyptians of all shades of political opinion, the Anglo-Egyptian Condominium, which enabled Britain to rule the Sudan during these years, was a betrayal of Egypt's historical rights, which embraced the entire Nile Valley. Egyptian nationalists viewed the condominium as an act of colonialist conquest, and the editor of *Al-Ahram* (January 26, 1899) denounced it in an editorial as "The Black Condominium of Sudan." Sa'd Zaghlul, Egypt's most notable nationalist leader in the post–World War I period, even stated that Sudan was more important to Egypt than Alexandria.[6] Though one shouldn't take Zaghlul's statement regarding Alexandria literally, it is nonetheless true that the united Nile Valley that embraced Sudan was viewed by Egyptian nationalists of all political shades as an absolute must.

Following Lord Allenby's ultimatum to the Egyptian government in the wake of the assassination of Sir Lee Stack, Sudan's governor-general, by an Egyptian nationalist in Cairo in November 1924, mutual relations and mistrust became even worse. Lord Allenby's subsequent ultimatum to Egypt led to the resignation of Sa'd Zaghlul's government and to the expulsion of the Egyptian army and most Egyptian officials from Sudan. In it Allenby threatened, without Whitehall's consent, that Sudan would be allowed to exploit as much of the Nile waters as it required, regardless of Egyptian needs. This threat, though never implemented, had an everlasting traumatic impact on Egypt, for it impressed upon its rulers that whoever ruled Khartoum could hold Egypt for ransom. Egypt therefore rejected all further British attempts to reach a compromise that would grant Sudan the right of self-determination, and continued to insist on its unity with Egypt under the Egyptian Crown. There was indeed a national consensus in Egypt between 1899 and 1955 that once the British were forced to abandon the Nile Valley, unity would prevail forever.

THE NILE AND THE HIGH DAM AFTER INDEPENDENCE

It was only after the Free Officers came to power in July 1952 that a more realistic policy toward Sudan was adopted in Cairo. President Muhammad Najib (Nagib)—himself half-Sudanese and educated in Sudan—realized that Sudan had to be granted the right to determine its own future. Nagib believed that self-determination would lead the Sudanese to opt for unity with Egypt. But despite the optimism prevailing in Cairo following the Anglo-Egyptian agreement of February 1953 and the first general elections in November of that year, in which the pro-unity National Unionist Party (NUP) won, Sudanese of all shades of opinion chose independence, and on January 1, 1956, the Republic of Sudan was born. Nagib laid the blame for the Sudanese change of heart squarely on the shoulders of Gamal Abdel Nasser. According to Nagib, Nasser's antidemocratic measures and his mistreatment of Nagib himself frightened even the most avowed pro-unity Sudanese who feared their fate under a Nasserist dictatorship. Moreover, the disbanding of all political parties, the public trials of leaders of stature, such as Mustafa al-Nahhas Pasha, and finally the mass arrests of the members of the Muslim Brothers discouraged Isma'il al-Azhari and Sayyid 'Ali al-Mirghani—the respective leaders of the NUP and the Khatmiyya Sufi order—from tying their fate to Egypt's political upheavals. 'Abd al-'Azim Ramadan concluded that this unfortunate turn of events was caused by the fact that "when the dawn of liberalism rose in the Sudan, it set in Egypt."[7]

Since 1956 Egypt was therefore faced with the reality of an independent Sudan. The allocation of the Nile waters to the two states had been raised already in 1955. Isma'il al-Azhari—the Sudan's first prime minister and until 1954 one of Egypt's closest allies—demanded a revision of the 1929 Anglo-Egyptian agreement regarding the respective shares of the two countries in the waters of the Nile. The Sudanese argued that the agreement was no longer valid because it had been reached by Britain and

Egypt without consulting with them and had discriminated against Sudan by granting it only one-twenty-second of the total annual flow of Nile water.[8] Sudan's request came at an inopportune moment for President Nasser, for at that time he was considering the feasibility of building the High Dam at Aswan for which he needed the goodwill and the consent of the Sudanese. In March 1955, Khidr Hamad, a staunch supporter of unity with Egypt, undertook his first trip to Egypt as the newly appointed minister of irrigation in al-Azhari's government. The Egyptians, represented by Major Salah Salim, who was put in charge of all matters relating to Sudan by the Revolutionary Command Council, objected to Sudan exploiting any additional waters before the completion of the High Dam. He claimed that this would entail less irrigation for Egypt and the death of thousands of its peasants. He promised, however, that once the dam was completed, there would be an additional 16 to 22 billion cubic meters per annum to be divided between Egypt and the Sudan. At this stage the Egyptians also withdrew from their previous agreement to enable Sudan to build a new dam at Rusayris, on the Blue Nile. They stated that their consent depended on Sudan's agreement regarding the High Dam at Aswan. According to Khidr Hamad, Egypt's obstinacy was partly the result of al-Azhari's decision to opt for an independent Sudan.[9] The growing tension between Egypt and Sudan included the movement of military forces to the Halayib Triangle and highlighted the centrality of the Nile in Egyptian-Sudanese relations. Only in October 1959, one year after the military coup that brought General Ibrahim 'Abbud to power in Sudan, a new Nile Waters Agreement was signed. It granted Egypt 55.5 billion cubic meters per annum while Sudan's share increased to 18.5 billion cubic meters. Work on the Aswan Dam started in January 1960 and was completed eleven years later when it was officially opened by Presidents Sadat and Podgorny. The dam and Lake Nasser, in which surplus waters were stored, increased Egypt's water storage capacity from 5.6 to 130 billion cubic meters. It was also predicted that some 1.2 million *feddans* (roughly the same size as acres) of land would be reclaimed for agriculture, and that cheap electricity, to the tune of 10 billion kwh per annum, would be provided until 1992.[10]

SADAT AND NUMAYRI: A BRIEF HONEYMOON

President Anwar al-Sadat focused Egypt's attention once again on the Nile Valley for political and economic reasons. Politically Sadat viewed Numayri as an important ally against Soviet designs on the Nile Valley. In the 1970s pro-Soviet regimes in Libya, Chad, Somali, and Ethiopia threatened—according to Sadat—to encircle Egypt, which had rid itself of

Soviet domination in July 1972. A friendly, anticommunist Sudan seemed essential to Sadat in order to forge his new alliance with the West. This was the regional and international setting for the *takamul* (integration) agreement signed by Presidents Sadat and Numayri in February 1974, which for the first time since 1956 revived the quest for a united Nile Valley. From then until Numayri's downfall in April 1985, Sudan became a dependable ally of Egypt and supported Sadat's policies against an almost united Arab and Muslim front. Sudan did not sever its diplomatic relations with Egypt in 1979 following the Camp David accords and Egypt's boycott by the Arab summit in Baghdad. Economically, cooperation between Egypt and Sudan flourished, and a number of joint projects were agreed upon, including the digging of the Jonglei Canal, which sought to save the waters of the White Nile from evaporating in the sudd. The integration charter, which had been worked out in detail during these years by a joint parliament of the Nile Valley, was finally signed by Presidents Mubarak and Numayri on October 12, 1982.[11]

During the 1980s there had been a noticeable decrease in the quantity of water that flowed into Lake Nasser. This had been caused partially by the continuing drought in East Africa, causing widespread starvation in Ethiopia, Sudan, and other countries, and by the uncontrollable wastage of waters in the sudd region of Bahr al-Ghazal. Throughout those years and despite growing concern, Egypt continued to exploit its full annual share of 55.5 billion cubic meters granted under the 1959 agreement that without Lake Nasser would have been impossible. How can the flow of waters into Lake Nasser be increased? One answer was to decrease the loss of water in the White Nile. In June 1978 Sudan started to dig the Jonglei Canal from the Sobat River to Malakal, a distance of some 360 kilometers. Once completed, the canal would have yielded an annual flow of 4.7 billion cubic meters of water, of which 3.8 billion were destined for Lake Nasser. About 267 kilometers of the canal were completed in February 1984. But digging came to an abrupt end due to an attack on the Sobat headquarters of the company by Sudan's People's Liberation Army under the command of Colonel John Garang. No further progress has been made since then, and the partially completed canal has turned into a useless ditch and has become a dangerous hazard to the inhabitants and wildlife in that region.[12]

The flow of waters in the Blue Nile had always been regarded as more reliable, for an average annual flow of 84 billion cubic meters had been recorded from 1899 to 1959. This too, however, declined considerably since 1977, when the average flow dropped to 72 billion cubic meters, with a low of 42 billion cubic meters recorded in 1984, to the dismay of both Egyptian and other experts. Indeed, between 1984 and 1990 the average annual flow remained at the low level of 52 billion cubic meters.[13]

These figures provided the background for the prophecies of doom both in Egypt and elsewhere mentioned above. Egypt was faced with an annual deficit of nearly 12 billion cubic meters of water in 1988 and with no alternative sources to bridge the gap. Its crucial concerns in this region are therefore self-evident. Unlike its relations with the Fertile Crescent, which are primarily of political and strategic importance, Egypt's links with its southern neighbors are vital for its survival, and any threat to the free flow of the Nile will not be tolerated in Cairo. In an interview with the weekly *Al-Musawwar* on May 13, 1988, Marshal Muhammad 'Abd al-Halim Abu Ghazala, then Egypt's minister of defense, asked himself the following questions: How will Egypt react if one of its southern neighbors attempts to divert the Nile waters? "Will we die of thirst or fight for the supreme interests of the homeland?" His response was that the Egyptian army would strike if the free flow of the Nile waters was tampered with.

DETERIORATING RELATIONS
AND THE RE-EMERGENCE OF CONFLICTS

Since Numayri's downfall in 1985 Egypt's relations with Sudan deteriorated rapidly. The integration agreement was abolished unilaterally by al-Sadiq al-Mahdi's government, and bilateral relations were at a low ebb. Irritation with al-Sadiq's policies made Cairo the first to recognize Colonel Hasan 'Umar al-Bashir when he overthrew Sudan's democratically elected government in a military coup on June 30, 1989. President Mubarak hoped, erroneously as it transpired, that the Bashir regime would soon resume Sudan's cordial relations with Egypt. But Bashir proved worse than his predecessor, and Egyptian authorities have ascribed much of Khartoum's bellicosity to the malign influence of Hasan al-Turabi, the fundamentalist Muslim leader who heads the NIF, and to Sudan's close relationship with Iran.[14] Bashir's government has turned to become the most hostile Sudanese regime ever faced by Egypt since Sudan became independent in 1956. This hostility has expressed itself primarily in the export of Islamic violent radicalism into Egypt, culminating in the attempt on President Mubarak's life, on June 26, 1995. However, it invariably brought about a conflict over the Nile waters and the Halayib border issue in the months that followed. To quote Hasan al-Turabi once again: "Egypt is today experiencing a drought in faith and religion . . . , [but] Allah wants Islam to be revived from Sudan and flow along with the waters of the Nile to purge Egypt from obscenity."[15]

Since 1995, when Turabi uttered this warning, many waters have flown in the Nile, and Sudan's internal, regional, and international situation is on the verge of collapse. A more realistic approach than the one uttered by

Turabi would view Sudan's future as a viable nation-state as rather questionable. Furthermore, it would regard Egypt's rather tolerant attitude toward Sudan as a sign of its strength and its unwillingness to become engrossed in the internal conflicts of its southern neighbor. All this may change overnight if those in power in Sudan will tamper with the free flow of the Nile waters without Egypt's prior agreement.

NOTES

This is an abbreviated version of a chapter published in *White Blood Black Blood,* edited by Stephanie Beswick and Jay Spaulding (Lawrenceville, N.J.: Red Sea Press, 1999).

1. "Ethiopia Puts Khartoum on Notice over Terrorism," *Sudan Democratic Gazette,* 64 (September 1995), p. 6; according to an Ethiopian investigation, completed in August 1995, all suspects were Egyptian nationals, two of whom had escaped to Sudan, and the Ethiopians demanded their immediate extradition. In a more recent report official Egyptian sources accused Sudan of not treating this issue seriously and of evading its responsibility for terrorism (*Al-Hayat,* 12 July 1996); I am grateful to Yehudit Ronen, from the Dayan Center, for drawing my attention to the Al-Hayat publication.

2. For details see Warburg, "The Nile in Egyptian-Sudanese Relations," pp. 565–572, and "Egypt and Sudan Wrangle over Halayib," pp. 57–60.

3. Milad Hana, "Azmat al-Sudan," *Al-Hayat,* 19 February 1997, p. 19. I am grateful to Professor Sasson Somekh, director of the Israeli Academic Center in Cairo in 1996–1997, for drawing my attention to this article.

4. 'Abd al-Hayy, *Al-Nil wa'l-mustaqbal.*

5. Ramadan, *Ukdhubat al-isti'mar al-Misri li'l-Sudan,* pp. 21–28, 64–66; see also Warburg, "The Turco-Egyptian Sudan: A Recent Historiographical Controversy," pp. 193–215.

6. Ramadan, *Ukdhubat al-isti'mar al-Misri li'l-Sudan,* p. 74; see also Yunan Labib Rizk, "Al-Ahram: A Diwan of Contemporary Life," *Al-Ahram Weekly,* 21–27 September 1995. Professor Rizk, a renowned authority on Sudanese history, published a series of articles on this issue between 7 September and 25 October in *Al-Ahram Weekly.* I am grateful to Dr. Uri M. Kupferschmidt, from Haifa University's department of Middle East history, for drawing my attention to this series.

7. Ramadan, *Ukdhubat al-isti'mar al-Misri li'l-Sudan,* pp. 165–181; see also Najib, *Kalimati li'l-ta'rikh,* pp. 193, 231. For a detailed study see Warburg, *Historical Discord in the Nile Valley,* pp. 62–124.

8. Ministry of Irrigation, *Waters Question: The Case for Egypt, the Case for the Sudan Nile,* Khartoum, 1955, pp. 2–3.

9. Hamad, *Mudhakarat Khidr,* pp. 202–204, 207–213.

10. Rizk, *Al-Ahram Weekly,* 19–25 October 1995.

11. 'Abd al-Ghani Sa'udi, *Al-takamul al-Misri al-Sudani;* see also "Integration Charter Concluded Between Egypt and Sudan," Cairo and Khartoum, 12 October 1982.

12. Collins, *The Jonglei Canal;* see also Collins, *The Waters of the Nile,* p. 90.

13. Collins, *The Waters of the Nile,* pp. 402–405.

14. For details on Turabi and the NIF see El-Affendi, *Turabi's Revolution.*

15. *Al-Sharq al-Awsat,* 6 July 1995. See Ronen, "Sudan," and Lowrie, *Islam, Democracy, the State and the West,* p. 89.

18

◆

Removing the Nubians: The Halfawis at Khashm al-Girba

Ismail H. Abdalla

This chapter assesses a resettlement and development project in eastern Sudan, the Khashm al-Girba project. It traces the story of relocating 50,000 or so Sudanese Nubians displaced by Lake Nasser in southern Egypt early in the 1960s and tries to determine the extent to which the resettlement project at Khashm al-Girba has lived up to the high expectations of its planners.

As with any major development scheme, there were many uncertainties in the 1960s with regard to the removal and resettlement of the Sudanese Nubians, or Halfawis. There was, to begin with, the difficult problem of the selection of the resettlement site. Of the six areas proposed for resettlement, only three seemed to appeal to the Nubians who would be displaced: the two proposed sites to the north and to the south of Khartoum, and the Wadi al-Khawi near Dongola.[1] If they had to move, they reasoned quite logically, they wanted to be as close as possible to the center of politics and finance, which was Khartoum, the capital. If for any reason the two proposed resettlement areas around Khartoum were excluded, the alternative was Wadi al-Khawi. To them, Wadi al-Khawi was not far from their original homeland, its ecosystem was familiar, and its inhabitants, the Dongolawis, were their distant kinfolk. However, they did not even consider Khashm al-Girba, where they finally were resettled against their own wishes. The place was strange to them in almost every respect, and the fact that they knew practically nothing about it made it even less attractive. But the Sudan military government of General Ibrahim 'Abbud had an altogether different plan in mind that had much to do with the larger issue of economic development in the country as a whole, a country for whose destiny the soldiers felt responsible since they usurped power in 1958 from a democratically elected government.[2] 'Abbud and his clique were under pressure to legitimize themselves in the eyes of the Sudanese. Thus, economic development that stressed elephantine projects like the one implemented at Khashm al-Girba was the preferred strategy to achieve their political goals. The Khashm al-Girba project and the resettlement there of the Nubians must therefore be understood in the context of the larger political and economic development of Sudan in the 1960s, and not merely as the relocation of unfortunate peoples who lost their land.

'Abbud's government faced stiff resistance on the part of the Nubians both in Nubia and in Khartoum,[3] but that made his government even more determined to succeed, if for no other reason than its own survival. In the end the government prevailed. On the one hand, harassment, intimidation, even imprisonment of "troublemakers" was liberally used by the government to silence opposition to the project. On the other, government officials went out of their way to sell the new site at Khashm al-Girba to the settlers. Propaganda depicted the proposed resettlement area as the land of opportunity. Its large expanse of virgin soil with a plentiful supply of water was ready to accommodate a land-hungry people hemmed in by the most inhospitable terrain in the Nile Valley. What is more, the Nubians were led to believe that the abundant electricity generated by the Khashm al-Girba Dam would usher them into the modern world of consumption. The site's nearness to Khartoum in the west and to Sudan's only port at Port Sudan in the east would ensure the settlers fast and easy communication. The government recognized their sacrifice, they were told, and would work with them to make their new home a model for Africa and the world.

But the government did not depend on propaganda alone to win the Nubians over. Its newly established Resettlement Commission headed by an able and dedicated administrator, Dawud 'Abd al-Latif, a Nubian himself, worked hard to convince skeptical Halfawis that the move to Khashm al-Girba was in their best interest. Truckloads of would-be settlers were shipped to the resettlement area where they toured the proposed site, especially the newly constructed villages with their concrete two- or three-bedroom houses ready for occupancy, the newly built sugar factory, the hydroelectric generator at the dam, and the Pilot Horticulture Farm, where new promising cash crops and plants were being developed. It is no wonder that many visitors returned to Old Halfa favorably impressed, if not by what they saw at Khashm al-Girba then certainly by the seriousness of the military government to settle them there and by its commitment to do everything possible to ensure their safety and prosperity in their new home.

The sustained, intense propaganda eventually paid off. Even the displaced people themselves began to share in the euphoria and general optimism that was in the air in the Sudan of the 1960s. They, too, believed that something pivotal in the destiny of their country was afoot, and they were proud to be part of it. They also believed that their newly independent country seemed to have a lot going for it at this point in history. The Sudanese had just obtained their freedom, and colonialism was on the retreat in the rest of the continent. At long last, the process of relocation started in January 1964, and by September of the same year almost all the 50,000 displaced Nubians were relocated at Khashm al-Girba in twenty-two newly constructed villages plus the town of New Halfa. Each family was provided with a place to live and a fifteen-acre tenancy. Those who had owned agricultural land in Nubia were granted twice the amount in freehold lands.[4]

The Sudanese career administrators, perhaps more than any group, were caught up in this euphoria and optimism and were hence determined to make the first resettlement project of its kind in Africa a success. The fact that the Sudanese army took power in Khartoum and aborted the first democratic experiment in the country barely two years after independence did not seem to dampen the optimism of those Sudanese bureaucrats responsible for the project. It was the largest planned transfer and resettlement of a population anywhere in Africa, and its designers knew that. They also relished the idea that they would spearhead sub-Saharan Africa's major economic drive to join the developed world. If Nasser of Egypt saw the successful construction of the High Dam as the litmus test of his Egyptian socialism and Arab nationalism, the soldiers in Khartoum and the seasoned civilian administrators on whom they came to depend perceived the execution of the resettlement project in the Butana "empty" lands as the vindication of their coup d'état. To them it was a test of will for the Sudanese people, and its implementation according to plan was the proof that the Sudanese deserved their freedom and independence.

Because planners were concerned primarily with agricultural development in Sudan as a whole and only secondarily with the immediate problems of the displaced people, they had casually dismissed the Nubians' own preference to be resettled elsewhere in Sudan. This was the first of a series of high-handed, top-down decisions that the 'Abbud military government and successive administrations made that are linked directly to the problems that have bedeviled the resettlement scheme at Khashm al-Girba since its inception. The lofty goals of productive settler farmers, integrated pastoralists of the Butana, and industrialization remain largely unfulfilled to this day. Mistakes in the original planning were compounded later by even more serious ones in management, the marketing of farm produce (mainly cotton), and the inability of the Halfawi settlers and the local Shukriyya nomads to coexist in the scheme in a state of harmony and cooperation.

Successful land settlements need several ingredients to succeed. They include:

1. Deciding on the project
2. Defining the objectives
3. Selection of the site
4. Distribution of land
5. Management of farms
6. Supply of services
7. Provision of production requisites
8. Integration within an overall development plan.[5]

Even if not included here, identifying willing settlers is by far the most important factor. This was lacking both in the resettlement of the displaced Halfawis, many of whom would rather have been elsewhere, and especially in the planned settlement of the nomadic Shukriyya, some of whose grazing lands were taken over by the resettlement scheme. The planners of the project presumed that the displaced Nubians would be lured by the prospect of the huge amount of farmland at Khashm al-Girba, and being farmers by profession, would actually till the plots assigned them once they were there. They were wrong on both assumptions. The Halfawis were not impressed at all by how much land was made available to them. There were interesting stories of many Halfawi tenants who, seeing how big a fifteen-*feddan* tenancy was, told officials they would do with only five-*feddan* plots. And not all the displaced people were farmers in Old Halfa. Indeed, in the land-hungry area of Batn al-Hagar to the south of Old Halfa, farming had never completely supported the sparse population that lived there and depended on substantial remittances from relatives working in Egypt or elsewhere in Sudan. As for tilling the soil themselves, most Halfawis preferred to see others, mainly farm laborers from western Sudan and the south, do the hard work of farming. As in the Gezira scheme, absentee landlords became a problem that undermined production at Khashm al-Girba.

In contrast, most of the Shukriyya in the Butana region were nomads who practiced only limited farming to supplement income. But this made no difference to planners, steeped as they were in ideas about development popular in the 1960s. Then the wisdom of settling nomads seemed self-evident. The pastoralist way of life was deemed backward and inefficient. Development was seen as synonymous with settled life. The Sudanese planners and their impatient government were convinced that the nomadic Shukriyya must be settled if they were to share in the fruits of modernity, and must turn to perennial agriculture instead of traditional farming, dependent as it was on unpredictable patterns of rainfall. Accordingly, the resettlement of "primitive tribal groups" and nomads was necessary for the "proper utilization of land, forests, and water resources."[6] As Salah el-Din Noah writes, "It seems inevitable for primitive tribal groups and nomadic herdsmen to undergo certain social readjustments leading to an optimum balance between their present primitive adaptations and the emerging economic needs of civilization."[7]

It is clear that resettlement projects were perceived as part of a more fundamental program of social engineering in Sudan. Planners saw themselves as agents of economic and social transformation in the country, and the Nubians and the Shukriyya were their guinea pigs. Unfortunately, neither the displaced Nubians nor their reluctant hosts believed that they were instruments of social or economic transformation. Indeed, the response of the Shukriyya to the scheme was clearly negative, at least in the beginning.[8] First, they bitterly resented the loss of their grazing lands, and opposed the new regulations restricting the movements of their animal herds in the settlement zone. They were also offended in particular by the fact that all government services, including housing, food rationing during the first months of settlement, health, and education, were the exclusive prerogative of the strangers from the north. When some of them finally agreed to settle down and farm, they were given 6,915 tenancies, though mostly in the remote sections of the scheme where irrigation proved to be difficult.

As a result of the 1959 Nile Waters Agreement between Egypt and Sudan, Sudan's share of the Nile waters jumped to 18.5 billion cubic meters measured at Aswan.[9] To utilize its share of the waters, Sudan began to implement several gravity irrigation projects of which Khashm al-Girba was one. The resettlement project was to develop 372,000 *feddans* on the west side of the Atbara River at Khashm al-Girba, about 350 miles east of Khartoum.[10] To irrigate these lands, a dam with a storage capacity of 1.3 billion cubic meters[11] was constructed by 1966 at a cost of £S 30 million (30 million piastres). About 26,000 *feddans* were set aside for vegetable gardens and forestlands, and 37,000 *feddans* for planting sugarcane, for which a new sugar processing factory was built.[12] Large-scale irrigation projects like the one under consideration here were, until very recently, favored by developers because they were easy to control, and because they invariably fostered further centralization of the administration and the bureaucracy.[13] For the governments of the newly independent African countries, which were unsure of themselves and their place in history, these large-scale projects were a God-sent salvation.

All indications at the time showed that the irrigation development project at Khashm al-Girba, which was to have an administrative structure not dissimilar from that of the Gezira scheme, would be an all-round success. Its large cost was seen as a better investment compared, for example, to limited investment in the rain-fed traditional agriculture.[14] This was so, it was argued, because the central government was more likely to collect taxes on a regular basis from the farm produce in irrigated schemes than from produce of rain-fed farming, notwithstanding the acknowledged fact that investment in traditional agriculture would benefit a much larger number of farmers than would an equivalent sum of money in irrigated schemes.[15] In other words, planners were interested primarily in the net return to the central government from capital investment through taxes and other miscellaneous revenue-generating activities, namely, rail transportation of export crops, and not in the overall benefits that might accrue to farmers in the rain-fed sector of agriculture. Bureaucrats in Khartoum then and now were in the business of governing principally for the benefit of the intelligentsia, and not for the well-being of poor farmers who happened to be the majority of the population. The only difference between the intellectual leadership of the early 1960s and the current leadership in Khartoum is one of orientation. The old guard was interested mainly in the economic and social transformation of the Sudanese society. The present government in Khartoum, led by the National Islamic Front, is committed to an ideological rebirth as well.

What is striking about this type of bureaucratic reasoning and economic planning early in the 1960s is that the contribution of the traditional agricultural sector to the gross domestic product was more than twice the contribution of what was called the "modern sector," meaning irrigated agriculture.[16] Statistics show that investment in irrigated farming costs ten times as much as in mechanized farming and twenty-five times as much as in investment in traditional farming.[17] Yet policymakers in this period preferred to completely ignore this fact in their drive to modernize agriculture, focusing mainly on gravity irrigation. They were willing, thus, to invest heavily in projects like that of Khashm al-Girba.

Barely fifteen years after being put into operation, the resettlement project already faced serious problems. The most severe was the rapid rate of sedimentation in the reservoir. A study conducted in 1977 found that the silting up had already reduced the reservoir's 1.3 billion cubic-meter capacity to 0.8 billion cubic meters, a loss of about 40 percent.[18] Even if the dam retained its storage capacity of 1.3 billion cubic meters, it would still be unable to meet the annual water consumption at the resettlement scheme estimated in 1977 to be 1.7 billion cubic meters and rising.[19] The repercussions of this development were not unknown to farmers, most of whom had experienced low or no supply of irrigation water during the critical periods of cultivation. Indeed, the same study also found that irrigation efficiency operated at only 37 percent of optimum capacity.[20] The result was a noticeable decline in cotton production per *feddan* during the period between 1967 and 1981, from a high of 1,449 pounds to about 825 pounds, a loss of 43 percent.[21] Some loss of productivity could be explained by factors other than water shortage, lack of fertilizers and pesticides, problems with weeds, and shortage of labor for harvesting, as well as the increasing salinity resulting from bad or nonexistent drainage. [22] But the main difficulty remained water shortage. So severe indeed was this problem that the last phase of the irrigation scheme was not implemented. The international consulting firm that did the above-mentioned studies even suggested that the relatively high water-consuming crops like wheat and groundnuts should be phased out entirely by the year 2009, while lands under cotton cultivation should be reduced from 109,000 to 7,600 *feddans* by 2010.[23] This was a clear indictment against a project for whose success its planners had had such high hopes.

"As a project," says the report of the German Agrar und Hydrotechnic consulting firm, "the scheme economics are only just satisfactory, output only marginally covering inputs. The economics at the farmer level are unsatisfactory: for cotton the average tenant has actually made a small loss in recent years. . . . The position is equally unsatisfactory for wheat and it is only from groundnuts that a satisfactory farm level return is obtained."[24]

Insufficient water supply led to corruption in the distribution of available water. Farmers with good connections to officials responsible for water allocation and to bank officers for credit proved to be more successful than those without such connections. The result was a much more stratified community in New Halfa than in Old Halfa.

Water shortage was just one of many problems that plagued the project from its inception. The other was management. Because of a lack of experience with large-scale resettlement, the government ran the Khashm al-Girba irrigation scheme as if it were an extension of the Gezira, with more or less the same rules and regulations and with similar crop rotation. This was a mistake. In the first place, though most Nubian settlers were farmers in their old home, farming was not their sole source of income. Many, as we have noticed earlier, depended on remittances from relatives. They should not, therefore, have been put on a par with settled farmers at the Gezira irrigation scheme, most of whom had lived there long before the Gezira was ever developed and were totally dependent on farming for a living. Again, the rigidity of the rules pertaining to crop rotation often flew in the face of efficiency and common sense. For example, it took the authorities fifteen years to realize that the Shukriyya tenants who made up half the population in the scheme actually preferred to produce sorghum, their staple food, than wheat, which was the staple food of the Nubians.[25] Part of the problem was that there were too many government departments involved in running the irrigation scheme at Khashm al-Girba, and they were rarely in agreement among themselves with regard to policies. The Engineering Department of the Ministry of Agriculture resisted for a long time the incorporation of sorghum in the crop rotation because it put additional water demands on an irrigation system that was just barely, if ever, able to meet existing water requirements.[26] The department believed rightly that irrigation water was too precious a resource to be spent on the cultivation of a crop that could be produced much more cheaply in rain-fed lands. In the end, however, the department had to agree, rather reluctantly, to legitimize what had long become a practice: the illegal cultivation of sorghum.

The management also failed to develop a sound policy that would integrate livestock in the scheme without detrimental effects on crops. The regulation of allowing only two animals per household made no sense to farmers, who simply ignored it. With diminishing returns from farming,[27] many Nubian settlers, like their neighbors, the Shukriyya,[28] owned livestock in increasing numbers. The nomadism that the original planners of the project considered an inefficient and backward mode of economic activity had now become a legitimate occupation.

To conclude, one can say that the whole resettlement enterprise would, undoubtedly, have had a better chance at success if the bureaucrats in Khartoum had involved the farmers themselves in the design and implementation of the irrigation project from the very beginning. But such an alternative would have been inconceivable in those days. Farmers, peasants, and nomads were to be led not consulted, and development projects were the sole concern of the technocrats and dictators who employed them. Civil society that was to become somewhat instrumental in governance in the Sudan—one that on two occasions brought down authoritarian rule— was yet to be born.

NOTES

1. Abdalla, "The Choice of Khashm al-Girba Area for the Resettlement of the Halfawis," p. 62.

2. Abdalla, "The 1959 Nile Waters Agreement in Sudanese-Egyptian Relations," p. 335.

3. Ibid., p. 67.

4. Salem-Murdock, *A Study of Settlement and Irrigation*, p. 26.

5. Hussain, "Problems in the Planning of Land Settlement," p. 80.

6. Noah, "Agricultural Extension," p. 161.

7. Ibid.

8. Salem-Murdock, *A Study of Settlement and Irrigation*, p. 26.

9. Waterbury, *Hydropolitics on the Nile Valley*, p. 321.

10. Ibid.

11. Ibid. River Atbara is a torrential river that rises in the Ethiopian highlands and joins with river Setit before reaching Khashm al-Girba. Its estimated annual flow is 1.2 billion cubic meters. However, only one-fifth of its water storage is available for irrigation every year. See Abdel Magid, "Nile Control for Agricultural Development in the Sudan," p. 323.

12. Wynn, "Water Resource Planning in the Sudan," p. 105.

13. Huntington, *The Clash of Civilizations and the Re-making of World Order,* p. 69.

14. Mirghani, "Problems of Increasing Agricultural Productivity," p. 100.

15. Ibid.

16. Department of Statistics, *Economic Survey,* Khartoum, 1964, p. 45. The bias against traditional farmers was common among Khartoum planners, as evident from statements like this: "The subsistence farmer is very conservative. He and his family live so close to a subsistence level that they cannot afford to experiment with new crops or new farming practices." Or "the traditional farmer measures income, work, and leisure on a scale different from that which the economist is accustomed to finding in more advanced agricultural societies. It is the social value of goods and services that is important to him, and not their economic value" (Mirghani, "Problems of Increasing Agricultural Productivity," p. 99).

17. Lees and Brooks, *The Economic and Political Development of the Sudan,* p. 49.

18. Agrar und Hydrotechnic, "New Halfa Rehabilitation Project: Phase 1," Ministry of Planning, Khartoum, 1978, p. 13.

19. Waterbury, *Hydropolitics on the Nile Valley,* p. 233.

20. Agrar und Hydrotechnic's report cited in Salem-Murdock, *A Study of Settlement and Irrigation,* p. 35.

21. Salem-Murdock, *A Study of Settlement and Irrigation,* p. 34.

22. Hulme and Trilsbach, "Rainfall Trends and Rural Change in Sudan Since Nimeiri," p. 10.

23. Salem-Murdock, *A Study of Settlement and Irrigation,* p. 35.

24. Agrar und Hydrotechnic, "New Halfa Rehabilitation Project: Phase 1," 1978, p. 22.

25. Salem-Murdock, *A Study of Settlement and Irrigation,* p. 55.

26. Ibid., p. 71.

27. Planners of the project estimated early in the 1960s that a farmer at Khashm al-Girba would make a net return of £S 38.00 per tenancy after the payment of water charges, and £S 86 without such payment. See Wynn, "Water Resource Planning in the Sudan," p. 111. Actual net returns from cotton, the main crop, were considerably lower, however, only £S 8.00 in 1960s, and £S 3.00 in the 1970s. See Salem-Murduck, *A Study of Settlement and Irrigation,* p. 32.

28. S. Hoyle has noticed, for example, that between 60 and 70 percent of the Shukriyya tenants in the scheme depended on raising livestock to supplement income. See Koyle, "The Khashm al-Girba Agricultural Scheme," pp. 116–131.

19

♦

In Search of the
Nile Waters, 1900–2000

Robert O. Collins

The peoples of Egypt and northern Sudan have been obsessed by the waters of the Nile since they were driven to its banks by the desiccation of the Sahara 5,000 years ago. But neither the pharaohs nor the kings of Kush, and certainly not their subjects, knew the source or the configuration of the lands beyond the deserts through which the waters flowed. Those intrepid centurions sent by the Roman emperor Nero in A.D. 61 were not much help when they reported that the empire did not need to acquire the sudd. After that stalwart Portuguese Jesuit, Pedro Paez, reached the holy spring of Sakala where the Blue Nile begins in Ethiopia, it was another half century before the Royal Society translated his description into English and another hundred years before James Bruce confirmed that source only to produce disbelief and not a little hilarity in the fashionable salons of eighteenth-century London. Another three-quarters of a century had to pass before that harbinger of nineteenth-century imperialism, Muhammad 'Ali, sent Salim Qapudan in 1841 to unravel the labyrinth of the sudd, and the multinational missionary Erhardt published his slug map of "The Sea of Uniamesis" to fill up the empty spaces of African maps hitherto occupied by trumpeting elephants. Mesmerized by the cartographic myopia of the great lakes of equatorial Africa everyone forgot about the Jesuits, James Bruce, and the Ethiopians as British explorers challenged one another in "The Nile Duel" to claim its source, until Henry Morton Stanley resolved "the greatest secret after the discovery of North America" by circumnavigating Lake Victoria and running the cataracts and war canoes on the Lualaba to end the Nile quest in 1878.[1] Four years later in 1882 the British imprisoned themselves in Egypt only to spend the next century trying to secure their release by deciphering the hydrology of the

Nile basin to regenerate the Egypt they had acquired in order to defend a distant empire.

Following in the vanguard of General Sir Garnet Wolseley's victorious British army in 1882 was Sir Evelyn Baring who, as Lord Cromer, provided the administrative leadership to secure Great Britain's occupation of Egypt and the defense of the Suez Canal by imposing "scientific administration" to cleanse the Aegean Stables of Turkish-Egyptian corruption with British officials. Their task was to increase agricultural production to create political passivity by renovating and expanding the perennial irrigation introduced by Muhammad 'Ali, and to devise schemes to provide water after the Nile flood had abated from January to July with stored water commonly known as "timely." To accomplish his objective Lord Cromer brought Sir Colin Scott-Moncrieff and his engineers from India, among whom were Sir William Willcocks and Sir William Garstin. Garstin was perceptive and affable; Willcocks was brilliant and erratic. Garstin's view of the Nile embraced the whole of its basin; Willcocks was the quintessential Egyptian who sought to produce timely water by a dam at Aswan.

By the end of the nineteenth century, barrages, diversion dams, and canals had raised the water level of the Nile to channel it into the fields along the river and through the latticework of conduits in the delta. The dam above Elephantine Island was completed in 1902 to supply the water required for perennial irrigation, but neither it nor the barrages downstream had the capacity to store additional water from one year to the next. Since the end of the Nile quest the great reservoirs of equatorial Africa were well-known; their relationship to the hydrology of the Nile basin was not. So long as the Khalifa 'Abdallahi and his followers dominated Sudan from Omdurman astride the confluence of the Blue and the White Niles in the middle of their extensive drainage, Garstin and his associates could not begin to collect the hydrological data required to understand the hydrological dynamics to prepare for the hydrological planning to use the waters of the Nile to the best advantage of the peoples of Egypt.

The year that the first stone was laid at Aswan the Anglo-Egyptian forces led by Sir H. H. Kitchener destroyed the soldiers of God and the Khalifa on the plains of Karari outside Omdurman on September 2, 1898. Kitchener had been sent to Khartoum not so much to defeat the Sudanese, who as defenders of the faith ironically became the protectors of the waters for their Christian enemy, but to challenge French pretensions to control the Nile and thereby recover at Fashoda Napoleon's dreams lost at Abukir and De Lesseps's monument sold in the bankruptcy court by the Khedive Isma'il. The folly of Fashoda was quickly resolved by the display of British military power, and then the subsequent occupation of Sudan enabled the British to bind Egypt and their East African colonies into a Nilotic empire to dominate virtually the whole of the Nile basin. The imposition of imperial authority in the last link of this imperial chain, southern Sudan, was contingent upon navigability through the sudd, the swamps of the Upper Nile the size of Belgium, irrespective of the prevailing ignorance of sudd hydraulics. Money was speedily found and undesirables rounded up in Omdurman to join the prisoners of war from Karari to clear the sudd obstructions from the Bahr al-Jabal and to reach open water and the parkland of Equatoria by May 1900. The river was now navigable for Sir William Garstin to steam south from Khartoum to the Nile source in order to determine the most advantageous utilization of its water for the benefit of the inhabitants downstream.

While Willcocks and that pragmatic, charming Scottish engineer Murdoch MacDonald toiled in the heat of Aswan, Lord Cromer turned to Garstin to unravel the dynamics of Nile control for Egypt and the security of Britain's position therein. Cromer was always suspicious of generals and particularly Kitchener, who was useful to frustrate the French but quite unsuitable to appreciate the totality of Nile control, which had been his reason to acquiesce in the expensive Anglo-Egyptian occupation of the Sudan. Six months after the victory at Karari and again in 1900 and 1901, he sent Garstin upriver to delve into the waters and again in 1903 to the lake plateau of East Africa, the swamps, lakes, and mountains that Great Britain had conquered by a cold and calculating strategy to secure Egypt and the Suez Canal, but in which the waters flowing from the Ethiopian highlands had not been a significant consideration.

Garstin's pioneering surveys between 1899 and 1903 and his two reports published in 1901 and 1904 established the foundation for Nile hydrological investigations to control and conserve its waters throughout the twentieth century.[2] Although the waters of the lake plateau—Albert, Edward, George, Kyoga, Victoria—were obvious reservoirs, it was equally apparent that their fresh waters would never pass through the swamps of the Nile without enormous loss from evaporation. Garstin did not require seventy-five years of sudd studies to determine that any plan for additional water in Egypt from the equatorial lakes would fail without a conduit through the sudd. He proposed, at the suggestion of J. S. Beresford, a massive canal, the Garstin Cut, from Bor, where the swamps begin, to the confluence of the Sobat and the White Nile south of Malakal, where they end. Ethiopia and the hydrology of the 'Atbara, the Sobat, and the Blue Nile were largely ignored. The absence of the Ethiopian connection was a serious flaw in a brilliant exposition of Nile hydrology, which remains an intimidating manifesto for Nile water development to this very day. After Garstin, the combined efforts of British, Egyptian, and Sudanese designs for Nile development remained focused on the river from Kampala to Khartoum to Cairo. After Garstin, all "the best laid schemes o'mice and men" converged upon the equatorial lakes, the sudd, and the White Nile.

The holy spring at Sakala, the emerald waters of Lake Tana, and the wine-dark flow of the Abbai remained an afterthought in the Anglo-Egyptian designs for Nile control.

Despite its unmeasured but substantial volume, British interest in Lake Tana and the Blue Nile receded proportionately to their geographical isolation, geological inaccessibility, and the fortress of Ethiopian xenophobia. After his enemy, the Khalifa, was defeated at Karari and his allies, the French, were discredited at Fashoda, Emperor Menelik quietly dropped his exaggerated claims to the east bank of the Nile. In 1897 the British envoy, Rennell Rodd, had been sent to Addis Ababa, to prevent by futile diplomacy, a French advance to the Nile from the east. Menelik had demanded the Nilotic plains from Khartoum to Lake Albert, but in 1902 he decided it was more prudent to curry favor with the victorious British by agreeing not to tamper with the waters of the Blue Nile without proper consultation. The next year Garstin sent C. E. Dupuis, inspector-general in the Egyptian irrigation service, to determine whether Lake Tana could be an alternate reservoir to Lake Albert. Dupuis concluded that a dam at Bahar Dar was feasible, as did G. W. Grabham and R. P. Black in 1921, but any reservoir would not substantially provide additional water to the Nile when the lake only contributed a paltry 7 percent of the Blue Nile flow.[3] Moreover, Menelik's growing senility, the conservatism of Empress Zwaditu, and the hostility of the feudal barons of Gojjam and Begemdir, who dominated the highlands above the water, discouraged any discourse with the Ethiopians about Nile development. Regent Ras Tafari, however, was determined to have a dam at Lake Tana, particularly after the Nile Waters Agreement of 1929 appeared to remove the political obstacles for Nile control, which presupposed the inclusion of the Blue Nile. Upon becoming Emperor Haile Selassie in 1930, he crushed the power of the highland *ras* in order to centralize his authority necessary to build a dam as a symbol of his policies of modernization. Suspicious of British intentions in northeast Africa after he learned that Great Britain was willing to support an exclusive Italian interest in western Ethiopia in return for the Lake Tana Dam concession, the emperor turned in 1927 to the American J. G. White Engineering Co. of New York to undertake the surveys and designs for the dam, the construction of which the British and the Egyptians promptly conspired to frustrate until the Italians were able to do it for them after their invasion of Ethiopia in 1936. Intent upon appeasing the new and resurgent Roman empire of Benito Mussolini with the sand of the Sara Triangle in the Libyan Desert, a governor-general in the palace at Khartoum friendly to Italy, and their indecent abdication of collective security against Italy at the League of Nations, the British government was silently satisfied with Mussolini's vague assurance that Italy would not interfere with the flow of the Nile waters. No one dared to press the triumphant Mussolini, whose king had now become emperor, for a more precise definition of Italy's hydrological intentions in Ethiopia, and the engineers and hydrologists in Egypt, Sudan, and Uganda expressed no serious concern since Ethiopia had become but a cipher in the equation of Nile control.

Garstin's magisterial report for the hydrological development of the Nile basin in 1904 was not amended until the publication by Sir Murdoch MacDonald of *Nile Control* in 1921, which was more a brief for the defense of his stewardship as adviser to the Ministry of Public Works than an expansion on the schemes devised by Sir William Garstin. To be sure, Sir Henry Lyons published his account of "Nile supply . . . periodicity . . . low stage . . . excessive floods," which incorporated what was known of the Nile basin and its hydrology at the end of the Cromer-Garstin era but did not provide any schemes or dreams of what to do with it.[4] The end of World War I witnessed a brave new world of astonishing technologies, aberrant ideologies, and a "lost generation" of which Sir Murdoch Mac-Donald was the very personification as the skillful engineer determined to utilize the new technology for the economic development, not only for Egypt but for Sudan as well. Thus, his proposal to build two dams in the Sudan, one at Makwar (Sennar) to provide water for the Gezira cotton scheme south of Khartoum, and another at Jabal Auliya to produce timely water for Egypt, created a storm of controversy from those Egyptian nationalists and engineers liberated, politically and spiritually, by the Great War during which their country had experienced a surfeit of British arrogance and the lowest Nile in a century. Lieutenant Colonel M. Ralston Kennedy Pasha, director-general of public works for Sudan and that stormy Nile goose, Sir William Willcocks, charged that MacDonald had deliberately falsified, then misinterpreted, Nile flows that had been incorrectly read and haphazardly collected to advocate schemes in Sudan for Nile control to the detriment of Egypt. He thundered: "The Sudan will take its share of the water high up the course of the river, and Egypt will receive much of its share on paper."[5]

The Egyptian opposition to MacDonald was not confined to his proposal for dams in Sudan but sharpened the frustration and discontent with British domination of the irrigation service whose officials were unaccustomed to pander to the psychoses of pompous politicians and ignorant fellahin. Enshrouded by measurements and equations, the British engineers of the irrigation service appeared to be a mysterious and devious clique, loyal to Britain and the empire and therefore not working in the best interests of Egypt. MacDonald was tried in the nationalist press, by the Egyptian public, the consular courts, and the Nile Commission, the appointment of which only confirmed Albion's perfidy. There was no Egyptian representative on that commission, and after its membership was announced no Egyptian could be convinced to serve. Not surprisingly,

MacDonald was found guilty by the politicians and the populace and innocent of any impropriety by the commission and the courts. The commission concluded: "There had been no falsification or intentional suppression of records nor any fraudulent manipulation of data or gauges by Sir Murdoch MacDonald or by anyone else."[6] The court found Willcocks guilty of defamatory libel against MacDonald and sentenced him to probation. Despite his vindication MacDonald's position as the adviser to the ministry was hopelessly compromised. He resigned a few months after the Willcocks trial and immediately decamped from Cairo for a seat in the House of Commons and a fortune as a consulting engineer.

MacDonald left behind in Egypt a vacuum in the leadership at the ministry with disastrous results for the hydrological development of the Nile Valley. His testament, *Nile Control,* was a hastily contrived collection of memoranda and computations composed more to deflate the rhetoric of Willcocks and to mollify his critics in Egypt than to inspire its readers with a grand design for the conservation of the Nile waters. There was little tangible construction for Egypt, a barrage at Nag Hammadi, and a regulator, if not a mirage, in the extreme heat at Jabal 'Auliya. Ethiopia was not completely forgotten. There was to be a mysterious dam, perhaps in the Blue Nile gorge, presumably at Lake Tana. The Garstin Cut was, of course, included, and a remote reservoir at Lake Albert that MacDonald hoped would assuage Egyptian concerns for the additional water that he was giving to the Sudanese at Sennar for the irrigation of the Gezira. No one understood the meaning of the Sennar Dam more clearly than the American member of the Nile Commission, Harry Thomas Cory. Cory was an engineer, a Hoosier, and something of a cowboy, later played in the cinema by Gary Cooper, who tamed the Colorado River into the Salton Sea in 1906 and sought from the Quran the principle that any additional water conserved from the Nile should be divided equally between Egypt and Sudan. The Cory Award, as it became known, was regarded by the Egyptians with open hostility; the reaction of the Sudanese was too inchoate to be observed as public opinion, but Cory's ghost was going to appear a generation later in Khartoum and a half century later in Kampala.

The resignation of Sir Murdoch MacDonald in 1921, combined with the political upheavals in Egypt, left the future planning of the Nile in disarray. His position as adviser to the ministry was never filled, and upon the independence of Egypt in 1922 the British high commissioner could no longer play the political and financial role of Cromer, Gorst, or Kitchener, while their successors became bogged down in the swamp of disputatious and frustrating negotiations between Britain and Egypt over their own political relationship and the peculiar position of each in the governance of Sudan. Leaderless, the younger British hydrologists and engineers faithfully amassed enormous quantities of information about Nile flows and almost mindlessly devised schemes to bring down the water from the equatorial lakes without any coherent plan for control of it. Ethiopia was all but forgotten. The boats of W. N. McMillan and B. H. Jensen had been swamped trying to run the rapids of the Blue Nile before World War I; Major R. E. Cheesman, the British consul at Debre Markos, was to traverse the canyon of the Blue Nile during his treks on foot between 1926 and 1929. As late as 1958 little was known of the Blue Nile from Tisisat Falls to the Sudanese frontier.

After the British government reluctantly declared Egypt a sovereign state in 1922, the planning and execution of a chain of major engineering works embracing thousands of miles of the Nile could not be ignored, despite the demise of the position of the adviser whose responsibility had been to supervise the direction and the realization of Nile control. Cory had recommended an "adjudication board," and C. E. Dupuis had suggested a "board of control." The Sudanese government decided to organize its own independent irrigation service after the assassination of Governor-General Sir Lee Stack and the financial and construction problems that were eroding the Sennar Dam. Both the British and Egyptian governments continued to exchange proposals for the direction of Nile development that were stillborn in the acrimony that characterized their relationship but made all the more obvious by the signing of the Nile Waters Agreement in 1929.

The agreement was a political armistice that derived its inspiration from *The Nile Commission Report* of 1926, "a practical working arrangement" for the engineers to administer the Nile until the politicians could determine its destiny.[7] It was not a plan for the hydrological development of the Nile nor the means to achieve it. Exhausted by years of tendentious bickering, both the British and the Egyptians were prepared to accept an agreement on the rates of abstraction of water behind the Sennar Dam to irrigate the Gezira and the amount of timely water from Jabal 'Auliya for Egypt. The agreement was regarded in Cairo as a substantial victory. Egypt's established and historic rights were preserved. Egypt had the right to review and thereby approve any future conservancy construction. Sudan received a modest increase in its allotment of the waters but mortgaged its future by the admission of the primacy of Egypt's future needs. With Olympian self-satisfaction, the British and the Egyptians appeared content with an incomplete document that had no provisions for a comprehensive plan for Nile control or the administrative machinery to achieve it.

Surrounded by a hostile physical and political environment, the British engineers and hydrologists on the Nile labored during the two decades between the world wars with no grand design to inspire them, no direction, and only their own rivalries that soon turned inward to collect data for no other reason than the intrinsic merit of the information itself. They were talented men, but they were cautious and conservative, suspicious of politicians, often contemptuous of their Egyptian employers. They loathed inefficiency, which was often a rationale for doing nothing. They were honest, incorruptible, sober, and responsible men. They were also dull, rigid, and unimaginative. Reports they could write; dreams they suppressed. Harold Edwin Hurst occupied a unique position among this intrepid band. Recruited by Sir Henry Lyons for the survey department in October 1906 to begin a career that spanned sixty-two years, he had come to Cairo from a lectureship in physics at Oxford and thereafter seemed to be more the university don than a British effendi in the Egyptian service. A modest and mathematical man, his scientific abilities propelled him from the magnetic survey of Egypt to the director-generalship of the Physical Department of the Ministry of Public Works in 1915. The Physical Department was responsible for the preservation, collation, and analysis of data throughout the whole of the Nile basin, with a view to the construction of yet-to-be-determined works for Nile control. Only when hard-pressed by his Egyptian employers did Hurst produce his major contribution to Nile development, *The Future Conservation of the Nile,* until his official retirement in 1946.

Hurst introduced the innovative concept of century storage but was more interested in the mathematical probabilities between yield and reservoir capacity, which became known as the "Hurst Phenomenon." Such abstruse abstractions had great practical application but by their very nature were not easily translated into the hydropolitics of the Nile Valley. His personality and his interests were such that Hurst never conceived of himself following in the footprints of Garstin or MacDonald nor would the Egyptians allow him to do so. In the end he remained a civil servant, not the adviser, and like a much beloved retainer he was kept on in the Egyptian service even after his contribution to Nile control had become compromised by a High Dam at Aswan.

In the spring of 1946 the Egyptian Ministry of Public Works published volume seven of *The Nile Basin* titled *The Future Conservation of the Nile* by H. E. Hurst, R. P. Black, and Y. M. Simaika of the Physical Department.[8] During the aimless interwar years Hurst, in cooperation with P. Phillips and later Black and Simaika, had published six volumes and several supplements under the general title of *The Nile Basin.* These volumes contained largely statistical material with little commentary and no profound proposals. They did, however, provide the data for a more comprehensive plan now demanded by the Egyptian government. The result was volume seven in the series by which Hurst and his associates presented the first comprehensive plan for Nile control from the information that Garstin did not possess and a rigor that had escaped MacDonald. The Egyptian minister of public works, 'Abd al-Qawi Pasha, wrote with relief and pride:

> This is the first time that the full development of Egypt has been consid-
> ered in detail and a new idea, that of "Century Storage" is introduced.
> The book makes it clear that we can no longer proceed by small stages
> leaving the ultimate development for future consideration. The new ideas
> show that on important points a decision must be made now. The main
> projects are seen to be closely connected parts of one whole, and their
> connection is a complicated one.[9]

Hurst's plan for Nile control demonstrated the interrelation between
the individual projects that had emerged in the variety of separate proposals during the preceding decades in order to provide for the most efficient
use of the Nile waters, which in turn required the total control and regulation of all the waters in the drainage basin of the Nile. The definition of
"the most efficient use" was not simply the production of additional quantities of water but the means to supply a constant flow that could be so reg-
ulated as to prevent floods. The unique feature of Hurst's proposal was
"century storage," a refinement of the concept advanced by MacDonald
for overyear storage by which water would be contained in the equatorial
lakes where the rate of evaporation is balanced by rainfall and the geological configuration permits an increase in the volume of water without a
substantial increase in the surface exposed to evaporation.

Hurst envisaged a great reservoir at Lake Albert supplemented by a
regulator at the outlets from Lake Victoria and Lake Kyoga. In order to
make efficient use of the lake reservoirs under the concept of century storage, however, a big canal, the Garstin Cut, would be required to carry the
large volume of water conserved past the sudd to prevent its loss from
evaporation. Dams as conservators and as regulators at Lakes Victoria,
Kyoga, and Albert appeared straightforward; the sudd canal was not.
Known as Jonglei, after the fishing village on the Bahr al-Jabal below Bor
where the canal would begin its passage to the mouth of the Sobat, this
conduit immediately became the lynchpin of Hurst's Nile control, but a
project complicated by the mysteries of sudd hydraulics and the impact
upon the inhabitants and the environment of the swamps and floodplain
through which the Jonglei Canal would be excavated.

Garstin proposed to reduce the loss of water in the sudd by the Garstin
Cut. Thereafter, British hydrologists had slouched through the swamps in
an effort to explain their mechanics, which resulted in numerous schemes
and many volumes of flow measurements. Despite these efforts or perhaps
because of them, a satisfactory explanation of sudd hydraulics remained
obscure until the research and publications of J. V. Sutcliffe after the independence of Sudan in 1956.[10] Although the sudd presented the greatest
obstacle to the conservation of the Nile waters, the means to reduce or
eliminate it thrust Jonglei into the very center of that part of Hurst's century

storage dealing with the whole of the Upper Nile basin and known as the Equatorial Nile Project. To be sure its dams were principally in Uganda, with little effect upon the inhabitants of the sudd. Not so for Jonglei, whose massive canal would have a significant impact upon the lives of the Nilotic peoples whose interests the British officials in Sudan were determined to defend.

Although British officials in southern Sudan had reported rumors that a Jonglei Canal was contemplated as an essential part of the Equatorial Nile Project, inquiries by British officials of the Sudan government at Cairo had been dismissed as premature. Consequently, the publication of *The Future Conservation of the Nile* astonished every official in Sudan, none of whom had been apprised of its preparation nor forewarned as to the projects envisioned for Sudan, particularly Jonglei. Angry but impotent, the Sudan government, in a feeble gesture, quickly appointed a Jonglei Committee to review Hurst's plans for Nile control. Indignation turned to outrage when the Egyptian government unilaterally adopted *The Future Conservation of the Nile* as its official policy for the development of the Nile basin of which the Equatorial Nile Project was the principal component. There was neither casual nor courtesy consultation with Khartoum. Presented with a fait accompli the Jonglei Committee accepted the Equatorial Nile Project with its big canal with resignation, apprehension, and not a little bitterness. As a symbol of defiance the committee created the Jonglei Investigation Team to assess the environmental impact and the damages to the inhabitants of the Upper Nile in order to improve their social and economic livelihood with schemes and money. Since the Equatorial Nile Project involved British territories other than Sudan, negotiations opened in June 1947 between Egypt, Sudan, and Uganda to seek an agreement that would enable its implementation. No one considered or desired Ethiopian participation for Hurst's inclusion of the Lake Tana Dam was peripheral to his century storage, whereas the Blue Nile was totally ignored until incorporated a dozen years later in the more comprehensive and sophisticated scheme for the Nile basin by H. A. W. Morrice and W. N. Allan in *Report on the Nile Valley Plan.*

Remembered today by only connoisseurs of Nile control, *Report on the Nile Valley Plan* is an extraordinary document published in Khartoum in June 1958.[11] The culmination of half a century of Nile studies, it combined the sweeping comprehension of Garstin without his prose and the hydrological analysis of Hurst without his timidity. Humphrey Morrice and Nimmo Allan had engaged the assistance of the British National Physical Laboratory at Teddington, IBM, SOGREAH, and MIT to "introduce a very powerful tool into the study of the Nile conservation projects" by which they produced a "classic study in computer simulation."[12] In 1946 Nimmo Allan was the director of the Irrigation Department of the Sudan government and after his retirement in 1947 its special consultant. His hydrological experience spanned several decades, his skill as a negotiator for water unmatched. Humphrey Morrice was the divisional engineer, Projects Division of the Sudan Irrigation Department, as brilliant at mathematics as he was at bridge. Pleasant without camaraderie, analytical without introspection, he ranks with Garstin, MacDonald, and Hurst as one of the great innovators in the search for the Nile waters. When the rumors of designs being drafted in the Ministry of Public Works for Nile control could no longer be completely ignored in Khartoum, the governor-general, Sir Hubert Huddleston, who had promoted his career by a visceral suspicion of everything Egyptian, ordered an independent Sudan investigation south of Malakal, "where Africa begins," and where Humphrey Morrice was duly sent in the summer of 1945. Thereafter he pondered the waters of the Nile and their mysteries until his untimely death in December 1959. Nimmo Allan chiseled his epitaph: "The whole of the Nile Valley should be treated as a hydrological unity."[13]

The origins of the Nile Valley Plan are to be found in a report by Morrice in 1954 in which he insisted that all projects should be planned so that they become part of a larger whole embracing all the riparian states.[14] On the one hand, the Nile Valley Plan was vintage Hurst, confirming the principle of century storage with the lakes as reservoirs and a large Jonglei Canal to bring down the water. On the other, it was more comprehensive by including additional dams for Lake Kyoga, Semna (the third cataract), and the High Dam at Aswan that had now become the centerpiece of Egypt's Nile water policy. Annual storage would be contained in reservoirs at Roseires, Sennar, and Khashm al-Girba. Unlike his predecessors Morrice did not neglect Ethiopia despite the dearth of hydrological data. The Lake Tana Dam was, of course, included, but there were conservancy works on the Baro, in the unexplored Blue Nile gorge, and the Balas scheme whereby a tunnel from Lake Tana to the Upper Balas Valley could produce far greater hydroelectric power than the turbines to be entombed in the Aswan High Dam.

Despite its elegant configuration, however, the Nile Valley Plan was a flawed document. Hydrologically, it was derived from measured flows from 1905 to 1952, whose volume could not be guaranteed in the future. Structurally conceived by mathematical formulas, the plan did not take into account the hydropolitics of the Nile Valley nor the economic requirements demanded from poverty-stricken countries for its construction. Adopted by Sudan as its proposal for Nile control, it was, in the abstract, the most efficient use of Nile water that has been devised in this century and which recognized the interests of the riparian states but not those of political reality. The Egyptians vehemently rejected the Nile Valley Plan. Simaika, the close colleague of Hurst, former undersecretary of state, and principal adviser to the Ministry of Public Works, dismissed the plan as "unacceptable" and liable to human error in its regulation to the detriment of Egypt.[15] Overwhelmed by the propaganda for the Aswan High Dam, the Nile Valley Plan was unceremoniously consigned to the dustbin of history.

Upon seizing power in Egypt on July 23, 1952, Gamal Abdel Nasser and his fellow officers needed a spectacular symbol to demonstrate the resurgence of revolutionary Egypt under their leadership. Within two months they found it in the proposal by Adrian Daninos, an Egyptian-Greek engineer, and the Italian Luigi Gallioli, who in 1948 conceived of one grand structure at Aswan to guarantee overyear storage for irrigation and to produce enormous quantities of hydroelectric power for industry. Daninos had tried for years to sell his idea to the Ministry of Public Works without success. Hurst could not accept the huge loss of water by evaporation in the torrid heat of Aswan; siltation, seepage, seismicity, and scouring were all discouraging. They did not matter. Politically, the High Dam was a gigantic, expensive, and daring scheme, a monument to the vision of the revolutionaries. Economically, it provided water and power. The decisive argument, before which all previous proposals for the development of the Nile basin were reduced to scientific obscurantism and dismissed as British vanity, was the indisputable location of the dam at Aswan within the territorial boundaries of Egypt. By providing overyear storage the High Dam would free Egypt from the imagined and real threat of being a hostage to upstream riparian states. There in the technical office of the Revolutionary Command Council in the autumn of 1952 the Aswan High Dam scheme was consummated, and after intense international controversy, bitter environmental and technical criticism, and objections from independent African states, completed on January 15, 1971. Hurst's century storage for Egypt and Sudan and Morrice's Nile Valley Plan for all the states of the Nile basin appeared very dead indeed.

The determination to build the High Dam was a unilateral decision by Egypt, but its construction could not be undertaken without an agreement with Sudan whose riverine lands in Nubia would vanish beneath the reservoir and whose expanding population required a substantial increase in the amount of water for irrigation. Contentious and competitive negotiations, which transcended the years from the Anglo-Egyptian Condominium into those of the independent Sudan, were characterized by unproductive discussions among British, Egyptian, and Sudanese engineers and acrimonious, rhetorical exchanges between their leaders. The Egyptians sought to bargain approval for their dam at Aswan in return for additional water behind the Sudanese dam at Roseires. No Sudanese minister in the euphoria of independence was willing to accept such an exchange until Major General Ibrahim 'Abbud, a gentle pragmatist, was invited to take over the Sudanese government from impotent politicians three weeks before the

Soviet Union offered to finance the High Dam. Negotiations between Cairo and Khartoum were immediately restarted, stimulated by Britain's feeble attempt to reassert its historic position in the Nile Valley by a desperate call for an international conference to establish an "International Nile Waters Authority" in which Great Britain would be a nonriparian member. More decisive was the decision in May 1959 by Eugene Black, president of the World Bank, that Sudan could expect no financial assistance from the West for Roseires or a dam at Khashm al-Girba for the displaced Nubians without a Nile Waters Agreement with Egypt. The agreement for the full utilization of the Nile waters was concluded with all deliberate speed on November 8, 1959, amidst handshaking, hugs, and kisses.

The agreement not only made possible the construction of dams at Aswan, Roseires, and Khashm al-Girba, but it established the principle of sharing on an equal basis any additional water obtained by future conservancy schemes, the old Cory Award, which the Nile Waters Commission of 1921 had refused to adopt after strenuous Egyptian objections. Both Egypt and Sudan unashamedly staked out substantial increases in their "historic and established" rights to the waters of the Nile, 7.5 billion cubic meters for Egypt, 18.5 billion cubic meters for Sudan. Since none of that additional water could be expected from Ethiopia, who not surprisingly was ignored, the 1959 Nile Waters Agreement dramatically revived the Equatorial Nile Project, the completion of which was quite impossible without the Jonglei Canal. In order to excavate the canal and to build the lake reservoirs to feed it, the agreement created the Permanent Joint Technical Commission, with its headquarters symbolically in Khartoum, to plan and implement all the conservancy schemes in the Upper Nile required for the completion of the Equatorial Nile Project. For the first time since the resignation of Sir Murdoch MacDonald in 1921, there was now a single body given the responsibility for directing Nile Valley water development, except, of course, in Ethiopia.

When Hurst's century storage (the Equatorial Nile Project) was conceived, the principal riparian territories in the Upper Nile basin were under British administration. Political unity made possible the comprehensive and rational development of the region, and this assumption was implicit in the Nile Valley Plan proposed by the independent Sudan in the spring of 1959. No sooner was the ink dry on the Nile Waters Agreement six months later than the British colonies of Tanganyika, Uganda, and Kenya became independent in 1961, 1962, and 1963, respectively. As the first British East African territory to become liberated, Tanganyika promptly asserted its sovereignty by invoking what came to be known as "The Nyerere Doctrine": "Former colonial countries had no role in the formulation and conclusion of treaties done in the colonial era, and therefore they must not be assumed to automatically succeed to those treaties."[16] Tanganyika specifically informed Great Britain, Egypt, and Sudan that it did not recognize the Anglo-Egyptian Nile Waters Agreement of 1929 and neither did Uganda and Kenya after independence. Egypt, not surprisingly, responded firmly that the agreement was in full force and would act upon its terms where applicable. The Nyerere Doctrine was not a new idea and in fact had been proposed in the context of that agreement by none other than Morrice in his capacity as the hydrological consultant for the British East African territories. The Nyerere Doctrine clearly undermined the legitimacy of the Equatorial Nile Project in international law, for henceforth any conservancy schemes in the great lakes would have to be negotiated by Egypt and Sudan with those states surrounding their shores.

Suddenly in 1957 the long shadow of the Ethiopian highlands spread across the plains and deserts of the Nile Valley. At best patronized, at worst ignored, the Ethiopians had been aroused by the independence of Sudan in 1956, concerned by the subsequent Nile waters negotiations between Khartoum and Cairo, and were soon to become thoroughly alarmed by the Nile Waters Agreement of 1959. In 1956 the imperial government had informed Cairo that Ethiopia "reserved its rights to utilize the water resources of the Nile for the benefit of its people"; the following year an indignant Haile Selassie decided on more aggressive action by enlisting the support of his American ally to launch a major study of the water resources of the Blue Nile for irrigation and hydroelectric power.[17] In August 1957 the United States Bureau of Reclamation of the Department of the Interior signed a contract with the Ethiopian Ministry of Public Works and Communication to begin a massive study of the water resources of the Blue Nile.

The Blue Nile Plan required five years of intensive investigation; it is in striking contrast to the more methodical, plodding, British-inspired studies of the Egyptian Irrigation Service. With characteristic conviction the Bureau of Reclamation included not just the river but the whole of the Blue Nile basin. A multitude of stream-flow measurements along the length of the river and its many tributaries were completed as well as aerial surveys and extensive mapping. Although a brief encounter compared to the efforts of the Egyptian Ministry of Public Works, in terms of pounds the seventeen volumes and appendices of *Land and Water Resources of the Blue Nile Basin: Ethiopia* outweigh the tomes of *The Nile Basin*.[18] The conservancy scheme espoused by the bureau would eliminate the annual flood of the Blue Nile by impounding its water behind four dams with a hydroelectric capacity three times that of Aswan so that the flow of the river out of Ethiopia would be constant. If managed as designed, the amount of water available to the downstream riparians would actually increase. Because the Blue Nile dams would be managed in conjunction with the Roseires reservoir, now freed from debris and siltation, water could then be released in May as timely water without sustaining the enormous loss by evaporation at Aswan. Egypt, however, would no longer be the beneficiary of additional water in years of high flood that would be stored in Blue Nile reservoirs with their low rate of evaporation and not at Aswan. Moreover, lowering the level of Lakes Nasser and Nubia to limit evaporable loss would concomitantly reduce hydroelectric power, but in return Egypt would receive additional water for irrigation to confirm the historic economy of Egypt as an agricultural nation with only marginal industry, a prospect the Egyptians could not be expected to view with equanimity. Ethiopia could, of course, malevolently withhold water it did not need in a year of low rainfall to threaten disaster in the Nile Valley.

Such a prospect could not but rekindle ancient Egyptian fears of Ethiopian control of the life-giving waters—a historic fable, to be sure, but one that is still firmly believed and which concrete could only make a reality. Here were the ghosts of Friar Jordanus, Prester John, Jean de Lastic, Ariosto, and James Bruce emerging from the mists of the past in the bizarre form of the Bureau of Reclamation to bestow upon the Ethiopians the plans by which to control or at least to intervene in Egypt's established rights to the Nile waters. This historic paranoia now came into conflict with the vigorous nationalism of the riparian states. First the demands of the Sudanese for additional water, then the Nyerere Doctrine, and finally the Blue Nile Plan all loomed as a threat to Egypt's precious water. And the Ethiopians would not let them forget. At the UN Water Conference at Mar Del Plata in 1977, Ethiopia reasserted its rights to the waters of the Blue Nile and in June 1980 at the meeting of the Organization of African Unity in Lagos.

While the scientists and engineers of the Bureau of Reclamation were toiling through the Blue Nile gorge, nature was capturing the attention of the hydrologists at the equatorial lakes. The sudden and unpredictable increase in the rainfall on the lake plateau of 20 percent between 1961 and 1964 raised the level of the equatorial lakes by 2.5 meters, producing extensive flooding around their shores and the disastrous inundation of the sudd floodplain. The East African countries studiously did nothing to alleviate the flooding of southern Sudan. In fact, they sought to relieve the areas surrounding Lake Victoria by an increase of 125 percent in the outflow at the Owen Falls Dam to the grief of the Nilotes downstream. Although the independent East African governments displayed little more than sympathy for their own flood victims, the extraordinary deluge elicited a proposal from the World Meteorological Organization for a hydrometeorological survey of the lake plateau financed by the UN, which the East African states promptly joined and "in the spirit of African unity" invited Egypt and Sudan to participate in as well.[19] This gesture was eagerly accepted, for Egypt and Sudan were only too happy to participate in a project by which they might obtain future claims to Nile water. As for the East Africans they were not interested in storing water for Egypt and Sudan but rather how to get rid of it in order to ameliorate the damage inflicted upon citizens of new and unsteady states.[20]

The prospect for Nile basin cooperation for water, or for that matter any concern, soon proved illusory. In 1977 Egypt and Sudan invited the East African states to join with them in a commission of all the riparian states to plan the development of the water resources for the whole of the Nile basin. The Africans were, not surprisingly, suspicious of any organization of nine sovereign states, seven with little power and less experience in matters hydrological that would be dominated by Egypt while their own hydrological energies were being committed to the development of the Kagera River basin. They resolved this dilemma by deflecting Egyptian and Sudanese interests without offense into the UNDUGU group, from the Swahili *ndugu* (Brotherhood), consisting of Egypt, Sudan, Uganda, Zaire, Rwanda, Burundi, and the Central African Republic, which soon delved into many furtive and unproductive conferences and ministerial meetings. Kenya, Tanzania, and Ethiopia were conspicuously absent, and without them there was little prospect for Nile basin cooperation. With financial assistance from the UN a consortium of Norconsult of Norway and Electrowatt from Switzerland began a detailed study of the Kagera basin reminiscent of the Bureau of Reclamation study in Ethiopia. In 1977 they produced a thirteen-volume report recommending a Kagera Basin Organization that was duly confirmed in the Rusumu Agreement of August 24.[21]

Rebuffed but determined (particularly the Sudanese), Egypt and Sudan continued to press for a Nile basin commission, but despite numerous meetings of ministers, heads of state, and a team from the Permanent Joint Technical Commission, which aggressively toured the capitals of the riparian states, their leaders stubbornly refused to gather collectively at the negotiating table. Egypt had little to offer the upstream states and as in the past, turned inward to proceed with its own ambitious master water plan unveiled in 1981.[22] Perhaps to emulate the Bureau of Reclamation the Egyptian Ministry of Public Works produced seventeen ponderous volumes. If the Americans had confined their investigations solely to the Blue Nile basin, the Egyptians appeared to be possessed by the spirits of Garstin, MacDonald, and Hurst, for they concentrated their search for new water on the Upper Nile basin. Ethiopia was ignored, for its Blue Nile Plan, like Sudan's Nile Valley scheme, was unacceptable and therefore irrelevant to any proposition to acquire water from the equatorial lakes. There were to be dams at Lakes Victoria, Kyoga, and Albert, and regulators on the Bahr al-Jabal and on tributaries in the Bahr al-Ghazal. Diversion canals coursed around the sudd to connect the Bahr al-'Arab and drain the Machar marshes into the White Nile. It was all very grand but dependent upon the Jonglei Canal to bring down the waters of equatorial Africa.

At the beginning of the twentieth century as well as at its end, Nile control of the equatorial lakes was dependent upon the Garstin Cut without which all the dams would be reduced to unrecoverable reservoirs. The heavy rains between 1961 and 1964 had demonstrated nature's ability to produce an amount of water Hurst had calculated would take decades. The High Dam had resolved, rather wastefully to be sure, the quest for century storage. Everyone from Garstin to the Permanent Joint Technical Commission had assumed a Jonglei Canal, but no one had devised the means to dig it. During the twentieth century canals were excavated by dredgers and draglines. Draglines were more efficient than dredgers, but to dig the longest navigable canal (280 kilometers) through the sudd of Sudan would require twenty years at enormous expense and demand the primacy of the Lake Albert Dam, not just for storage but as an essential regulator to control the outflow into the Bahr al-Jabal. The invention of the bucketwheel dramatically changed all these worrisome assumptions. Adapted from iron strip-mining in Germany by Orenstein and Koppel for the French conglomerate Compagnie de Constructions Internationales (CCI), and then modified for use in the sudd by Pierre Blanc and Guy Charlère, the bucketwheel could excavate the Jonglei Canal at a rate of 2 kilometers every six days at only 14 percent the cost of dredgers and draglines. The bucketwheel suddenly made Jonglei economically possible in less than one-third the time previously required to dig a ditch that would carry 25 million cubic meters of water a day and eliminate the need for the Lake Albert Dam as a regulator.

Now technically and economically feasible, the more Delphic political negotiations resumed to a successful conclusion on July 28, 1976, when the Egyptian and Sudanese ministers of irrigation signed a contract with CCI to excavate a canal 50 meters wide, 7 meters deep, and 280 kilometers long to increase the annual yield at Aswan by 3.8 billion cubic meters, all for a pittance of $43 million.[23] The Jonglei Canal was extended to Bor for a total length of 360 kilometers when it was learned that the Bahr al-Jabal river bottom between Bor and Jonglei was unstable. The revised cost of the canal increased to $125 million, precipitated by the dramatic rise in the price of fuel, for the bucketwheel consumed 40,000 liters a day.[24] Even before the bucketwheel had taken its first bite of the infamous "cotton soil" at the mouth of the Sobat in June 1978, however, the reality of a Garstin Cut produced three dramatic reactions: the understanding of sudd hydraulics in relationship to the canal; the environmental concerns and exaggerations; and the political awakening of southern Sudanese to political realities, until then the preserve of southern elites.

J. V. Sutcliffe had carried out the research for his doctoral dissertation at Cambridge in the sudd during the 1950s. Twenty years later the effects of the proposed Jonglei Canal upon the hydrological workings of the sudd had to be recalculated as much to determine the amount of water saved for

Egypt and Sudan as for the impact the revised hydraulics would have on its inhabitants and their environment. His studies revealed the dynamics of the sudd. Because the volume of water lost by evaporation is determined not by the rate of evaporation, which is constant, but by the area of flooding over which the evaporation takes place, whatever the volume of water entering the sudd at Bor, the outflow from the edge of the sudd at Malakal is relatively constant. The greater the flow from the equatorial lakes, the greater the flooding, and thus the greater the volume lost by a constant rate of evaporation so that the discharge will not increase in proportion to the inflow. In years of large flows, the Jonglei Canal would act as a regulator to limit flooding, and in the years of low flows it would draw off released water from the lake reservoirs.[25]

The environmental hue and cry over Jonglei began in 1945 when Morrice had been sent to Malakal to begin an assessment of the effects of the canal on the region, which was followed by the establishment of the Jonglei Investigation Team led by P. P. Howell, a former Nuer District commissioner, whose report, published in 1954, laid the foundation for all subsequent environmental impact studies of the Upper Nile. A remarkable account of the hydrology, ecology, and the peoples of the Upper Nile and the consequences of the canal upon them, the report was in fact to provide the information by which to assess damage and hence the monetary compensation to the Sudanese government and its Nilotic citizens.[26] It had nothing to do with Nile control. Thorough and thoughtful the Jonglei Investigation Team may have been in the early 1950s, not so the environmentalists of the late 1970s. Emanating from the UN Environmental Programme in Nairobi, a steady stream of copy, sometimes sincere, often strident, and frequently ignorant, poured forth from the media, led by a coalition of environmental groups in Europe and the United States known as the Environmental Liaison Center, demanding a moratorium on construction in the canal zone. In 1977 the UN Conference on Desertification held in Nairobi provided a global forum for those who grimly denounced the canal for turning the sudd into "Africa's next desert."[27]

Much of the criticism about the canal was nonsense, but it directly contributed to the political ferment in southern Sudan. Two years before the signing of the contract Jonglei had become the rallying cry, not only for southern resentment against northern Sudanese but a call by the opposition in the southern regional government led by Equatorians to bring down the government of Abel Alier and his fellow Nilotes. When the rumor that 6,000 Egyptian fellahin were being escorted by Egyptian troops to settle in the canal zone, students and Equatorians from Juba rioted for two days, leaving three dead and much damage. The regional government stood firmly behind the canal. Abel Alier declared that if he had to drive his people to paradise with sticks, he would do so for their own good and the good of those who come after them. He was quick to promise ambitious programs for social and economic development to be planned and implemented by agencies that were never provided with the skilled personnel or the resources required to create paradise. By 1983 the canal had become a reality by means of the bucketwheel, but there was not a single viable socioeconomic project in the canal zone. The southern regional government had been dismantled by a contemptuous President Ja'far Numayri; drought now decimated the people and their herds who had perished twenty years before from floods; and Colonel John Garang and his followers in the Sudan Peoples Liberation Movement resumed the war between the governments in Khartoum and the southern Sudanese, now more determined than in the previous conflict between 1955 and 1972 to preserve for the southerners the newfound oil and water of the sudd from the ill-disguised designs of the northern Sudanese. Garang had argued in his doctoral dissertation at Iowa State University that the future agricultural development for the south could only be achieved by rain-fed, mechanized agriculture and not irrigated water from the Jonglei Canal.[28] In order to demonstrate his thesis, capture the sympathies of his disgruntled Nilotes, and strike a blow—both symbolic and tangible—against Numayri's government, he unleashed the Sudan Peoples Liberation Army, which promptly destroyed the CCI base camp at Sobat on February 10, 1984, and immobilized the bucketwheel. The excavation of the canal ceased. All that remained of the Jonglei Canal was a big ditch and shattered dreams of Nile control.

While the bucketwheel collapsed like a dead elephant at kilometer 267, Nile planning accumulated just about as much rust. Jonglei had been the lynchpin for the Egyptian master water plan as it had been for Hurst's Equatorial Nile Project, and the prospect of its revival appeared remote in a land consumed by war and whose survivors now perished from disease and starvation. The spirit of African brotherhood and unity, during which the flame of cooperation among the riparian states had flickered briefly in the 1960s, was dissolved within the decade by growing distrust and fear over fundamental differences for Nile water development between Arabs and Africans, northerners and southerners, Muslims and Christians. Internally, rebellions and civil war in the lake plateau paralyzed the development of East African water resources, leaving the Kagera River basin plan dormant amidst genocide. The Nile Waters Agreement of 1959 officially bound Egypt and Sudan together, but their cooperation, symbolized by the Permanent Joint Technical Commission, died with the bucketwheel. In the 1990s the regime of General 'Umar Hasan Ahmad al-Bashir in Khartoum has remained anathema to the Egyptians and hydrologically hostile for its support of Ethiopia's demands for Blue Nile water and a unilateral declaration for a dam north of Khartoum.

In 1971 the East Africans had deflected the initiative of Egypt and the Sudan for an international Nile agency of all the riparian states by the creation of the UNDUGU commission, which held sixty-six meetings at the technical and ministerial level between 1977 and 1992 with more rhetoric than results. This dismal record of achievement could not continue despite civil strife in the lake plateau. The 250 million people living in the Nile basin were rapidly increasing at 3.6 percent a year, and the extensive environmental degradation could no longer be ignored. Egypt responded to these needs with a policy of confidence building by offering assistance for regional projects in the upstream states as much to divert their attention from the fundamental but contentious issue of the division of available water as to curry their goodwill. In 1993 at their sixty-seventh meeting in Aswan the ministers for water resources reorganized UNDUGU into the Technical Cooperation Committee for the Promotion of the Development and Environmental Protection of the Nile (TECCONILE) to meet annually as the Nile 2002 Conference.

TECCONILE was at first concerned with the water quality of the equatorial lakes and then drafted the Nile River Basin Action Plan, (NRBAP) which was not so much a plan as "an expression of commitment by the basin states," but enthusiastically approved at the third meeting of the Nile 2002 Conference at Arusha in February 1995.[29] During his opening remarks to the conference Cleopa Msuya, the Tanzanian prime minister, announced that his government was committed to the principle of "equitable entitlement" to the water resources of the Nile, which formally challenged the opposing Egyptian principle of "historic needs and established rights."[30] This fundamental difference has always been and always shall be that which determines the projects for Nile control. Like the Nyerere Doctrine in 1961, the principle of equitable entitlement advocated by Tanzania in 1995 elicited strong support from its neighbors. The following year, in May 1996 at the fourth 2002 Nile Conference in Kampala, an international basin association was proposed to include Eritrea, the members of which fervently blessed the spirit of cooperation, on the one hand, while defending their self-interests, which would destroy it, on the other.

Nine months later in February 1997, at the seventy-first meeting of TECCONILE held in Cairo to approve twenty-two projects mostly for environmental protection contained in NRBAP, Egypt strongly supported the U.S.$100 million needed to carry out the NRBAP activities, hopefully to placate the opposition to its historic needs and to demonstrate confidence building among the upstream riparians who would gather a week later at Addis Ababa for the fifth annual Nile 2002 Conference. Egypt's cooperation and support for the environmental concerns of their upstream neighbors could not disguise the fundamental issue of Nile control—who was going to obtain the Nile waters and how? In his opening address to the 300 representatives from the ten riparians and international agencies, Shiferaw

Jarso, the Ethiopian minister for water resources, insisted that "as a source and major contribution of the Nile waters, Ethiopia has the right to have an equitable share of the Nile waters and reserves its rights to make use of its water."[31] There was nothing dramatically new in this declaration except a half century. In 1956 the imperial Ethiopian government officially declared that Ethiopia "would reserve for her own use those Nile waters in her territory."[32] Now in 1997 the Ethiopians were simply demanding an "equitable share." Indeed, Minister Shiferaw's position at the end of the century appears to be more in keeping with the theme of the conference—"Comprehensive Water Resources Development of the Nile Basin: Basis for Cooperation"—than the declaration by Haile Selassie fifty years before. Neither pious pronouncements for cooperation nor clarion calls for confidence building could disguise the incompatibility between equitable shares and historic needs and established rights, which was no nearer to a resolution at the end than at the beginning of the twentieth century. The demand for an equitable share is hopelessly obscured by its very definition and can hardly be reconciled to needs and rights translated in A.D. 2000 into ever more Egyptians requiring ever more entitled water to sustain them.

In that extraterrestrial year, 2001, the development of the earth's water resources in the Nile basin will undoubtedly remain shackled by historic rivalries, ethnic and religious antagonisms, erroneous perceptions solidified by emotions, and hostilities perpetuated by ignorance. To be sure, there have been projects to satisfy parochial populations and special interests often to the detriment of the commonwealth—the High Dam, Sennar and Roseires, Owen Falls—but the evolution of any grand design for Nile control has been defeated in our century by the forces of ethnic, racial, and religious nationalism and sustained by the hypnotic fear instilled from time to time by nature. History is awash with the ironies of the Nile civilizations and their myths; and there is no greater irony than when we stand today, as the proverb prescribes, to drink once again the waters of the Nile from those coy fountains of Herodotus at the foot of tall mountains in this new century of self-determination and democracy in preparation for navigating the long and perilous passage down the river from the shimmering surface of great lakes, through the Stygian sudd, along narrow defiles of deep canyons, to the terror of turbulent cataracts and the sea, without the skill, experience, and vision of an imperial river guide.

NOTES

1. Johnston, *The Nile Quest.*
2. Garstin, *Report as to Irrigation Projects on the Upper Nile;* Garstin, *Report upon the Basin of the Upper Nile.*

3. Dupuis, "A Report upon Lake Tana and the Rivers of the Eastern Sudan," pp. 209–236; Grabham and Black, *Report of the Mission to Lake Tana 1920–21.*

4. Lyons, *The Physiography of the River Nile and Its Basin.*

5. Sir William Willcocks to H. E. High Commissioner, Lord Allenby, 18 July 1918, Sudan Archives, Durham University, England, 108/7.

6. "Report and Opinion of Judge Booth," in *Report of the Nile Projects Commission.* Cairo, 1920.

7. MacGregor and Suleiman, *The Nile Commission Report,* para. 21, Sudan Archives, Durham University, England, 500/3/28.

8. Hurst, Black, and Simaika, *The Future Conservation of the Nile.*

9. Ibid., p. vi.

10. Sutcliffe, "A Hydrology of the Sudd Region of the Upper Nile," and "A Hydrological Study of the Southern Sudd Region of the Upper Nile."

11. Morrice and Allan, *Report on the Nile Valley Plan.*

12. Hurst and Barnett, "Planning for the Ultimate Development of the Nile Valley," pp. 291, 294. IBM is International Business Machines, SOGREAH is Société grénobloise d'études et d'applications hydrauliques, and MIT is Massachusetts Institute of Technology.

13. Allan, "Discussion on Planning for the Ultimate Hydraulic Development of the Nile Valley," p. 314.

14. Morrice, "The Development of the Main Nile for the Benefit of Egypt and the Sudan."

15. Simaika, "Discussion on Planning for the Ultimate Hydraulic Development of the Nile Valley," p. 309.

16. Okidi, "International Laws and the Lake Victoria and Nile Basins," p. 422.

17. Quoted in Whiteman, *Digest of International Law,* pp. 1011–1012.

18. *Land and Water Resources of the Blue Nile Basin: Ethiopia,* 17 vols. (Washington, D.C.: United States Department of the Interior, 1964).

19. Hon S. A. Maswanya, Minister for Home Affairs, Tanzania, speech at the Meeting of the Hydrometeorological Survey, 27 February 1967, in *Hydromet,* Entebbe, 1968, p. 21.

20. UN Development Program and World Meteorological Organization, *Report of the Hydrometeorological Survey of the Catchment of Lakes Victoria, Kyoga and Mobutu Sese Seko: Project Findings and Recommendations* (Geneva, 1982).

21. Norconsult A/S and Electrowatt Engineering Services, Ltd., *Kagera River Basin Development, Phase II,* 13 vols. (New York: United Nations Development Programme, 1976); see also Executive Secretariat of the Kagera River Basin Organization and United Nations Development Programme, *Development Programme of the Kagera River Basin, Final Report,* 5 vols. (February 1982).

22. *The Nile Master Water Plan,* 17 vols. (Cairo: Ministry of Public Works, 1981).

23. *Jonglei Canal Project,* Nanterre (FR), Ministry of Irrigation and Hydroelectric Power, Sudan, 28 July 1976.

24. *Jonglei Canal Project: Eastern Alignment to Bor,* Nanterre (FR), Ministry of Irrigation and Hydroelectric Power, Sudan, 13 March 1980.

25. Sutcliffe and Parks, "A Hydrological Estimate of the Effects of the Jonglei Canal on Areas of Flooding"; and Sutcliffe and Parks, "Hydrological Modelling of the Sudd and Jonglei Canal."

26. Howell, *The Equatorial Nile Project and Its Effects in the Anglo-Egyptian Sudan.*

27. R. Odingo, Environmental Liaison Center Press Conference, University of Nairobi, Nairobi, September 1977.

28. Garang, "Identifying, Selecting and Implementing Rural Development Strategies for Socio-Economic Development in the Jonglei Projects Area, Southern Region, Sudan."

29. Jackson Makwetta, minister for Water, Energy and Minerals, Tanzania, quoted in "Development Plan Approved for Nile Basin States," 13 February 1995, Xinhua News Agency, Item No. 0213102.

30. Cleopa Msuya, Prime Minister, Tanzania, quoted in "Review of International Laws on Nile River Waters Urged," 14 February 1995, Xinhua News Agency, Item No. 0214130.

31. Shiferaw Jarso, minister for Water Resources, Ethiopia, quoted in "Ethiopia Stresses Equitable Use of Nile Waters," 24 February 1997, Xinhua News Agency, Item No. 0224259.

32. Statement by the Imperial Ethiopian Government, *Ethiopian Herald,* 6 February 1956.

20

◆

Conclusion:
Historical Legacies and
Present Concerns

Haggai Erlich & Israel Gershoni

The chapters provided in this volume are but a sample of the historical versatility of the Nile and of its riparian peoples. We believe they reflect the centrality of the river in the formation and reformation of culture, religion, and national identity, and in the shaping of their interrelationships. We also contend they assert the validity of our premise that the Nile basin should be redressed academically as a theater of common political relevance, a civilizational microcosm of diversity and mutuality, and a cultural polysystem.

Indeed, the general historical picture is that of continuous, meaningful linkage among the cultural entities. Each one—the Egyptian, the Ethiopian, the Sudanese—is in itself a system of cultural diversity, the various inner components of which contributed to and enriched the all-regional intercultural dynamism. One major theme, for example, was the religious Ethio-Egyptian dialogue. The Islamic core of Egyptian culture had its connections and significant influence on the Islamic minorities of Ethiopia and the Horn of Africa, whereas the Orthodox Church of Ethiopia, from its very incipience, had been a bishopric of the Coptic Church of Egypt. We underline such dimensions of historical mutuality for two reasons: first, in order to emphasize our plea for an enlivened academic curiosity in the greater Nile basin and an enhanced study of its inner multifaceted historical interconnections. Second, to observe that during the past generation or two, some of these cultural bridges, and much of the eye contact between the said civilizations, especially along the Ethiopian-Egyptian axis, have been damaged and blurred.

We have not covered this contemporary rupture in the present volume. We have merely mentioned a number of relevant cases, and briefly at that.

Most of them developed and culminated during the 1950s. In 1959 Ethiopia opted for a complete and final disconnection from the Egyptian Church, ending spiritual relations of political importance that had begun in the fourth century. Turning to the then re-energized spheres of African identity and continental diplomacy, Ethiopian leadership practically declared the old Egyptian-Ethiopian religious and cultural bond irrelevant. The Egyptian leadership, on its part, worked to promote mutual irrelevance and in no lesser an area of ancient connection. During the same year, the Egyptians opted for a water agreement with the Sudanese, bluntly ignoring the Ethiopians. Constructing the High Dam in Aswan, Egypt's leaders seemed to assume that the new Lake Nasser would replace the Ethiopian Abbay as the main source of the Nile. The Islamic Egyptian-Ethiopian connection, perhaps equally as old and meaningful as the Christian link, also seemed to change in 1959. The *riwaq al-jabartiyya,* the Ethiopian Muslims' old little corner in the Cairene Islamic university of al-Azhar, had trained Islamic functionaries and religious leaders for Ethiopia and the Horn of Africa for many centuries. During the 1950s, however, it became the base of a new generation of Arab revolutionary nationalists who established the Eritrean Liberation Front in Cairo in 1959. The struggle they began in Eritrea in the name of Arab revolutionarism and against Ethiopia's imperial legitimacy further alienated Ethiopians and Egyptians. Again, in the same year, the Ethiopians retaliated by allying themselves with Israel, importing and expanding the Arab-Israeli wall of alienation, further heightening the "dams" and conceptual barriers along the Nile.

Each of these issues, as well as other realities of the contemporary scene, deserves extensive research and should be included in future Nile studies. In our introduction we indicated the academic change of the 1960s, which, in combination with the cultural-political rupture mentioned above, contributed to the widening gap. We think it is high time the relevant academic communities address the greater Nile basin as a historic polysystem, interpreting its current developments against the legacies of its rich past.

All of the relevant countries have undergone essential changes since that culmination of rupture. From Gamal Abdel Nasser to Anwar al-Sadat to Husni Mubarak, from Ibrahim 'Abbud to Ja'far al-Numayri to Hasan al-Turabi, from Haile Selassie to Mangistu Haile Mariam to Meles Zenawi, amid the ever-quickening historic pace, Egypt, Sudan, and Ethiopia have re-examined and reinterpreted their very identities. Nearly all the definitions of nationalism prevalent during the 1950s and 1960s, of social revolutionarism, of religious politics, of state and society, concepts that separated Cairo and Addis Ababa some forty years ago, are no longer valid. New definitions of self, and therefore of the other, have already contributed to reconstructing some old bridges and reopening neighborly dialogues.

The importance of today's dialogues can hardly be exaggerated. Robert Collins's chapter, "In Search of the Nile Waters," re-emphasizes the fact that in terms of hydropolitical analysis, the Nile is indeed a single unit. This calls for unified action, where cooperation is perhaps the only road to survival. In coping with water scarcity and demographic increase, a shared concept of common all-Nile discourse is vital. This, we contend, does not contradict but rather complements the main message of this book. Only by redressing the past, by demystifying its myths, by deciphering its legacies, by deriving inspirations and attaining perspective can humankind better cope with the challenges. Only by recognizing diversity and legitimizing pluralism can regional cooperation and unity of action be achieved.

◆

Bibliography

Abbink, J. "The Enigma of Beta Israel Ethnogenesis: An Ethnohistorical Study."
Cahiers d'etudes africaines 30, no. 4 (1990).

'Abd al-Ghani Sa'udi, Muhammad. *Al-takamul al-Misri al-Sudani*. Cairo: n.d.

'Abd al-Hayy, 'Abd al-Tawwab. *Al-Nil wa'l-mustaqbal*. Cairo: Dar al-Ahram.
1988.

Abdalla, Ismail H. "The Choice of Khashm al-Girba Area for the Resettlement of
the Halfawis." *Sudan Notes and Records*, Vol. 2 (1970).

———. "The 1959 Nile Waters Agreement in Sudanese-Egyptian Relations." *The
Middle East Journal* 7, no. 2 (1971).

Abdel Magid, Yahya. "Nile Control for Agricultural Development in the Sudan."
Agricultural Development in the Sudan. Khartoum: Sudan Philosophical Society, 1964.

Abdussamad Ahmad. "Gojjam: Trade, Early Merchant Capital and World Economy, 1901–1935." Ph.D. thesis, University of Illinois, Urbana, 1986.

———. "Ethiopian Slave Exports at Matamma, Massawa and Tajura ca. 1830–
1885." Paper presented at the Symposium on Long Distance Trade in Slaves
Across the Indian Ocean and the Red Sea in the Nineteenth Century. London,
School of Oriental and African Studies, 1987.

Adams, W. Y. *Nubia: A Corridor to Africa*. Princeton, N.J.: Princeton University
Press, 1977.

———. "The Kingdom and Civilization of Kush in Northeast Africa." In *Civilizations of the Ancient Near East*, edited by Jack M. Sasson. Vol. 2. New York,
1995.

Adorno, Jean. *Itinéraire d'Anselme Adorno en Terre Sainte (1470–1471)*. Translated and edited by J. Heers and Georgette de Groer. Paris: Editions du Centre
National de la Recherche Scientifique, 1978.

Ajayi, J. F. A. *Christian Missions in Nigeria*. London: Longmans, 1965.

Alamayyahu, Haddis. *Feqer eska maqaber. Leb wallad tarik* (Love to the grave: A
novel). 7th edition. Addis Ababa 1989.

Allan, W. N. "Discussion on Planning for the Ultimate Hydraulic Development of
the Nile Valley." *Proceedings of the Institute of Civil Engineers*, Vol. 14 (1959).

Alvarez, Francisco. *The Prester John of the Indies.* Vol. 2. London: Hakluyt Society, 1958.

Amanu, Adugna. "The Ethiopian Orthodox Church Becomes Autocephalous." B.A. thesis, Addis Ababa University, Institute of Ethiopian Studies, 1969.

Amare, Girma. "The Imperative Need for Negotiation on the Utilization of the Nile Waters." Paper presented at the Fifth Nile 2002 Conference, Addis Ababa, 24–28 February 1997.

APF. (Archivo dell Sacra Congregazionedi Propaganda Fide/Scritture riferitre nei Congressi). "P. Etienne to Propaganda Fide," 25 July 1852. SC/Etiopia, Vol. 4.

———. "Poussou to Fransoni," 25 May 1852. SC/Etiopia, Vol. 5.

———. "Sapeto to Propaganda Fide," 30 November 1842. SC/Etiopia, Vol. 4.

———. Tobia Gheresghier to the Pope. SC Etiopia-Arabia, Vol. 3.

———. "Istruzioni fatte in Sinodo da Mons. G. Massaja." SC/Etiopia, Vol. 6.

———. "Brenier to Havett." SC/Etiopia-Arabia, Vol. 5 (1848–1857).

Arbel, B. "The Port Towns of the Levant in the Sixteenth Century Travel Literature." In A. Cowan, ed., *Mediterranean Urban Culture.* Forthcoming.

Arens, G. *Evangelical Pioneers in Ethiopia.* Stockholm: EFS, 1978.

Ariosto, Ludovico. *Orlando Furioso.* Translated by B. Reynolds. Harmondsworth, London: Penguin Books, 1977.

Arnold, Heinz Ludwig, ed. *Adolph Freiherr Knigge.* München, 1996.

Atkinson, Geoffroy. *The Extraordinary Voyage in French Literature Before 1700.* New York, 1920.

———. *Les Nouveaux horizons de la Renaissance française.* 1969. Reprint, Geneva: Slatkine Reprints, 1969.

Ayalon, David. "Aspects of the Mamluk Phenomenon." *Der Islam* 53 (1976).

———. "The Nubian Dam." *YSAI* 12 (1989).

Ayandele, E. A. *The Missionary Impact on Modern Nigeria.* London: Longmans, 1966.

al-'Azm, Sadiq al-Muayyad. *Rihlat al-habasha.* Cairo, 1908.

Baeteman, J. *Dictionnaire Amarigna-Français. Suivi d'un vocabulaire Français-Amarigna.* Derre Dawa, 1929.

Baines, John. "Origins of Egyptian Kingship." In *Ancient Egyptian Kingship,* edited by David O'Connor and David P. Silverman. Leiden, 1995.

Baker, A. *Morning Star: Florence Baker Diary of the Expedition to Put Down the Slave Trade on the Nile, 1870–1873.* London, 1972.

Baker, Samuel. *Ismailiya.* 2 vols. London, 1877.

———. *The Nile Tributaries of Abyssinia.* London, 1867.

Bakr, Muhammad Num. *Italy in Her Colonies* (Arabic). Cairo, 1936.

al-Baladhuri. *Futuh al-Buldan.* Leiden, 1866.

Baron, S. W. *The Social and Religious History of the Jewish People.* Philadelphia: The Jewish Publication Society, 1983.

Basset, R. "Etudes sur l'histoire d'Ethiopie." *Journal Asiatique* 17 (1881).

Baykadane, Gabra Heywat. "Ate Menilekenna Ityopeya" (Emperor Menilek and Ethiopia). In *Berhan Yekhun* (Let it be light), edited by O. Eriksson. Asmara, 1912.

Beazley, C. R. *The Dawn of Modern Geography.* Vol. 1. 1897. Reprint, New York, 1949.

Beccari, C. *Notizia e saggi di opere e documenti inediti riguardanti la storia d'Etiopia durante i secoli XVI, XVII e XVIII.* Rome: Casa Editrice Italiana, 1903.

———. *Rerum Aethiopicarum Scriptores Occidentales.* Vols. 2 and 15. Rome: C. de Luigi, 1903–1907.

Beckingham, C. F., and E. Ullendorff. *The Hebrew Letters of Prester John.* Oxford: Oxford University Press, 1982.

Beckingham, C. F., and and G. W. B. Huntingford, eds. *Some Records of Ethiopia.* London: Hakluyt Society, 1954.

———. *The Prester John of the Indies.* Vol. 1. London: Hakluyt Society, 1958.

———. "An Ethiopian Embassy to Europe, c. 1310." *Journal of Semitic Studies* 14 (1989); reprinted as "Essay 10," in *Prester John, the Mongols and the Ten Lost Tribes,* edited by C. F. Beckingham and Bernard Hamilton. Aldershot, England: Variorum, 1996.

Beke, Charles, T. *An Essay on the Nile and Its Tributaries.* London, 1847.

———. "Mémoire en réhabilitation des P. P. Paez et Jer. Lobo, missionaires en Abyssinie, en ce qui concerne leur visite à la source de l'Abai (le Nil) et à la cataracte d'Alato." *Bulletin de la Société de Géographie* (April-May 1848).

———. *The Sources of the Nile.* London, 1860.

Bell, Stephen. "The Ruins of Mertule Maryam." From *Proceedings of the Eighth International Conference of Ethiopian Studies.* Vol. 1. Addis Ababa and Frankfurt: Institute of Ethiopian Studies and Frobenius Institute, 1988.

Belon, Pierre. *Le Voyage en Egypte de Pierre Belon du mons 1547,* edited by S. Sauneron. Paris: Institut Français d'Archéologie Orientale du Caire, 1970.

Ben-Amos, Paula Girshick. "The Promise of Greatness: Women and Power in the Edo Spirit Possession Cult." In *Religion in Africa,* edited by Thomas D. Blakely et al. Portsmouth, N.H.: Heinemann, 1994.

Ben-Jochannan, Yosef A. A. *Africa—Mother of Western Civilization.* Baltimore, Md.: Black Classical Press, 1988.

Berger, H. *Geschichte der wissenschaftlichen Erdkunde der Griechen.* Leipzig: Verlag von Veit und Co., 1903.

Bernier, François. *Travels in the Mogul Empire, 1656–1668.* 3d edition. Translated by Irving Brock, edited by Archibald Constable. New Delhi, 1972.

Berque, J. *Egypt: Imperialism and Revolution.* London, 1989.

Bernal, M. *Black Athena.* New Brunswick, N.J.: Rutgers University Press, 1987.

Berry, A. C., and R. J. Berry. "Origins and Relationship of the Ancient Egyptians. Based on a Study of Non-metrical Variation in the Skull." In *Population Biology of the Ancient Egyptians,* edited by D. R. Brothwell and B. A. Chiarelli. London: Academic Press, 1973.

Beyene, Yaqob, ed. *Fesseha Giyorgis—storia d'Etiopia.* Naples, 1987.

Bitterli, Urs. *Die Entdeckung des schwarzen Afrikaners.* Zürich, 1970.

Blaut, J. M. *The Colonizer's Model of the World: Geographical Diffusionism and Eurocentric History.* New York: The Guilford Press, 1993.

Blochet, E. "Neuf chapitres du 'Songe du viel Pèlerin' de Philippe de Mézières relatifs à l'Orient." *Revue de l'Orient chrétien* 4 (1899), 5 (1900).

Borghonst, Joris F. "Magical Practices Among the Villagers." In *Pharaoh's Workers: The Villagers of Deir El Medina,* edited by Leonard H. Lasko. Ithaca, N.Y.: Cornell University Press, 1969.

Bowdich, A. *An Essay on the Superstitions, Customs, and Arts Common to the Ancient Egyptians, Abyssinians and Ashantees.* Paris, 1821.

Breasted, James. *A History of the Ancient Egyptians.* New York, 1908.

Brentjes, Burchard. *Anton Wilhelm Amo. Der schwarze Philosoph in Halle.* Leipzig: Koehler and Amelang, 1975.

Brockelmann, C. *Geschichte der Arabischen Literatur.* Leiden: E. J. Brill, 1943.

Bruce, J. *Travels to Discover the Source of the Nile*. 4 vols. Edinburgh: G. G. J. and J. Robinson, 1790.

Budge, E. A. Wallis. *The Nile. Notes for Travellers in Egypt*. London, 1898.

———. *The Book of the Saints of the Ethiopian Church*. Cambridge: Cambridge University Press, 1928.

———. *A History of Ethiopia, Nubia and Abyssinia*. London: Methuen, 1928.

———. *Osiris and the Egyptian Resurrection*. 2 vols. New York, 1937.

Bulliet, Richard. *The Camel and the Wheel*. New York: Columbia University Press, 1990.

Bunbury, E. H. *A History of Ancient Geography*. Vol. 2. 2d edition. New York: Dover Publications, 1959.

Burckhardt, Jacob. *The Civilization of the Renaissance in Italy*. 4th edition. Translated by S. G. C. Middlemore. London: Phaidon Press, 1951.

Butzer, Karl. W. *Early Hydraulic Civilization in Egypt: A Study in Cultural Ecology*. Chicago: University of Chicago Press, 1976.

Buxton, C. *Memoirs of Sir Thomas Fowell Buxton*. London, 1851.

Buxton, T. F. *The African Slave Trade and Its Remedy*. London: J. Murrey, 1840.

Calvesi, M. *Il mito dell'Egitto nel Rinascimento. Pinturicchio, Piero di Cosimo, Giorgione, Francesco Colonna*. Florence: Giunti, 1988.

Campbell, M. B. *The Witness and the Other World. Exotic European Travel Writings, 400–1600*. Ithaca, N.Y.: Cornell University Press, 1988.

Caraman, P. *The Lost Empire—The Story of the Jesuits in Ethiopia*. London: Sidgwick and Jackson, 1985.

Castelli, P. *I geroglifici e il mito dell'Egitto nel Rinascimento*. Florence, 1979.

Celenko, Theodore, ed. *Egypt in Africa*. Indianapolis: Indianapolis Museum of Art in cooperation with Indiana University Press, 1996.

Cerulli, E. "Il 'Libro del Conoscimiento' e le sue notizie sull'Etiopia." *Bollettino della Regia Società Geografica Italiana*, serie 5a, 6 (1917).

———. *Folk-Literature of the Galla of Southern Abyssinia*. Cambridge, Mass., 1922.

———. "Il volo di Astolfo sull'Etiopia nell'Orlando Furioso." *Rendiconti della R. Accademia Nazionale dei Lincei* 8 (1932).

———. *Il libro etiopico dei miracoli di Maria*. Rome: Giovanni Bardi, 1943.

———. *Etiopi in Palestina. Storia della communità etiopica di Gerusalemme*. 2 vols. Rome: Libreria dello Stato, 1943–1947.

Cheesman, R. E. *Lake Tana and the Blue Nile, an Abyssinian Quest*. London: Cass and Co., 1936.

Chevalier, R. "Le Voyage archéologique au XVIe siècle." In *Voyager à la Renaissance, Actes du Colloque de Tours, Juillet 1983*, edited by J. Ceard and J. C. Margolin. Paris: Maissoneuve et Larose, 1987.

Chojnacki, Stanislaw. "Day Giyorgis." *Journal of Ethiopian Studies* 7, no. 2 (July 1969).

Clagett, Marshall. *Ancient Egyptian Science/A Source Book*. Vol. 1, 2 tomes. Philadelphia: American Philosophical Society, 1989–1995.

Clark, Daima M. "Similarities Between Egyptian and Dagon Perceptions of Man, God and Nature." In *Kemet and the African Worldview*, edited by Maulana Karenga and Jacob H. Carruthers. Los Angeles: University of Sankore Press, 1986.

Clarke, John Henrik. "Cheikh Anta Diop and the New Concept of African History." In *Great African Thinkers*, edited by Ivan van Sertima. Vol. 1. New Brunswick, N.J.: Transaction Books, 1992.

Cohen, Morris R., and I. E. Drabkin. *A Source Book in Greek Science*. New York, 1948.

Collins, R. O. *The Jonglei Canal, the Past and Present of a Future.* Durham: Durham University, 1987.

———. *The Waters of the Nile, Hydropolitics of the Jonglei Canal, 1900–1988.* Oxford: Clarendon Press, 1990.

Connah, G. *African Civilizations—Pre-colonial Cities and States in Tropical Africa: An Archaeological Perspective.* New York: Cambridge University Press, 1987.

Conti Rossini, C. "Il 'Libro del Conoscimiento' e le sue notizie sull'Etiopia." *Bollettino della Regia Società Geografica Italiana,* serie 5, 6 (1917).

———. "Leggende giudaiche del IX secolo (Il Sefer Eldad)." *Bollettino della Regia Società Geografica Italiana,* serie 6, 2 (1923).

———. *Storia d'Etiopia.* Bergamo, 1928.

———. *Etiopia e genti di Etiopia.* Florence: R. Bemporad, 1937.

———. "Le sorgenti del Nilo azzurro e Giovanni Gabriel." *Bollettino della Regia Società Geografica Italiana* serie 7, 6 (1941).

———. "Geografica I. L'Africa orientale in carte arabe dei secoli XII e XII. II Carte Abissine. III Gli itinerari di Alessandro Zorzi." *Rassegna di Studi Etiopici* (1943).

———. *Gli atti di re Na'akueto La'ab.* Rome: Tipografia del Senato, 1943.

Cowley, A. E. *Aramaic Papyri of the Fifth Century B.C.* Oxford: Clarendon Press, 1923.

Crawford, Keith W. "The Racial Identity of Ancient Egyptian Populations Based on the Analysis of Physical Remains." In *Egypt Revisited,* edited by Ivan van Sertima. New Brunswick, N.J: Transaction Publishers, 1991.

Crawford, O. G. S. "Some Medieval Theories About the Nile." *Geographical Journal* 114 (1949).

———. *Ethiopian Itineraries Circa 1400–1524, Including Those Collected by Alessandro Zorzi in Venice in the Years 1519–24.* Cambridge: Cambridge University Press, 1958.

Creone, F. "La Politica orientale di Alfonso di Aragone." *Archivio Storico per le Provincie Napolitane* 27 (1902).

Cromer, Lord. *Rapport de Lord Cromer sur L'Egypte et le Soudan pour l'année 1904.* Cairo, 1905.

Crowther, Samuel, and John Christopher Taylor. *The Gospel on the Bank of the Niger.* London, 1859.

Crummey, D. "Imperial Legitimacy and the Neo-Solomonic Ideology in 19th Century Ethiopia." *Cahiers d'etudes africaines* 28, no. 1 (1988).

Curlander, Harold. *A Treasure of African Folklore.* New York, 1996.

Davidson, Basil. *The African Genius.* Boston, 1969.

———. *African Civilization Revisited.* Trenton, N.J.: Africa World Press, 1991.

———. "The Ancient World and Africa: Whose Roots?" In *The Search for Africa: History, Culture, Politics,* London: Times Books, 1994.

De Barros, Philip. "Changing Paradigms, Goals and Methods in the Archaeology of Francophone West Africa." In *A History of African Archaeology,* edited by Peter Robertshaw. Portsmouth, N.H., 1990.

De Birch, W. G. *The Commentaries of the Great Dalbuquerque.* Vol. 4. London: Hakluyt Society, 1875–1884.

De Coppet, M. ed. *Chronique du règne de Ménelik II, Roi des rois d'Éthiopie.* Paris, 1930–1931.

Diffie, B. W., and G. D. Winius. *Foundations of the Portuguese Empire 1415–1580* Minneapolis: University of Minnesota Press, 1977.

Diop, C. A. *The African Origin of Civilization: Myth or Reality.* New York: Lawrence Hill and Co., 1974.

————. "Africa: Cradle of Humanity." *Journal of African Civilization* 6, no. 2 (1987).

————. *Precolonial Black Africa.* Translated by H. Salemson. New York: Lawrence Hill Books, 1987.

————. "Origin of the Ancient Egyptians." In *General History of Africa,* Vol. 2, edited by G. Mokhtar. UNESCO International Scientific Committee for the Drafting of a General History of Africa, 1981.

————. *Civilization or Barbarism: An Authentic Anthropology.* Translated by Yaa-Lengi Meema Ngemi. New York: Lawrence Hill Books, 1991.

Doresse, J. "L'Éthiopie et le patriarcat copte." In *L'Empire du Prêtre-Jean,* Vol. 2, edited by J. Doresse. Plon, 1957.

Du Bois, Burghart. "Egypt." In *The World and Africa,* edited by Burghart Du Bois. New York: International Publishers, 1992.

Dupuis, C. E., "A Report upon Lake Tana and the Rivers of the Eastern Sudan." In *Report upon the Basin of the Upper Nile,* by W. Garstin. London: HSMO, 1904.

Ehret, Christopher. "Ancient Egyptian as an African Language, Egypt as an African Culture." In *Egypt in Africa,* edited by Theodore Celenko. Indianapolis: Indianapolis Museum of Art in cooperation with Indiana University Press, 1996.

El-Affendi, Abdelwahab. *Turabi's Revolution, Islam and Power in Sudan.* London, 1991.

Erlich, Haggai. *The Struggle over Eritrea, 1962–1978.* Stanford: Hoover Institution, Stanford University, 1983.

————. *Ethiopia and the Challenge of Independence.* Boulder, Colo.: Lynne Rienner, 1986.

————. *Students and University in 20th Century Egyptian Politics.* London, 1989.

————. *Ethiopia and the Middle East.* Boulder, Colo.: Lynne Rienner, 1994.

————. *The Middle East Between the World Wars.* Vol. 4, *The 1930s: Crisis and Revolt.* Tel Aviv: Open University of Israel, 1996.

————. *Ras Alula and the Scramble for Africa.* Revised edition. Lawrenceville, N.J.: Red Sea Press, 1996.

————. "Ethiopia and Egypt—Ras Tafari in Cairo, 1924." *Aethiopica* (Hamburg) 1 (1998).

————. "Egypt and Adwa." In *Proceedings of the Adwa Centenary Conference,* edited by Bahru Zewde and Richard Pankhurst. Addis Ababa: Addis Ababa University Press, 1998.

————. "Periphery and Youth—Fascist Influence in the Middle East." In *Fascism Outside Europe,* edited by Stein Larsen. Forthcoming.

Fabris, A. "Note sul mappamondo cordiforme di Haci Ahmed di Tunisi." *Quaderni di studi arabi* 7 (1989).

Fauvelle, François-Xavier. *L'Afrique de Cheikah Anta Diop: Histoire et idéologie.* Paris: Edition Karthala, 1996.

Fawzi, Mahmoud. *Suez 1956: An Egyptian Perspective.* London, 1986.

Figliuolo, B. "Europa, Oriente, Mediterraneo nell'opera dell'umanista palermitano Pietro Ranzano." In *Europa e Mediterraneo tra Medioevo e prima età moderna: l'osservatorio italiano,* edited by S. Gensini. San Miniato: Pacini Editore, n.d. (Centro di studi sulla civiltà del tardo medioevo, San Miniato, Collana di Studi e Ricerche, no. 4).

Finch, Charles S., III. "Nile Genesis: Continuity of Culture from the Great Lakes to the Delta." In *Egypt Child of Africa,* edited by Ivan van Sertima. New Brunswick, N.J.: Transaction Books, 1991.

———. "The Works of Gerald Massey: Studies in Kamite Origins." In *Egypt Revisited,* edited by G. I. van Sertrud. New Brunswick, N.J.: Transaction Publishers, 1991, pp. 401–412.

Finkelstein, A. A., ed. *Sifre on Deuteronomy.* New York, 1969.

Fuglestead, F. "The Trevor-Roper Trap or the Imperialism of History, an Essay." *History in Africa* 19 (1992).

Gabra-Haywat, Kidana-Mariam. *Yader Sultan ba'irusalem.* Addis Ababa, 1957.

Gabre-Yohannes, Hailu. *Innatkin Belulgn.* Stockholm, 1989.

Gaffuri, L. *Africa o morte.* Milano: Unicopli, 1997.

Gamst, Frederick C. *The Qemant, a Pagan-Hebraic Peasantry of Ethiopia.* New York: Holt, Rinehart and Winston, 1969.

Garang, John de Mabior. "Identifying, Selecting and Implementing Rural Development Strategies for Socio-Economic Development in the Jonglei Projects Area, Southern Region, Sudan." Ph.D. dissertation. Ames: Iowa State University, 1981.

Garstin, Sir W. *Report as to Irrigation Project on the Upper Nile.* London: Parliamentary Accounts and Papers, 1901.

———. *Report upon the Basin of the Upper Nile.* London: HSMO, 1904.

Gaudefroy-Demombynes, M. *Ibn Fadl Allah Al-'Umari, Masalik al-Absar fi Mamalik al-Ansar.* Paris: Librarie Orientaliste Paul Geuthner, 1927.

Gershoni, Israel. *Light in the Shade: Egypt and Fascism, 1922–1937* (in Hebrew). Tel Aviv: Am Oved, 1999.

Gershoni, Israel, and J. Jankowski. *Egypt, Islam, and the Arabs: The Search for Egyptian Nationhood, 1900–1930.* New York, OUP, 1986.

Gilles, Pierre. *The Antiquities of Constantinople.* Translated by J. Ball, edited by G. Mustso. New York: Italica Press, 1988.

Gillings, Richard J. *Mathematics in the Time of the Pharaohs.* New York, 1972.

Grabham, G. W., and R. P. Black, *Report of the Mission to Lake Tana 1920–21.* Cairo: Ministry of Public Works, 1925.

Grafton, A., ed. "The Ancient City Restored: Archaeology, Ecclesiastical History, and Egyptology." In *Rome Reborn.* Washington, D.C.: Library of Congress, 1983; Vatican City: Biblioteca Apostolica Vaticana, 1983.

Guidi, I. "Due nuovi manoscritti della Cronaca Abbreviata di Abissinia." *Rendiconti della Reale Accademia dei Lincei* 2 (1926).

Gum'a, Muhammad Lutfi. *The African Lion and the Italian Tiger.* (Arabic). Cairo, 1935.

Habla-Selassie, Sergew. *Ya'amarena yabeta Krestyan mazqaba qalat* (Church Lexicon in Amharic). Heidelberg, 1989.

Hafiz, Sabri. "The Egyptian Novel in the Sixties." In *Critical Perspectives on Modern Arabic Literature,* edited by Issa Boullata. Washington, D.C., 1980.

Haile Selassie, Emperor. *Fre kanafer* (Fruit of the lips). Book 5. Addis Ababa, 1969.

———. *My Life and Ethiopia's Progress.* Translated and annotated by E. Ullendorff. Oxford: Oxford University Press, 1976.

Hallo, William W., and William Kelly Simpson. *The Ancient Near East: A History.* New York: Harcourt Brace Jovanovich, 1971.

Hamad, Khidr. *Mudhakarat Khidr; Hamad al-haraka al-wataniyya li'l-istiqlal wama ba'dahu.* Maktabat al-sharq wa'l-gharb, Al-Sharika, 1980.

Hamann, Günther. *Der Eintritt der südlichen Hemisphäre in die europäische Geschichte.* Wien, 1968.

Hamilton, A. "Eastern Churches and Western Scholarship." In *Rome Reborn. The Vatican Library and Renaissance Culture*, edited by A. Grafton. Washington, D.C.: Library of Congress, 1993; Vatican City: Biblioteca Apostolica Vaticana, 1993.

Hamilton, Bernard. "Continental Drift: Prester John's Progress Through the Indies," Essay 13. In *Prester John, the Mongols and the Ten Lost Tribes*, edited by C. F. Beckingham and B. Hamilton. Aldershot, England: Variorum, 1996.

Hamrush, Ahmad. *M'araqat al-suwis—Thalathun 'aman* (The Suez campaign—thirty years). Cairo, 1988.

Hancock, Graham. *The Sign and the Seal*. London: Mandarin, 1993.

Hanseberry, William Leo. *African History Notebook*. Vol. 2, *Africa and Africans as Seen by Classical Writers*, edited by Joseph E. Harris. Washington, D.C.: Howard University Press, 1981.

Harb, Muhammad Salih. *Wahdat Wadi al-Nil*. Cairo, 1946.

al-Hashimi, Taha. "The Battle of Adwa." In *Al-Risala*, Part 1, 28 October 1935.

Haykal, Muhammad Hasanayn. *Milafat al-suwis* (The Suez files). Cairo, 1986.

Hayton (Hethum). "La Flor des Estoires de la Terre d'Orient." *Recueil des historiens des Croisades. Documents Arméniens* 6 (1906).

Heberer, Michael. *Voyages en Egypte de Michael Heberer von Bretten, 1585–1586*, edited by O. V. Volkoff. Paris: Institut Français d'Archéologie Orientale du Caire, 1976.

Hecht, E.-D. "Ethiopia Threatens to Block the Nile." *Azania* 23 (1988).

Hegel, G. W. *The Philosophy of History*. Translated by S. Sibree. New York, 1956.

Heine, Peter, and Ulrich van der Heyden, eds. *Studien zur Geschichte des deutschen Kolonialismus in Afrika*. Pfaffenweiler: Centaurus, 1995.

Heitsch, Ernest, ed. *Die Dichterfragmente der Römischen Kaiserzeit*. Vol. 1. Göttingen, 1963.

Helck, Wolfgang, ed. *Kleine Ägyptische Texte: Der Text des "Nilhymnus."* Wiesbaden, 1972.

Henze, D. "Leonhart Rauwolff." Introduction to *Aigentliche Beschreibung der Raiss in die Morgenlaender*, by Leonhart Rauwolff. Graz: Akademische Druckverlagsanstalt, 1971.

Henze, Paul B. *Ethiopian Journeys, Travels in Ethiopia 1969–72*. London: Ernest Benn, 1977.

Herodotus. *The Histories*. Translated by Aubery de Selincourt. New York: Penguin Books, 1972.

Hertslet, E., ed. *The Map of Africa by Treaty*. 3d edition. 1909. Reprint, London, 1967.

Hilliard, Asa G. III. "The Meaning of KMT (Ancient Egypt) History for Contemporary African-American Experience." *Clark University Review of Race and Culture* 49, nos. 1, 2 (spring, summer 1992): 10–22.

Hobsbawm E., and T. Ranger. *The Invention of Tradition*. London, 1969.

Holl, Augustin. "West Africa: Colonialism and Nationalism," In *A History of African Archaeology*, edited by O. Robertshaw. London, 1990.

———. "African History: Past, Present, and Future: The Unending Quest for Alternatives." In *Making Alternative Histories*, edited by Peter R. Schmidt and Thomas C. Patterson. Santa Fe, N.M.: School of American Research, 1996.

Holt, P. M. "The Nilotic Sudan." In *The Cambridge History of Islam*. Vol. 2. Cambridge, 1970.

Howe, Stephen. *Afrocentrism: Mythical Pasts and Imagined Homes*. London: Verso, 1998.

Howell, P. P., et al. *The Equatorial Nile Project and Its Effects in the Anglo-Egyptian Sudan: Being the Report of the Jonglei Investigation Team*. Khartoum, 1954.

Hugon, Anne. *The Exploration of Africa: From Cairo to the Cape*. Translated from the French by Alexandra Campbell. London, 1992.

Hulme, Mike, and A. Trilsbach. "Rainfall Trends and Rural Change in Sudan Since Nimeiri: Some Thoughts on Environmental Changes and Political Control." In *Sudan After Nimeiri,* edited by Peter Woodward. London: Routledge, 1991.

Huntington, Samuel P. *The Clash of Civilizations and the Re-making of World Order.* New York: Simon and Schuster, 1996.

Hurst, H. E., and M. P. Barnett. "Planning for the Ultimate Development of the Nile Valley." *Proceedings of the Institute of Civil Engineers* (UK) 16 (July 1960).

Hurst, H. E., R. P. Black, and Y. M. Simaika. *The Future Conservation of the Nile.* Vol. 2: *The Nile Basin.* Cairo: Ministry of Public Works, 1946.

Husayn, Abdalla. *The Ethiopian Question* (in Arabic). Cairo, 1935.

Hussain, Altaf. "Problems in the Planning of Land Settlement." In *Agricultural Development in the Sudan.* Khartoum: The Philosophical Society of the Sudan, 1966.

Huzayyin, Sulayman. *Hadarat Misr: Ard al-Kinana.* Cairo, 1991.

———. *Ard al-'Urbua: Ru'yat Hadariyya fi al-Makan wa al-Zaman.* Cairo, 1993.

———. *Mustaqbal al-Thaqafa fi Misr al-'Arabiyya.* Cairo, 1994.

Ibn 'Abd al-Hakim. *Futuh Misr wa-Akhbaruha.* New Haven, Conn., 1921.

Ibn ad-Athar. *Al-Kamil fi al-Ta'rikh.* Vol. 11. Beirut, 1966.

Ibn al-A'tham. "Mémoire sur la Nubie." In *Mémoires géographiques et historiques sur l'Égypte et sur quelques contrées voisines.* Vol. 2. Translated by E. Quatremère. Paris, 1811.

Ibn Hamadû, Nu'aym. *Kitab al-fitan.* Beirut, 1993.

Ibn Khaldun. *The Muqaddimah: An Introduction to History.* Vol. 1. Translated by Franz Rosenthal. London: Pantheon Books, 1958.

Institute of Archeology. *Ya'atse lalibala gadl. Kage'ez wada amarena yatataragwama* (The hagiography of Emperor Lalibala translated from the Ge'ez into the Amharic). Addis Ababa, 1960.

Isaac, Ephraim, and Cain Felder. "Reflections on the Origins of Ethiopian Civilization." In *Proceedings of the 8th International Conference of Ethiopian Studies,* Vol. 1, edited by Taddese Beyene. Addis Ababa: Institute of Ethiopian Studies, 1988; Frankfurt: Frobenius Institute, 1988.

al-Istakhri. *Kitab Masalik wa'l-Mamalik.* Leiden, 1927.

Iverson, E. *The Myth of Egypt and Its Hieroglyphs in European Tradition.* Copenhagen: Gec Gad Publishers, 1961.

Iyob, Ruth. *The Eritrean Struggle for Independence: Domination, Resistance, Nationalism (1941–1993).* Cambridge: Cambridge University Press, 1995.

Janseen, J. *The Ancient Egyptian Ships Logs.* Leiden, 1961.

Johnson, Samuel, trans. *A Voyage to Abyssinia by Father Jerome Lobo . . . Continued by M. Le Grand.* 1789. Reprint, London, 1978.

Johnston, H. H. *The Nile Quest.* London: Lawrence and Bullen, 1903.

Joinville, Jean de. *Chronicles of the Crusades.* Translated by M. R. B. Shaw. Harmondsworth, England: Penguin Books, 1980.

Jones, A. H. M., and Elizabeth Monroe. *A History of Ethiopia.* Oxford, 1962.

Jumhuriyyat Misr, al-'Arabiyya. *Harb al-'udwan al-thulathi* (The Tripartite War) Arab Republic of Egypt, Ministry of Defense, Cairo, n.d.

Kamil, Mustafa. *Al-Khutub,* edited by 'Abd al-'Azim Ramadan, Matba'at al-Hi'yya al-'Amma lil-Kitab. Cairo, 1987.

———. *Al-Maqalat,* edited by 'Abd al-'Azim Ramadan, Matba'at al-Hi'yya al-'Amma lil-Kitab. Cairo, 1987.

Kammerer, A. *La Mer Rouge, l'Abyssinie et l'Arabie depuis l'antiquité.* Le Claire: Société Royale de Géographie d'Egypte, 1929.

Kane, T. L. *Amharic-English Dictionary.* Wiesbaden, 1990.

Kaplan, S. "The Origins of the Beta Israel: Five Methodological Cautions," (in Hebrew). *Pe'amim* 33 (1987).

————. "The Beta Israel (Falasha) Encounter with Protestant Missionaries, 1860–1905." *Jewish Social Studies* 49, no. 1 (1987).

————. *The Beta Israel (Falasha) in Ethiopia: From Earliest Times to the Twentieth Century.* New York: New York University Press, 1991.

Karrow, R. W., Jr. *Mapmakers of the Sixteenth Century and Their Maps: Bio-Bibliographies of the Cartographers of Abraham Ortelius, 1570.* Chicago: Speculum Orbis Press for the Newberry Library, 1993.

Kees, Herman. *Ancient Egypt: A Cultural Topography.* Translated from the German by E. D. Morrow. Chicago: University of Chicago Press, 1961.

Kefle, Kidana Wald. *Mashafa sawesew wages wamazgaba qalat haddis nebabu bage'ez fechchew bamareña* (A book of grammar and verb, and a new dictionary. Ge'ez entries with Amharic definitions). Addis Ababa, 1955.

————. "Haymanota Abaw la foi des pères anciens. I: Texte Ethiopien." *Studien zur Kulturkunde* 79 (1986).

Keita, S. O. Y. "The Geographical Origins and Population Relationship of Early Ancient Egyptians." In *Egypt in Africa,* edited by Theodore Celenko. Indianapolis: Indianapolis Museum of Art in cooperation with Indiana University Press, 1996.

Kessler, David. *The Falashas.* 3d revised edition. London: Frank Cass, 1997.

Kete Asante, Molefi. *Kemet, Afrocentricity and Knowledge.* Trenton, N.J.: Africa World Press, 1992.

al-Kindi. *Kitab al-Wulat.* Beirut, 1908.

Knigge, Adolph Freiherr. "Erstausgabe." *Benjamin Noldmanns Geschichte der Aufklärung in Abyssinien,* in *Sämtliche Werke,* Vols. 1, 2, edited by Paul Raabe. Nendeln: KTO Press, 1978.

Knigge, Adolph von. *Ausgewählte Werke in zehn Bänden.* Translated by Wolfgang Fenner. Hannover: Fackelträger, 1991.

Kogel, Jörg-Dieter. *Knigges ungewöhnliche Empfehlungen zu Aufklärung und Revolution.* Berlin: Oberbaum, n.d.

Kohler. "Documents relatifs à Guillaume Adam, Archevêque de Sultaniyeh, puis d'Antivari et à son entourage (1318–46)." *Revue de l'Orient Latin* 10 (1903–1904).

Koyle, S. "The Khashm el-Girba Agricultural Scheme: An Example of an Attempt to Settle the Nomads." In *Land Use and Development,* edited by Phill O'Keefe and Ben Wisner. London: International African Institute, 1977.

Kranz, W. *Stasimon: Untersuchungen zu Form und Gehalf der griechischen Tragödie.* Berlin, 1933.

Krapf, J. L. *Travels, Researches, and Missionary Labours, During an Eighteen Years' Residence in Eastern Africa.* London: Trübner, 1860.

Kraus, Gerhard. *Human Development from an African Ancestry.* 2 vols. London: Karnak, 1990.

Krzyzaniak, Lech, Michat Robusiewicz, and John Alexander. *Environmental Change and Human Culture in the Nile Basin and Northern Africa Until the Second Millennium B.C.* Poznan, 1993.

La Broquière, Bertrandon de. *Le Voyage d'Outremer,* edited by C. Schefer. Paris: E. Leroux, 1892.

Lamma, Mangestu. *Matshafa tezzeta za'alaqa lamma haylu walda tarik* (The book of reminiscences of Alaqa Lamma Haylu Walda Tarik). Addis Ababa, 1966.

Landstrom, Bjorn. *Ships of the Pharaohs: 4000 Years of Egyptian Shipbuilding.* New York, 1970.

La Roncière, Charles de. *La Découverte de l'Afrique au moyen age.* Vol. 2. Cairo: Société Royale de Géographie d'Egypte, 1924–1927.

Lees, Francis A., and Hugh C. Brooks. *The Economic and Political Development of the Sudan.* Boulder, Colo.: Westview Press, 1977.

Lefevre, R. "L'Africa Orientale nella cosmografia patristica e nella cartografia genovese del '300.'" *Rivista delle colonie* (1939).

———. "Roma e la Comunità etiopica di Cipro nei secoli XV e XVI." *RSE* 1 (1941).

———. "Note su alcuni pellegrini etiopi in Roma al tempo di Leone X." *RSE* 21 (1964).

———. "L'Etiopia nella stampa del primo Cinquecento." *Africa* 20, no. 4 (1965).

———. "Note su alcuni pellegrini etiopi prima di Concilio de Firenze del 1439." *RSE* 23 (1967–1968).

———. "Presenze etiopi in Italia prima di Concilio di Firenze del 1439." *RSE* 23 (1967–1968).

Lefkowitz, M. R. "Ancient History, Modern Myths." In *Black Athena Revisited,* edited by M. R. Lefkowitz. Chapel Hill: The University of North Carolina Press, 1996.

Le Grand, M. J. *Voyage historique d'Abissinie du R. P. Jerome Lobo.* Paris: P. Gosse and J. Neaulme, 1728.

Lemma, Legesse. "Ethiopia and Egypt: Towards an Appraisal of Nile Water Sharing in the Context of the Helsinki Rules." In *Proceedings of the Eleventh International Conference of Ethiopian Studies,* Addis Ababa, April 1–6, 1991, edited by Bahru Zewde, Richard Pankhurst, and Taddesse Beyene. Addis Ababa: Addis Ababa University Press, 1994.

Leonessa. M. Da. *S. Stefano Maggiore o degli Abissini.* Rome: Tip. Vaticana, 1928.

Lesinski, Markus. "Zwischen Mutter- und Schwesterkirche. Orthodoxe in Eritrea streben nach kirchlicher Eigenständigkeit." In *Glaube in der 2. Welt. Zeitschrift für Religionsfreiheit und Menschenrechte* 3 (1994).

Leslau, Wolf. *Falasha Anthology.* New Haven, Conn.: Yale University Press, 1951.

Letts, M. *The Pilgrimage of Arnolf von Harff.* London: Hakluyt Society, 1946.

Levine, D. "Menilek and Oedipus: Further Observations on the Ethiopian National Epic." In *Proceedings of the First US Conference on Ethiopian Studies,* edited by H. Marcus. East Lansing, Michigan State University Press, 1975.

Levine, Molly Myerowitz. "Bernal and the Athenians in the Multicultural World of the Ancient Mediterranean." In *Classical Studies in Honor of David Sohlberg,* edited by Ranon Katzoff. Ramat Gan: Bar-Ilan University Press, 1996.

Lichtheim, Miriam. *Ancient Egyptian Literature.* Vol. 1, *The Old and Middle Kingdoms.* Berkeley: University of California Press, 1975.

Lifchitz, D. "Un Sacrifice chez les Falachas, Juifs d'Abyssinie." *Terre et la vie* 9 (1939).

Lloyd, A. B. *Herodotus Book II, Commentary 1–98.* Leiden: Brill, 1976.

Lobo, J. *A Voyage to Abyssinia.* London: John Hawkins, 1789.

Lowrie, Arthur L. *Islam, Democracy, the State and the West, a Round Table with Dr. Hasan Turabi.* Tampa, Fla.: World and Islam Studies Enterprise, 1992.

Lucas, J. O. *The Religion of the Yoruba.* Lagos, Nigeria, 1948.

Lucchetta. G. "Viaggiatori e racconti di viaggi nel Cinquecento." In *Storia della cultura veneta, vol 3: Dal primo Quattrocento al Concilio di Trento.* Part 2. Vicenza: Neri Pozza Editore, 1980.

———. "I viaggiatori veneti dal medioevo all'età moderna." In *Viaggiatori veneti alla scoperta dell'Egitto. Itinerari di storia e arte*, edited by A. Siliotti. Venice: Arsenale Editrice, 1985.

Lucretius. *De Rerum Natura*. Translated by W. H. Rouse. Loeb Classical Library, 1959.

Ludolf, Job. *Historia Aethiopica*. Frankfurt, 1681.

———. *A New History of Ethiopia*. London: Samuel Smith, 1682.

———. *Ad suam historiam Aethiopicam Commentarius*. Frankfurt, 1691.

———. *Les Chroniques de Zar'a Ya'eqob et de Ba'eda Maryam*. Paris: Emile Bouillon, 1893.

Lyons, H. G. *The Physiography of the River Nile and Its Basin*. Cairo: Ministry of Public Works, 1906.

Macgaffey, Wyatt. "Concept of Race in the Historiography of Northeast Africa." *Journal of African History* 7, no. 1 (1966).

MacGregor, R. M., and Abdel Hamid Suleiman. *The Nile Commission Report*. Cairo: Ministry of Public Works, 1926.

Maffei. *Historiarum Indicarum libri xvi*. Lyon, 1637.

Mahtama-Selassie, Walde-Masqal. *Yabbatochqers* (The Heritage of the Fathers). Addis Ababa, 1969.

al-Makin. *Historia sarracenica*. Leyden: Thomas Erpenii, 1625.

Makweriya, Takla Tsadeq. *Ya'ityopeya tarik. Nubya aksum zagwe eska atse yekunno amlak zamana mangest* (A history of Ethiopia: Nubya Aksum Zagwe until the reign of Yekunno Amlak). Addis Ababa, 1959.

al-Maqrizi. *Al-Khitat wa'l-athar*. Cairo, 1853.

Marrassini, P. "Insieme contro Maometto. Europa ed Etiopia dal Medioevo all'età moderna." *Storia e dossier* 54 (September 1991).

Maryam, Tayya Gabra. *Ya'ityopeya hezb tarik* (A history of Ethiopian peoples). 6th edition. Addis Ababa, 1966.

Mas'ad, Bulus. *Ethiopia or Abyssinia in a Turning Point in Her History*. Cairo, 1935.

Massaja, G. "Letter of G. Massaja to Card. Alessandro Barnabo," April 1865. In *Lettere e scritti minori*, Vol. 3, edited by A. Rosso. Rome: Ist. Storico Cappuccino, 1978.

———. *I miei trentacinque anni di missione nell'alta Etiopia*. Rome: Tip. Ploglotta di P. Fide, 1885–1895.

Massey, Gerald. *Book of the Beginning*. Vol. 2. Kila, Mich.: Kessinger Publishing Company, 1992.

al-Mas'udi. *Muruj*. Vols. 2, 3. Paris, 1861–1877.

McCann, James. "Ethiopia, Britain, and Negotiations for the Lake Tana Dam, 1922–1935." *International Journal of African Historical Studies* 14, no. 4 (1981).

Mehrez, Samia. *Egyptian Writers Between History and Fiction: Essays on Naguib Mahfouz, Sonallah Ibrahim, and Gamal al-Ghitani*. Cairo, 1994.

Meinardus, O. F. A. "A Brief History of the Abunate of the Ethiopian Church." *Zeitschrift für die Kunde des Morgenlandes* 58 (Wien, 1962).

———. *Christian Egypt, Faith and Life*. Cairo, 1970.

———. "Ethiopian Monks in Egypt." *Publ. de l'Inst. d'Ét orient* 11 (1962).

———. *Monks and Monasteries of the Egyptian Deserts*. Revised edition. Cairo, 1992.

Mekonnen, Kefyalew. "A New Basis for a Viable Nile River Water Allocation Agreement." Paper presented at the Fifth Nile 2002 Conference, Addis Ababa, 24–28 February 1997.

Melloni, A. "Facteurs involutifs et lignes de développement dans l'historiographie relative au christianisme africain." In *Eglise et histoire de l'Eglise en Afrique. Actes du colloque de Bologne 22–25 octobre 1988,* edited by G. Ruggeri. Paris: Beauchesne, 1990.

Mercier, Roger. *L'Afrique Noire dans la littérature française.* Dakar, 1962.

Meyrowitz, E. L. R. *The Divine Kingship in Ghana and Ancient Egypt.* London, 1960.

Mika'el, Tasamma Habta. *Ya'amareña mazgaba qalat* (An Amharic dictionary). Addis Ababa, 1959.

Milanesi, M. "Introduction" to *Navigazioni e viaggi,* Vol. 1, by Giovanni Battista Ramusio. Turin: Giulio Einaudi Editore, 1978.

Ministry of Information. *Ya'abbay weha lemat majammarya masarat* (Foundation of the first phase of development of the Nile waters). Addis Ababa, 1959.

Mirghani, Abdel Rahim. "Problems of Increasing Agricultural Productivity in the Traditional Sector." *Agricultural Development in the Sudan.* Khartoum: Sudan Philosophical Society, 1966.

Mitchell, Timothy. *Colonising Egypt.* Berkeley: University of California Press, 1991.

Momigliano, Attilio. *Storia della Letteratura Italiana dalle origini ai nostri giorni.* 8th edition. Milano-Messina, 1958.

Mondon-Vidailhet, C. "Une tradition Éthiopienne." *Revue sémitique 12* (1904).

———, ed. *Chronique de Théodorus II Roi des Rois d'Ethiopie (1853–68).* Paris, 1904.

Monges, Miriam Ma'at-Ka-Re. *Kush—The Jewel of Nubia: Reconsidering the Root System of African Civilization.* Trenton, N.J.: Africa World Press, Inc.

Morenz, Siegfried. *Egyptian Religion.* Translated by Ann E. Keep. Ithaca, N.Y.: Cornell University Press, 1973.

Morrice, H. A. W. "The Development of the Main Nile for the Benefit of Egypt and the Sudan." Morrice Papers, Sudan Archives, Durham University.

Morrice, H. A. W., and W. N. Allan. *Report on the Nile Valley Plan.* 2 vols. Khartoum: Ministry of Irrigation, 1958.

Moses, Wilson Jeremiah. *Afrotropia: The Roots of African American Popular History.* Cambridge University Press, 1998.

Mulatu, Ayyalnah. "Teqqur abbay." In *Yagetmoch madbal (ka'asra sabat gatamyan serawoch)* (The rose pen: An anthology of poems [from the works of seventeen poets]), edited by Tsegereda Be'er. Addis Ababa: Ethiopian Printing Corporation, 1984.

Murdock, George. *Africa: Its Peoples and Their Cultural History.* New York, 1959.

Musto, G. "Introduction" to *The Antiquities of Constantinople,* by Pierre Gilles. Translated by J. Ball and edited by G. Musto. New York: Italica Press, 1988.

Myers, Charles. S. "Contributions to Egyptian Anthropometry II—The Comparative Anthropometry of the Most Ancient and Modern Inhabitants." *Journal of the Anthropological Institute of Great Britain and Ireland* 35 (1905).

———. "The Anthropometry of the Modern Mahommedans." *Journal of the Royal Anthropological Institute* 35 (1906).

Najib, Muhammad. *Kalimati li'l-ta'rikh.* Cairo: Dar al-Kitab al-namudhaji, 1975.

Newman, James L. *The Peopling of Africa: A Geographical Interpretation.* New Haven, Conn.: Yale University Press, 1995.

Noah, Salah el-Din. "Agricultural Extension: Its Role and Importance in Agricultural Development in the Sudan." *Agricultural Development in the Sudan.* Khartoum: The Philosophical Society of the Sudan, 1966.

Nora, Pierre. "Between Memory and History: *Les Lieux de mémoire.*" *Representations* 26 (spring 1989).

Nougera, Anthony. *How African Was Egypt? A Comparative Study of Ancient Egyptian and Black African Cultures.* New York: Vintage Books, 1976.

al-Nuqrashi, Mahmud Fahmi. *Qadiyyat Wadi al-Nil.* Cairo, 1947.

O'Connor, David. "Ancient Egypt and Black Africa—Early Contacts." *Expedition* (fall 1971).

———. *Ancient Nubia: Egypt's Rival in Africa.* The University Museum of Archaeology and Anthropology, University of Pennsylvania, 1993.

Okidi, Charles O. "International Laws and the Lake Victoria and Nile Basins." *Indian Journal of International Law* 20 (1980).

Pais (Paez), Pero. *Historia da Etiopia.* Vol. 3. Porto: Libraria Civilizacao, 1945.

Pankhurst, R., ed. *The Ethiopian Royal Chronicles.* Oxford: Oxford University Press, 1967.

Pankhurst, S. *Ethiopia. A Cultural History.* Woodford Green, Essex: Lalibela House, 1955.

Paulus, H. E. G. "J. M. Wansleb bisher ungedruckte Beschreibung von Aegypten im Jahr 1664." *Sammlung der merkwürdigsten Reisen in den Orient.* Vol. 3. Jena, 1794.

Paviot, J. "Autour de l'ambassade de d'Aramon: Erudits et voyageurs au Levant 1547–1553." In *Voyager à la Renaissance, Actes du colloque de Tours, juillet 1983,* edited by J. Ceard and J. C. Margolin. Paris: Maissoneuve et Larose, 1987.

———. "The French Embassy of D'Aramon to the Porte: Scholars and Travelers in the Levant 1547–1553." *Studies on Ottoman Diplomatic History* 1 (1987).

Perruchon, J. *La Vie de Lalibala, roi d'Ethiopie.* Paris: Ernest Leroux, 1892.

———, ed. *Les Chroniques de Zar'a Ya'eqob et de Ba'eda Maryam, rois d'Ethiopie de 1434 à 1478.* Paris, 1893.

Pick, Christopher. *Egypt: A Traveler's Anthology.* London, 1991.

Polotsky, H. J. "Aramaic, Syriac, Ge'ez," *Journal of Semitic Studies* 9 (1961).

Porten, B. *Archives from Elephantine.* Berkeley: University of California Press, 1968.

Pritchard, J. B., ed. *Ancient Eastern Texts Relating to the Old Testament.* Translated by J. A. Wilson. 3d edition. Princeton University Press, 1969.

Prutsky, Remedius. *Prutsky's Travels in Ethiopia and Other Countries.* Translated and edited by J. H. Arrowsmith Brown and annotated by Richard Pankhurst. London: Hakluyt Society, 1991.

Quatremère, E. *Mémoires géographiques et historiques sur l'Egypte.* Paris: F. Schoell, 1811.

Quirin, J. A. *The Evolution of the Ethiopian Jews.* Philadelphia: University of Pennsylvania Press, 1992.

Quraishi, Z. M. *Liberal Nationalism in Egypt.* Delhi, 1968.

al-Rafi'i, 'Abd al-Rahman. *Fi A'qab al-Thawra al-Misriyya.* Vol. 3. Cairo, 1951.

Ramadan, 'Abd al-'Azim. *Ukdhubat al-isti'mar al-Misri li'l-Sudan.* Cairo: Al-hay'a al-Misriyya al-'ama li'l-kitab, 1988.

Ramusio, Giovanni Battista. *Navigazioni e viaggi.* 2 vols. Edited by M. Milanesi. Turin: Giulio Einaudi Editore, 1978–1979.

Ranger, T. "The Invention of Tradition Revisited." In *Ripensare la storia coloniale, Cagliari 18–19 aprile, Atti del Convegno,* edited by B. M. Carcangiu. Cagliari, 1995.

Redford, Donald B. *Pharaonic King-Lists, Annals and Day-Book: A Contribution to the Study of Egyptian Sense of History.* Mississauga: Benben Publications, 1986.

Reid, D. M. "Nationalizing the Pharoanic Past: Egyptology, Imperialism, and Egyptian Nationalism, 1922–1952." In *Rethinking Nationalism in the Arab Middle East,* edited by J. Jankowski and I. Gershoni. New York, 1997.

———. "The Egyptian Geographical Society: From Foreign Laymen's Society to Indigenous Professional Association." *Poetics Today* 14, no. 3 (fall 1993).

Reinisch, L. *Ein Blick auf Aegypten und Abessinien.* Inaugurationsrede gehalten am 26. Vienna, 1896.

Renfrew, Colin. *Archaeology and Language: The Puzzle of Indo-European Origins.* London, 1987.

Rey, C. F. *In the Country of the Blue Nile.* London: Duckworth, 1927.

Röhricht, R. "Le Pèlerinage du moine augustin Jacques de Vérone (1335)." *Revue de l'Orient Latin* 3 (1895).

Ronen, Yehudit. "Sudan." In *Middle East Contemporary Survey, 1995,* Vol. 20, edited by Bruce Maddy-Weitzman. Boulder, Colo.: Westview Press, 1997.

Rosen, Felix. *Eine deutsche Gesandtschaft in Abessinien.* Leipzig, 1907.

Rossi, E. *Storia della Marina dell'Ordine di S. Giovanni di Gerusalemme, di Rodi et di Malta.* Rome, 1926.

Rossini, Conti C. "Il Libro del Conoscimiento' e le sue notizie sull'Etiopia." *Bollettino della Regia Societá Geografica Italiana* 5, no. 6 (1917).

———. "Leggende giudaiche del IX secolo (Il Sefer Eldad)." *Bollettino della Regia Società Geografica Italiana* 7, no. 2 (1923).

———. "Geografica I. L'Africa orientale in carte arabe dei secoli XII e XII. II Carte Abissine. III Gli itinerari di Alessandro Zorzi." *Rassegna di studi Etiopici* (1943).

Sadji, Uta. *Der Negermythos am Ende des 18. Jahrhunderts in Deutschland. Eine Analyse der Rezeption von Reiseliteratur über Schwarzafrika.* Frankfurt: Peter Lang, 1979.

al-Sakhawi, *Al-Tibr al Masbuk.* Cairo, 1896.

Salem-Murdock, Muneera. *A Study of Settlement and Irrigation: Arabs and Nubians in New Halfa.* Salt Lake City: University of Utah Press, 1989.

Salt, H. *A Voyage to Abyssinia.* London: F. C. and J. Rivington, 1814.

Sauneron, S., ed. *Le Voyage en Egypte de Pierre Belon du mons 1547.* Paris: Institut Français d'Archéologie Orientale du Caire, 1970.

Schefer, "Le voyage d'Outremer de Bertrandon de la Brocquière, premier écuyer tranchant et conseiller de Philippe le Bon, duc de Bourgogne." *Recueil de voyages et documents pour servir à l'histoire de la géographie depuis le xiiie jusqu'à la fin du xvie siècle* 12 (1892).

———. "Le Voyage d'Outremer: Égypte, Mont Sinay, Palestine, de Jean Thenaud, gardien du couvent des Cordeliers d'Angoulême." *Recueil de voyages et documents pour servir à l'histoire de la géographie depuis le xiiie jusqu'à la fin du xvie siècle* 12 (1892).

Seligman, Charles. *The Pagan Tribes of the Nilotic Sudan.* London, 1932.

Seyberlich, R. M. "Beziehungen und Abhang igkeibverhaltnisse zwischen der koptischen und der Ethiopischen Kirche." In *Koptologische Studien in der DDR. Wissenschaftliche Zeitschrift der Martin-Luther-Universitet in Halle-Wittenberg,* 1965.

Sharpe, E. J. *Comparative Religion: A History.* London: Duckworth, 1986.

Shavit, Yaacov. *History in Black.* London: Frank Cass, forthcoming.

Shelemay, K. K. *Music, Ritual and Falasha History.* East Lansing: Michigan State University Press, 1986.

Shinnie, P. L. "The Legacy to Africa." In *The Legacy of Egypt,* edited by J. R. Harris. 2d edition. Oxford: Clarendon Press, 1971.

———. "Christian Nubia." In *The Cambridge History of Africa.* Vol. 2. Cambridge, 1972.

Shuqayr, Na'um. *Tarikh al-Sudan al-qadim wal-hadith wa jughrafiyatuhu.* Beirut: Dar al-Thaqafah, 1967.

Sigali. "Viaggio al Montes Sinai." In *Etiopi in Palestina. Storia della communità Etiopica di Gerusalemme.* 2 vols. Rome: Liberia dello Stato, 1943–1947.

Simaika, Y. M. "Discussion on Planning for the Ultimate Hydraulic Development of the Nile Valley." *Proceedings of the Institute of Civil Engineers* 14 (1959).

Singer, Milton. *When a Great Tradition Modernizes: An Anthropological Approach to Indian Civilization.* New York, 1972.

Sitran Gasparini, L. "L'Egitto nella rappresentazione cartografica." In *Viaggiatori veneti alla scoperta dell'Egitto,* edited by A. Silotti. Venice, 1985.

Slessarey, V. *Prester John. The Letters and the Legend.* Minneapolis: University Press of Minnesota, 1959.

Smidt, Heinrich. *Berlin und West-Afrika. Ein Brandenburgischer See-Roman.* 6 vols. Berlin, 1847.

Smith, A. D. *The Ethnic Origins of Nations.* Oxford, 1986.

Smith, C. Elliot. *Migration of Early Culture.* Manchester, 1915.

Smith, Robert S. *Kingdoms of the Yoruba.* 3d edition. Madison: University of Wisconsin Press, 1988.

Sorenson, John. *Imagining Ethiopia: Struggles for History and Identity in the Horn of Africa.* New Brunswick, N.J.: Rutgers University Press, 1996.

Spencer, Diana. "Travels in Gojjam: St. Luke Icons and Brancaleon Rediscovered." *Journal of Ethiopian Studies* 12, no. 2 (1974).

Spindler, M. R. Spindler, "Writing African Church History 1969–1989: A Survey of Recent Studies." *Exchange Journal of Missionological and Ecumenical Research* 19, no. 1 (1990).

Steindorff, George, and Keith C. Seele. *When Egypt Ruled the East.* 2d edition. Chicago: University of Chicago Press, 1957.

Stella, G. C. *Il viaggio in Etiopia di Michelangelo Pacelli.* Ravenna, 1986.

Suriano, Francesco. *Treatise on the Holy Land.* Translated by. T. Bellorini and E. Hoade. Jerusalem: Franciscan Press, 1949.

Suriyal, Antuni. *'Dir al-Sultan bi'al-Quds* (A documented study of the Coptic-Ethiopian rivalry over the convent). Cairo, 1991.

Sutcliffe, J. V. "A Hydrology of the Sudd Region of the Upper Nile." Ph.D. dissertation, Cambridge University, 1957.

———. "A Hydrological Study of the Southern Sudd Region of the Upper Nile." *Hydrological Sciences* 19 (1974).

Sutcliffe, J. V., and Y. P. Parks. "A Hydrological Estimate of the Effects of the Jonglei Canal on Areas of Flooding." Wallingford, UK: Institute of Hydrology for the Food and Agricultural Organization (UN), 1982.

———. "Hydrological Modelling of the Sudd and Jonglei Canal." *Hydrological Sciences Journal* 32, no. 2 (1987).

al-Tabari. Ta'rikh al-Rusul. Leiden, 1879–1901.

Tafla, Bairu. "Atsma Giyorgis and His Work: History of the Galla and the Kingdom of Shawa." *Äthiopistische Forschungen* 18 (1987).

Tal, David. "Israel's Road to the 1956 War." *International Journal of Middle East Studies* 28, no. 1 (February 1996).

Tamrat, Tadesse. *Church and State in Ethiopia 1270–1527.* Oxford: Clarendon Press, 1972.

———. "Ethiopia, the Red Sea, and the Horn." In *The Cambridge History of Africa.* Vol. 5. New York: Cambridge University Press, 1977.

Tegegne, Muse. *"Gojjam" the Stigma: The Abyssinian Pariah—Sociology of Hope.* Geneva, 1993.

Thevenot, Jean de. *Voyages de M. de Thevenot en Europe, Asie et Afrique.* 3d edition. Amsterdam, 1727.

Tilahun, Wondimneh. *Egypt's Imperial Aspirations over Lake Tana and the Blue Nile.* Addis Ababa, 1979.

Trasselli, C. "Un Italiano in Etiopia nel XV secolo. Pietro Rombulo da Messina," *Rassegna di Studi Etiopici* 1–2 (1941).

Trevisan-Semi, E. *Allo specchio dei Falascia: Ebrei ed etnologi durante il colonialismo fascista.* Firenze: Giuntina, 1987.

Trigger, Bruce G. "Nubian, Negro, Nilotic?" In *Africa in Antiquity I, The Arts of Ancient Nubia and the Sudan: The Essays,* edited by S. Hochfield and E. Riefsthal. New York: The Brooklyn Museum, 1978.

———. "Egypt and Early Civilizations." In *Egyptology and Social Sciences,* edited by K. Weeks. Cairo: American University in Cairo Press, 1979.

Trimingham, J. S. *Islam in Ethiopia.* Oxford: Oxford University Press, 1952.

Troutt Powell, Eve M. "Egyptians in Blackface: Nationalism and the Representation of the Sudan in Egypt, 1919." *Harvard Middle Eastern and Islamic Review* 2 (1995).

Ullendorff, E. *The Ethiopians. An Introduction to the Country and People.* London: Oxford University Press, 1960.

———. *Ethiopia and the Bible.* Oxford: Oxford University Press, 1968.

Vanderkam, J. C. *Textual and Historical Studies in the Book of Jubilees.* Missoula, Mont.: Scholars Press, 1977.

van der Merwe. "The Advent of Iron in Africa." In *The Coming of the Iron Age,* edited by T. A. Wertime and J. D. Mubly. New Haven, Conn.: Yale University Press, 1980.

van Donzel, E. *Foreign Relations of Ethiopia 1642–1700.* Leiden-Istanbul, 1979.

van Sertima, Ivan, ed., *Blacks in Science: Ancient and Modern.* New Brunswick, N.J. Transaction Books, 1991.

———, ed. *Egypt Revisited.* Transaction Publishers: New Brunswick, N.J. 1991.

———, ed. *Great African Thinkers.* Vol. 1, *Cheick Anta Diop.* New Brunswick, N.J.: Transaction Books, 1992.

Varthema, Ludovico di. *The Travels etc.* 1863. Reprint. New York: Burt Franklin, n.d.

Vatikiotis, P. J. *The Modern History of Egypt.* London: Weidenfeld and Nicolson, 1969.

———, ed. *Chronique de Théodoros II, Roi des rois d'Ethiopie* (1853–68). Paris, 1904.

Vincent, A. L. *La Religion des judéo-arméens d'Elephantine.* Paris: P. Geuthner, 1937.

Voigt, G. *Die Wiederbelebung des classischen Altertums oder das erste Jahrhundert des Humanismus.* Vol. 1. 4th edition. Berlin: Walter de Gruyter and Co., 1960.

Volney, M. C-F. *Voyage en Syrie et en Egypte.* Paris, 1787.

von der Gröben, Otto Friedrich. *Orientalische Reise-Beschreibung Des Brandenburgischen Adelichen Pilgers Otto Friedrich von der Gröben. Nebst der Brandenburgischen Schiffahrt nach Guinea und der verrichtung zu Morea.* Marienwerder: Simon Reinigern, 1694.

Vossius. *De Nilo et aliorum fluminum origine.* Hagae Comitis, 1666.

———. *Dissertation touchant l'origine du Nil.* Paris, 1667.

Wald, Dasta Takla. *Addis yamareña mazgaba qalat bakahnatenna bahagara sab qwanqwa tatsafa* (A new dictionary of Amharic. Written in accordance with the parlance of the clergy and the peasants). Addis Ababa, 1970.

Waldman, Menachem. *The Jews of Ethiopia.* Jerusalem: Joint Distribution Committee, 1985.

Walda-Selassie. Heruy. *Yale'lat wayzaro Manan mangad ba'iruslemna bamisr.* Addis Ababa, 1923.

———. *Dastana kibir* (A diary of Ras Tafari's trip to Europe). Addis Ababa, 1924.

———. *Ba'adame masinbat hulun lamayet.* Addis Ababa, 1934.

Warburg, Gabriel. "The Nile in Egyptian-Sudanese Relations." *Orient* 32, no. 4 (1991).

———. "The Turco-Egyptian Sudan: A Recent Historiographical Controversy." *Die Welt Des Islams* 31, no. 2 (1991).

———. *Historical Discord in the Nile Valley.* London: C. Hurst, 1992.

———. "Egypt and Sudan Wrangle over Halayib." *Middle East Quarterly* 1, no. 1 (1994).

Warmbold, Joachim. *Germania in Africa. Germany's Colonial Literature.* New York: Peter Lang, 1989.

Warqu, Makuriya. *Messaleyawi annagagar* (Proverbial expressions). Addis Ababa, 1989.

Waterbury, John. *Hydropolitics on the Nile Valley.* Syracuse: Syracuse University Press, 1979.

Welsby, Derek A. *The Kingdom of Kush: The Napatan and Meroitic Empires.* London: British Museum, 1996.

Whiteman, Marjorie D. *Digest of International Law.* Vol. 3. Washington, D.C., 1964.

Wiet, G. "Les Relations Égypto-Abyssines sous les sultans mamelouks." *Bulletin de la Société d'Archéologie Copte* 55 (1928).

Wild, Johann. *Voyages en Egypte.* Edited and translated by O. V. Volkoff. Paris: Institute Française d'Archeologie Orientale du Caire, 1973.

Wilkinson, Charles K., and M. Hill. *Egyptian Wall Paintings: The Metropolitan Museum of Art's Collection of Facsimiles.* New York, 1979.

Wilkinson, J. Gardiner. *The Ancient Egyptians, Their Life and Customs.* London, 1994.

Wright, J. K. *The Geographical Lore of the Time of the Crusades.* 2d edition. New York: Dover Publications, 1965.

Wüstenfeld, F. "Die älteste Ägyptische Geschichte nach den Zauber und Wundererzählungen der Araber." *Orientalia und Occidentalia* 1 (1861).

Wynn, R. F. "Water Resource Planning in the Sudan: An Economic Problem." *Agricultural Development in the Sudan.* Khartoum: Sudan Philosophical Society, 1964.

al-Ya'qubi. *Kitab al-Buldan.* Leiden, 1860.

———. *Ta'rikh.* Vol. 1. Leiden, 1901.

Yaqut. *Mu'jam al-Buldan.* Vol. 4. Cairo, 1906.

Yorca, Frank J. "Were the Ancient Egyptians Black or White?" *Biblical Archaeological Review* 15, no. 5 (September/October 1989).

———. "Black Athena: An Egyptological Review." In *Black Athena Revisited,* edited by Mary R. Lefkowitz and Guy MacLean Rogers. Chapel Hill: University of North Carolina Press, 1996.

Zerubavel, Y. *Recovered Roots: Collective Memory and the Making of Israeli National Tradition.* Chicago, 1995.

The Contributors

Ismail H. Abdalla   Associate professor at the College of William and Mary, specializing in modern Sudanese and African history. He has published on cultural, anthropological, and medical aspects and mainly on their connection to Islam and politics.

Benjamin Arbel   Associate professor of early modern history in the Department of History, Tel Aviv University. Former chief editor of the *Mediterranean Historical Review,* he is the author of over fifty publications on various aspects of European presence in the eastern Mediterranean.

David Ayalon, 1914–1998   Professor emeritus, Department of Islamic and Middle Eastern Studies, the Hebrew University of Jerusalem. He specialized in medieval and late medieval Islamic societies. (See also the Introduction).

Uoldelul Chelati Dirar   Assistant professor at Asmara University, chair of the Department of History. He specializes in cultural aspects of colonial history.

Robert O. Collins   Professor of history, Emeritus, at the University of California, Santa Barbara. His various books on the Nile and the Sudan include *The Waters of the Nile: Hydropolitics and the Jonglei Canal* (Oxford 1990, Princeton 1996), *The Waters of the Nile: An Annotated Bibliography* (Oxford 1991), and *The Nile* (Yale, forthcoming).

Haggai Erlich   Professor of Middle Eastern and African history at Tel Aviv University, specializing in Ethiopia and Egypt. His recent books include *Ethiopia and the Middle East* (Boulder 1994), *Ras Alula and the Scramble for Africa* (new edition, New Jersey and Asmara 1996), and *Youth and Politics in the Middle East—Generations and Identity Crises* (Tel Aviv 1998, in Hebrew).

Israel Gershoni   Professor of history in the Department of Middle Eastern and African History at Tel Aviv University. He has published numerous books on cultural aspects of Egyptian and Arab nationalism. His most recent books include *Redefining the Egyptian Nation, 1930–1945*, with J. Jankowski (Cambridge 1995), and *Light in the Shade: Egypt and Fascism, 1922–1937* (Tel Aviv 1999, in Hebrew).

Paul Henze   A retired diplomat and a resident consultant with the Rand Corporation, Washington, D.C. His publications on Ethiopian history and culture include *Ethiopian Journeys* (1977), *Rebels and Separatists in Ethiopia* (Santa Monica 1985), *The Horn of Africa from War to Peace* (London 1991), and *Layers of Time, A History of Ethiopia* (London 1999).

Steven Kaplan   Associate professor of African studies and comparative religion and chairman of the Institute of Asian and African Studies at the Hebrew University, Jerusalem. His publications include *The Monastic Holy Men and the Christianization of Early Solomonic Ethiopia* (Wiesbaden 1984) and *The Beta Israel (Falasha) in Ethiopia* (New York 1992).

Nehemia Levtzion   Professor of the history of Muslim peoples at the Hebrew University, Jerusalem, and former president of the Israel Oriental Society. His publications include *Ancient Ghana and Mali* (London 1973) and *Eighteenth-Century Renewal and Reform in Islam*, with J. Voll (Syracuse 1987).

Yoram Meital   Chairman of the Department of Middle East Studies at Ben Gurion University, Beer-Sheva. He is the author of *Egypt's Struggle for Peace: Continuity and Change, 1967–1977* (Gainesville 1997), and presently engaged in studying cultural aspects of Nasserism in Egypt.

Richard Pankhurst   Founder of the Institute of Ethiopian Studies and a history professor at Addis Ababa University. He has published numerous books on social, cultural, and economic aspects of Ethiopian history, and is the winner of the 1974 International Prize for Ethiopian Studies.

Yaacov Shavit   Professor of Jewish history and chairman of the department at Tel Aviv University. His books include *The New Hebrew Nation* (London 1987), *Athens in Jerusalem: Classical Antiquity in the Making of* *the Modern Jew* (London 1997), and *History in Black—African-Americans in Search of Ancient Past* (forthcoming).

Bairu Tafla   Professor of history at the Institut für Afrikanistik und Athiopistik, University of Hamburg, specializing in cultural history and oral traditions. His publications include *A Chronicle of Emperor Yohannes IV (1872–1889)* (Stuttgart 1977) and *Ethiopia and Germany: Cultural, Political and Economic Relations, 1871–1936* (Wiesbaden 1981).

Eve Troutt Powell   Assistant professor in the History Department of the University of Georgia, where she specializes in cultural history of the modern Middle East.

Emery van Donzel   He is the editor of *The Encyclopedia of Islam*. His publications on Ethiopia include *Foreign Relations of Ethiopia, 1642–1700* (Leiden 1979) and *A Yemeni Embassy to Ethiopia, 1647–1649* (Stuttgart 1986).

Gabriel Warburg   Professor emeritus of Middle Eastern history and former rector of Haifa University. He has published extensively on the histories of Egypt and the Sudan. His latest book is titled *Historical Discord in the Nile Valley* (London 1993).

Joachim Warmbold   A senior lecturer in the Department of Languages, Tel Aviv University, he specializes in German colonial literature. His publications include *Germania in Africa* (Frankfurt 1989).

Index

About the Book

Intercultural relations have revolved around the River Nile throughout recorded history: sharing the river's waters, Egyptians, Ethiopians, and Sudanese have developed rich dialogues of mutual cultural enrichment, as well as misconceptions and conflicts. This volume represents a rigorous scholarly attempt to trace these complex relations, exploring the multifaceted representations of the Nile, both in the region and in the West, from early medieval times to the present.

Underlying the authors' analysis is their recognition that the resurgent nationalism and sociopolitical revolutions of the present have aggravated historical conflicts and often reinvented traditional images. Their hope is that reconstructing the continuum of the Nile's history, its changes, and its cultural reciprocity will enhance mutual understanding as the region faces the acute water problems predicted for the future.

Haggai Erlich is professor of Middle Eastern and African history at Tel Aviv University. **Israel Gershoni** is professor of Middle Eastern history at Tel Aviv University.